HERMANN BECKH (1875-1937) studied Law and later Sanskrit, becoming Professor of Oriental Studies at the University of Berlin. A master of ancient and modern languages, he wrote extensively on religious and philosophical subjects, including Buddhism, Indology, Christianity, Alchemy and Music. In 1911, he heard a lecture by Rudolf Steiner and was inspired to join the Anthroposophical Society, where he soon became a valued co-worker. In 1922, he helped found The Christian Community, a movement for religious renewal. His many books are gradually being translated from the original German and published in English.

JOHN'S GOSPEL
THE COSMIC RHYTHM
STARS AND STONES

Hermann Beckh

Translated by Alan Stott

TEMPLE LODGE

Temple Lodge Publishing Ltd.
Hillside House, The Square
Forest Row, RH18 5ES

www.templelodge.com

Published by Temple Lodge in 2021

First published in English by Anastasi Ltd., Herefordshire, in 2015

Originally published in German under the title *Der kosmische Rhythmus, das Sternengeheimnis und Erdengeheimnis im Johannesevangelium* by Rudolf Geering Verlag, Basel, in 1930

This revised edition © Temple Lodge Publishing 2021
Translation © Alan Stott 2021

This book is copyright under the Berne Convention. All rights reserved. Apart from any fair dealing for the purpose of private study, research, criticism or review, no part of this publication may be reproduced, stored in a retrieval system, or transmitted in any form or by any means, electronic, electrical, chemical, mechanical, optical, photocopying, recording or otherwise, without the prior written permission of the copyright owner. Inquiries should be addressed to the Publishers

The rights of Alan Stott to be identified as the author of this translation has been asserted in accordance with sections 77 and 78 of the Copyright, Designs and Patents Act, 1988

A CIP catalogue record for this book is available from the British Library

ISBN 978 1 912230 81 5

Cover by Morgan Creative
Typeset by Symbiosys Technologies, Visakhapatnam, India
Printed and bound by 4Edge Ltd., Essex

*In memory of my sister Marie,
†25 February 1929*

Contents

Dedication	v
Table of Zodiac Signs	xii
Foreword	1
Translator's Note	3
INTRODUCTION	9
The Essence of the Gospel Rhythm: Sign and Constellation	9
Twelve World-Conceptions	11
Star Script	14
Sign and Constellation	15
Coincidence of Sign and Constellation	17
Birth Constellations	19
Overview: The World of the Stars, the Earth and the Human Being	20
Mark's Gospel	21
PART ONE: MYSTERY OF THE STARS: THE COSMIC POINT OF DEPARTURE FOR CONTEMPLATIONS ON JOHN'S GOSPEL	23
John's Gospel	
1. The Zodiac in the Cosmic Rhythm of Mark's Gospel (overview)	25
The Goat and the Waterman (♑ ♒)	25
The Fishes (♓)	26
The Ram (♈)	27
The Bull (♉)	27
The Twins (♊)	29
The Crab (♋)	29
The Lion (♌)	30
The Virgin (♍)	30
The Scales (♎)	31
The Scorpion (♏)	32
The Archer (♐)	33

2. The Planetary Aspect: the Spirit of the Planets ... 35
    Stars and Planets ... 36
    Geocentric and Heliocentric Conceptions: the outer
        planets and fixed stars ... 37
    Planetary Influences ... 40
    The Spiritual Hierarchies ... 42
    The Planetary Characters: Planetary Regions ... 43
    Ephesian Mysteries verse ... 44

3. The Planetary Aspect in the Cosmic Rhythm of the Gospel ... 47
    Saturn ♄ ... 48
    Jupiter ♃ ... 49
    Mars ♂ ... 49
    Venus ♀ ... 50
    Mercury ☿ ... 51
    Moon ☽ ... 52
    Sun and Mercury ☉☿ ... 53
    Venus ♀ ... 54
    Mars ♂ ... 57
    Jupiter ♃ ... 58

4. The Cosmic Rhythm in John's Gospel (overview) ... 59

5. John's Gospel and the other Gospels, observed from the
    Cosmic Rhythm ... 71

6. John's Gospel as Christ's Message of the 'I' ... 83

7. The Star-Mystery of the Eternal Name: the Book of Life
    and the Book of Destiny ... 91
    The Mystery of the Eternal Name ... 91
    The Apocalypse of John ... 93
    True Faith ... 94
    The Mystery of the Name ... 97
    Human Origins in the Spirit ... 99
    The Polarity of M and N ... 101
    Dwellings and Abiding ... 106
    Internalize ... 108
    The *Amen-Amen* sayings ... 110
    Summary ... 112

The Birth Horoscope and Astrology	113
The Fall of man	115
John 8 and earthly *karma*	116
John's Gospel and the Stars	120

PART TWO:
FROM THE RIDDLE OF THE STARS TO THE RIDDLE OF THE EARTH: THE RHYTHMIC STRUCTURE OF JOHN'S GOSPEL IN DETAIL — 123

I. The Descent of Christ (John 1–5)	125
1. The Word in the Primordial Beginning (John 1:1-18)	125
2. The Meeting at the Jordan (John 1:19-51)	138
The Baptist	140
The Disciples	142
3. The Marriage-Miracle in Cana (John 2)	147
4. The Conversation with Nicodemus (John 3)	160
5. The Samaritan Woman at the Well (John 4:1-42)	170
6. The Healing of the Nobleman's Son (John 4:43-54)	187
7. The Invalid of Bethesda (John 5)	191
II. The Crisis (John 6–10)	200
1. Essence, Cause and Outbreak of the Crisis; Feeding of the Five Thousand and Storm on the Lake (John 6 & 7)	200
Balancing opposite forces	206
The Feeding of the Five Thousand	209
Voyage on the Lake	210
The Scales and Christ	210
The Great Dispute	212
Living Water	216
Nicodemus	216
2. The Woman caught in Adultery and Stoning (John 8)	218
Judgment and Crisis	219
Stoning	221
Crystals	222
Virgin and Scorpion	224
The Woman, Johannine Initiation and the Magdalene	225
Writing in the Earth	227

3. The Healing of the Man Born Blind (John 9)	232
Metamorphosis through Christ	235
Change in John and the Disciples	236
4. The Good Shepherd (John 10)	238
Yoga and the Tree of Life	240
Thieves and Robbers	243
III. The Raising of Lazarus (John 11 & 12)	247
1. The Invalid (John 11:1-6)	247
2. The Grave of Bethany (John 11:7ff.)	257
Christ's Deed	261
The Forces of Decay	264
From 'I' to 'I'	265
The Mystery of Love	267
Thomas	269
3. He who was raised. Mary Magdalene (John 12)	273
IV. The Last Supper and Leave-taking from the Disciples (John 13–16)	278
V. The Great Intercession (John 17)	290
VI. Suffering and Dying (John 18 & 19)	297
1. The Mystery of the Earth	297
2. Gethsemane (John 18)	303
3. Ecce homo (John 19:1-15)	305
4. Golgotha (John 19:16ff.)	310
VII. Resurrection (John 20 & 21)	318
Thomas	327
The Paradisal Garden, the Stream & the Holy City	329
Fishing, feeding and the future	330
The Figures of the Zodiac	334

APPENDICES:

Hermann Beckh: Rhythmical Events in the Gospel	341
Hermann Beckh: The Indian Yoga Mystery and the Awakening Deed of Bethany	348

Hermann Beckh: The Heavenly Jerusalem   358
Hermann Beckh: John and the Word   373
Rudolf Steiner's Last Address   379
Book Reviews   388

Bibliography   395
The Works of Prof. Hermann Beckh   399

Endnotes   405

Table of Zodiac Signs

♈ The RAM (Aries)
♉ The BULL (Taurus)
♊ The TWINS (Gemini)
♋ The CRAB (Cancer)
♌ The LION (Leo)
♍ The VIRGIN (Virgo)

♎ The SCALES (Libra)
♏ The SCORPION (Scorpio)
♐ The ARCHER (Sagittarius)
♑ The GOAT (Capricorn)
♒ The WATERMAN (Aquarius)
♓ The FISHES (Pisces)

Table of Planetary Signs

♄ = Saturn
♃ = Jupiter
♂ = Mars
☉ = Sun

☿ = Mercury
♀ = Venus
☽ = Moon

Foreword

In the 'Last Address' which Rudolf Steiner, already very ill, held on the evening before Michaelmas Day 1924 in Dornach before a large group of participating friends, the Mystery of that person, to whom we are indebted for the inspiration of John's Gospel, was once more gently touched on. What the name *John* signifies for the consciousness of humanity, we saw ourselves called to receive deeply into our consciousness. It was presented not as a dogma but rather like a riddle whose solution should be unlocked in the seeking forces of the heart. It causes us once more to consider what anthroposophy should be in the age of knowledge, what its founder meant it to lead in the hearts of people—*a way of knowledge, that would lead the spiritual in the human being to the spirit in the universe*. Given in the form of people's thinking of today, anthroposophy would lead up to a cosmic thinking, a *thinking relating to the stars*. A stellar impulse lives in it as the most inner seed for the future. To search in John's Gospel itself for this impulse was the concern of the present work.

From this farewell hour, significant for humanity, from all the feelings of gratitude for the founder of anthroposophy that sounded through it, the gratitude of the writer turns to another, for him, personally significant hour. From early youth his sister inwardly united in spiritual endeavour, after a long and difficult illness passed over into the spiritual world. In this work she took part with the deepest forces of her heart. The earlier part on Mark's Gospel she experienced as she was dying; her dying spiritually flows into this second part on John's Gospel.

Finally, the well-earned, deeply felt thanks to the publisher, Herr Rudolf Geering of Basel, whose magnanimous sacrificial sense directed to high human aims, after the appearance of the first part of this work, has now made it possible that the second part also appears.

Hermann Beckh
Stuttgart, 8 July 1930

Translator's Note

Hermann Beckh (1875-1937) acknowledges a debt to the spiritual researcher Rudolf Steiner, explaining the context of his own contribution. He was present at Steiner's 'Last Address' (Dornach. Michaelmas Eve, 28 Sept. 1924), included as an Appendix here, along with accounts from others who were present on p. 379ff. and in *Mark's Gospel: The Cosmic Rhythm* (hereafter: MG), Appendix 4. The task remains to acknowledge Beckh's own contribution almost 90 years on. Indeed, the present translation may be seen as part of a sustained effort to re-assess Beckh's whole output. Translations forming the *Collected Works* are appearing in good time for the centenary of the first editions and that of the founding of the non-sectarian Movement for Religious Renewal, which Beckh served from its founding, The Christian Community (2022).

We may be in a better position today to suggest why Beckh himself felt at times misunderstood. Readers can now judge for themselves whether Beckh's whole contribution may be viewed as potentially even more important for the twenty-first century. In the present work, he writes about 'the key' he found—freely offered—and could consequently use so fruitfully (p. 250f.):

> In the present work lies the attempt in such a way to employ what Steiner has given; it lies already in that which in the presentation on Mark's Gospel could be said on the Mystery of John [MG 45ff., 48ff., 122ff., 208ff., 238ff.]. Intellectual 'evidences and proofs'—with which in such cases we do *not* have to do—want to force the understanding to accept a statement or other, whereas the essence of a *key to the Mysteries*—which is what we have been given by Steiner—consists in leaving the soul free, that it remains to the active soul-forces to work further on the matters, to test the worth of knowledge of what has been communicated. Only such a 'key' is not beneficial when it falls into the hands of those who take everything again 'dogmatically', who are themselves coerced and want to coerce other people. This attitude of mind, still widely prevailing both within and without theology, stands in contradiction to that of John's Gospel. There, through the whole work of *knowledge of the truth in the light-filled consciousness (aletheia)*, Christ wanted to lead to freedom, to the 'I'.

As with the translation of his book on Mark's Gospel, while acknowledging Beckh's lecturing style, the need was felt to break up his over-long sentences. Repetition, after all, may be less a tedious phenomenon of a lecturing style, much more a welcome help when an author is trying to describe processes. Moreover, it can help to support detailed study of the gospel, taken chapter by chapter—which, of course, is a well-tried method of Bible-study and the 'quiet hour'. With the text, I have added more paragraph breaks and some sub-titles, occasionally adopted bullet points for lists, and, because they usually contain important points, have included some footnotes in the text. For preference, I have used verbal forms where obviously appropriate in English. I have respected Beckh's use of the subjunctive mood and the self-evasive use of the passive voice.

Consistency is the aim with capitals for technical names: Spirit-man, Earth, Sun, Imagination, Mystery, Lake [of Galilee], Bible, Fall of man, and so on. In English, we face apparent inconsistencies with pronouns such as 'He'/'he', and so on, for the divinity. Published translations of the New Testament use the lower case. For *das Ich* I have usually translated as 'the "I"', sometimes 'the ego'. Despite being another foreign word, the word 'ego', preferred by earlier translators of similar texts, is still used today. Alternative possibilities, 'identity', 'individuality', 'self' and so on, were considered. English readers of many translated works are getting used to the unusual noun-form with the quaint quotation marks for this cardinal concept. In this connection, Beckh's translation of Psalm 23, beginning 'He who says "I" in me …', speaks volumes. Again, Beckh explains below:

> The 'I' Christ means is the lost or forgotten divine Self of the human being, the divine in the human being. This today but slumbers as a seed of a new, becoming future 'member of the human being'. In biblical language it is often called 'the Son of man' [p. 83].

Beckh is inclined to present almost everything as a *Mysterium* or *Geheimnis*; the latter derives from Luther as a translation of the Lat. *mysterium*. But a moment's reflection justifies this technical term 'Mystery', which in English goes back to the thirteenth century as a religious term (however ungainly, I have capitalized the almost 900 uses in this book of the word 'Mystery' or 'Mysteries' in a religious context). But the use became broader, and today, for example, music is a 'mystery' until you study it: pitch, rhythm and beat and how to notate them are themselves all 'mysteries'. Then with the keys on the circle of fifths Beckh saw the correspondence to the zodiac—here, the universal scholar tells us, he found the key to the Archetypes. Now, we note (following on from C.S. Lewis,

Studies in Words [1960/67]) that it is possible to describe, but not *define* all the basic things: 'life', 'light', 'love', 'rhythm', 'heat', 'light', 'electricity' ... Technically, these are all 'mysteries'. Consequently, Prof. Beckh is employing exact science when he uses the term I have translated as 'Mystery' or the plural and sometimes as 'secret'. With 'Mysteries' *meaning itself* is inherent, waiting to reveal itself to a proactive approach. The example of music is most apt; one famous concert pianist claimed he only played music that he 'could not play', that is, he felt he could not do it complete justice—there is always more to discover. Mysteries, we can establish, can be revealed but not 'explained away'. We are speaking here, claims Beckh, of the Mystery of John, who found the 'lost word'; it is the Mystery of ourselves, of which no end is in sight.

Now to mention a few details: we speak of the 'ancient' world, from our point of view the world as it was a long time ago. Yet, in itself, the infancy of the race clearly came 'early', as the use of the word by the 'early music' movement has made us aware. With this matter, I have tried to steer a reasonable course. Then, another word: occasionally, following George MacDonald, I have risked 'becoming' as a noun. Again, I tend to think *Wesen*, 'being', usually adds little in English to other nouns, but here some sensitivity has been shown in this text. This and other examples of problems of translation might fill a good few pages; I can claim no novel solutions.

Beckh's lasting contributions?

Not for nothing, it seems, did destiny lead Beckh to a lecture by Rudolf Steiner on the prophet Elijah (Berlin, 14 Dec. 1911, in GA 61. 194-220). What struck Beckh most deeply about this first meeting was Steiner's appeal to the freedom of his listeners.[1]

> One recognized suddenly the spiritual reality active behind the Biblical pictures ... The letters became alive. It was like scales falling from your eyes. Everything fell away that until then laid over the Bible like a veil of traditional notions ... The Old Testament, whose picture-world like a forgotten archetypal memory of humanity shone into my early childhood and then for decades was almost dismissively shelved, was as given afresh through this lecture.

The lecture, it seems sure, provided the occasion for a contemporary retake on Elijah's experience of the 'still, small voice', or as the LXX puts it, 'the voice of thin silence'. Thirteen years later, the circle for Beckh closed with Steiner's 'Last Address' that left him, and others, with the Mystery of the 'two Johns'. It has to be noted that Beckh—whose expositions, early in the field, are far in advance of most subsequent researchers—has been largely marginalized by these people, including certain colleagues, who, whether inspired or terrified by him, should have known better. The academic attacks by the theologians of the day, both Reformed and Roman Catholic, took on Friedrich Rittelmeyer, Emil Bock and Rudolf Frieling, but declined the task of approaching Beckh. Wilhelm Hauer in *Werden und Wesen der Anthroposophie*, 1921/22/2004 degenerates into slander and gossip. Beckh's biographer,[2] moreover, mentions a letter of 13 May 1941 from Heinrich Himmler, leader of the SS during the Third Reich, who admits that Beckh was:

> an excellent researcher. In his younger years he wrote one of the best books on Buddhism, then he came under the influence of Rudolf Steiner and during the course of about a decade he landed up in absurdities which one can only call abnormal.

On 1 Sept. 1937 Himmler wrote:

> The two volumes on Buddha by Beckh are very good. But after these ... Beckh no longer wrote anything proper. Through anthroposophy and The Christian Community he has been led so hopelessly into error that I can only view him as a psychiatric case.

The Language of Tonality was pulped by the Nazis, and no doubt other titles as well. One wonders what Owen Barfield (1898-1997), a member of the Inklings and—like Beckh a philosopher of language and a universal scholar—would have said about a fellow worker on the Continent, whom he apparently never met. In his later years Barfield was distressed that not enough attention was being paid to what he termed R.U.P., the 'Residue of Untransformed Positivism'. Like Beckh, he saw a grim future for civilization without some balance attempting a change of consciousness. Beckh, in the lecture of 1921 delivered to the Humboldt University of Berlin, as mentioned earlier (boycotted by his colleagues), gave his reasons for a career-change to devote his energies as a freelance lecturer for anthroposophy. It did not take long (as a later colleague, Alfred Heidenreich, points out) before an iron broom swept Europe, ... and today? R.U.P. won't disappear, as C.S. Lewis (1898-1963) and the other Inklings knew. But Johannine, cosmic Christianity is also there (certainly subversive, but 'abnormal', 'deviant'?)—and permanently there until the end of the world. Lewis chose fiction to clothe his cosmic vision for posterity, not only in the adult 'space trilogy' novels, above all in the apocalyptic *That Hideous Strength* (1945), but also the Narniad (1950-56). 'The characters of the planets, as conceived by medieval astrology,' wrote Lewis,[3] 'seem to me to have a permanent value as spiritual symbols.' The planetary moods are still experienced in the days of the week, and, as Michael Ward has shown,[4] they underpin the seven books of the Narniad, known throughout the world.

Beckh's whole attempt with the two volumes on *The Cosmic Rhythm* in the gospel was written in response to his colleagues' wish to answer the notions of the materialistic humanist, Arthur Drews (1865-1935). Drews took a superficial, dismissive view on Mark's Gospel as an 'astral myth', concluding that the Incarnation did not happen. In this situation, only one man could take on this challenge. With his progressive habits of thinking assisted by his solid legal background, it cannot be claimed that Beckh lacks the equipment to write intelligibly on the influence of the stars.

Today, almost one hundred years on, the *Collected Works of Rev. Prof. Hermann Beckh* approaches completion. It is now possible to suggest more than the simple fact that the Professor has been met with a general bewilderment. There is space here to mention a few things to draw together the threads of this Introduction.

Firstly, concerning the highly important theme that solicited Beckh's profound contributions, there are in fact *four Johns*: the Baptist, Lazarus-John, John the apostle and John Mark. As in *any* meaningful human situation, to participate here at the birth of the second half of Earth-evolution emphatically more is demanded than a clever intellect and more than a simple devotional attitude.

Secondly, we find in Beckh the pioneer for whom musicality was not only a way of life but brought the comprehensive *methodical knowledge* to appreciate the 'key' to research ultimate Johannine Mysteries. A complete commentary on the Book of Revelation was unfortunately never penned, yet along with the work on the gospel, Beckh did write a poetic piece, 'The New Jerusalem', which he mentions at an important point in discussing John 8.

Among Beckh's unique qualities was his unparalleled grasp of the cosmic order which left his colleagues Rittelmeyer and Bock worrying and Frieling pleased. *Only* Beckh knew about *ṛta*, *maat*, *asha* and the *berit olam;*[5] only Beckh could demonstrate that the life of the Buddha went through twelve stages;[6] Beckh alone realized the relationship of the tropical zodiac to the musical keys (*Weltenstimmungen*);[7] Beckh could write movingly about Lazarus and his sister, inspired (as he tells us in his Foreword) by his own sister Marie, who had recently died. For the titles of the studies on Mark and John, he put first *Der kosmische Rhythmus*. He went on to write *The Language of the Stars*, the first attempt to found a new 'Christened' wisdom of the stars, intended for publication, perhaps his crowning contribution, then as his death approached the last books on music, something, he felt sure, for the future: 'The cosmic rhythm in tonality. This really lives in me; this is my theme.'[8] In all this, it is time to recognize Beckh's unparalleled achievement.

My bilingual wife pounced on several blunders in the draft of this English version, which is a revision of the first edition, and my editor, Neil Franklin, Ph.D., the original source of the project to issue the *Collected Works*, deserves my profound thanks for inspiration, those more than felicitous suggestions, and never-failing support.

The underground spiritual stream—the term 'Neoplatonic' covers many diverse traditions—always did nourish our thinkers and poets. Norman Nicholson, either knew or, as we say, 'intuited' much concerning creation and re-creation. He concludes his 'Carol' with a fourth verse touching on the ultimate Mystery discussed in these pages on John's Gospel.[9]

> Mary nursed her Child beside
> The gardens of a grave —
> And by the death within His bones
> The dead became alive.

Alan Stott, Michaelmas Eve, 2014 (rev. 2020).

(Written 90 years after Rudolf Steiner's 'Last Address' to the Members of the Anthroposophical Society.)

Introduction

The Essence of the Gospel Rhythm
Sign and Constellation

Many ways could lead us closer to understand John's Gospel. Alongside and with the Apocalypse it is the most profound of all the documents of humanity, with the most difficult content and the one that carries most the future of humanity. Here we take the way that results from looking at the 'cosmic rhythm' in Mark's Gospel.

'The Gospel of Mark as the way to John; the Gospel of John as the way to Christ'—so in all brevity and decisiveness runs the fundamental thought of this whole work, dedicated in its first part to Mark's Gospel and, beginning the second part on John's Gospel here.[10]

The term 'cosmic rhythm' was found in the considerations of Mark's Gospel to bear its spiritual construction and the inner connections; it can be recognized as resting in itself, shedding its own light. A *spiritual concept of twelve* in this *rhythm* is revealed in its individual motifs or 'signs': in passing three times through the twelve sections of the gospel events; returning to the same 'sign' also links to the same event, or one connected in meaning. The spiritual meaning of the individual 'signs', and therewith of the whole rhythm, is directly understandable *out of itself*. The same kind of context on the circular path returns in the three rounds of those twelve motifs or 'signs'.

The governing rhythm in the events of the gospel is none other than the great rhythm of the Earth and of the human being. It forms the basis of everything in the cosmos and the Earth, revealed in the eternal alternation of blooming and wilting, of growth and fruiting, of becoming and passing away, life and death, sleeping and waking, summer and winter, day and night. We can pursue this rhythm right into music, even into the spatial world, and right into the harmonic construction of the human body (MG 26ff.).[11]

This rhythm is decisive also for that spiritual path of the unfolding and graded development that here we always call 'Initiation' for the 'development of Spirit-man', in particular in the Christian-Johannine Initiation. The threefold progress through the unity of the twelve heavenly signs in the narration of Mark's Gospel not only reveals a secret of the life of Christ but a fact of the Johannine

Initiation—as we recognized in the earlier exposition. In the name 'John' itself we recognized the secret of three stages on this path of becoming (MG 46ff.).

This rhythm is revealed especially clearly and significantly in blooming and withering, of growth and decay during the course of the year. Initially it is a *Sun-rhythm*. The annual path of the Sun in its heavenly course takes place with the circuit of the events of the year. (The point here is not about Copernican problems but concerns the simple description of heavenly events as they are presented to the observer on the Earth.) We observed a *star-rhythm*. In this, its annual movement, the Sun describes a circuit through twelve heavenly regions. Respecting tradition, this is always called the *twelve constellations of the zodiac*. Each of these twelve zodiac constellations describes a section or a 'sign' of the Sun's course and the yearly events. Regardless of all tradition, though, the 'unity of twelve' of the signs naming the sections of the Sun's course and the events of the year result from the further observed fact that the Sun-rhythm and a Moon-rhythm unites a *circuit of twelve months* with the circuit of the year (taken as a pure Moon-rhythm it does not completely tie into the Sun-rhythm) [because the lunar calendar consists of 13 months—*Tr.*].

Thus for this whole earthly and cosmic rhythm *Sun, Moon and stars* initially are nothing other than *the cosmic clock*, on which we read the timing of earthly events, measuring all the earthly moments of time. According to it, in the last resort, we all unite to set our tiny earthly clocks and watches. The course of the day is the reflection in small of the course of the year (MG 25). The dial of the most simple watch contains an indication of the unity of twelve cosmic signs.

Thus, without considering the stars and the constellations, we can gain a spiritual overview of the rhythm always meant here and of its twelve 'signs'. We need fully to grasp the different moods of the twelve monthly sections of the circle of the year, to recognize what degree is revealed of blooming and withering, of growth and bearing fruit, of becoming and passing away as revealed with each of these twelve sections of the year. (The respective transition does not lie around the first day of the month, but rather around the 21st day, around the time in which also the equinoxes and solstices lie.) Moreover, like the course of the day and the course of the year, the musical facts of the circle of keys knows a light and a dark side, a day-side and a night-side. This, too, allows us to conceive the *spiritual unity of twelve* as such, independent of the starry heavens.

Twelve world-conceptions

It is to the greatest degree worth noting how Rudolf Steiner speaks of the twelve main world-conceptions. These directions of thought express the *spiritual zodiac*.

> The Sun appears to move through the zodiac and the other planets appear to move through the zodiac. Likewise, it is possible for the human soul to move through a *spiritual circle* that contains twelve world-conceptions.

This expresses the 'spiritual signs of the zodiac' (Rudolf Steiner: *Human and Cosmic Thought*. Lecture 3, Berlin, 22 Jan. 1914. GA 151). For example, 'Idealism' characterizes the world-conception of the Ram. It is expressly said that this relationship, to be conceived purely spiritually, is not identical to the zodiac constellation assigned to an individual birth-horoscope. It is not about horoscope matters.

For this spiritual zodiac, this 'twelve spiritual signs of the zodiac', the zodiacal starry constellations shining in the heavens, initially at all events, is only a picture or comparison. (The list and explanations of the names are found in MG 36ff.) Precisely when concerned with questions on the gospel and its cosmic rhythm, it is important that we can achieve such a spiritual zodiac as Steiner suggests. With the names of the individual 'signs' of the stellar zodiac always used here, only a pure spiritual view is meant. Everything has been discussed in detail in the exposition on Mark's Gospel. Thus, we experience in the Parable of the Sower, the Feeding [of the 5000] and the Last Supper as the meaning of the sign of the Virgin (the 'Last-Supper constellation'). It is simply the *reception of a spiritual seed*, but intensifying through three different stages of the great rhythm. In the ensuing pictures of the Voyage on the Lake, the Storm on the Lake, and so on, this 'struggle for inner balance' is experienced as the meaning of the sign of the Scales. Precisely with the 'Scales' it is not difficult to understand the meaning of the word purely spiritually, independent of all astronomy. And it can awaken the impression that after the 'reception of the spiritual seed' there always follows such a 'struggle for inner balance'. The spiritual rhythm from the sign of the Virgin apparently always leads to a 'struggle for inner balance' in the sign of the Scales. This corresponds in the familiar order of the zodiac.

The correct pictures and grasp of the concept of a 'spiritual zodiac' will be of determining significance for expounding the gospel. Here we feel how these spiritual 'signs' mean something not only for earthly man—its original meaning was divine-spiritual. The gospel allows us from the highest of all possible viewpoints to behold this 'spiritual unity of twelve'—or 'twelvefold spiritual signs'. We are allowed to approach most directly the *original divine meaning*, the actual primordial motif *of these twelve signs*. Not out of some kind of traditional 'astrology' do we draw teaching for the spiritual understanding of the gospel, but rather a spiritual astrology—never to be mistaken with mere horoscope casting—receives new aspects through the Christian gospel.

***

If we have correctly understood the spiritually universal meaning of the zodiac rhythm as meant here, then in the light of the ancient wisdom saying, 'As above, so below'—can also run, 'As below, so above'—which can explain how that which governs what is revealed in all the contexts of earthly time has ultimately to reveal itself in the starry widths themselves. We have completely to free ourselves from the one-sided material notion of the starry world entertained by many people. In the progress of natural-scientific research, not a single one of the wonderful and super-material, supersensory manifestations of physical and astronomical facts compels such a materialistic manner of picturing things. They are found much more in certain 'popular', basically ignorant and unscientific presentations [of 'materialist humanism'], than in the much more careful, even if not positively spiritual, results of a true scientific pursuit. Where they are still found today, they actually appear only as an opaque residue from the nineteenth century, no longer as contemporary thinking.

Spirit and life on the Earth are not only sporadic appearances of man, plant and animal in the midst of an otherwise dead environment. Spirit and life could not reveal themselves unless they were also present in the cosmos. This means, in the starry worlds—to which our Earth also belongs. With this, however, a spiritual-realist view of the 'zodiac', of the starry worlds in general, is acknowledged. A direct observation of this fact is gained only through supersensory perception, through a clairvoyant 'knowledge of higher worlds', as presented in a contemporary way in Rudolf Steiner's book with that title. A *firm grasp* of the fact is also possible without clairvoyant vision. The whole exposition given in the book on Mark's Gospel basically deals with such a path of knowledge. Even without stepping on the path of knowledge itself, today through opening up a life in anthroposophy, in knowledge of supersensory research in general, an understanding can be unlocked for the soul that divines the living element and the spirit-reality in the cosmos.

In order to understand all this, it is not at all necessary to 'ignore the material element' or to regard it as unimportant. Thereby we would only close ourselves off from the actual depths of Johannine knowledge. Even the word 'materialism' has not at all to be taken always and only in the sense of a lower and crude materialism. In the above-mentioned lecture-course *Cosmic and Human Thought*, Rudolf Steiner shows how 'materialism' can also be understood as one of the twelve possible and justifiable main world-conceptions. It is the world-conception corresponding to the spiritual zodiac sign of the Crab. And in the book on *Mark's Gospel: The Cosmic Rhythm* (MG 243f.), we attempted to show how in a real penetration of the Mystery of matter, in the manner that took place on the cross on Golgotha, a higher Johannine, alchemical 'materialism' can be found, one that transubstantiates the Earth and earthly matter. For this reason John's initiation ends in the sign of the Crab. In the course of the exposition on John's Gospel, it will be seen how we are led here from the cosmic heights ever deeper into the depths of the Earth, from the riddle of the stars into the depths of the riddle of the Earth.

If we have found access to this 'Mystery of matter', to this *revelation of the spirit in all so-called matter*, to this Johannine knowledge of matter, then there exists no further occasion to resolve the starry heavens into mere abstractions. We will only be clear nonetheless that in no other realm than the astronomical realm does the crude sensual kind of thinking of our time work so catastrophically with its materialistic pedantry, so spiritually denying and destructive of the 'I', the human self. Indeed, to such undermining thinking that forms certain all-too-earthly and earthly-material notions of space, stellar space, all elevated spirituality has finally to succumb, all inner harmony of the soul, all true humanity, even the health of the body. The overcoming of one-sided materialistic thinking in order to make an advance, consequently, is in no realm more important than in this decisive area.[12]

It has been said elsewhere [Hermann Beckh, 'Genesis', in *From the Mysteries*, TL 18f.], that in order to comprehend the starry heavens the habit of thought of today takes concepts and views from earthly life and transposes them into space. To overcome this thinking, the main thing is that we ourselves have to grow into a stellar consciousness; we no longer measure the cosmic with the earthly but re-introduce cosmic criteria into earthly life. Then we will sense from the stars not this earthly life, but how *Cosmic Life, Cosmic Love, and Cosmic Being are raying down from them to us.*

Star Script

As long as we sought the zodiac rhythm only in the earthly situation, above all in the course of the year, the stellar worlds of Sun, Moon and stars were for us only something like a great cosmic clock. If we have gained the spiritually alive concept of the starry cosmos, just characterized, then we do not remain at a standstill. Then this still somewhat mechanical imagination changes for us and looks for the transition into something other, something more alive, into the imagination of a 'spiritual starry script', as, for example, Novalis suggests in the Introduction to his poetic prose work *The Novices of Sais*:

> Mankind travels along all sorts of pathways. He who pursues and compares them will perceive the emergence of certain strange figures; figures that appear to be inscribed in that massive script in cipher that one beholds everywhere and in everything: on wings, eggshells, in clouds, in the snow, in crystalline and stone formations, in frozen waters, on the outside and within the mountain-ranges, of plants, beasts, people, *in the lights of heaven*, in contiguous and expansive panes of pitch and glass, in the clustering of iron filings around the magnet, in the extraordinary conjunctions of chance. In these one may glimpse an intimation of the key to this wondrous text, its very grammar-book … .

Where spiritual influences are at work in cosmic existence, they create for themselves form, they are revealed in form; consequently, the arrangement of the stars in the cosmos cannot be arbitrary. We have to recognize meaning and harmony in the cosmic whole and all its realms. This and nothing else is what the expression 'cosmic script', 'starry script' means. In this way the spirituality of the Ram, the Bull, the Twins, and so on, is really revealed in the corresponding constellation, that is, in the picture of the corresponding group of stars. For previous ages of human consciousness this was still a living, pictorial view; today it is taken as an abstract and arbitrary naming from an obsolete mythology.

'As above, so below'—the spirituality of the Ram, the Twins, the Scales and of the Scorpion truly revealed in the constellations is ultimately the same as we experience in the different earthly revelations (of the course of the year, and so on), experienced in the earthly *signs*. The Bull, the Crab, the Scales, the Archer, and so on, as spiritual entities—as beings of the higher hierarchies—express and reveal themselves in the actual stellar world, in the world of the fixed stars.

Sign and Constellation

At this point, for a proper understanding of everything that follows, for the viewpoint of the earthly revelation and effect of the 'signs', it appears important to distinguish the living entity in the stellar worlds. Thus we find, for example, the spirituality of the *Ram* in the course of the earthly year is revealed today as for millennia, when with the spring equinox the bright part of the year begins and the Sun reveals its enlivening power. (This is said from the viewpoint of the Northern Hemisphere. In the Southern Hemisphere the autumn/fall begins at that time, which would actually be the sign of the Scales. With each sign there works at the same time the counter-sign—this happened repeatedly in the exposition of Mark's Gospel—and in the Southern Hemisphere the emphasis of sign and counter-sign is reversed.)

The *Crab* is revealed in the course of the earthly year—today, as for millennia—when in the summer solstice the Sun takes up its retrograde motion; 'it continues crabwise' when, in the Northern Hemisphere, the life of nature starts to recede. Likewise, in the Northern Hemisphere, the *Scales* is the sign of the autumn equinox. Day and night are temporarily equally as long again, they have 'entered into the Scales'. In this sense the *Goat* would be the 'sign' of the winter solstice. If today, however, we want to decide the segment of the Sun's actual course corresponding to this 'sign', then we find that for a long time the two no longer go hand in hand. Here, for the earthly course of the year, 'the sign of the Ram' stands essentially already in the constellation of the Fishes—that is, it is oriented in the heavens to the Fishes (only a few degrees of the sign of the Ram still lie today in the constellation of the Ram)—likewise the sign of the Crab is oriented today towards the constellation of the Twins; the Scales lies completely in the constellation of the Virgin, and so on. (The varying size of the *constellations* also plays a part; their boundaries are frequently taken differently, and parts of a constellation project into another, as does, for example, the sting of the Scorpion into the Archer; the *signs*, however, corresponding to the equal measure of the course of the year, are all taken in the same size as a twelfth of the whole circle, that is, 30°.)

The situation today has to do with the reverse movement of the spring equinox, which in the course of about 25,920 years (here and there the number given varies somewhat) travels through all the constellations of the zodiac. (This movement was frequently mentioned in the book on Mark's Gospel.) Astronomically and mathematically this movement, this change in the starry heaven, is explained from the change in the Earth's axis. During the course of this great 'cosmic year', it turns to ever-different regions of the stellar cosmos. Thus the rhythm of the course of the earthly [single] year is faced by another, greater rhythm of the 'great cosmic year'. In this, however, the sequence of individual zodiac constellations, through which the Sun takes its course, is the reverse of the usual course of the [single] year.

- In the exposition of *John's Gospel* will be shown what significance this 'rhythm of the great cosmic year' holds precisely for this gospel, whereas
- the rhythm of *Mark's Gospel* is completely oriented to the earthly course of the year.

(Clarity has to exist with all this, so that when it is said the Sun, or a planet, stands in this or that sign or constellation, the spatial reference is never to the fixed stars, but always only that our Sun, or a planet of our solar system, in its apparent movement is to be seen moving through some specific constellation of the heavenly course.)

The time in the rhythm of the year in which the spirituality of the Ram, or of one of the other zodiac signs, rules is today *not* the spirituality of that zodiac entity ruling the *constellation* through which the Sun passes. Much rather are both today already visibly out of sequence by as much as a whole sign, about a twelfth of the whole cycle. The disparity will increase till the two once more coincide after more than 20,000 years have passed. Consequently, the *sign*—as a specific segment of the rhythm of the year—differs from the *constellation*, that is, the sign can no longer be spatially placed with the constellation, even when the spiritual entity of sign and constellation are ultimately the same. Consequently, the stellar names are retained for the spatial differently oriented 'signs', because of the precession of the spring equinox.

- The 'sign' points to earthly connections and events [tropical zodiac].
- The 'constellation' points to the starry worlds [sidereal zodiac].
- A planet expresses its position in a specific 'sign' not in relation to the fixed stars, but *how it stands towards the Earth*.

Sign and constellation are as different as the earthly world and stellar world—which in no way excludes the mutual relationship. Only this relationship, which as spiritual relationship always remains today, because of the precession of the spring equinox, is no longer directly spatial; in future it will become ever less so.

Coincidence of Sign and Constellation

For the question of John's Gospel—as the further presentation will show even more clearly—this *differentiation of sign and constellation* is not without significance. The problem that we have initially presented purely astronomically, will become pushed increasingly into a more spiritual sphere. We will initially feel something of this spiritual sphere by asking, 'When actually did sign and constellation, which are moving apart, coincide; when did the "signs", so to speak, receive their names from the starry constellations, and which in the times following have remained with them? When, as a consequence of the shifting of the spring equinox, was the direct, spatial relationship of sign and constellation increasingly no longer true?'

Now, this concerns a purely astronomical fact, not, for instance, some kind of 'spiritual-scientific' communication. *The hour when this coincidence of sign and constellation was no other than that when the Mystery of Golgotha took place.* At this point the spring equinox of the Sun had gone through the Ram and entered the constellation of the Fishes.

There are calculations that reckon this moment in time fifty or eighty years earlier. We have to remember, as already mentioned, the constellations vary in size, the signs on the other hand are the same as each other. Mathematically, then, precise coincidence is not possible. Moreover, with the boundaries of the individual constellations there is no common agreement; one part of one constellation encroaches on that of another. Finally, the retrograde motion of the spring equinox is very slow, only noticeable over long periods of time. Viewing all these facts in the right way, for a spiritual view it becomes clear without more ado that the transition of the spring equinox from the Ram into the Fishes can really as precisely as possible be taken as occurring at the Turning Point of Time. The boundaries of the constellations are simply to be taken according to the position of the spring equinox.

Furthermore, this astronomical transition of the beginning of spring, from one zodiac sign or stellar constellation into the other, is to be distinguished from the usual anthroposophical way of calculating the historical 'cultural epochs' of history. According to this calculation given by Rudolf Steiner, the transition from the age of the Ram to the age of the Fishes took place in 1413 CE. The new sign then only makes a decisive impression into the cultural epoch when astronomically about half of the respective sign is reached—or, as in this case, is far overstepped. With regard to the event of Golgotha, this likewise sufficiently shows how far the transition of the astronomical sign in a true sense means a spiritual turning point.

At that time, the spring equinox was beginning in the constellation of the Fishes, or just before. Today it is located almost at the end of this constellation, ready to enter the constellation of the Waterman in the not-too-distant future. At this moment, just before entering the Waterman, the sign of the Ram will coincide as completely as possible with the constellation of the Fishes, just as at the time of Golgotha, before the passing over of the beginning of spring into the Fishes, when sign and constellation of the Ram coincided as completely as possible.

The time when Christ walked the Earth was the time when sign and constellation coincided most completely. At that time, in that epoch—in the 'fourth', the 'Greco-Latin cultural epoch', as it is termed in the anthroposophical view of history—the earthly signs received their names out of the cosmos, from the constellations. The spirituality of the cosmic Ram was stamped on the earthly surroundings.

(Of course, the movement of the spring equinox is permanent. For example, in the Ancient Egyptian cultural period preceding the Greco-Latin period, the spring equinox—the 'sign of the Ram', in the sense intended here—lay in the constellation of the Bull that is spiritually deeply connected with the whole Egyptian Isis-Venus cult, the Mysteries of Isis. In the Ancient Persian epoch it lay in the constellation of the Twins; in the prehistoric Ancient Indian epoch it lay in the sign of the Crab. The much earlier coincidence of the sign of the Ram and the constellation of the Ram would lead to a far-distant past. Yet in *Christ and the Spiritual World*, Leipzig 1913 [GA 149], Rudolf Steiner shows how in such a far-distant past other Christ-events—[sacrifices] not then taking place in the physical world—preceded the earthly, historical Christ-event in Palestine.)

In the last lecture of the Leipzig lecture-course [GA 149], which is of basic significance for all questions of a new, star-wisdom penetrated by Christ—an astrology and astrosophy—Rudolf Steiner, with a singular emphasis, three times quotes the words of the astronomer Kepler, the discoverer of the famous 'planetary laws': '*A certain picture of the zodiac and the whole firmament is imprinted by God into the soul of the Earth.*' And Steiner again summarizes Kepler's insight in the words: 'And today we see how this picture of the zodiac is imprinted into the soul of the Earth, *into the aura of the Earth.*' This stellar picture, as it were, firmly imprinted into the 'aura of the Earth' would be the 'sign' of today, which remains unaffected by the change of the constellations.

Birth Constellations

Is not this event of the 'hour of birth of the "I" of the Earth'—for in spiritual science this is the hour of Golgotha—in great measure the same as in any hour of birth when, following the indications Rudolf Steiner gives in his booklet *The Spiritual Guidance of Man and Mankind* [GA 15], the stellar constellation of the heavenly firmament of the hour of birth is imprinted at that moment into the 'brain-aura' of the infant, to remain the 'birth firmament' or 'birth horoscope' of that person for their whole earthly life?

The destiny of an earthly life is to a large extent determined through this constellation at birth. Rightly understood, this does not contradict 'human freedom'. What is expressed in the horoscope is simply what someone has themselves woven in earlier earthly lives as a specific configuration and constellation of 'astral' tensions, harmonies and disharmonies. To a high degree this manifests things of a destiny-carrying and destiny-demanding nature. What the 'self' does with this 'self-woven' astral weaving of destiny is a matter of freedom—*as far as such a matter has already been achieved.*

In the horoscope there stands not the self, but only that tapestry woven by the self before birth, much less what the self will then make out of this tapestry. One could say with the Indian Buddhists, the 'householder' does not stand in the birth horoscope, but only the house that he built. Or, speaking in the technical, astrological sense, the specific constellation of the house and configuration of the house is shown by the birth-firmament. It is evident to everyone that for everything that the earlier builder of the house and present householder in the house takes on, the state, character and arrangement of the house to a great extent is decided. Likewise, that the 'freedom' of the householder to do just what he wants is not affected. Only it is quite obvious that this 'freedom' can manifest only within certain limits determined by the situation. There exist rather clumsily built, restricting houses, that make it difficult to take on any intended profession or activity, whereas a well-situated, cleverly built and well-furnished house, well-orientated to all the directions of heaven, benefits the free unfolding of the householder.

In the above-mentioned lecture-cycle, also in a significant passage in *Man in the Light of Occultism, Theosophy and Philosophy*, Christiania, 2-12 June 1913 [GA 137], Rudolf Steiner explains the principle of astrology out of the fact that the human being is born out of the whole cosmos, that he is an extract of the whole cosmos. Everything expressed here should not be taken as a 'fixed dogma' but initially as a stimulus for our own thinking, and because in the progressive exposition of John's Gospel we will be led repeatedly to this issue.

In any case, what has been presented could throw light on the difference between *sign* and *constellation* emphasized here. For everything practical in this realm, it was and is something always self-evident—a *Christ-event of the most significant kind*, a fact expressed in the Mystery of Golgotha.[13]

Overview: The World of the Stars, the Earth and the Human Being

With all this we had assumed to make the distinction between:

(i) an *earthly zodiac of signs*, and
(ii) an actual stellar zodiac, a *zodiac of stellar constellations, as two different revelations of one and the same spiritual order*—consequently also the whole justified use of the same names. With the one, the earthly zodiac of signs, we are actually only in the rhythmic surroundings of the Earth, in the aura of the Earth, in that sphere in which especially the life of the year takes place and the cultic experience that follows this. (The Indian Vedic word ṛta—spoken 'rita', cf. Latin *ritus*—names the cosmic rhythm in the course of the stars, in the events of the course of the year and in the rites of the rituals of offering, based on this cosmic lawfulness. Cf. the mentioned article, Appendix 1.) Only with the zodiac of the constellations are we in the actual stellar world. The 'spirituality of the zodiac' shared by both is revealed precisely in the earthly and in the stellar world.

If we proceed from the anthroposophical fourfold human being, we feel in the physical body the relationship to the solid Earth, to the mineral earth; in the etheric body the relationship to the rhythmical surroundings of the Earth, to the earthly aura—to that sphere where the 'zodiac of signs' is to be thought. In the astral body we feel the relationship to the planetary world, to the closer world of the [wandering] stars of our solar system; in the 'I', or ego, the relationship to the whole stellar cosmos, to the world of the fixed stars as the actual 'stellar world'. This is that world, to which belongs also the 'zodiac of constellations', the actual stellar zodiac.

Mark's Gospel

Looking once more from the point at which we have arrived to the exposition of Mark, we find there we have to imagine the zodiac initially not at all as the 'stellar zodiac'. The sphere of Mark's Gospel is basically the earthly zodiac [tropical zodiac], the rhythmical earthly aura, that sphere in which we also stand in living the course of the year and in the [seasonally changing aspect of the] ritual of the Christian liturgy. Consequently, the sequence of the signs here also corresponds to the yearly course of the Sun and the events of the year. Only John's Gospel—whose element is the 'I', as Mark's element is the etheric—raises us into the actual spheres of the stars—in order to lead us from these cosmic heights ever deeper and more decisively down into the Mysteries of the depths of the Earth. To understand Mark's Gospel, it is still sufficient in a certain way to look at the earthly zodiac of the signs. With John's Gospel we are increasingly led from the earthly zodiac towards the stellar zodiac, towards the Mystery lying between *sign and constellation*.

We can in this sense understand the spirituality of Mark's Gospel in its essence already from the yearly events, the yearly rhythm, out of the [earthly] zodiac of the signs. The fact is also evident that the experiences described there of the threefold rhythm, the course of the Sun traversing the twelve signs, do indeed lead us to the 'three years of Christ's earthly life', to that time when *signs* and *constellations* coincided in the most complete way, when the cosmic element of the stellar zodiac was impressed into the earthly zodiac. Thus far, then, behind the earthly zodiac (sign-zodiac) of Mark's Gospel, the stellar zodiac was possible and permissible, the zodiac of the starry constellations. Consequently, for this reason it could be and was permitted in the exposition of Mark at clearly defined places (e.g. MG 147, 339f.) nevertheless to point to the stellar constellations, to the real view of the starry heavens.

Since the cosmic rhythm of the signs of the zodiac found for Mark's Gospel also serves as an important key for the questions of John's

Gospel—although the use of this key leads there to quite a different rhythm—it appears important at the beginning of this exposition to recall in a short summary and in retrospect that rhythmic construction of Mark's Gospel and the *gospel sense of the individual zodiac constellations* that sheds light on this rhythm important for all subsequent presentations (also considering the reader who is not yet familiar with Part 1 of this work). To this rhythmic, cosmic aspect of the zodiac signs, a new planetary point of view is added in Chapter 2, serving as a further key for the cosmic connections and starry Mysteries of John's Gospel.

PART ONE

MYSTERY OF THE STARS
THE COSMIC POINT OF DEPARTURE FOR CONTEMPLATIONS ON JOHN'S GOSPEL

1.
The Zodiac in the Cosmic Rhythm of Mark's Gospel (Overview)

The important cosmic rhythm of the zodiac signs was found earlier as the key for the contexts of Mark's Gospel—where it takes its course in three great rounds or 'octaves'—and also for those of John's Gospel, the Mystery of the angel always goes before. It forms a prelude to the events with Christ in the sign of the Fishes.

(♑ ♒)

The mystery of the angel who prepares the way for the Christ-event on the Earth ('Behold, I send my messenger [= angel] before thy face, who shall prepare thy way;' Mark 1:2), the angel-Mystery of John the Baptist (the 'Elijah-John being' or 'entelechy') prepares for Christ's work on Earth. To this 'Elijah-John prelude' belong both zodiac signs of the *Goat* and the *Waterman*. With the mountain Goat (♑), which in earlier astrology was called the 'heavenly wilderness', the motif of the 'preacher in the desert' (as Luther translates), of the 'voice crying in the wilderness' (for the 'wilderness' is, apart from that of the lands east of the Jordan, also the soul-loneliness of the Baptist, in which he encounters the heavenly 'I'). John's *motif of the baptism by water* is linked with the Waterman (♒). It was shown in the earlier exposition, how the 'Change your thinking!' (Gk. μετανοεῖτε, usually translated 'repent'), which, in a later round, returning again in the sign of the Goat, appears in the mouths of the disciples (in whom the Elijah-John being now begins to reveal himself, Mark 6:12 and MG 134). The Goat—to which on the human figure knee and elbow belong—is on the one side the sign of self-wilfulness, of dark self-will: it appears thus in the story of Herod and Herodias. In the 'change of thinking', when the knee is bent in prayer, the other side of this being and sign is revealed as devotion to the divine.

In all three 'rounds' or 'octaves' these signs, Goat and Waterman, are united with the sacrifice of John the Baptist (the Elijah-John being). Such a sacrifice already lies in the devotional being of the Baptiser of Christ in the Baptism in the Jordan. Furthermore, it lies—in the second round—in the sacrificial death of John, which then enables the disciples to work with new forces out of the spiritual world (Mark 6).

In the third round, in the Transfiguration (at the same time the third stage, that of Intuition, MG 189, 195f.), a new stage of devotion is revealed of the Elijah-John being for the Christ-event and, from then onwards, we find the disciple John increasingly as bearing this Christ-event.

Already beyond the 'third octave', in the story of Golgotha leading to the Resurrection event, the Goat as the sign of turning becomes the Turning Point of the World. The Waterman, in the first octave still the sign of John's Baptism with water, stands in the second octave, where the depths of the water and of the etheric have already become the depths of the grave of the Earth, as the sign for the entombment of John (the Mystery of death already sounds also in the third octave with the Elijah-event of the Transfiguration), and in the transition to the Resurrection the Waterman becomes the sign for the entombment of Christ Himself.

(♓)

The Goat and the Waterman are two 'dark' signs, belonging to the lower, dark part of the zodiac. The Fishes (♓), too, belong still as a 'nocturnal sign' to the semicircle of the *five lower, dark zodiac signs* (to which, as shown in MG, the 'five loaves' of one of the Feedings relate), even if therein the transition to the upper, brighter part of the zodiac already takes place, to the *seven, bright zodiac signs* (see Fig. 1). As things above and things below, summer and winter, day and night, *heaven and earth* meet in the zodiac sign of the Fishes.

- This is the sign in which the Sun stood in the heavens in the cosmic primordial past when Sun and Earth parted; it is the sign in which with the Baptism in the Jordan in the descent of Christ, the spiritual life of the Sun was once again united with the Earth. (It should be said that the sign of the Fishes stands *spiritually* over the events at the River Jordan, without thinking that the stellar constellation for the events in question stands over the outer events, over the time of year, even though relationships are possible here.)
- In the second octave the nocturnal sign of the Fishes is connected to a nocturnal Feeding, narrated in Mark 6 (that is, to be thought of as a 'night-experience', as a mediation experience). A new stage lies in this, a new revelation of Christ's earthly deeds, of the heavenly 'events of the Grail'.
- The next degree is realized in the third octave, in the Transfiguration of Christ, where the 'saying of the Son of the Sun' first heard at the Baptism in the Jordan 'Thou art my beloved Son' [Mark 1:11] appears again at the

Transfiguration, 'This is my beloved Son' [Mark 9:7]), where already the real dying of Christ into the Earth begins.
- Finally, the Fishes appear once again on the Resurrection Morning.

(♈)

In the *Ram*, in the sign of the initial ministry, after the first encounter with the earthly realm has taken place in the Fishes, the entrance of Christ into active work on the Earth takes place. Already in Mark 1 there follows the healing of those possessed, so characteristic of this gospel. Upon the re-appearance of the Ram in the third octave, so significantly connected with the Transfiguration, we find in Mark 9 the 'healing of the possessed ['epileptic'] boy', whom the disciples cannot heal, who is then healed by Christ. Here the characterizing words *of getting up and standing upright* also appear in the gospel for the *meaning of the sign of the Ram* ('and lifted him up, and he arose', Mark 9:27). The only healing of someone possessed in Mark's Gospel that does not stand in the sign of the Ram—because it has to do with a more spiritual event, for which the healing of those possessed is but a picture—is that of Mark 5, standing in the sign of the Scales, that is, not in any other sign but in the spiritually connected *counter-sign* to the Ram. Already in Mark's Gospel the relationship of sign and counter-sign, to be observed everywhere, gains in John's Gospel an enhanced significance.

As the Fishes belong to the Christ-cross, or 'Cross of the Son', to the 'Cross of Etheric' (MG, Appendix, p. 343ff.), the Ram belongs to the 'Cross of the Father', to the 'Cross of the Physical'.[14] In this sense, the Ram in the second octave characterizes the arrival on solid land after the Storm on the Lake (Mark 6, towards the end). The storm pictures the storm in the soul, the inner crisis; this 'arrival on the solid land' pictures the secure conveying of the spiritual experiences of the night to the shore of daytime consciousness. And this viewpoint is decisive in the Ram, with the healings of those possessed, for conveying those sick of a disturbed consciousness to normal day-consciousness, into the normal system of the physical forces.

(♉)

The Fishes belong to the 'Cross of the Etheric', the Ram to the 'Cross of the Physical'. The Bull (♉) that follows belongs to the 'Cross of the Astral', to the 'Cross of the Spirit'. In the sense of Indian Theosophy, this would be the Cross of the death-bringing and healing

Rudra-Shiva. On the one axis of this cross (the other is formed through the already-mentioned sign of the Waterman with that of the Lion) we find the Bull, the power of the healing word (on the human form the sign of the Bull is ordered to the organ of speech, the larynx), in an opposition to the death-sign of the Scorpion. (The Scorpion is the sign of the primordial phenomenon death; the Archer for death as fulfilment.) The Mysteries of health and illness, life and death are expressed in this axis of the zodiac.

Corresponding to this in the gospel, already in the first and then in the following octaves, we find the revelation of the divine, healing power active in the word. Christ's healings of the sick, when they take place on the Sabbath, become the cause of that ever-recurring dispute in the gospels, the dispute of Christ with the scribes and Pharisees. The healing power of the living, divine Word—so we can take the nature of these disputes—stands in this constellation facing the rigid and deadly rules of Jewish Pharisaism. This has killed the living revelation once given to Moses on Mount Sinai out of the heights of the Divine. The power of life and the power of death—as we can also say—stand opposed. The healing, divine power of life and of love at work in the word, on the one side, here faces on the other side what is dead, past, on which the Father-principle is brought to rigidity, the power resisting the living power of love of the Son.

As to other signs, to other motifs of the gospel-rhythm, other gospel words belong, to the Bull simply the word 'word' belongs (e.g. Mark 2:2). On the second stage of the rhythm, the word becomes *Inspiration* to the disciples. In the concluding picture of the healing of the deaf man governing Mark 7, the essence of the sign of the Bull is revealed as governing the whole section. All the other episodes of this chapter, especially the initially puzzling behaviour of Christ towards the Syrophoenician woman (Mark 5:25ff. MG 158ff.), become understandable from the motif of the word in the sign of the Bull.

The whole Johannine depths of the 'Word' opens on the third stage, of *Intuition*, where what was lost to humanity in the Fall of man, the Word also once again slipped away from the disciples in their initiation, and finally passes to the one becoming John as the only one penetrating through to the Christ-Initiation (Mark 9:31–10:31). All the tests and crises he still has to pass stand under the sign of the word, of the Bull (MG 208ff.). In his initiation John unites himself completely with the divine creative Word of Christ. The union of the self to the essence of the divine Word owes its inner power to the beginning of John's Gospel, 'In the primordial beginning the Word already was ...'. In this sense there stands over the Prologue to John's Gospel the sign of the word of the Bull.

(Ⅱ)

In the rhythm of the signs of the zodiac, after the Bull there follows the exalted sign of the *Twins*. In the presentation of the zodiac in the Appendix (initially MG 362f.) we can recognize the *sign of the Fishes* as the *beginning of the Deeds of Christ* (the 'heavenly ascendant'); the *Twins* form the *middle of the heavens (medium coeli)*, which in the spiritual sense they are. The region of the zodiac which one calls the 'sacred Mount of the Heavens'— as can really be seen in the constellation—culminates in the 'heavenly Twins' (Castor and Pollux), rising on winter nights over Sirius-Orion. In the gospel the Twins are the sign of the sacred Mount of Inspiration and of Initiation. Here, where they first appear, the words of Mark's Gospel belong, 'And he went up on the mountain, and ... appointed Twelve' (Mark 3:13f.). When on the second stage the motif should appear again, we find the corresponding words at the parallel passage in Matthew's Gospel (Matthew 15:29). In a special sense, in connection with the passages in question, in Mark's Gospel the two 'sons of Zebedee' James and John appear as the 'heavenly Twins'. With these 'sons of Zebedee' we have to think not of the earthly, but of the Mystery-personality of the two disciples. (On the Mystery-personality especially of John in connection with the earthly personality, see MG 45ff., 220ff., 272ff. etc.) This appears in the light of day on the third stage of the rhythm, when the 'sons of Zebedee' present their mysterious request to Christ (Mark 10:35ff., and MG 231ff., where it is attempted to show how everything is based on a Mystery-experience of John).

(♋)

After the exalted sign of the Twins, there follows the sign of turning and of descent: the *Crab*. Here we step from the Christ-Son cross of the etheric, to which the Twins belongs, to enter again the earthly physical cross. The descent from the spiritual mountain heights towards the depths of humanity, the lowlands of the illness of mankind, of human blindness and of human darkness is in Mark's Gospel the meaning of this sign, to which corresponding words of descent to humanity into the depths are allotted, as in Mark 3:19 the words, 'And he went home' (there soon follows the meeting with His mother and brothers, characteristic for the Crab, where the narrowness of blood relationships faces the embracing human love of Christ). In the third octave (Mark 10:46) the motif of descent appears in the picture of the descent from the uplands to the depths of Jericho [258 m/ 846 ft below sea level], where the healing of the blind man then follows, emphasizing the blindness of humanity (MG 249). In the sign of the Crab the Initiation of John is completed, who therein becomes the conqueror of the Crab, that is, of the negative side of this sign. *Metamorphosis of matter*, transubstantiation, becomes the higher, Johannine meaning of this sign. In the dying of the old and that which is past there is revealed the becoming of the future-bearing [principle]; in the destruction of matter [arises] the resurrection of the spirit. From the sign of mere descent to the depths, the Crab becomes the sign of turning to the spirit (note here the opposition to the Goat, to the other 'sign of turning': the Goat the Mystery of the early, pre-Christian Initiation; the Crab is united with that of the new, the Christian Initiation). To this higher, Johannine meaning of the sign of the Crab are then revealed the words in John's Gospel, 'He must increase, but I must decrease' (John 3:30), in a section that can be thought of as belonging to the sign of the Crab.

(♌)

The *Lion*, which in the first place governs the whole of Mark's Gospel and its cosmic rhythm, here unlike the other signs does not have sections outwardly aligned to it, but stands more in the background as the sign of higher overcoming, of sovereignty in the 'I'. Therewith, it is also the sign of alchemical change, of transformation of the physical through the fire of the spirit right into the depths of the blood. With Mark, the Lion belongs in a special sense more to the centre than to the periphery of the circle. Yet the motif of this sign appears in opposition to the Waterman in all clarity in the words of the gospel, 'I baptize you with water; *but he will baptize you with the Holy Spirit*' (Mark 1:8; with Matthew 3:11: 'he will baptize you *with the Holy Spirit and with fire*').

(♍)

The *Virgin*, the most etheric of all the signs, with its counter-sign the Fishes, the Christ-Son Cross of the middle, forms that 'Last-Supper constellation' so important for the Christ-Event in the gospel. In the early Mysteries it was the bearer of the 'bread of life', the forces of the cosmic life-ether; it will become this again in a new sense through the 'I'-power of Christ (cf. the Johannine, 'I am the bread of life'). The relationship of the three stages (rounds, or octaves) of the cosmic rhythm is here especially clear and evident.

The Zodiac in the Cosmic Rhythm of Mark's Gospel (Overview)

- On the first stage of Imagination, the Mystery of the cosmic Last-Supper event (the future development of the Earth and of humanity, of the 'kingdom of heaven') appears still as in a seed in the pictures of the sower and the seed (Mark 4).
- On the second stage of Inspiration, what was then received in picture and seed form for the disciples has already become an active soul-force, which enables them to progress from receiving to giving, to administer to famished humanity the bread of life, as took place then in the 'Feeding of the Four Thousand' (Mark 8). In the gospel picture of bread and fishes in both Feeding stories—the first, feeding at night in Mark 6, that of the 5000, stands in the nocturnal sign of the Fishes; the other [the 4000], to be thought of as a day-experience, in the bright daylight of the Virgin—is seen in the constellation Virgin–Fishes.
- On the third stage, that of Intuition, the meaning of the sign of the Virgin is then revealed in Christ's Last Supper itself (Mark 14); as it were the incarnated Virgin—Mary Magdalene appears (the name is only given in John's Gospel), who anointed the feet of Christ Jesus (in Mark the head).

(♎)

The sign of balance, the *Scales*, itself standing in the bright half, conveys the transition from the upper, bright part to the lower, dark part of the zodiac. It appears everywhere in the gospel where, in the pictures of the Storm on the Lake and the storm in the soul, we find the struggle for inner balance. (With the episode in Mark 6 of the Storm on the Lake primarily aligned to the Ram, the Scales as counter-sign is strongly involved.) There sounds significantly in this connection Christ's I-AM (Mark 6:50, cf. John 6:20). And in John's Gospel there appears the great 'I', the I-AM of Christ everywhere as the motif of the Scales. From the Storm on the Lake of the first experience of the Scales (Mark 4:35ff.), the disciples on the second stage (Mark 8) advance to the calm voyage on the lake. Yet there appears as summer lightning the signs of fresh soul-difficulties and crises, in which the death-sign of the Scorpion already casts its gloomy shadow (MG 173ff.).

On the third stage, the Scales—Gethsemane—we see Christ, abandoned by the disciples in the utmost anxious world-hour, struggling for the inner spiritual-physical balance for the possibility to achieve the Mystery of Golgotha, to stay with the earthly body, threatening premature dissolution. From the Last Supper Christ-Jesus is basically already a dying man; in Gethsemane already struggling in full agony; a dying man having to set all the forces of heaven into movement in order still to 'experience' the death on the cross, to keep Himself alive in the earthly body up to the Martyrdom of the cross. We see Him bringing the wavering and shuddering of the Scales of the world into balance, to win the victory of inner balance enabling all advance of the evolution of the Earth over the dark counter-forces.

(♏)

In the cosmic rhythm of the signs of the zodiac, the Scales leads over to that sign that has the serious and critical significance before all others as the 'death sign' in the whole Initiation story of Mark's Gospel, in the Christian-Johannine Initiation as such. Mysteries are hidden in this sign of the source of life, of the 'Eagle of the Sun', that first with the Fall of man became the Scorpion carrying the sting of death (♏). Already the story—to be thought under the Scales—the story of those possessed in Mark 5 allows the critical surroundings to be clearly felt, the influence of the death-bringing sign and its daemonic forces. In its opposition to the Bull, the prevailing relationship is expressed that also exists physiologically between the human forces of speech and the sexual forces [the male voice breaks, etc.]. Both signs belong significantly to the 'Cross of the Astral'.

Healing, the healing force of the living word, is revealed in the sign of the word, of the Bull. In the Scorpion the power of death is revealed, which is also the cause of illness. The two cases of illness narrated in Mark 6, standing in a sympathetic connection with the 'natural man', of which the second, the case of Jairus' daughter, has led close to the border of death, clearly point to the realm governed physiologically by the Scorpion (MG 117).

In the initiation story of the disciples, the Scorpion is the consciousness-darkening power, through which the initiation is brought into crisis. Already the story of those possessed in Mark 5, inwardly connected with the story of the Storm on the Lake in Mark 4, when taken as the picture for spiritual events, allows a premonition of this crisis. It comes fully to expression in the second round, in the darkening of Peter's consciousness at Caesarea Philippi directly after his 'confession' of Christ (MG 178ff.), and then becomes completely evident in Mark 9 in the inability of the disciples to heal the possessed boy.

Like Judas and Peter, Pontius Pilate is also under the negative influence of this sign. Judaism and Romanism reveal in their behaviour to Christ the power of death of the Scorpion. Only John in the overcoming of the power of death realizes the aim of Christian Initiation. Imaginatively speaking, he metamorphoses the Scorpion again into the Sun-Eagle—to which, as the evangelist, he is aligned in early ecclesiastical images. In overcoming and transforming, he regains the lost virginal state of the human being. For this reason, within the zodiac, the Virgin especially appears as the sign of John. Already in the first round it can be seen how this fact is revealed in the raising of Jairus' daughter. In the presence of the three disciples, in the wakeful witness especially of John, Christ speaks the words, 'Young maid, I say to you, arise!' [Mark 5:41]. Here, in something that happens outwardly, something definite also takes place in John's consciousness.

The darkening of consciousness in the meaning of the sign ♏ speaks especially out of the words in the gospel about the 'flight in winter' (Mark 3:18; MG 317). A darkening of consciousness which otherwise is a mental derangement, as the *night* of consciousness, in the corresponding picture taken from the rhythm of the year appears here as the *winter* of consciousness. The flight of the disciples in Gethsemane (Mark 14:50) is in this sense a 'flight in winter', in the night of consciousness. The motif of 'flight' plays a decisive role in John's Gospel, the dispersion and separation through the power of death darkening the consciousness. We can compare Christ's indication of the flight of the disciples at the end of the Farewell Discourses (John 16:32) and previously in John 10:12, where the adversary of the 'I' is spoken of as the 'wolf snatches them [the sheep] and scatters them'. Right into the language we find here in both passages in the Greek σκορπίζειν (*skorpizein*) the indication to the Scorpion as the sign governing the events in question.

(♐)

The Scorpion reveals the cause of death; the *Archer* reveals the accomplished death. The Archer appears first with the death of John the Baptist in Mark 6; in the second round with the 'Transfiguration' (Mark 9) it denotes in these events already the beginning of the dying of Christ; finally in the third round (Mark 15), the fulfilment of the Mystery of death, the death on Golgotha. Thus, as the other signs of the zodiac are aligned to specific *words* of the gospel, we experience in the Archer the curtailing of the word, the consecrated completion on the cross. From the 'cross of the astral', to which the Scorpion is the sign of the cause of death, we have again stepped over to the Christ-Son cross of the middle, which is also that of the Last-Supper constellation, the 'cross of the etheric'. In death, as in the Mystery of the 'deep midnight' with the Archer in the rhythm of the day, the Mystery of the source of life is revealed, of the eternal, stream of life carrying the future.

In this way, in the gospel the meaning of the twelve heavenly signs is presented, seen purely out of the gospel itself. The Sun in the circuit of the year moves through the ring of the twelve signs of the zodiac; hence is revealed in the cosmic rhythm of Mark's Gospel, in the triple progress through each of the twelve heavenly signs, the Mystery of the Sun-life of Christ and the initiation leading into this life. In witnessing and receiving the inner rhythm contained in the I-A-O of John's name itself (MG 46) the becoming of John, the Johannine Initiation, is completed to attain that level of consciousness from which the inspiration of John's Gospel has then flowed.

2.
The Planetary Aspect: The Spirit of the Planets

Weltensprossenes Wesen, du in Lichtgestalt ☉☽ Von der *Sonne* erkraftet in der *Mond*gewalt,	Offspring of all the Worlds! Thou Form of Light, Firm framéd by the *Sun*, with *Luna's* might,
♂ Dich beschenke des *Mars* erschaffendes Klingen ☿ Und *Merkurs* gliedbewegtes Schwingen,	Endow'd with sounding *Mars'* life-stirring song, And swift-wing'd *Mercury's* motion in thy limbs.
♃ Dich erleuchte *Jupiters* erstrahlende Weisheit ♀ Und der *Venus* liebetragende Schönheit	Illumin'd with radiant *Jupiter's* all-wisdom And grace-bestowing *Venus'* loveliness—
♄ Dass *Saturns* weltenalte Geist-Innigkeit Dich dem Raumessein und Zeitenwerden weihe!	That *Saturn's* ancient memoried inwardness Hallow thee to the world of Space and Time!

(Ephesian Mystery verse, according to Rudolf Steiner)

(Rudolf Steiner. *The Easter Festival in Relation to the Mysteries*. 'The Mysteries of Ephesus, the Aristotelian Categories.' Lecture, Dornach. 22 April 1924. GA 233a. Tr. based on that of George Adams.)

Before adding the planetary aspect to the cosmic rhythm of the signs of the zodiac in the gospel that results from looking for the 'governing' planet in the respective sign (that is, aligned to it in a special sense), it appears advisable to preface a few things on the whole way a *spiritual influence* of the planets is discussed. This, similar to the subject of the zodiac, differs from the purely astronomical way of looking at the matter.

Stars and Planets

We find ourselves with the zodiac, as we experienced it in the cosmic rhythm of Mark's Gospel, initially still in the 'earthly zodiac', in the 'aura of the Earth', in the auric, rhythmical periphery of the Earth. (Concerning the relationship of sign and constellation, earthly zodiac and star-zodiac, see the Introduction.) In looking to any planet and its spiritual activity standing in one of the signs of the zodiac, we raise ourselves to the *astral* of our solar system ('astral' from *astrum* 'forehead', Gk. *astron*). And with these 'planets' we are still far from the actual 'starry world' (with which a spiritually exact observation always understands only the world of the fixed stars), not in the 'star zodiac', but always only in the wider periphery of the Earth and the periphery of the Sun.

'A planet stands in this sign or starry constellation', does not mean it should be in the real neighbourhood of the fixed stars of that constellation, but that it finds itself in that part of the periphery of the Earth, which through the respective sign or constellation is determined mathematically and spatially for the eye. (When it is said, for example, 'The planet stands in the *sign* of the Ram', considering the displacement of signs and constellation, one sees it shining today in the *constellation of the Fishes*.)

The matter concerns the *constellation* as seen from the Earth, what is called the *aspect*. (When we have to do with the spiritual *effect* of one or another planet, it does, of course, depend on this *aspect*, with the position of the planet in relation to the Earth.) 'Planets' in the sense meant here are not at all 'stars in the narrow sense' (however much Venus, Jupiter, Mars, and so on, in ordinary discourse are called 'stars'—one thinks of [the planet Venus as the] 'Morning Star' and 'Evening Star'). 'Stars', according to the retained linguistic usage that has prevailed, are only the 'fixed stars'. 'Planets' are those heavenly bodies that, to our eyes looking from the Earth at the heavenly events, move on their courses in the zodiac on the ecliptic ['wandering stars']. However, not only the 'astronomical planets' Mercury, Venus, Mars, Jupiter, Saturn [visible to the naked eye], as well as those seen telescopically Uranus and Neptune [with Pluto, discovered 1930, Eris, discovered 2005, and other smaller objects], but also the Sun. The Sun from the objective, astronomical (the Copernican, heliocentric) viewpoint is taken as a fixed star. And the Moon, from the same viewpoint likewise appears not as a 'planet' (that is, a satellite of the Sun), but as the satellite of the Earth.

Geocentric and Heliocentric Conceptions: the Outer Planets and Fixed Stars

However justified and obvious for astronomical and mathematical observation and reckoning the heliocentric system is—that is, the viewpoint that places the Sun in the middle-point—the geocentric system (the viewpoint that observes things from the Earth, that is, in a certain sense places the Earth in the middle-point) is just as natural and obvious for every spiritual observation, for every spiritual or other stellar influence. The basic geocentric viewpoint obvious for all early astrology is consequently still justified when not the astronomical, mathematical reckoning, but the spiritual reckoning, some influences or other of the stars, come into question. Not only early astrology and Mystery wisdom, but also a recent spiritual way of investigating cosmic questions, in particular anthroposophy, too, speaks of 'seven planets'. Here apart from Mercury, Venus, Mars, Jupiter and Saturn also the Sun and the Moon belong. This does not exhibit some kind of 'ignorance' or 'non-scientific' pursuit. With a justified variety of viewpoints that rest on other viewpoints, in *its* realm a spiritual view is in no way detrimental to the likewise fully justified astronomical and mathematical notions.

Some 'experts' in astronomical things might perhaps object that in accepting this 'planetary' unity of seven, nevertheless there lies something incorrect, 'not scientific'. It appears not to recognize the facts—or, as it appears, in any case ignores them. For example, beyond Saturn there are two planets, *Uranus* and *Neptune*, very distant from the Sun, the duration of whose orbits exceed that of Jupiter and Saturn several times over.[15] Or have these two planets, far distant from the Sun, perhaps nothing more to do with the spirit-side of our solar system? One view that comes into consideration draws on the spiritual nature of the entire cosmos, therewith also the spiritual nature of the stars. The scientific explanation was given in the Introduction. It is clear that the acceptance of the spiritual in the stars cannot stop with Uranus and Neptune. It is only always pointed out, also by Steiner, that both these distant outer 'wandering worlds' originate from a different cosmic context than our solar system. The purely astronomical facts already suggest this. The moons of these planets move in retrograde motion, differing from [all] the moons of the planets nearer the Sun. Here, as otherwise, it is important not to neglect the facts of a purely empirical science; rightly considered, this will not contradict a genuine spiritual research but actually confirm it.

Both those planets, far-distant from the Sun, Uranus and Neptune, as Steiner always presents it, came later to our solar system, even if it was in the far distant past. To understand this properly we have to rise to imagine a more etheric character of the planetary system in the cosmic primordial history that preceded the form of today. The spiritual character and activity of the far-distant planets *Uranus* and *Neptune*—for all confirming experiences in this area are readily available, here nowhere denied—appear as *mediators between the planetary world of our solar system and the actual world of the stars* (the world of the fixed stars). Like a 'greeting out of the world distances' the late discoveries in recent times (Uranus 1781, Neptune 1846) can be felt for both planets invisible to the naked eye. It is as if the 'spirit of the age' only led to this discovery when something in humanity—initially perhaps only in a few individuals—began to become receptive for those fine and distant rays from the cosmos.

Saturn as the original boundary marker of our solar and planetary system—for this reason it is also the 'guardian of the cosmic primordial memory', the 'original cosmic spiritual inwardness' in the sense of the Ephesian Mystery verse [quoted above]. Saturn is the guardian of everything on Earth that leads to consolidation, manifesting in earthly gravity. In the realm of the consolidated minerals, the metals of the Earth, the influence of Saturn appears as lead, the Sun's rays as gold, and the Moon's rays as silver.[16]

In the forces of Saturn, or at least in one side of its manifestation, there lies the *earthly* element. The subtle rays of Uranus and Neptune point human beings to the cosmos, to the *star-element*, the actual stellar worlds, to those regions to which in their innermost being they originally belong, but from which in their conscious being they have increasingly fallen.

For this reason, Uranus and Neptune do not belong, spiritually seen, to the narrower solar system, the [family of] 'seven planets' which as such holds its own, despite the later additions of more outer planets. These appear much rather as sent by the actual 'starry world'. In future they will have increasingly more to say to human beings. As they become more receptive for the fine cosmic raying that brings revelations of subtler forces of nature and of the spirit, new ways to advance are revealed. Thereby the spiritual nature and influence of these two planets far distant from the Sun are fully recognized, and yet at the same time the fact set forth and established that they stand *outside the system of seven planets* and why this is so.

Some people take these two planets as a 'higher octave' of the two inner planets that are closer to the Sun, Mercury and Venus; in some respects Uranus would be placed with Venus rather than with Mercury. In any case, it is important to distinguish various planetary categories. Apart from:

(i) the 'two lights' Sun and Moon (not counted as planets in the astronomical sense),
(ii) the two *inner* planets *close to the Sun* (whose spheres for the geocentric view crosses in multifarious ways) between the Sun and the Earth, then
(iii) the *outer* planets Mars, Jupiter, Saturn beyond the Earth's orbit (seen from the Earth, beyond the Sun's course), of which Mars is distinguished through its proximity to the Earth, divided from Jupiter and Saturn by the belt of asteroids (according to Steiner the debris of a former planet): Jupiter and Saturn are planets far distant from the Earth;
(iv) finally, the planets *most distant* from the Sun, Uranus and Neptune, which we already feel as dispatched from, and mediators [to and from] the actual 'starry world'. Also in their extremely slow 'wandering'— the movements in the heavens of the resting, or 'fixed stars', is only perceptible over long periods of time—these two planets resemble the stars.

Seen from all these viewpoints, the name *Uranus* has been meaningfully chosen. Uranus, *uranós* (οὐρανός) means in Greek the 'starry heaven', or, to distinguish it from the planets of the actual solar system the 'upper starry sky' as it was spiritually seen and experienced from an earlier Mystery-wisdom. This spiritual entity Uranós still *stands above Saturn* and precedes it cosmogonically. Uranos in the Greek myth is the father of Saturn-Cronos, who is the father of Jupiter-Zeus: out of the semen of Uranos that had fallen into the sea to become the froth of the sea, Venus-Aphrodite was born. We distinguish Uranós in the spiritual sense, the spiritual Uranus-sphere,[17] as the sphere of the upper heavens beyond Saturn, from the mere 'Uranus planet'. This telescopic 'planet Uranus' (only just visible to the naked eye, as a 'star of 6th magnitude') was discovered by Herschel in 1781. The Uranós, the upper Saturnian heaven as spiritual sphere, was already known in ancient pre-Christian Mysteries: in Friedrich Creutzer (*Symbolik und Mythologie der alten Völker*, Bk. 2, p. 49) we find the indication that in the Egyptian Mysteries *eight planetary gods* or 'Kabiri-gods' were spoken of; over the planetary seven (Sun, Moon, Mercury, Venus, Mars, Jupiter and Saturn) the *starry firmament* was revered as the eighth Kabiri-god. This exactly corresponds to the Greek *uranós*, from which in modern times the planet beyond Saturn discovered by Herschel received its name.

And this distinguishing quality is in a certain sense at the same time that which links. For as a boundary-stone of the world beyond Saturn of the 'upper heavens' (Uranós) that planet Uranus can be seen as in a completely natural and intimate way. One felt or had an inkling for the connection simply existing here as the name was given to the newly discovered planet. The name 'Uranus' can be felt as if inspired by the Spirit of the Age. And the Mystery of this *spiritual Uranus-sphere of the early Mysteries*, the 'upper starry heavens' (*uranós*), on which it reminds us, is raised in John's Gospel (note especially the word οὐρανός *uranós* in John 3:12-3 and 6:31-3, 38, 41-2, 50-1, 58) in a very significant manner *into* the *Christ-sphere*.

Planetary Influences

With this differentiation—not excluding the mutual relationship—of the outer planet Uranus (discovered in 1781) from the 'spiritual sphere of Uranus' (already known in the early Mysteries), at the same time a general, and for the further exposition important viewpoint is presented. Everything said here or elsewhere about the spiritual entity of the planets and the planetary influence should not be too closely and one-sidedly connected with the *visible planet*. The visible planet is, as it were, but the sensory reflex of this entity, the zodiac field in the earthly-auric sense as the etheric field of forces and area of influence appearing in the periphery of the Earth. The spiritual nature of a planet is revealed in the whole ('astral') sphere, evident and felt in its rays. In order to explain, for example, the obvious connection of the Moon and its phases with the tides of ebb and flood of the sea, we do not need to assume some 'magical remote control' of the Moon; it only depends on raising the accustomed physical concept into the direction of a finer, higher, 'etheric' realm of forces (as described in Guenther Wachsmuth's *The Etheric Formative Forces: Cosmos, Earth and Man*). Then one sees in the whole sphere between Earth and Moon (or the Moon's orbit) the activity of the spiritual-etheric Moon. 'Moon' in this sense is then not only the astronomical Moon visible as the Earth's satellite, but the whole of the sphere bounded by the Moon's orbit, with the Earth at the centre.

It is similar with the 'astral' influences of the Moon, felt even more in the soul element; it is similar, too, with the etheric and astral spiritual influences and essences of the planets. Venus, in the sense meant here, is not only the visible Morning and Evening Star, but the whole sphere whose centre is the Earth and which is bounded approximately by the orbit of Venus. It is similar with all the others, with Mercury, Sun, Mars, Jupiter, Saturn, Uranus and Neptune. For contemplation looking at the spiritual spheres of the planets, the Earth always stands in the middle. For the spiritual view this 'geocentric' viewpoint is just as natural as the purely astronomical-mathematical view is for the other view. From a still higher viewpoint, the initially 'geocentric' appearance of this manner of viewing, with a gentle alteration of the letters, becomes *ego-central* (that is, here not 'egoistic', but in a completely objective, justified sense placing the 'I' in the centre). A spiritual contemplation can only and always proceed from the 'I'; this 'I' (or the place of this 'I') is always the middle. Through the connection of the World-'I' with the earthly in the Mystery of Golgotha, the fact just presented can be present in the consciousness in a still more elevated sense.

The point, then, where Sun, Moon and planets stand in the heavens, is only, as it were, a dragging into visibility of the spiritual, etheric and astral essence and activity filling the whole of space. This [portion of 'outer'] space is bounded by the planetary orbits whose middle-point is the Earth. Inasmuch as the word 'space' is used, there still adheres to it much of an earthly way of imagining things, much Maya ['illusion', or more accurately 'delusion']. All these things are bridges, [models] to an understanding. For a higher understanding, a consciousness approaching reality, 'space' would be overcome, only the *spiritual* activity of the stars would still remain present. This applies in a certain sense also for the experience of soul and spirit between death and a new birth: space, time and material, as we experience them *here*, only belong to the time-span between birth and death. The worlds of the stars *there* are entered into as spiritual spheres.

Out of this purely spiritual encounter with the spirit of the planetary and stellar spheres in the 'life between death and a new birth', the fact of birth-horoscopes become understandable (already touched on in the Introduction). For the human being is born out of the starry cosmos.[18]

The Spiritual Hierarchies

Rudolf Steiner develops the connection of the spiritual planetary fields with the sphere of the spiritual beings, the heavenly hierarchies (*The Spiritual Hierarchies and their Reflection in the Physical World.* Düsseldorf, 12-18 April 1909. GA 110). He shows how the whole construction of interpenetrating planetary spheres of the planetary 'heavenly ladder' corresponds to the spiritual hierarchies (from the Angels to the Cherubim and Seraphim, initially to the Thrones).

- The Moon-sphere as the one lying nearest to us (what is meant is the sphere bounded by the orbit of the Moon, with the Earth as the middle-point) coincides with that of the Angeloi (Angels);
- the sphere of Venus and Mercury coincides with that of the Archangeloi (Archangels) and Archai ('Primordial Powers');
- the Sun-sphere itself (that is, the sphere between Earth and Sun)[19] with that of the 'Spirits of Form';
- the Mars-sphere (which at the same time would correspond to that of 'Ancient Moon' (the third incarnation of planet Earth], named thus in Steiner's *Esoteric/ Occult Science.* GA 13, MG 84) with that of the 'Spirits of Movement';
- the Jupiter-sphere (that would correspond to 'Ancient Sun' in *Esoteric/ Occult Science* [the third incarnation of planet Earth]) coincides with the sphere of the 'Spirits of Wisdom';
- the Saturn-sphere coincides with that of the Thrones ('Spirits of Will'). At the same time, this 'Saturn-sphere' essentially corresponds with 'the sphere of Ancient Saturn' [the first incarnation of planet Earth] described in *Esoteric/ Occult Science*, with what would astronomically simply be the 'solar system' (but limited to the 'seven planets'), the comprehensive sphere that, as the seventh, embraces all the others.

The two still higher hierarchies, Cherubim ('Spirits of the Light') and Seraphim ('Spirits of Love') point beyond Saturn to the regions of the 'upper starry heavens' (*uranós*), the actual cosmos of stars. We do not, for instance, have to arrange it simply with the spiritual sphere of Uranus and Neptune, but yet recognize how in these two planets far-distant from the Sun there is already the essence of the actual 'starry heavens' (consequently the name Uranus), announced by the cherubinic and seraphic presence.

The Planetary Characters: Planetary Regions

Of the nature of the planets, like that of the zodiac rhythm, little is to be found in the world of the stars as conceived in astronomy. Yet like the zodiac rhythm, *the spirituality of the planets is revealed everywhere, as above so below,* as in the heavens so on the Earth, as in the stars, so in the stones, plants, the human being and the animal. Concerning the revelation of the planets in the lap of the Earth, in the metals—Sun gold, Moon silver, Saturn lead, Mars iron, etc.—this has already been mentioned, and also the recent scientific work to show the connection purely empirically. For the 'star', that, as it were, is dragged into visibility as etheric-spiritual rays is present in *all* realms. *Its most prominent, all-comprehensive revelation, however, is the human being.* Everything expressed in the human being from the physical up to soul and spirit, and all relationships of human beings to each other, is in some way or other revealing planetary spirituality. Here we meet these planets most directly. The time will one day arrive when all physiology and psychology will be fructified in a decisive way by this knowledge. Directly from human nature one can get to know the Mars-nature, the Jupiter-nature, the Sun-like quality (in the sense of soul and spirit), the Venus (grace, revealing love and beauty), and so on.[20]

- One only has to see how in everything revealed directly from the human being of a graceful, loving nature; an amiable, artistic nature; a soul-filled charm and engaging quality is revealed, how precisely the same spiritual qualities are also expressed in the rays of the *Venus*-star. Not for nothing does language contain expressions like *'Stern des Auges'*, 'star of the eye'—what beholds us out of the eye of a human being, is for a deeper observation in the last resort really the same as that which is revealed in the rays of a specific planetary star.
- Even the martial, the Sun-like expression, and so on, can be found located in an eye. In the strong, forward pressing, energetic, also in the passionate aspect of the human being, *Mars* can be revealed, just as in a more persuasive, convincing power of the word (the *soulful* element of the word is *Venus*);
- in the aspect of understanding, the many guises of *Mercury*,
- *Jupiter* dominates in wisdom, then
- leading into earthly gravity, the dual nature of *Saturn*, carrying in itself the forces of [old] age, relates to the cosmic preserver of boundaries,

or 'Guardian of the Threshold' between the Earth and the cosmos, as discussed above.

- Even the manifestations of *Uranus* and *Neptune* can be found in the human constitution at least here and there already today, where developed people have evolved a receptivity for distant and fine cosmic rays—for these two planets really point to cosmic regions.

It is neither easy nor simple without more ado, or at all possible, to encapsulate the spiritual nature of the planets with a short slogan. For such a thing language basically does not lend itself; today's language is too abstract. Only in looking up to the spiritual planetary beings, raising ourselves from the abstract to the really tangible—above all in psychology—for this reason these planetary beings are something very real, speaking about them much more than a mere 'mystical playing around'. The value of expounding the gospel consists here as everywhere in raising what otherwise easily remains in the abstract to the highest living level, at least to a spiritual vision encountering the divine primordial grounds. What it is able to achieve in this connection for spiritual knowledge of the zodiac, it can do also for that of the planetary entities. In the gospel we shall recognize most clearly, in the most living way, the *divine primordial motifs* of the individual planetary beings.

Ephesian Mysteries Verse

A help for us can be the verse placed as a motto at the head of this chapter, given by Rudolf Steiner as the 'Ephesian Mysteries verse'. In this work, making a link to this verse is all the more justified as it was indeed the Mystery-centre of Ephesus from which the inspiration of John's Gospel was received in the evangelist's maturity. John's Gospel is completely penetrated by the spirit of a Christened star-wisdom and planetary wisdom, which we may bring into a very close relationship with the planetary wisdom of the Ephesian Mystery-centre. As always, a more philological contemplation may ponder thereon, for a deeper research penetrating into the spiritual connections it is completely illuminating that not only John's Gospel but also John's Apocalypse flowed from the same source of inspiration. It was the same unique Johannine spirit—regardless who, seen outwardly the 'author' of the document or fragments that we have today as the 'Apocalypse', the 'Book of Revelation', might have been. Right into important details of expression—still to be encountered in the exposition of this book—this is clearly shown. John's Gospel and John's Apocalypse inwardly belong together in style and content; they mutually carry and support each other; the one document is for the other the most important source of interpretation.

Thus, serving John's Gospel as one of its sources of inspiration the Ephesian Mystery and planetary wisdom finds its expression, for example, in the Apocalypse 5:12, in the 'song of the four creatures/ beasts', which in Luther and RSV, as representative, somewhat indifferent translations, run: 'Worthy is the Lamb who was slain, to receive power and wealth and wisdom and might and honour and glory and blessing!' (already quoted in MG 223). A look at the Greek original allows us to recognize quite clearly in the partly rather unclear and tautological current translations seven attributes of the Lamb (Christ) in this Ephesian Mystery verse containing 'seven planetary virtues'.

Ἄξιόν ἐστιν τὸ ἀρνίον τὸ ἐσφαγμένον
Worthy is the Lamb — having been slain

λαβεῖν τὴν δύναμιν καὶ πλοῦτον καὶ σοφίαν
to receive the power and riches and wisdom

καὶ ἰσχὺν καὶ τιμὴν καὶ δόξαν καὶ εὐλογίαν.
and strength and honour and glory and blessing

- δύναμις (*dynamis*) signifies '*power, moving force*' pointing to the strength of the Moon;
- ἰσχὺς (*is-chys*) 'strength' to the strength of the Sun-'I' and spiritual revelation of the Sun (note, even if it cannot be the meaning for the linguist-researcher, the sound with ichthys, 'fish', the Sun-sign ♓);
- πλοῦτος (*plutos*) 'riches'—in the spiritual sense, as 'riches of cosmic primordial recollection'—is the planetary virtue of Saturn,
- σοφία (*sophia*) 'wisdom', that of Jupiter,
- εὐλογία (*eulogia*), quite literally, 'the talent to speak well' is the planetary virtue of Mars (not to be confused with its other, more daemonic revelation),
- τιμὴ (*timé*) 'honour, esteem', the deliberative, estimating attitude of the two bowls of the weighing scales, is the planetary virtue of Mercury,
- δόξα (*doxa*) 'the light of revelation, the splendour of revelation, revealed beauty' is Venus.

Thus we now recognize the Johannine, Christened meaning of the Ephesian Mystery verse:

Weltensprossenes Wesen,	Offspring of all the Worlds!
du in Lichtgestalt	Thou Form of Light,
Von der *Sonne* erkraftet (ἰσχὺς ☉)	Firm framéd by the *Sun*, with
in der *Mond*gewalt (δύναμις ☽)	*Luna's* might,
Dich beschenke des *Mars*	Endow'd with sounding *Mars'*
erschaffendes Klingen (εὐλογία ♂)	life-stirring song,
Und *Merkurs* gliedbewegtes	And swift-wing'd *Mercury's*
Schwingen (τιμὴ ☿)	motion in thy limbs.
Dich erleuchte *Jupiters*	Illumin'd with radiant *Jupi-*
erstrahlende Weisheit (σοφία ♃)	*ter's* all-wisdom
Und der *Venus* liebetragende	And grace-bestowing *Venus'*
Schönheit (δόξα ♀)	loveliness—
Dass *Saturns* weltenalte	That *Saturn's* ancient memo-
Geist-Innigkeit (πλοῦτος ♄)	ried inwardness
Dich dem Raumessein und	Hallow thee to the world of
Zeitenwerden weihe!	Space and Time!

3.
The Planetary Aspect in the Cosmic Rhythm of the Gospel

The spirit of the planets and also the zodiac, discussed in the previous chapter, is revealed in the most varying earthly and cosmic realms, inasmuch as the characteristics and effects of the individual planetary beings expressed particularly in the individual signs of the zodiac unfold their activity in a special way there. People consequently speak of 'houses' of the individual planets in the zodiac, as of signs in which the essence and activity of a particular planet is expressed most purely and strongly. Thus:

- the relationship of the Sun to the sign of the Lion—where, as in the August-sign, the Sun unfolds purely outwardly its strongest activity on the [northern] most populated half of the globe—as already mentioned in the exposition on Mark's Gospel (MG 99f. 280f.).
- Likewise the Moon, of the wandering stars [the most] rapid in manifesting its waxing and waning, is connected with the Crab, with the sign of the decline of the day after its previous increase (MG 239), which then in a higher sense is also the sign of change and transformation (MG 278).
- Likewise with the arrangement of the Sun to the Lion, one thinks not only of the unfolding of the outer Sun's warmth in high summer, but of the revelation of a spiritual solar activity and soul-warmth in the region of the human heart that is aligned to the Lion (MG 21f., 99f., 280f.). In the Lion, in its esoteric sign (MG 99), the Sun is the 'Lord of the house' (cf. Mark 13:35; 3:27. MG 280f.).[21]

The 'houses' of the other planets are found in an early [Western] tradition of humanity in this way, that they proceed from the ☉ Sun (Lion) and ☽ Moon (Crab)—these two have each only *one* house in the zodiac. The planets are arranged to the individual signs of the zodiac in their sequence from the nearest to the Sun to the farthest from the Sun. As *houses* there appear:

☿ Mercury, Virgin and Twins,
♀ Venus, Scales and Bull,
♂ Mars, Scorpion and Ram,
♃ Jupiter, Archer and Fishes,
♄ Saturn, Goat and Waterman.

With this arrangement, we see the 'seven planets' distributed over the twelve positions of the zodiac.

Initially, we take this whole arrangement as hypothetical. The point everywhere here is not to take dogmatically some view from early tradition, but to check it with the gospel, waiting to see what results out of the gospel itself regarding the spirit of the planets and the connections with the individual signs of the zodiac.

If one wants to extend the arrangement in question to include both outer planets far distant from the Sun, Uranus and Neptune, then by securing Sun-Lion as the point of departure, we find for Uranus the Waterman and for Neptune the Fishes as the 'house' in which the respective planet would unfold its strongest activity. Because we already know the Waterman as a 'house' of Saturn, and the Fishes as a 'house' of Jupiter, there would be in the Waterman alongside the activity of Saturn (which in the Goat is the only or strongest governing sign), an activity of Uranus, in the Fishes, alongside the activity of Jupiter there would be an activity of Neptune.[22]

♄

We turn from here, from the aspects of the signs of the zodiac, to the already developed rhythm of Mark's Gospel, in order to consider this rhythm also from the planetary aspect. Immediately, we are struck how the signs of the zodiac, the Goat and the Waterman, the planetary 'houses of Saturn', always appear in the rhythm of Mark's Gospel as belonging together, as the two 'Elijah-John signs', and as such always as a preparation, forming a 'prelude' to the events of Christ in each round. Through combining both zodiac signs ♑ and ♒ with the same planet Saturn, the zodiac duality is dissolved into a planetary unity. In the dark Goat, in the 'heavenly wilderness' and loneliness, Saturn rules alone. Here we find the Baptist John, as he experiences the consciousness of humanity at the threshold of time facing the soul-loneliness and 'I'-abandonment of the 'I' (Christ). Here, at this cosmic threshold of Saturn, the Baptist holds his sermon on changing one's thinking. The cosmic day of Saturn is to pass over into the cosmic Sun-day of Christ.

In this other Elijah-John sign, in the Waterman, in the sign of the baptism by water, Uranus is the co-governor with Saturn. Here we already feel the proximity of Christ, Who descends out of the spirit of the upper star-world, of *uranós*, in the sense of John's Gospel (as that, too, of the Greek Mysteries).[23] The 'water of the etheric' always to be experienced in the Waterman, of the etheric of human origins is still shining, connected to a bright stellar being. Here the light-ether is active, with which Uranus is connected in a special way (see previous endnote). John the Baptist himself, as we saw, is still deeply united with this etheric origin of the human being.

♃

The actual union of Christ with the Earth takes place in the sign of the Fishes. The *'Kyrios Christus'* [the Lord Christ], the 'Sun-spirit of wisdom' comes to the Earth. We discussed above the connection of the 'Spirits of Wisdom' (Gk. *Kyriotetes*) with the Jupiter-sphere. The 'wisdom' itself is represented in Jupiter, whose house is the Fishes. We often call this sign the 'Sun-sign', because the Jupiter-sphere [with its satellites-cum-planets is a 'memory' of that incarnation of planet Earth] (this cosmogony is described in Rudolf Steiner's *Esoteric/ Occult Science*) termed 'Ancient Sun' (see MG 84). Out of this realm of 'Ancient Sun', the spiritual primordial Sun, the Christ descends to the Earth. He brings it spiritually with Him; the planet Jupiter, which is housed in the Fishes, appears as the boundary mark for this realm.

This connection of Jupiter with the sphere of 'Ancient Sun' appears especially strongly with the revelation of Christ's Sun-splendour in the 'Transfiguration on the Mount' (MG 189ff., esp. p. 192f.) which embraces both Jupiter-signs, the Fishes and the Archer—between them the two Saturn-signs Goat and Waterman are connected to the revelation of Elijah-John.

According to an already mentioned astrological viewpoint—co-governor with Jupiter in the sign of the Fishes is Neptune, far distant from the Sun. Does it link with a sound from the farthest cosmic distances to the experiences of the Christ-Sun? This would apply to the event in the Jordan and the Transfiguration, as well as the 'Grail experience' of the Feeding of the Five Thousand, which also stands in the Fishes. The Fishes belong to what is called the 'triangle of the element of water', that is ordered to the sound-ether (MG 361ff.) and is also the 'Johannine triangle'. The Johannine relationship to the sound-ether and cosmic music comes out everywhere. This again is related to the Sun-distant planet Neptune, whereas with Uranus the light-ether stands in the foreground.

♂

The descent of Christ into the earthly realm takes place in the Fishes; the *beginning of His earthly ministry* takes place in the following sign of the Ram. In Mark's Gospel (Mark 1:21) this coincides with the beginning of His teaching in Capernaum. *Mars in the Ram* is the planet in question (εὐλογία, 'ability to speak well' in the Ephesian Mystery verse) and the active unfolding of power, whereas in the dark Scorpion the daemonic side of Mars comes more to expression. In Mark's Gospel the healings of those possessed in the section in the Ram are significant. The motif of becoming upright and the returning of the sick into the normality of the earthly forces corresponds here to the positive side of Mars' influence in the Ram, whereas in those possessed already the daemonic side of Mars chimes. This is especially the case with the grotesque story of the daemoniac in Mark 5 ['Legion'], where alongside the Scales, the counter-sign of the Ram, the daemonic side of Mars in the Scorpion can be more felt.

♀

The message of Mars leads outwards. The deeper soul-force of the word is bound with *Venus*, who is at home in the Bull, in the sign of the word, and the organ of speech initially unfolds more its earthly activity (according to Steiner in his lecture on the planetary beings, Dornach 27 July 1923). And so we find in the gospel the healings of the sick by Christ in the word-sign of the Bull at the same time revealing the activity of the divine-healing forces of love, *Venus*. Wherever the forces of the word and of love are inwardly connected, there is revealed the influence of Venus. (In the little book: Hermann Beckh, 'Genesis' in *From the Mysteries*, TL 2020, it is pointed out how the same configuration of sounds which in Hebrew mean 'to speak' (*amor*) mean in Latin 'love'.) In this sense the sections of the gospel in the Bull are at the same time sections in Venus.

Where in the sign of the word of the Bull the 'dead leaven' of the Pharisees opposes the living word of Christ, where scribes and Pharisees always want to kill what is living in words, there appears everywhere the opposition of Bull and Scorpion in the planetary influence of Venus and Mars. On the axis of this contrast we find in John's Gospel above all in Chapter 5 the healing of the paralytic at the Pool of Bethesda with the clash with the Pharisees.

In this opposition, this 'standing over the cross'[24] of Venus and Mars in the zodiac sign of Bull and Scorpion, a fact is revealed of the 'Fall of man'. The activity of Mars is the actual reason that the human soul no longer purely recognizes and loves Venus as a being; love is entangled in sexuality and is mistaken for it. Here Mars and Venus appear in an impure link and connection. With the influence of Mars from the Scorpion everything that is daemonic stands connected, tending to pull downwards in this area, whereas the Moon is the high cosmic regulator of the life of the genders and its rhythms. In Mars there lies moreover the aggressive male aspect, in the Moon the female aspect of this subject. Venus, the aloof, maidenly planet—expounded by Rudolf Steiner in above-mentioned lecture—has originally nothing to do with it. Its realm is the manifesting, love-bearing beauty (δόξα), radiating, shining love. Only through the Christ-impulse, out of the depths of Johannine-Christian recognition, can this being, Venus, darkened by the Fall of man through the activity of the Scorpion and Mars be restored and experienced in its purity.[25] For this reason Venus is hidden from all others, the most 'occult', the *esoteric* amongst the planets—as H.P. Blavatsky rightly recognizes in her *Secret Doctrine* (II, 31ff.).

This knowledge of the being of Venus in her original purity and beauty, John finds on the path of his initiation-experience that reveals the return of the Taurus-Venus sign on the third round of the rhythm of Mark's Gospel. Especially the section Mark 10:2-16, as the earlier exposition showed (MG 213ff.), can be understood in this light. This passage does not deal with a conventional 'sermon on divorce'. It concerns the primordial Mysteries already touched on in Genesis, of the masculine-feminine principle in human nature. The Christian disciple in the making, John, growing into an Intuition bestowed on him by Christ Himself, John in the knowledge of this secret, or Mystery, won back the childlike, virginal purity of human nature (on this Mark 10:14-16, MG 217f.). Lost primordial Mystery wisdom, the *Mystery of Isis and Osiris* (called the Egyptian Mystery), lives again in this knowledge. In a Christian context, Isis is revealed afresh in her original purity; in her planetary aspect she is none other than Venus (the fixed-star aspect of Isis is Sirius [the brightest star in the sky]). (See Friedrich Creutzer. *Symbolik und Mythologie der alten Volker*. II. 46 [e-book of all four volumes available free on several internet sites].) 'But when the Sun is in the sign of the Bull, she is in *domicilio Veneris*, or, Egyptian: in the house of Isis.' Isis is the Egyptian name for Venus, as Istar-Astarte is the Babylonian name. We met her in a decadent form in the episode of the Syrophoenician woman and her degraded Mystery-centre (Mark 7).

☿

With the zodiac sign of the Bull, Isis-Venus as the planetary governess of this sign stands over the whole flowering of the early Egyptian Mysteries. The origin of these Mysteries belongs to a still earlier (prehistoric) primordial age, when the spring equinox stood in the sign of the Twins governed by Hermes-Mercury. Here Hermes Trismegistos, the mystical inaugurator of the Egyptian Mysteries, appears as the representative of the divine-planetary Hermes-Mercury. And we shall touch ever again on the Mystery, already mentioned, of an original close union of the Venus-sphere with the Mercury-sphere (for the geocentric conception it already exists to a certain extent purely astronomically) in the word *hermaphrodite* ([Gk.] Hermes-Aphrodite = [Lat.] Mercury-Venus), when not taken in its pathological sense of today, but understood in its divine primordial meaning from Mark 10:6 with Genesis 1:27. And the usual planetary signs (☿ Mercury, ♀ Venus) express the relationship meant here. The one Mystery lies in the difference between the beings Venus and Mars—who governs the actual sexual factor—the other Mystery lies in its original union of being with Mercury. One then understands why Venus has one of its houses today not, as one would presume, in the Virgin, but in the Scales; and Mercury, not as one would presume, in the Scales, but in the Virgin. (The other Mercury house is in the Twins.) A relationship of Venus to the Virgin, of Mercury to the Scales, stands in the background even today.

☽

In the gospel, in the sign of the Twins that follows the Bull, Christ leads the disciples on the *Mount* and there begins with them the work of *Initiation* (Mark 3:13ff; MG 86ff.; 231ff.). This completely agrees with that which was said previously on the role of Hermes-Mercury, the planet governing the Twins, as the initiator and inaugurator of the great pre-Christian Mysteries. In the sign of the Twins, of Hermes-Mercury, in which the great pre-Christian Mystery-impulses were given, Christ Jesus also moves for the initial preparations of Christian Initiation. The significance of Hermes-Mercury as the great initiator is fulfilled in Christ and in John, the disciple of Christ. The mysterious sign of the Mercury staff stands over the early Egyptian and the early Indian Yoga-initiation[26] as well as standing over Christian initiation. The Mystery of Venus-Mercury originally indicated in the word 'hermaphrodite', the leading back of love into the divine in the highest Christ-sense, is achieved in the union of John with the Mother under the cross (John 19:26, 27). There the becoming of the disciple of love is achieved.

In the sign following the Twins, the sign of the Crab that descends and turns, amongst the planets the *Moon* is revealed. This has frequently been mentioned both here and in the previous exposition (see especially MG 239f. and what is said about Jericho as the 'City of the Moon'). The tendency of the Crab-Moon sign to drag down and solidify into the earthly-material element is that which John overcomes in his initiation. The high *alchemy of the Earth* is revealed in the Johannine metamorphosis (transubstantiation) of the earthly element. The lunar element of this sign in its higher, alchemical meaning appears in the third round of the initiation of John (MG 238).[27]

We see the alchemical metamorphosis of the earthly element with the Moon-sign of the Crab working with the Sun-sign of the Lion (MG 280f.). The Lion, unlike the other signs of the zodiac, does not have its own section in Mark's Gospel, but esoterically is taken as the heart-centre of the entire rhythm. All this becomes clearer through the planetary aspect when the frequently-mentioned fact is taken into consideration that the Lion is the house of the Sun.

☉ ☿

With the Sun in the Lion, we reach the other solar point of departure for allocating the other planetary houses. In the sign following the Lion, the Virgin, we find the planet nearest the Sun, *Mercury*. And looking at the gospel, the question arises: How are the sections standing in the sign of the Virgin linked with the planet Mercury, that is,

> in the first round the Parable of the Seed and the Sower,
> in the second round the 'Feeding of the Four Thousand',
> in the third round the Last Supper of Christ?

Initially, certainly insofar as Hermes-Mercury is the Priest-Initiator, and the events in question have to do with the specific degrees of the life of the disciples' initiation (as is shown in detail in the exposition of Mark's Gospel).

To all this, certain very significant specific aspects are brought to our attention by Friedrich Creuzer in his *Symbolik und Mythologie der alten Völker*. We find in the gospel narration of the Parable of the Seed the passage, 'To you has been given the secret of the kingdom of God, but for those outside everything is in parables; so that they may indeed see but not perceive, and may indeed hear but not understand' (Mark 4:11 RSV. See MG 104f.) and 'he did not speak to them without a parable, but privately to his own disciples he explained everything' (Mark 4:34 RSV). The *exoteric teaching* in pictures and parables for the people appears here set opposite the *esoteric* explanation for the disciples. This touches on Mysteries of Hermes-Mercury, about which we read in Creuzer,[28] whereby we observe that it has initially to do with Egyptian conditions there: 'Hermes has to take on two forms. Not all knowledge and all wisdom is for everyone; the best has to remain in the halls of the temple, only priests and kings are able to enjoy it.[']'[29] They are the *esotericists*; the rest of the knowledge is for the people, the *exotericists*. So, too, the script. This is twofold: a closed system of animal signs, hieroglyphs, only legible to the initiates; and an open, public system of letters, recognizable to everyone. Through the Mystery of Golgotha, *this* way of differentiating the exoteric from the esoteric—not the difference itself—indeed ended. In the Christian era the connections in this realm lie differently than in the Egyptian pre-Christian era, whereby, however, it is to be borne in mind that the Parable of the Sower was told, as everything that took place during the three years of Christ's earthly ministry, precisely *before* Golgotha. Christ created what was actually *new* for the world only through His *death*. In everything that took place *prior* to this (for example, even in the raising of Lazarus) moments from the earlier [traditions] and the earlier initiation play in.

A further Mercury-motif of the sign of the 'Virgin with the sheaf'[30] lies in the *individual grain* itself, in the grain of wheat, which then later becomes the bread of the Feeding and of the Last Supper. We find Creuzer (ibid. 116) on this:

> But he (Hermes) as agrarian intelligence is the eternal bread ... He is the drink offering from the chalices of grace. Whoever receives him into themselves, is an initiate; whoever drinks from his cup is refreshed, his longing is satisfied; to whose lantern he lights, he is in the light; whoever sees in his mirror, sees through all natures and creatures. Such a person is the priest alone; he is Hermes. He reads in the stars, he writes the script of the heavens, the hieroglyphs ...

♀

The next sign, the *Scales*, appears in the gospel narration:

- for the first time in the episode of the Storm on the Lake (Mark 4:35-41). In the following story of the daemoniac ['Legion'] in Mark 5, motifs of the Scorpion play in (MG 112ff.).
- The Scales are strongly emphasized in the second round, lying on the zodiac axis Ram–Scales, in the episode of the second Storm on the Lake with the 'Walking on the Lake' (Mark 6:47-51) following the 'Feeding of the Five Thousand' (MG 188). In John's Gospel the episode of the Storm on the Lake of Mark 6 with Christ's Walking on the Waves stands clearly in the Scales.

- In the third rhythmic round of Mark's Gospel, the struggle of Christ in Gethsemane, decisive for the end of the Earth's destiny, stands in the sign of the Scales (MG 347ff.).

Venus in the Bull reveals its more earthly side; its more heavenly side as *Venus Urania* is revealed in the sign of the Scales belonging to the Uranus-trigon of the light-ether. This is most beautifully, most revealingly expressed precisely in the section of the gospel devoted to the Scales. Nowhere does the connection of the Mysteries of Christianity with the pre-Christian Mysteries appear more deeply and significantly than where we look from the revelation of the sea of Venus-Aphrodite to *Mary*, the *'star of the sea'*, where, in and behind the Christian Mary, the Christened Isis-Venus-Mystery is gently announced (the Mystery that in the Apocalypse/ Revelation 12 has found its strongest, most revealing expression, cf. MG 264).

Venus-Aphrodite, the heavenly-virginal element in the life-ether and in the higher light-ether[31] is the essential quality in the etheric realm, whose earthly pictures are the waters of the sea's depths, the *blue surging sea*. The Greek myth was mentioned previously, in which Venus-Aphrodite, 'she who is born out of the foam of the waves of the sea', comes into being out of the starry semen of Uranos. The star shining in the watery depths, the picture of the etheric in the rays of the light and of the primordial Mysteries of the virginal Earth (the *prima materia* of the alchemists), is the revelation of the goddess Venus Urania, fathered by the heavens (Uranos), born out of the depths of the sea.

Also the Hebrew-Christian name *Mary* (Latin *Maria*, Hebrew *Mirjam*) speaks of the Mysteries of water and of the sea (Heb. *jam*, sea, and reversed: *maj*, water; Lat. *mare*, sea), the Hebrew name, as it appears, also of the bitterness of salt,[32] and the connection of all these secrets sounds to us in the text of the following Vespers hymn to Mary found in ninth-century manuscripts:

Ave, maris stella,	Hail, star of the sea,
Dei mater alma,	Nurturing Mother of God,
atque semper virgo,	And ever Virgin
felix cœli porta.	Happy gate of Heaven.
Sumens illud «Ave»	Receiving that 'Ave' (hail)
Gabrielis ore,	From the mouth of Gabriel,
funda nos in pace,	Establish us in peace,
mutans nomen Evæ.	Transforming the name of 'Eva' (Eve)

(Eva[33] reversed into Ave also points to the metamorphosis from the pre-Christian into the Christian age that also takes place in the form *Isis-Mary*.)

Venus-Aphrodite, the 'one born of the foam of the waves', Leukothea, the white goddess in Homer's *Odyssey* who throws the saving veil to Odysseus, wrestling with the salty waves of the sea, the visionary picture appearing in Act 3 of *Tristan and Isolde*, of Isolde walking over the blue, flowery billows of the sea—she too is a carrier of the higher element of life—all these pictures are completed in the Christian 'star of the sea', in Isis-Mary (for not simply the earthly Mary is meant) pointing towards the Mysteries of the etheric where the soul frees itself and feels released from the pressure and insistence of earthly physicality.

Darkness over the storm-whipped sea—recalling John 6:17, 18—is a picture of the darkness of the soul and inner unrest, of the fear and passion of the soul. This element of the inner storm and soul-storm, in which the soul wrestles for its balance, belongs in the cosmic rhythm of the gospel to the *Scales*. One thinks of the connection in German of *Wage* (scales) and *Woge* (wave); *Wage* and *wagen* (to dare), of *wagen* and *Woge*. In the Parable of the Sower, Christ placed the disciples before a higher life-element in the etheric element of time; in the meditation experience of the Feeding [of the Five Thousand] they directly experienced this life-element. These are deeply moving, inwardly stirring experiences; here they have to wrestle for their inner balance, for their inner certainty in that higher life-element. This is the deeper spiritual meaning of the episode in the gospel of the Storm on the Sea carried by the sign of the Scales, which in the rhythm always follows the other experiences in the Last-Supper constellation.

This, the fifth of the seven great 'signs' of Christ in John's Gospel, the stilling of the Storm on the Lake and the Walking on the Waves, corresponds to the fifth of the seven Christian sacraments, to *marriage*. The sacrament of marriage is concerned that marriage is not to sink into the one-sided physical aspect, into the sexuality of the daemonic Mars-forces working from the Scorpion, but that it can again access a higher etheric element of life. Not only in the physical, but the union of the marriage partners continues into the etheric, into this higher element of life. Both etheric streams: light-ether and warmth-ether as the stream of the masculine, sound-ether and life-ether as the stream of the eternal-feminine, of the higher element of life,[34] both streams ripped apart in the Fall of man, are to be found once again in the union of the marriage partners.

Only in this higher union lies the actual *Venus-element* of matrimony and raises marriage over the lower Mars-element of sexuality. From this it can likewise be understood how far the planet Venus in the sign of the Scales governs the episodes of the Storms on the Lake in the gospel.

To this revelation of the *heavenly* Venus, Venus Urania in the sign of the Scales, having become divine again in Christ, belongs the 'I AM' of Christ, the words of Christ walking over the waves appearing in Chapter 6 of both Mark and John (in the Greek appears only ἐγώ εἰμι [not 'It is I'], but 'I AM': 'I AM, be not afraid'.) Here we are allowed to see *Venus in the sign of the Scales*, how *in this I-AM of Christ a ray of eternal Love breaks through the dark clouds of the earthly realm* comparable with the star, which as Morning Star and Evening Star shines so benevolently over all earthly darkness.

The highest intensification of the crisis lies in the Scales in the third round of the rhythm in Mark's Gospel, in Christ's struggle in Gethsemane, where, as it were, the cosmic Scales threatened in its balance itself wavers and quakes, until Christ in the most significant and most difficult of all world-victories re-establishes the cosmic balance (MG 291ff.). Only the highest divine Love, incorporated in the John-angel (MG 300), is able here to support the disintegrating earthly body of the struggling Christ Jesus in full agony against the full assault of the powers of darkness. It is not by chance that this highest of all revelations of Venus-Urania in the Christian gospel, in narrated precisely in Luke's Gospel, very much turned towards the virginal secrets of the eternal feminine, of the life-etheric (Luke 22:43): 'And there appeared to him an angel from heaven, strengthening him.'

♂

Venus is revealed in the Scales as in a radiant ocean blue; in the following revelation *Mars in Scorpion* in cloudy, dark colours. Already in the story of the daemoniac in Mark 5 we saw this motif at work, the daemonic side of Mars in the Scorpion casting its gloomy shadow. In John's Gospel, as the coming exposition shows, the contrast of the Martian facing the Venus qualities is expressively conveyed. The power of death of the Scorpion appears in the planetary influence of *Mars*, and from this source unfolds the daemonic side of its nature. The crisis always approaching the disciples from the death-sign of the Scorpion climaxes in Judas' betrayal, Peter's denial and the flight of the disciples in Gethsemane. The three figures Judas, Peter and Pilate in Mark's Gospel clearly appear in the Scorpion (MG 303). How obvious all this is, for example, with Pontius Pilate and Imperial Rome that he represents. The Scorpion on the uniform of the Roman legionnaires was mentioned in the exposition of Mark's Gospel (MG 322). Without the forces of Mars of Imperial Rome the Mystery of Golgotha would not have come to effect; the Mystery itself, the whole martyrdom of the Crucified clearly shows this impact of Mars. Even the daemonic side of Mars was necessary in order to realize the highest good, the divine redemption in the events affecting mankind.

♃

In the Jupiter-sign of the *Archer* death is accomplished; the Mystery itself is fulfilled. Both 'houses' of Jupiter, the Fishes and the Archer, lie on the night-side of the zodiac, in the 'Cross of the Etheric'. With the *Transfiguration on the Mount*, where they both appear, this appears in all clarity. Here are revealed cosmic Mysteries of the 'deep midnight', in which, as a sublime 'beholding of the Sun at midnight', the *spiritual, primordial Sun* shines. (The relationship of Jupiter to 'Ancient Sun' was mentioned above.) Taking into account with this also both Elijah-John signs ♑ and ♒ governed by Saturn, we see the four signs of the zodiac standing over the experience of the Transfiguration through the planetary viewpoint resolve into a duality (Jupiter–Saturn).

All this appears in the highest intensification on Golgotha itself. There we saw in the Jupiter-sign of the Archer the new stream of life springing forth. (Compare here in Rudolf Steiner's poetic work on the zodiac, the 'Twelve Moods',[35] the words for ♃ in ♐: '*Im Sterben erreift das Weltenwalten*', 'In dying, there ripens prevailing of worlds'.) Beholding this new stream of life, this future-bearing revelation of life helps one at the same time to penetrate into the Mystery of the cycles of time, in Rudolf Steiner's *Esoteric/ Occult Science* called the future *Jupiter incarnation* of planet Earth.

***

For observations on John's Gospel, this addition of the planetary viewpoint to the signs of the zodiac will increasingly reveal its significance. It can be compared to that which in speech the vowels add to the consonants, or in music the addition of harmony to melody. Here too is revealed out of the nature of words and of harmony that which in John's Gospel plays such an important role. In what follows, after the present retrospect on the cosmic rhythm in Mark's Gospel, a kind of overview will be given of the cosmic rhythm in John's Gospel.

4.
The Cosmic Rhythm in John's Gospel (overview)

In what follows, we shall attempt in a short overview using the offered key in Mark's Gospel to show how the rhythm in John's Gospel is formed. We shall have to keep in mind that all actual indications of 'proof' in what is presented have to be reserved for the second part of this book, where the full evidence of the contexts can be given.

Like Mark's Gospel, the first chapter of John's Gospel presents the Christ-Mystery at the River Jordan. The signs of the zodiac correspond to this; both initial chapters of Mark and John lie in the zodiac-axis Fishes–Virgin, on the arms of the Son-cross that is also the 'etheric cross', the Christ-cross of the middle (MG 348ff.). A difference between both gospels is only in what precedes the Baptism in the Jordan. In Mark's Gospel we find the frequently-mentioned Elijah-John prelude to the Christ-event in both Saturn-signs of the Archer and the Waterman. Here the gaze is initially turned to the figure of the great forerunner and preparer of the way for Christ and His earthly ministry.

John's Gospel as the actual Christ-gospel no longer has to do with such a 'prelude' looking into the past of mankind. Here the prelude, if we find one here, can only be concerned with Christ, with the Eternal; it can only be a *cosmic prelude*: 'In the primordial beginning was the word ... and the word became flesh ... and we have beheld his revealed glory ...' (John 1:1-14). If we seek here the connection to the zodiac we can only find it in the sign of the word, in the *Bull*, which in esoteric science at the same time is the sign of the 'primordial beginning of the Earth'. The Bull is the sign of the *Word in the primordial beginning*; the Ram is the sign of the earthly activity, the entering into the earthly realm. 'And the word became flesh' (v. 14), and only with John 1:19 would the entry into the zodiac axis Fishes–Virgo be given that governs everything else within the opening chapter.

Still more than in Mark's Gospel, we find in John's Gospel the involvement of the respective counter-sign; more than in Mark the whole zodiac-*axis* seems to be emphasized, especially the opening verses. Already here we can recognize *how the rhythm in John's Gospel*, at the beginning at least, *has a different direction of movement*.

Here it does not correspond to the annual rhythm of the sign from below upwards, but the reverse, corresponding to the rhythm of the cosmic year from above downwards. In Mark 1 the zodiac-axis Fishes–Virgo was reached from below, from Goat–Waterman; in John's Gospel from above, from the Bull.

All this becomes clearer when we move on to John 2. There the 'changing of the water into wine' with the marriage at Cana places us immediately into the polarity of the words of John the Baptist (initially Matt. 3:11, similar to Mark 1:8): 'I baptize you with water for repentance, but He (Christ) who is coming after me is mightier than I, ...; he will baptize you with the Holy Spirit and with fire.' The water of the etheric realm, a bearing element of all pre-Christian Mysteries, becomes changed through the Sun-Ego of Christ into the wine of the human personality. This polar opposite, however, seen from the viewpoint of the zodiac, is that of the Waterman and the Lion (MG 31f., 61). With the Waterman we find the baptism with water, the 'water of the etheric realm', the [etheric] element of the 'human being of the primordial beginning'. The Lion, the sign of the heart, of fiery warmth and of the blood, is at the same time the sign of Spirit-man (atma), of the physical body changed by the 'I' right into the blood and breathing. Here the higher wine of life of the 'I' is revealed in the 'change of water into wine'. Those standing in the pre-Christian Mystery-contexts had to be anxious concerning the fate of the temple of the body with such a demand, for them unheard-of, of bringing the 'I' into the higher experience; they saw the body in danger of disintegrating. Only the real higher 'I-AM' of the Christ caused the renewal, the resurrection, of the physical body. For this reason, there is Christ's saying about re-building the disintegrated temple of the body precisely in this connection. The 'cosmic rhythm' proves itself here as a direct aid to recognize the contexts of the gospel. From the planetary viewpoint the contrast of ♒ – ♌ governs this chapter [John 2] as that of Saturn and the Sun. Therein lies a new, more revealing viewpoint to understand the Mystery-events of Cana.

***

Different from Mark's Gospel, the rhythm in John's Gospel unites far more with the chapter divisions as they have come down to us. From the descending rhythm of the great cosmic [Platonic] year, the first five chapters are arranged each one to another sign, or to another axis of the zodiac. The progress of this rhythm has to lead from the constellation Waterman–Lion in John 2 to the constellation

The Cosmic Rhythm in John's Gospel (overview) 61

Goat–Crab in John 3. We actually find in the conclusion of this chapter the Johannine saying characteristic for the spiritual meaning of the sign of the Crab: 'He must increase, but I must decrease' (John 3:30) (MG 95f., 274). In the Baptist John at the Jordan there stands the last representative of the pre-Christian traditions facing the Bringer of the new. Pre-Christian initiation climaxes in the Goat—here Buddha, too, finds his 'illumination'; the new, the Christian-Johannine initiation is fulfilled in the Crab (MG 238ff.).

This whole contrast, and with it the same constellation, also governs the beginning of John 3, the conversation at night of a Mystery-nature between Nicodemus and Christ. Nicodemus senses the new, what is coming, yet cannot comprehend it. A difficulty is prepared for him, especially the Mystery of the new birth, the birth from above from the forces of the starry heavens (*uranós*), from which Christ descended to the Earth. The Mysteries of birth and motherhood, however, always stand in the sign of the Crab. Nicodemus is not able to comprehend the new Christened meaning of this sign and its secrets of birth; he would like to remain with the old, with the sign of the Goat–Saturn, in which the earthly birth of Jesus of Nazareth, for which reason in the annual rhythm Christmas takes place in the Goat. But here in John 3, Christ speaks of a quite different birth.

In each of the first chapters of John's Gospel, in ever different forms and with ever fresh nuances, this contrast of pre-Christian and of Christian, the old and the new Mysteries appear. In John 4 this contrast comes to a certain height of destiny, with the meeting of Christ and the Samaritan woman at the well. Here we have to think of the hierophant of an old, decadent Mystery-centre. The new source of life meets us as the contrast of the old and the new. The meeting takes place in the 'sixth hour', that is (according to Hebrew reckoning), in the hot midday hour. We feel something quietly chiming-in from the Mysteries of the 'great midday of Zarathustra', whose greatness as the primordial inspirer of all the great post-Indian, pre-Christian Mysteries we still feel behind this decadent Mystery-centre. The zodiac-axis Archer–Twins lying over the whole chapter (in the rhythm it follows the axis Goat–Crab of John 3) speaks in its upper counter-sign, the Zarathustra-sign ♊, the Twins, of these Mysteries of Zarathustra; in the Archer here again the secrets are indicated, there are new sources of life springing forth on Golgotha—in the rhythm of John's Gospel it is always the lower, dark sign that is primarily emphasized. Above, in the sublime sign of Zarathustra, there sprang the earlier source of life, whose water then became progressively more sparse, until it finally ceased. Below, in the Archer, the death of Christ defeated the mind-deadening forces that had brought this source of life of primitive times to desiccation.

Through Christ, the negative side of the Archer is turned into a positive. This motif also governs the ending of the chapter, the healing of the nobleman's son through Christ. The contrasting features of life, good and evil, male and female, initially expressed in Zarathustra's great teaching of light and darkness, with the crisis of puberty have entered into the life of the child, forces of sensuality have killed the previously-existing life. This lies in the same constellation: the negative side of ♊ is intellectual doubt, of ♐ sensuality and sensory-bound thinking. Christ, the mediator, creates the balance out of the higher 'I'.

The continuation of the rhythm leads in John 5 to the axis Scorpion–Bull. This is expressed most clearly in the story of the healing of the paralytic of Bethesda and the ensuing clash with the Pharisees on breaking the Sabbath. As always in Mark's Gospel, so too here in the Scorpion the source of the illness appears in the power of death; in the Bull (here awakening the 'will in the "I"') the healing strength of the word and the divine power of love appear. Against which in the clash with the Pharisees in the Scorpion, the representatives of what is old want to oppose by holding fast to the dead letter of the law. It was already said how the planetary aspect in the opposition Mars–Venus finds its expression.

***

The rhythm of John's Gospel has led from the Fishes in John 1, through all of the five dark zodiac signs (MG 24f., 26, 35f., 40) until the death-sign of Scorpio. With this a first larger section of John's Gospel finds a close. It is followed by a further section, which again embraces five chapters, 6–10. In the exposition on Mark's Gospel the connection was already pointed out of the five lower, dark signs of the zodiac for the one Feeding [MG 34]. It is consequently not without meaning, or an inner connection with the whole composition of the gospel, that precisely in a new pentad introduced by John 6, following the first pentad, this Feeding with the five loaves is also narrated. It appears like a pictorial summary governing the five dark signs of the preceding rhythm. Mysteries of Christian initiation light up, which also lay hold of the lower, darker, will nature of the human being that is open to the forces of evil—from the Scorpion right down to the Fishes, the feet.

The Cosmic Rhythm in John's Gospel (overview)

If we look back from this point to the beginning of John's Gospel, we can find how in these first five chapters Christ, before He enters on the common stage of humanity, goes through a sequence of Mystery-encounters and Mystery-spheres which all lie still above the common, earthly human level. Here, in a certain way, Christ's descent into humanity is completed, which but begins in the Jordan baptism. John 5, lying already within the greatest depths of the human situation, still carries in itself certain Mystery-contexts and motifs. Consequently, from this viewpoint, we can summarize these first five chapters as 'Mystery-Chapters', contrasting the next five (6–10) as 'Chapters on Humanity'.

***

From the evidence of the descending rhythm found in the first five chapters of John's Gospel, it does not follow that this rhythmic tendency continues in the same way, passing now through the five dark signs of the zodiac, which then would lead up from the dark signs of the zodiac towards the bright ones. Investigation in this matter depends on repeatedly testing against the facts what has been found at each point.

Already that which inwardly connects the five dark signs of the zodiac in the first five chapters with the Christian-Johannine initiation, causes us to expect a certain ending. There also comes into consideration the fact that in John's Gospel, more than with Mark, always the whole zodiac-axis (sign and counter-sign) is emphasized. If we take the 'cosmic prelude' (♉) of John 1, we return in John 5 (axis ♏ – ♉) already to the initial constellation, but now emphasized from below, from the dark sign.

After we have arrived from the Fishes at the Scorpion in John 5—if we base the rhythm on the human body, all this would progress *up*wards—the continuation of the rhythm would lead over in John 6 to the *Scales*. This corresponds with the facts of the gospel. Only after the gospel-rhythm has reached the Scales, as a kind of resting stage, it enters the whole following pentad of five chapters. Initially this will be placed here as an hypothesis, only as a key-thought to investigate the tangible gospel facts. Hereby in the details, various things need clarifying.

First of all, at the beginning of John 6, the objection or question arises whether the story of the Feeding [of the Five Thousand] told there is to be aligned to the zodiac-axis Fishes–Virgin. In the parallel narration Mark 6 it is the Fishes, and with the other Feeding [of the Four Thousand] of Mark 8, not narrated in John's Gospel, the Virgin is primarily emphasized (MG 147, 169). From Mark's Gospel the clear enlightening meaning of the individual signs of the zodiac remains our key also for John's Gospel. In John's Gospel, too, seen on its own, the story of the Feeding [of the Five Thousand] is clearly shown on the axis Fishes–Virgin—on which later, in John 13, we actually find Christ's Last Supper.

Now, in John's Gospel, however, much more than in Mark's Gospel, the individual chapters are closed, rhythmical entities. Not the Feeding as such, but the crisis of the disciples released into consciousness through the experience of the Feeding, manifested in the picture of the Storm on the Lake, forms the middle-point and the decisive content of John 7. In the narration of both gospels (Mark 6 and John 6) there sounds out of the mouth of Christ, walking on the waves, the words: 'I AM, do not be afraid.' The connection of this I-AM saying of Christ with the sign of the Scales was already recognized and expressed (MG 119). In this sense the Scales is strongly present in Mark 6—with the Storm on the Lake in Mark 4 it is the sign primarily emphasized—and in John's Gospel, as the *gospel of the 'I'*, emphasis on the Scales is here completely decisive, not only for this chapter; it also dominates all the following Chapters 7–10.

In these chapters, the crisis that began with the group of disciples grows to the great *crisis of humanity*. Here the I-AM of Christ in the sign of the Scales stands in the middle throughout. Here Christ, as the *Representative of Humankind*, of full humanity, as its lost, forgotten higher 'I', stands everywhere before the spiritual eye between the adversaries, the adversary to the right and the adversary to the left (cf. MG 343f.). The words of Luke's Gospel (4:30): 'But passing through the midst of them he went away', the sense of which is repeated almost in every chapter of John (6:15, 7:30, 7:44, 8:59, 10:31, 10:39), appears as the sublime leitmotif of the whole gospel passage (John 6–10). And this meaning and this picture links to the meaning and picture of the sign of the Scales, which as the *sign of the great 'I'* and the Christ 'I-AM' is at the same time the *sign of the human being and of humankind*. Amongst the four zodiac triangles (see 'The Figures of the Zodiac'), which also align to the four apocalyptic beings (Rev. 4:7)—Bull, Lion, Eagle, and Human Being—and thus at the same time to the four evangelists, the Scales, along with the Waterman and the Twins, belongs to the *triangle of the human being*. The first five chapters of John's Gospel are Mystery-Chapters, lying above the usual human sphere. The chapters of the second pentad (6–10) are *Chapters on Humanity*. Their heavenly sign is the *sign of humanity, the Scales*, which at the same time is

The Cosmic Rhythm in John's Gospel (overview)

the sign of the I-AM of Christ. Here, the great 'I' in the sign of the Scales, by appearing within humanity, in the great conflict of humanity, manifests the great crisis of the human race in a deeply moving manner.

Thus, taken as a whole, John 6 stands in the sign of the Scales.

- On the one side stand those who, under the impressions of the experience of the Feeding, not yet understood in their hearts, and against the meaning of the true Kingdom of Christ in the 'I', want to raise Christ Jesus to a false earthly sovereignty in the sense of Jewish Messianic ideas.
- On the other side stand those who raise stones against Christ, who want to stone the Representative of Humankind, to murder their own higher 'I' (John 8:59, 10:31, also 7:30, 7:44, 10, 39).

In a false kingship the deviation of the adversary to the left side wants to place the false 'I' in place of the true 'I'. In raising stones against the bearer of the true 'I' lies the hardening of the heart, the deviation of the adversary to the right side. Between both deviations and adversaries the great 'I', the I-AM of Christ, asserts itself upright in the middle, in the Scales. This is the meaning of the sign of the Scales, which we assign to the chapters from the beginning of John 7 up to John 10.

And yet the above-mentioned relationship to the constellation Fishes–Virgin of the story of the Feeding [of the Five Thousand] at the beginning of John 6 should not be overlooked. The 'remaining standing in the Scales' (John 6–10) is to be understood *cum grano salis*—with a grain of salt. It has to be seen that it does not involve a complete resting. Far rather, after the rhythm of John's Gospel has reached the Scales, this is not simply a standing still, but, as it were, a rocking, an oscillating, touching alternately the two opposites between which it is placed. Like the balancing scales we know in daily life, the pans still move, oscillating; the pointer, or needle, still sways before a resting balance is finally reached. Only we may not take the cosmic matter schematically and abstractly, but if possible concretely and livingly imagined; in relying on pictures and imaginations we need not fight shy of the purely earthly: 'As below, so above.'

The luciferic deviation points upwards, and the ahrimanic downwards. The divine of the sign of the Virgin, in and for itself, which is a bright sign, brings Lucifer into the turbid, earthly-sensual view of things. Like the Scales between the other two signs, Christ stands here in this chapter between the two adversaries, between light (♍) and darkness (♏). This is especially evident in the Healing of the Blind Man in John 9.

In John 6, alongside the luciferic deviation, the divine meaning of the Virgin is emphasized where she appears as the sign of the bread of life: 'I am the bread of life.' But the bread of life, the etheric nourishment of life is now received in the 'I'. For this reason the Scales, the sign of the 'I', stands everywhere here decisively in the middle; in the motif of the bread of life the Virgin appears merely accompanying. Similarly in John 8 the 'I'-motif of the Scales holds the middle between the Scorpion and the Virgin—alongside that of the stoning, the death power of the Scorpion [♏] was at work in the hearts of the dark accusers, and whose daemonic Mars-side also brought the maidenly quality (♍) into error with the woman caught in adultery. Christ, who in the Scales, in the divine 'I', can say: 'I am the light of the world', raises the fallen one again to the heights of the level of divine virginity. The Scales in John 10 shows the way of the 'I' ('I am the door') as the right way of the middle, precisely between the deviations of both adversaries. The adversary who violates the 'I', in the meaning of this chapter, is the 'wolf' who 'snatches and scatters the sheep' (John 10:28, cf. MG 314).

In the *Scales*, which has always been the sign and symbol of 'judgment', there takes place in John's Gospel (Chapters 6–10) the division between light and darkness, which through the Christ–'I' leads to and causes the great division of spirits, the *crisis* [κρίσισ], as the event is called in the original text of the gospel, the 'judgment' (as KJV/AV translates it).[36] This is the shared motif of these chapters, which we called the 'Chapters on Humanity'.

The rhythm in the first five chapters, moving downwards through the dark signs of the zodiac, reaches the Scorpion. Then, reaching the Scales in John 6, it maintains the given direction. This sign between the upper bright and the lower dark signs likewise forms the transition to the side of autumn/ the fall, as the Fishes do the side of the spring. The Fishes, itself a dark sign, because it leads to the bright side we could regard as a 'half-bright' sign; the sign of the Scales, in itself bright because it leads down to the dark side, we could regard as a 'half-dark' sign. At the point where the rhythm of John's Gospel reaches the Scales, it remains stationary therein through five chapters, yet in such a way that the Scales stand continuously struggling with the upper bright (♍) and the lower dark signs (♏), as it were, oscillating between them. It is thoroughly characteristic of the rhythm of John's Gospel that—at the most with *one* exception in John 17—everywhere it actually orients itself towards the dark portion of the zodiac, the region of the Christian-Johannine Initiation.

***

In John 10 the Johannine path of initiation is set forth in the word; in *John 11 this initiation becomes deed in the raising of Lazarus*. (The detailed explanation of this fact will be given in the second part of this book, in the chapter on the raising of Lazarus. There the connections will also be made with the initiation story of Mark's Gospel.) Already in the exposition of Mark's Gospel (MG 49ff., 208ff., 238ff.) we attempted to recognize how in the initiation process described there—between the lines of the gospel—the awakening and opening up of the consciousness of John takes place from stage to stage. Already there it was pointed out how these spiritual events stand inwardly connected with this mysterious process, which John's Gospel narrates as the 'raising of Lazarus'.

In the *dying of Lazarus*—thus we can possibly summarize the motif of this gospel, of *both* gospels—the *becoming of John* takes place, the awakening of the disciple of Christ. The awakening of John's consciousness, described in Mark's Gospel, occurs in the upper, light-filled signs of the zodiac—beginning in ♉ and ending in ♊ ♋ ♌. With these processes of consciousness, the 'dying of Lazarus' goes hand in hand with the outer event in the corresponding lower, dark zodiac signs lying opposite. That is, that we connect the sign that normally is related to illness and death, the ♏, the counter-sign of the ♉, with the 'illness of Lazarus' (John 11:1). Here ♐, as otherwise, is the actual dying, ♑, the 'sign of turning' lying opposite ♋, signifies what here takes place, the decisive turning point of mankind, the transition from the old to the new initiation. Here ♒ means, as otherwise in the gospel—with John the Baptist as with Christ—the entombment, the lying in the grave. In the ♓ then occurs—as also with Christ—the resurrection out of the grave. Thus, what is presented in Mark's Gospel as the process of initiation-consciousness from the upper side, in John's Gospel is presented from the lower, dark side.

The dying of Lazarus is led through the same dark signs of the zodiac through which the dying of Christ Himself, the Mystery of Golgotha, is led. In the second part of this book it will become clearer how the inner spiritual context completely corresponds to this context in the cosmic rhythm, how the dying and awakening of Lazarus is connected most closely with the Mystery of Golgotha itself, how it already carries in itself the whole process of Christ's dying.

The oscillation of the Scales in the previous passage of the gospel, mentioned above, now becomes more understandable. After the rhythm of John's Gospel has reached the Scales, we see it does not simply remain at rest, but the Scales swings between the upper and lower signs, as it were, hither and thither, *because now the whole direction of movement changes*. The Scales, the sign of the I-AM of Christ, is, as it were, the point that gives the direction and aim of the entire rhythm. Here Christ, descending from cosmic heights, has placed Himself completely into the forces of the Earth and into humanity. That which now takes place lies completely in the earthly element, the descent into the Earth itself that takes place in the Mystery of Golgotha. The direction of movement goes down again towards the lower, dark signs of the zodiac; the rhythm is no longer the great cosmic year descending from cosmic heights, but the rhythm of the earthly course of the year.

The first five chapters of John's Gospel form an enclosed unity as the 'Mystery-Chapters'; the following five chapters form the 'Chapters on Humanity'. We will now regard John 11 and 12 belonging together as the two 'Lazarus Chapters'. They are the only ones where the name [or term] 'Lazarus' is mentioned. In John 11 we look at the entombment and awakening, in John 12 at the 'resurrected Lazarus'. The constellation of the previous chapter has led up to the Fishes, the sign of resurrection and awakening (also in the daily rhythm, ♓ is the sign in which we awaken, ♈ the sign in which we get up). The twelfth chapter, placing before us the awakened one, with its Mary Magdalene and its virginal last-supper scene at the beginning [John 12:2], lies clearly in the constellation ♓—♍, in the Last-Supper constellation.

With the background of Christ's Last Supper, we shall find this constellation decisive also for the subsequent chapters of farewell to which it clearly leads us; at the beginning of these chapters, the Washing of the Feet plainly points to the sign ♓. Once again we recognize a pentad of chapters as something inclusive. What is the new, shared element of these chapters?

Initially, looking back at the two 'Lazarus-Chapters' (John 11 and 12), we can find this related pair are once again 'Mystery-Chapters'. After Christ's encounter with the various early Mysteries and their initiates narrated in the first five chapters of John, the transition in Chapters 11 and 12 from the old to the new initiation takes place; the new, Christian-Johannine Initiation contrasts with the old, pre-Christian Mystery. These two chapters form the actual central Mystery, the actual main section of John's Gospel. Thus through these two pre-eminently 'Mystery-Chapters', the pentad of the first Mystery-Chapters is supplemented to a septenary.

The common viewpoint for the five subsequent Chapters (13–17), initially still in the Last-Supper constellation ♓–♍ is this: Christ, after

The Cosmic Rhythm in John's Gospel (overview)   69

the initiation and raising of the *one* disciple, turns to the others who could not find initiation, who failed in the initiation, who are now about to leave their Master. They don't know this yet, but the end of the 'Farewell Discourses' in John 16 precisely contains the clear indication of it. And not for nothing does the first of these chapters contain the clear foreseeing of Judas' betrayal and Peter's denial. Christ's love, which towards the *one* disciple whose secret is hidden behind the Lazarus story, could prove itself as an *awakening love*, is revealed to the others as the *carrying and protecting love*. It concerns those who initially failed where they should have formed the connection between Christ and humankind, nevertheless, through the carrying love of Christ they are retained and kept safe for their task for the future of humanity.

In this sense, the four actual chapters of farewell (the Farewell Discourses of Jesus, John 13–16) joined by the Great Intercession of the 'High-Priestly Prayer' (John 17), makes these five chapters the 'Chapters on the Disciples'. The disciples with their whole relationship to Christ form here the spiritual middle-point. Regarding the 'rhythm' of this chapter carrying the 'Last-Supper constellation' as a whole, it should be said that reasons can be suggested to allocate the cosmic abundance of light of the last of these five chapters, of John 17—in certain regards standing alone as the most esoteric chapter of John's Gospel—to allocate it to the bright sign of this constellation (♍) and from there to understand the further progress of this rhythm.

These five 'Chapters on the Disciples' are followed by the pair of chapters on Christ's Passion (John 18 and 19), once again a doubling. At the beginning of John 18, there is revealed in the I-AM of Christ, before Whom the pursuers fall to the ground, once more the sign of the Scales (following the Virgin in the rhythm). After a resting place was reached from John 12 onwards in the Last-Supper constellation (♓–♍), in Christ's Passion it proceeds downwards through the dark signs again, and the Scales again forms the transition in this descent. It was already pointed out how the exact correspondence of the Lazarus-events with Christ's Passion is revealed in the zodiac signs.

Facing Christ's I-AM in the Scales in a deeply moving, tragic way, stands Peter's 'I-am-not' in the sign of the Scorpion (John 18:17 & 25. MG 309). The *Ecce Homo* ['Behold the Man'] at the beginning of John 19 we still allocate to the Scorpion (MG 330); the Crucifixion itself stands, as always, in the death-sign of the Archer; the Entombment stands in the Waterman.

The two Lazarus-Chapters supplement the pentad of the first 'Mystery-Chapters' to form a septenary; the two 'Passion-Chapters' supplement the pentad of the 'Chapters on Humanity' (6–10) to another septenary. The 'crisis of humanity', so deeply movingly presented in John 6–10, finds in Golgotha its resolution. The stone-throwing of the Jews (John 7, 8 and 10) already contains the cross of Golgotha in itself, with its fateful consequences. The self-sacrifice of the God 'resolves' the *crisis*, which had awakened the 'I' placed by the living Christ-Jesus amongst humanity and which this humanity was no longer able to bear.

The two final chapters of John's Gospel, the Resurrection Chapters (John 20 & 21), lead again into the Last-Supper constellation ♓–♍. Already at the beginning of John 20, with the appearance of Mary Magdalene the Virgin is clearly connected with the Fishes, already discussed in its relationship to the resurrection; the experience of the meal with bread and fishes at the end of John 22 clearly points to the Last-Supper constellation. John's Gospel ends in the same constellation with which it began—if we disregard the cosmic Prologue.

We saw how the rhythm of this gospel essentially always moves in the five lower signs of the zodiac: after the downward moving rhythm in the direction of the cosmic year has reached the middle in the Scales, it turns in the opposite direction—following now the usual annual rhythm—again towards the dark signs, to the Fishes. This descent at first connected with the events of Lazarus, is repeated in Christ's Passion. In this way it proceeds twice from the middle point downwards. Unlike the rhythm of Mark's Gospel, the rhythm of John's Gospel is not a *circulation*, but the *swinging of a pendulum*. And if with Mark, with the Lion we feel reminded of the *circulation of the blood*, with John the Eagle, we can think of the *'beating of the Eagle's wings'*.

In the two final Resurrection Chapters, the disciples stand once again in the centre. Christ's carrying and protecting love (John 13–17) made it possible for those who did not recognize the Living One, who abandoned Him, to behold Him after His death, to *meet the Resurrected One*. What is experienced there is completed in the event of Pentecost.

- The pentad of the first *Mystery-Chapters* (John 1–5) is supplemented to a septenary through the two Lazarus-Chapters (John 11–12).
- The pentad of *Chapters on Humanity* (John 6–10) is supplemented through the two Passion-Chapters (18 and 19).
- The pentad of *Chapters on the Disciples* (13–17) is supplemented through the Resurrection-Chapters [John 20 and 21] to a septenary.

5.
John's Gospel and the other Gospels observed from the Cosmic Rhythm

The circulation of the heart's blood picturing the rhythm of the 'Lion' Mark, can be compared with the three circling 'rounds', always leading through all twelve zodiac signs. We could also compare the [ascending, lemniscate movement of the] Eagle's wing-beat with the rhythm of John's Gospel. This rhythm leads through the *dark* zodiac signs downwards, and then, from the middle, the Scales, it swings back through the same dark signs of the zodiac. This directs our gaze towards the marked differences and the mutual relationships of the four gospels, in which these differences are again revealed.

In the centre of all our observations there stands a figure of the whole zodiac at the beginning of the book on Mark (MG 364). It is reprinted again in 'The Figures of the Zodiac' of the present book. The second figure, taken from Günter Wachsmuth's book on the etheric formative forces (Vol. 2, *Die Ätherische Welt in Wissenschaft, Kunst und Religion*, Dornach 1927, 15), especially through the colouring makes visible the unique characteristic of the four triangles. With this the twelvefold nature of the zodiac is divided in its relationship to the four elements and the four different ethers, warmth-ether, light-ether, chemical or sound-ether, and life-ether. This fourfold concept is also mirrored in the fourfold concept of the biblical gospels. The relationship of the four heavenly triangles, once recognized, offers an explanation of the gospels deeper than any other viewpoint. In the third figure of 'The Figures of the Zodiac', the coloured indication of the four different kinds of ethers is retained and is listed:

   red—warmth-ether,
   yellow—light-ether,
   blue—chemical, or sound-ether,
   violet—life-ether.

This connects with the content of Fig. 1; the 'three crosses' are no longer differentiated through the colour, but only through dotted lines (for everything else see in the Appendix of the book on Mark. MG 343ff.).

The point of view of the four elements and the kinds of ether can also be linked to the four temperaments. With the gospels this may not be too superficially and schematically applied. As in real life, here too the various kinds of temperaments join and intermingle. An ultimate viewpoint, already taken by Rudolf Steiner, relates the four gospels to the fourfold human being:

> Matthew's Gospel to the human physical element,
> Mark's Gospel to the human etheric,
> Luke's Gospel to the human astral,
> John's Gospel to the 'I'.

These four members of the human being mutually penetrate and together form a whole; the four gospels do likewise. In them and their quaternary, we behold the *comprehensive human being*, the *eternal gospel*.

***

The human *physical body* formed of earthly substance is that human member through which it is united with the Earth, to earthly material and to the earthly contexts. In this sense the Gospel of Matthew is also the one in which especially the earthly figure of Jesus of Nazareth stands in the centre; the earthly, historical connections, including those between the New and the Old Testaments, are taken into account. In this sense, with Matthew the viewpoints of Judaism and its view of the physical connections and laws are especially evident. On the other hand it presents the figure of the Apostle Peter, of the 'rock of the church' and the carrier of the visible church. He carries the physical body of the church, as John carries the invisible church, or esoteric Christianity. Matthew's Gospel, like the human 'physical body', relates in particular to the visible world.

The human *etheric* body, or 'life-body'—the 'Sun dress' in the Grimms' fairytale '*Allerleirauh*', or 'All-kinds-of-fur'—as 'colour-aura' is only perceptible to the clairvoyant eye, but in its spiritual essence it can also be comprehended in thinking. It stands closely connected with the activity of thinking itself. This human member is allocated to the cosmic realm. Unlike the physical body that connects the human being with the earthly physical, to the Earth, the etheric body connects with the 'aura of the Earth', with the living realm of the etheric in the plant, human and animal kingdoms, and with the living realm of the whole cosmos. The 'etheric body' [as the body of formative forces] is not to be understood out of merely spatial, earthly relationships, but out of cosmic relationships. It can be understood out of the essence and activity of the starry world with its lawfulness and cosmic rhythms. These influence the germination and growth of plants, and the essence of all time processes. As a cosmic 'being of time', not an earthly being of space, the etheric or life-body is to be conceived.

In the little book 'Genesis', in *From the Mysteries*, 17ff., the author discusses how the essence of the etheric can be understood out of the secrets of the biblical creation story, Goethe's archetypal plant, and the possibility to form an understanding from the processes of plant growth and development.

Amongst the gospels, Mark's Gospel is allocated to the same cosmic realm and its rhythms. With John's Gospel this 'cosmic rhythm' is not so obvious. It is only found through looking at Mark's Gospel, at all the various relationships that in particular connect the Gospels of Mark and John.

Mark's Gospel relates to the etheric; Luke's Gospel relates to the human soul-astral realm. In the fairytale '*Allerleirauh*', the 'astral body' appears as the 'Moon-dress', which like the 'Sun-dress' and the 'star-dress' can be contained in a nutshell, that is, they are of a very fine, tender, super-earthly nature. This human 'astral body' is initially woven out of the essence of the starry, lunar, and planetary elements. The human being shares the physical body, the 'dress made out of all kinds of furs' in the fairytale picture, with animal, plant and stone, the ether-body with animal and plant. The astral body, the bearer of conscious feeling, of the actual soul-element, is shared with the animals. Human beings are distinguished from the animals through the 'I' as the self-conscious human member. Naturally, because it is penetrated by the 'I' or ego, the soul-element of conscious feeling is different with human beings than with animals. With the animals it is on the one hand duller, on the other hand, however, more cosmic—think of the wonderful feeling instinct of migratory birds. The 'astral element', the actual starry nature, appears stronger here. With the human being this starry, 'astral' element is obscured through the earthly consciousness of the lower ego.[37]

The ether-body points us more towards the outer cosmic realm; the astral body points more to the inner soul, the 'inner starry world'. This inwardness has always been felt with Luke's Gospel as something essential.

Matthew's Gospel belongs in a certain way to the human physical body, Mark to the etheric, Luke to the astral; John's Gospel belongs to the innermost principle, to the 'I' or ego. John's Gospel is pre-eminently the gospel of the ego, the great message of the 'I'. We have to take the 'I' in the sublime, divine sense about which we actually only learn again out of John's Gospel. The next chapter will show how regarding the Mysteries of this 'I' as a new member of the human being, initially present only in seed-form in its potential, John's Gospel speaks to humanity in all its chapters from ever new viewpoints. In the great I-AM sayings of Christ, in which all the future developments of humanity are included, this 'I'-Mystery has found its most concentrated expression. We saw this great 'I', this I-AM of Christ, aligned to the heavenly sign of the Scales, to the same sign governed by Venus Urania, by heavenly love. Venus in the Scales as the *love in the 'I'* is the governing motif of the whole of John's Gospel. One has only understood this 'I', this Johannine meaning of the 'I', when it is recognized how within it the *most inner place of the interior realm* lovingly joins together with the whole cosmic circumference.

In the language of the fairytale:

- the physical body is the 'dress of animal fur' (the 'coat of all kinds of fur'),
- the etheric body is the 'Sun-dress',
- the astral body is the 'Moon-dress',
- the 'I' is the *'starry body'*, woven out of the rays of all the stars, and yet, like the Sun-dress and the Moon-dress, it can be hidden in a nutshell.
- The *physical* as the *earthly dress of the body,*
- the *etheric* as the *Sun-dress of life,*
- the *astral* as the *Moon-dress of light,*
- receive the 'I' as the *starry dress of love*, the fourth member of the human being, raising the individual to true humanity.

These pictures taken from the language of the fairytale really do agree with the inner being of John's Gospel. We only need to think of the Prologue (or 'cosmic Prelude') and, when we link the *Word in the primordial beginning* with the 'Love in the primordial beginning' (Dante's *'il primo Amore'*), the Incarnation of the Word (John 1:14) with physical corporeality, we find the whole fourfold human being (from which we proceeded in this section) as *body, life* (v. 4), *light* (v. 6), and *love*. And we may think of Novalis' words: '*Love really is the "I"*, the ideal of every endeavour.'

***

John's Gospel and the other Gospels observed from the Cosmic Rhythm 75

From the 'four human members' lines of communication proceed to the 'four elements' and kinds of ether:

- The 'I' is ignited at the inner fire (at the warmth-ether),
- the astral relates to the light, the 'light-ether',
- the ether-body to the sound-ether (for the Indians, pre-eminently *the* ether),
- the physical body to the element of earth and to the life-ether.

From the triangle-figure on p. 334 all this becomes clear (compare also MG, Appendix 1). Mark, as we see, has the element of the circulation of the blood; he belongs to the element of fire, to the triangle of the warmth-ether. With the temperaments, choleric would correspond, to which also the compressed, hearty style of Mark's Gospel urging onwards also points in a certain sense.

From the three points of Mark's triangle, the point of the Lion belongs to the 'Cross of the Spirit', the 'astral cross'; the lower point belongs in the Archer to the 'Cross of the Sun', the 'etheric cross', of the 'Christ-cross'; the third point with the Ram belongs to the 'Cross of the Father', the 'physical, or Earth-cross' (on all these distinctions see MG 343ff.).[38]

The three points of the triangle of Mark, as we perceive from the chapter on the planets, are governed by the Sun (in ♌), Mars (in ♈) and Jupiter (in ♐), so that from here we can also understand why Mark is the only evangelist to present the Sun-rhythm.

The element of fire, or the 'warmth-ether', from which we proceed in the exposition as Mark's element, condenses below to the element of air, and sublimates above to the light-ether, so that the element of air and the light-ether stand in a certain connection. (All the facts of the etheric world touched on here are discussed in the frequently-mentioned book by Günther Wachsmuth.) The 'air-triangle', or 'triangle of the light-ether', is the one triangle with the point ♊ standing upwards in Figs. 1 & 3, pages 334 and 336. Through its point in Waterman (this is, the spiritual, primordial human being), it is the triangle of Matthew's Gospel. This sign belonging to the 'Cross of the Spirit', or the astral element, as explained in the chapter on the planets, is governed by Saturn-Uranus; the two other points are formed through the Mercury-sign Twins (in the 'Cross of the Etheric') and through the Venus-sign Scales in the Earth-Cross. The whole triangle, which we could also call the triangle of the human being, is (as mentioned above) in a certain sense the Uranus-trigon, or Uranus-triangle.

As the human being raises his brow (*Stirn*) to the stars (*Sternen*) (ἄνθρωπος, *anthropos* ... 'the one looking up to the heights'), this Matthew-triangle of the human being with its apex, or zenith, in the sign of the heights, the Twins, and of the 'sacred Mount' is turned towards the upper starry heavens, Uranos. Consequently, it is significant how the *Star of Bethlehem* stands at the entrance to Matthew's Gospel that leads the wise priests and astrologers of the East to the birthplace of the Redeemer of the world. This is the more remarkable, for otherwise in the gospel the stars are not directly mentioned—with the exception of the 'little apocalypse' Mark 14 = Matthew 24 = Luke 21, which has to be taken as an anticipation of the Apocalypse that brings us to a full view of the starry heavens. Even John's Gospel, as much as in its inner spiritual being it is also the gospel of the 'I' and at the same time the actual star-gospel, does not once contain the word 'star'. Perhaps we could say, that Matthew's Gospel, which with its trigon is governed by Uranus, by the upper starry heaven—in the story of the Star of Bethlehem—permits inclusion of the *old astrology*, whereas John's Gospel contains the astrology to be developed out of the 'I', the *'astrology of the "I"'*.

***

Warmth-ether and light-ether, to whose trigons the Gospels of Mark and Matthew align, are the two 'lower kinds of ether', the element of the male. The two other ethers, the sound-ether (or, chemical-ether) and life-ether, are the 'upper kinds of ether', the element of the eternal-feminine.

We quote here a passage from Günther Wachsmuth's book (Book 2, p. 77f.), because it connects with the deeper backgrounds precisely of John's Gospel:

> With the male human being, in the body the lower pole, the active radiating formative forces are used for building up and make the organism function. With the human female, for the same, it is the formative forces that draw in, as it were passively. The *male* organism consequently uses more the formative forces of the light-ether and warmth-ether; the *female* organism more the forces of the chemical-ether and light-ether ... It is the primordial principle of all living beings that ... those formative forces which are not used up for the bodily functions in the organism can freely serve the functions of soul and spirit ...
>
> - The *male* organism is fashioned so that at the bodily-creative pole warmth-ether and light-ether are at work; the chemical-ether and life-ether work at the spiritually-creative pole.

- The *female* organism is fashioned so that at the bodily-creative pole the chemical-ether and life-ether are at work; light-ether and warmth-ether work at the spiritually-creative pole.

In other words:

- with the male, in the spirit and soul element a female etheric body is active;
- with the female, in the spirit and soul element a male etheric body is active.

Only the synthesis of the male and female etheric body lying in the supersensory realm renders spiritually the synthesis of all etheric forces. When human beings in their *spiritual* activity at the upper pole of consciousness unite *all* the etheric forces, they are also able to produce within themselves the cosmic harmony that exists externally ... The 'Fall of man', the division into the two genders, works on in the division of the etheric formative forces and their function in human beings.

These sentences are added here because they relate to the deeper background of John's Gospel. Here one could arrive at the thought that John's Gospel as the 'highest gospel' could be aligned to the life-ether, as the 'highest' ether. But the facts repeatedly show that conclusions of this kind lead one astray, for in reality the facts are different. To the highest ether, the life-ether, the trigon of Luke's Gospel is aligned (violet in Fig. 1); John's Gospel is aligned to the trigon of the chemical-, or sound-ether (blue in Fig. 1). Certainly, John's Gospel is the highest gospel and the life-ether is the highest ether. But here another viewpoint is decisive. The chemical- or sound-ether is not the 'highest' but the most effective. As 'alchymical' ether it contains the magical force of forming and transforming matter, of metamorphosing the Earth that is also the element of John's Gospel. This at the same time is the gospel of the Cosmic Word and Cosmic Harmony, of Cosmic Music. Similarly, the chemical-ether is at the same time the sound-ether—in *sound* there originally lies the fashioning, ordering and differentiating force that is mightily revealed in the chapter on creation in the biblical book of Genesis.

Nothing is more understandable than the fact that *John's Gospel* and the essence of the chemical-ether, or sound-ether, inwardly belong together. Nothing can illuminate so deeply out of the esoteric background the character of this gospel. *Luke's Gospel* is aligned to the life-ether because it is the most intimate gospel, not because it is the 'highest'. As content, this gospel contains in particular the intimate Mysteries of the Eternal Feminine, to which the life-ether belongs, the Mystery of the Virgin and Mother. Already the infancy stories at the beginning point in this direction. The 'Mystery of the Virgin and Mother' is linked in the trigon of this gospel to the sign of the Virgin in the cross of the etheric, in the Christ-cross, whereas the Saturn-sign of the mountain Goat points in the Earth-cross to the Christmas-Mystery (♑ is the Christmas-sign); the Venus-sign ♉ points to the femininity of the Earth (other links of Luke's Gospel with the Mysteries of the female in MG 359). And often comparative gospel-research finds how the most intimate questions of the gospel, of John's Gospel too, do not find their key in the latter, but in Luke's Gospel (cf. MG 300).

In relationship to the higher ether there lies an *esoteric* moment of Luke's and John's Gospels. Opposite this, the Gospels of Matthew and Mark, whose trigons are aligned to the lower etheric (light-ether and warmth-ether) as the element of the male, there lies the *exoteric* moment. In the birth-stories of Matthew's Gospel one notices that the *father*, and in Luke's Gospel the *mother*, stand in the foreground. We can respectively differentiate both 'Jesus gospels' as the gospel of the father and that of the mother. Mark's and John's Gospels both omit the infancy stories of Jesus. To summarize their viewpoint: they narrate only the three years of Christ's earthly ministry. John's Gospel is the actual *Christ-gospel*. Mark's Gospel with its presentation of the Johannine Initiation forms a kind of preliminary stage for John's Gospel. For other connections, the viewpoint of the 'Jesus gospel', Matthew's Gospel forms a preliminary stage to Luke's Gospel.

***

The trigon of the chemical-ether, or sound-ether, aligned to John's Gospel is called the 'water-trigon' in an older designation. Relating downwards,

- the light-ether belongs to the air,
- the sound-ether to the water,
- the life-ether to the earth,

that is, the highest ether belongs to the lowest element. Of the three points of the 'water trigon',

- the apex belongs to the Moon-sign of the Crab, to the Earth-cross. We recognized metamorphosis of the Earth, Earth-alchemy as the Johannine meaning of this sign.

- In the 'etheric cross', in the Christ-Son-cross, lies the Jupiter-sign and Christ-Sun of the Fishes. That John's Gospel is the Christ-gospel is expressed above all in this sign.
- The third, the actual esoteric point of this trigon lies in the Scorpion that was once the Sun-Eagle. Through John it is transformed back into the Eagle (on the meaning of this Imaginative expression, see MG 122, etc.).

The whole Mystery of the Christian-Johannine Initiation, the overcoming of the power of death, is expressed in this transformation, or metamorphosis. This most critical of all signs, the 'death sign', is at the same time also the highest, most rich in Mystery; only on the highest stage of the Johannine Initiation does it reveal its highest meaning. At this point of the zodiac John stands as the Eagle-evangelist, whereas on the other hand the overcoming of the Scorpion's sting of death finds its expression in the Virgin (♍) that, unlike the Scorpion-Eagle, does not belong to the Johannine trigon. The Scorpion is governed by the planet Mars [see Chapter 2 on the planets]. Overcoming the sting of death is at the same time overcoming the Mars daemon.

***

The viewpoint of the temperaments that with 'Mark the Lion' leads to the choleric (fire-element, warmth-ether), would, according to the outer scheme, lead with John to phlegm as the water-element; one might think of the 'rest in the "I"' corresponding to the 'gospel of the "I", or ego'. In reality we would like to feel him as the melancholic—admittedly in a very changed and elevated sense of this word. Of course, it lies in the essence of every path of initiation, not least the Christian-Johannine, to harmonize all four temperaments. Already in the name John (MG 46, 53), we can indeed find all twelve heavenly signs reconciled with the universal, cosmic harmony. The individually fateful [or fixed] quality of each temperament is overcome through the Johannine Initiation in the most comprehensive manner. But an intimate trait lies in how in his whole image and being the conqueror of Bethany still carries a faint memory of the overshadowing deep melancholy of the former 'invalid' (MG 220, 222, 272ff.).

What was then suffered has deeply engraved itself into his whole being. To all this, there comes at the end the participation in the suffering of Christ's Passion, the standing under the cross. There the disciple of Christ felt all human suffering and all human tragedy. Those who have gazed into such depths of life, into such chasms of suffering will still carry in the entire harmony of their being, only recognized by the intimate gaze, that gentle trait of melancholy that is so characteristic of the pictures of John by Leonardo da Vinci. The 'melancholic gaze of love' that Nietzsche believed he perceived in Wagner's Prelude to *Parsifal* [see the author's *The 'Parsifal' Christ-Experience in Wagner's Music Drama*, Anastasi 2015, p. 46; TL forthcoming] is something deeply Johannine. And in John's Gospel itself this gentle trait of a sacred melancholy can certainly be most movingly felt in the 'Farewell Discourses' of Jesus.

John stands before us, not as the melancholic in the normal sense of the word, but as the one who metamorphoses the melancholic, the most obstinate and the most difficult of all the temperaments, into something higher. As the earthly temperament, melancholy points towards the element of earth. If one asks, *through which forces* the disciple John has metamorphosed and overcome this element of earth in the melancholic temperament, then one comes again to the transforming forces of the sound-ether and word-ether of the chemical, alchymical, magical ether. Then it becomes apparent how the aspect of the earth-temperament inwardly connects with the water-element, whose sublimation is the chemical- or sound-ether. Everywhere this ether in particular, the chymical, or sound-ether proves to be the actual Johannine element.

***

A final aspect allows us to connect the four gospels with the fourfold human being, with the four elements and the four temperaments, with the four kinds of ether, as well as with the fourfold dramatic structure of the great cosmic dialogue that takes place in the *eternal sacrifice of the Mass* between human beings and the divine, of the four main parts of the Mass (which, as such, are again present in The Act of Consecration of Man of The Christian Community, the contemporary form of the sacrifice of the Mass):

> Proclamation of the Gospel,
> Offertory,
> Consecration (Transubstantiation), and
> Communion.

- The first part, the Proclamation of the Gospel, points in a special sense to John's Gospel as the actual gospel of the word, towards the form of the gospel that reaches most towards the 'eternal gospel'; the Prologue of this gospel, 'In the beginning was the word … ', can be especially felt as the gospel of all gospels.

John's Gospel and the other Gospels observed from the Cosmic Rhythm 81

- Mark's Gospel with its looking up to the cosmic element awakens the picture of the cosmic sacrificial altar, of the Offertory.
- Over Luke's Gospel with its Mystery of the Eternal Feminine lies the chalice-Mystery of metamorphosis in a specially intimate sense (we recall how in the Grail Mysteries, the chalice is the feminine and the lance the masculine symbol). Also from this viewpoint, Luke's Gospel creates intimate possibilities of understanding for the chymical element in John's Gospel.
- The 'Communion' we will find especially in Matthew's Gospel in the emphasis on the earthly figure of Jesus which points us towards the union, the communion, of the divine with the human realm.

This explanation shows us how in a certain relationship *each* of the gospels is the highest gospel; they mutually complement and carry each other.

- John's Gospel is the highest gospel as the gospel of the 'I', or ego, and the actual Christ-gospel;
- Luke's Gospel as the gospel of the Mother, the most *intimate* gospel;
- Mark's Gospel is the predominantly *cosmic* gospel;
- Matthew's the predominantly *human*, the gospel of the human being, which as the 'gospel of the stars' has the astrological, the *Uranus-aspect*.

Matthew	Communion	Physical body	Watery temperament (phlegmatic)	Air element	Light-ether
Mark	Offertory	Etheric body	Fiery temperament (choleric)	Fire element	Warmth-ether
Luke	Consecration (Transubstantiation)	Astral body	Airy temperament (sanguine)	Earth element	Life-ether
John	Gospel (word)	'I', or ego	Earthly temperament (melancholic)	Water element	Sound-ether (chemical ether)

6.
John's Gospel as Christ's Message of the 'I'

> But this is the life of eternity, that they recognize You (Father) as the Divine resting in the omnipresence of the never-extinguished consciousness, and the One as the Christ, the Saviour Jesus Who is sent, arisen out of your star-radiance.
>
> John 17:3

The essential content of John's Gospel as the Christ-gospel and the gospel of the 'I' is Christ's message of and from the 'I', but not in the way the world understands this 'I'. The 'I' Christ means is the lost or forgotten divine Self of the human being, the divine in the human being. This today but slumbers as a seed of a new 'member of the human being' in the future, already evolving. In biblical language it is often called 'the Son of man'. It also has to do with this 'message'—gospel actually means 'message'—not about a theoretical communication or abstract teaching. The essential thing, how Christ speaks about the 'I', is that he does not say, or need to say: 'The "I" (or, the I-AM) is the light of the world', but simply says, or can say: 'I am the light of the world.' As far as we plainly and simply speak about ourselves as 'I' in the first person, not as an abstract concept as with many mystic, gnostic theoreticians, but in living immediacy, the great cosmic 'I' speaks out of and through Christ (through Christ-Jesus), when He says 'I'. This is the world-historic thing about Christ.

Certainly, the same Being spoke out of Him that revealed Himself to Moses in the Burning Bush: 'I am the I am' (*ejeh asher ejeh*) [perhaps best rendered, 'He who causes to be']; in Egyptian: 'I am everything that is, what was, and what will be.' Human beings today have but forgotten, or are no longer conscious of how actually in each 'I' is revealed the divine in the human being—one recalls especially the moment when children for the first time say 'I' [when not imitating others]. To no other being on Earth than the human being is this 'I' given. In the 'I-am' in general lies the communion of the divine with the human being, who again only in Christ becomes revealed. For this reason we leave the I-am sayings of Christ in John's Gospel simple and tangible as they are, without making them abstract through an artificial translation:

- 'I am the bread of life' (John 6:35);
- 'I am light of the world' (John 8:6);
- 'I am the door' (John 10:7 & 9);
- 'I am the good shepherd' (John 10: 12 & 14);
- 'I am the resurrection and the life' (John 11:25);
- 'I am the way the truth and the life' (John 14:6);
- 'I am the vine' (15:1).

Note: Here lies the main difficulty for all 'translations' of John's Gospel. People feel the deep, cosmic backgrounds of this 'I am' and would like to express this in the translation. [In some translating attempts into German], one comes from the simple 'I am ...' to the higher sounding 'The I is ...' or 'The I-am is ...' or even, 'The I-am-the-I-am is ...' People themselves then feel this inflated and try again to simplify, until by roundabout ways they arrive again at the simple 'I am' of the earlier translations [e.g. John 6:35 '*Ich bin das Brot des Lebens*' (Luther 1540); English versions: 'I am breed of liif' (Wiclif 1380); 'I am that breed of life' (Tyndale 1543); 'I am the breed of lyfe' (Cranmer 1539), etc.].

A similar difficulty is presented at the place: 'I am the one who speaks to you' (4:26) and 'I am, be not afraid' during the Storm on the Lake (6:20). Luther's translation gives the correct outer meaning; in the Greek it stands simply, Ἐγώ εἰμι ('I am') that allows the cosmic backgrounds to survive, which the little German word '*es*', English 'it' ['I am it'], in this case immediately kills. Is this problem of translation at all able to be solved? Attempts at new and contemporary translation of John's Gospel must one day come. Rudolf Steiner indicated several ways towards this and made a beginning, but here to arrive at the full truthful and faithful rendering in the spiritual sphere seems like 'squaring the circle'.

The final I-AM saying of Christ recorded in John's Gospel: Ἐγώ εἰμι ἡ ἄμπελος ἡ ἀληθινή (John 15:1), 'I am the true vine', shows most clearly the inner core of the Mystery of the 'I' in all of these saying, the essence of the 'I' always meant here. It is the *reality of the inextinguishable consciousness grounded in itself, anchored in the eternal.* Luther's translation '*Ich bin der rechte Weinstock*' ['I am the right vine'] says nothing at all. The dictionary version corresponds: '*Ich bin der* wahrhaftige *Weinstock*' (or, '*der Weinstock des Wahrhaftigen*')—'I am the true vine' (or 'the vine of the true people'). But the words ἀλήθεια (*a-létheía* from λήθη: 'forgetting', 'extinguishing consciousness') and ἀληθινός (*a-lethinós*) signify 'truth' and 'truthful', not simply as we use these words today lightly and superficially, but truth in the Johannine sense (see especially John 3): that which is the primordial meaning, the primordial significance of the Greek word, when we take this word again in its *completely literal meaning*: that which is far removed from forgetfulness, which one cannot extinguish, which is the inextinguishable consciousness that will remain before the light of the divine world and the consciousness of the divine, standing its ground and justifying itself, because it is itself anchored in the divine consciousness.

We take the words today lightly and abstractly; we can only *speak* truth and untruth. With Christ there also exists an ἀλήθειαν ποιεῖν, a '*doing* the truth'. Human *actions* are also challenged, whether cosmic truth or cosmic deceit speaks through these actions and is revealed. Here human action, the whole way a human being stands in life, can be something like a lie (John 3:20f.): 'lest his works *come to consciousness*'. 'But everyone who does evil hates the light, and does not come to the light, lest his works *come to consciousness*.³⁹ *Whoever does the truth* comes to the light that his works may be revealed; for they are performed in God.'

From this core-saying of Christ revealing the 'I'-Mystery and ego itself, 'I am (the I-am is) the vine of the never-extinguishable consciousness', the last I-am-saying of John's Gospel, a spiritual line of communication is drawn to the I-am-saying at the beginning of the Apocalypse, 'I am the Alpha and the Omega, he who is, and was and is to come'. The consciousness resting in itself is the actual reality of the world, is the beginning and end of all things—and *ultimately* everything real is consciousness. This also is a key to all the observations given here on the starry worlds. Only where the *reflection* of this reality of consciousness is taken for the reality itself, the shadow for the light, the negative of the world for the positive,⁴⁰ does the illusion arise of matter (as the presumed reality), that illusion that the Indian calls *maya*. Zarathustra called the being whose influence darkens consciousness the power of darkness (Ahriman). It is the same power (Satan-Ahriman), which in Mark's Gospel (Mark 8:33) wants to wipe out the consciousness of the disciple [Peter], and is addressed by Christ (MG 183f.). Ahriman, once active in the plan of creation as the most advanced power, is now the Un-spirit, the *adversary of the 'I'*. The whole initiation narration in Mark's Gospel is a struggle between light and darkness, a *struggle for the 'I'*. It is important to make oneself aware that the 'I' revealed in Christ and which is proclaimed by John is not achieved without struggle.

This *struggle for the 'I'* is the content of the history of mankind, its essential and decisive motif. The appearance of Christ on the Earth, in Whom the lost and forgotten 'I' is placed again into humanity, is the decisive turning point in this 'I'-drama of world-history. The key to understand this drama of mankind is John's Gospel linking to the Apocalypse of John. John's Gospel places before us the Mystery and essence of the 'I' as the one side of the revelation of the 'I'. The Apocalypse shows, how, through what birth-pains the Earth and crises of humanity the 'I', this new, becoming-human member gradually comes to unfold and develop during the course of the historical becoming. The greatest part of this development lies still in the future for us today. John's Gospel contains, as it were, the natural history—more correctly, the higher spirit-dynamic—of the 'I'; the Apocalypse of John reveals its *history*—which here is essentially a future-history, not a history of the past.

***

From chapter to chapter, John's Gospel leads us through Christ's revelation of the 'I', illuminates from ever-new sides the unique manner of being of this new, becoming member of mankind and the Mystery of its active forces.

- Thus *John Chapter 1* shows how in the event of the Jordan the *descent of the 'I'* out of higher worlds takes place, and in this descent of the 'I', in the 'birth of the Son' the heavens open again; how in the 'I' the connection is achieved to the starry spheres of the heavenly hierarchies. During the time of the descent of mankind Jacob still beheld a dream-experience of the 'heavenly ladder' [alluded to in]: 'Truly, truly, I say to you [the 'I' says to you], you will see heaven opened, and the angels of God ascending and descending upon the Son of man' (John 1:51). The 'I' speaks out of Christ, in which the innermost interior unites in love with the starry periphery of all the worlds. Only to the degree that this consciousness also awakens in humanity does the 'I' progress closer to its fulfilment; only then is the 'starry dress of love' being woven (see the previous chapter, p. 73ff., on the 'I' as *starry dress of love* in the language of fairy-tales). Furthermore, we keep in mind how Christ introduces His words with 'Amen, amen' ('Truly, truly, I say unto you'), especially when He speaks out of the consciousness of the unity of the 'I'-centre with the starry periphery of the worlds ('I and the Father are one').
- In *John 2*, with the miracle at the Wedding in Cana, Christ shows how the true 'I', encountering again the power of the Father, the starry-'I' of humanity, metamorphoses the water of the etheric-astral realm into

the *higher wine of life*: 'One day the stars, down dripping,/ Shall flow in golden wine' [Novalis] ... 'out of the "I" the new wine of life, the new Dionysus'. This we can place as a motif for this chapter.

- In *John 3*, the Nicodemus-Chapter lying in the birth-constellation (♑–♋), we experience the motif, 'in the "I" the new birth, the birth from above, out of the upper starry world, the worlds of freedom and of the life-creating Breath'.
- In *John 4*, the conversation of Christ with the Samaritan woman with its meaningful Mystery-backgrounds, has to do with the contrast of the old and new source of life. The one that streamed from primordial times is now close to drying up; the other springing from the hour of birth of the 'I' flows in ever-wider streams into the 'life of the cycles of time to come'. We can briefly call the motif of this chapter, 'Out of the "I" the new source of life'.
- In *John 5*, in the healing of the invalid of Bethesda, the 'I' of Christ awakens in the sick man the 'will in the "I"', which then becomes the actual course of the healing. The motif of this chapter lying clearly in the axis (♏–♉)—the power of death and the power of life—is 'out of the "I" the overcoming of sickness, the new health'.

In the second section of John's Gospel (Chapters 6–10) the 'I' revealed through Christ becomes the awakener of the crisis (rendered as 'judgment' AV/KJV) of humanity, of the great 'I'-crisis of humanity. We can call this more negative 'I'-motif of this section leading to the tragedy and conflict of humanity, 'out of the "I": the verdict, the crisis, the division of spirits'.

Alongside, there stands in each individual chapter specific positive revelations of the 'I':

- In *John 6*, the 'I'-motif sounds, flowing from the miracle of the Feeding: 'I am the bread of life', that is, 'Out of the "I" the new bread of life, the re-enlivening of the life-ether'. The nourishment of life was once revealed, giving itself out of the cosmic circle of stars. During the time of the descent of humankind its final decadent surplus was the 'manna in the desert' (John 6:31). It is now newly received in Christ out of the source of the 'I'.
- In *John 7*, in the first great 'chapter of conflict', Christ speaks the great saying: 'Whoever believes in me [whoever sinks the security of his heart in the "I"], as the scripture has said, "Out of his heart shall flow rivers of living water" [John 7:38]. Not only receiving but also passing on the stream of life that blesses, is spoken of here. 'Out of the "I" the all-blessing stream of life' is the motif that sounds here.

- *John 8*, beginning and ending with the motif of stone-throwing, of all the 'chapters of crisis' is the 'chapter of judgment'; seen outwardly, too, it concerns matters of judgment. Christ shows the heartless judges, who only judge according to the dry, dead letter of the law, how *He* judges. The 'I'—anchored in cosmic Love, rayed through by the cosmic 'I' of the [spiritual] Sun—*richtet*—judges, in the sense of *aufrichtet*, setting upright, set in order. Christ raises the fallen one, damned by the people, to the heights of His cosmic Light. Thus He reveals 'the divine judging out of the "I"'. Significantly, over this chapter stands the Scales as the [universal] sign of earthly justice, as the heavenly sign of Venus Urania, of the Christ-Love in the 'I'. At the same time there sounds the motif 'the new, higher purity, or virginity, out of the "I"'. In the further clash between Christ and the Pharisees, the motif sounds of 'the truth, out of the word of the "I" [that is, the consciousness able to keep hold of itself living in the cosmic Light], freedom out of the knowledge of the truth'; in short, 'in the "I" the inner freedom'.
- To this is added in *John 9*, the chapter on the Healing of the Blind Man, the motif: 'Out of the "I"—encountering the earthly forces—the new vision that overcomes the inherited spiritual blindness.' The motif working and sounding on from Chapter 8 of 'I am [the 'I' is] the light of the world' arrives here at its highest earthly manifestation.
- With the previous 'I'-motifs, all the forces are indicated that lead from the impulse bearing 'I'-development to the 'portal of initiation'. The *path* of this new, Christian-Johannine Initiation is one that is trod out of the forces of the bright, awake consciousness in the 'I', to its fulfilment in the 'I' of Christ. Christ speaks of it in *John 10*. Unlike certain pre-Christian 'ways', Christ's path of initiation does not lead through the 'hidden door' of subconscious forces of life, but through the 'open door' of the full consciousness in the 'I'. 'I am the door' (the 'I' is the door), the word of Christ sounds here. 'Through the "I" is the entrance to life, the true entrance to the path' could summarize here the 'I'-motif of the chapter. The entire initiation-story of Mark's Gospel shows how this path, the battle for the 'I', sought by the disciples, found only by John, encloses in itself the struggle with the forces that want to darken consciousness decisively, to extinguish the 'I'. The first chapters of John's Gospel were concerned with the forces of the 'I' as a yet distant and future 'human member', revealed in Christ for humanity itself. Now in John 10, the way to find this 'I' of Christ presented, and in all openness, before human beings, is primarily shown before the disciples.
- This 'showing of the path' initially still remains teaching, it remains a proclamation. The further step, still to be taken, the Initiation indicated in John 10, is now really to be carried out; the proclamation is to become deed, to become '*Ereignis*' an event (*Erreichnis*, 'attainment'). The 'I' hitherto

only revealed in Christ Himself can also be in another, that the spark of the 'I' can, as it were, leap over to another. *This forms the content of John 11.* Precisely in this leaping over of the divine spark *Christ the Initiator* reveals the highest authority and *magic of the 'I'*. This takes place in the *Raising of Lazarus*. In the one called, the one prepared by Christ Himself with endless care, led right through unutterable tests, temptations and crises, finally through the most narrow of all portals, right through the portal of death itself, the Christ-'I' now awakens. With this the greatest of all the revelations of the 'I' that have hitherto been brought about through Christ, *in John the place is found where the divine spark of the Christ-'I' begins to ignite in humanity*. The power of death that held mankind in bonds—initially they still lie on the other disciples—is overcome by him who in the dying of Lazarus found the resurrection in Christ and became John, who is raised living out of the grave of Bethany. 'I am the resurrection and the life', the saying of Christ sounds here: 'out of the "I" the resurrection, the new life', is the great 'I'-motif of this chapter.

- With this we have passed over from the realm of revealing teaching to that of deed, the practical realization. For this reason in *John 12*, Christ answers those who still expect further revelations that the time for such would now be past. Out of the 'I' of Christ there progressively matures the great decision to die, ungraspable to the other disciples apart from John. And in the Anointing of Christ Jesus through Mary Magdalene in John 12, as in the Washing of the Feet of the disciples by Christ that takes place in John 13, the great progress to death is already prepared. Out of the great conflict of humanity, out of the *Ego-Crisis* of mankind narrated in the second section (John 6–10), in the Event of Golgotha, comes the great tragedy of mankind, the *tragedy of the 'I'*. We experience this tragic element especially where we see sinful humanity with this Event of Golgotha and view the Event as the fault of humanity and the suffering of humanity.

The *tragedy of the 'I'* in the Mystery of Golgotha is followed in the Resurrection by the *triumph of the 'I'*. We saw earlier how the two Lazarus-Chapters (John 11 & 12) form with the five first 'Mystery-Chapters' of John's Gospel a septenary; the two Passion-Chapters of the 'tragedy of the "I"' (John 18 & 19) are inwardly connected with the five chapters of the 'crisis of the "I"' (John 6–10). Now the two Resurrection-Chapters—or Chapters of the 'Great Reunion' (John 20 & 21)—inwardly join with the Chapters of the Farewell Discourses and Chapters on the Disciples (John 13–17) to form another septenary.

Like a summary of what was revealed earlier about the 'I' and at the same time as a revelation of the resurrection-future, two sayings of Christ still appear in the 'Farewell Discourses': 'I am the way, the truth and the life' (John 14:6) and 'I am (the 'I' is) the vine of the unquenchable consciousness' (John 15:1). Through this 'I'–power in Himself, of the unquenchable consciousness, the carrying and protecting love of Christ leads the disciples. Their consciousness still lay in the darkening; their 'I' shows it is still incapable of bearing [anything]. Christ's love carries them right through their crisis and preserves them for the later fulfilment of their great task for humanity. Through the 'love till the end' (John 13:1), right to the festive fulfilment, He leads those who failed in consciousness. Those for whom the great parting, the great separation, will almost break the heart (John 16:22), He leads to the *great reunion* in the Resurrection after victoriously withstanding the night of death. 'I am the resurrection', the truth already revealed in the raising of Lazarus, becomes through the Resurrection of Christ the point of departure for the renewing of the Earth and mankind. We could call the 'I'-motif of these two final, future-bearing chapters of John's Gospel *'out of the "I" the great re-union, the re-union in Eternity'*. Even the 'Appearances of the Risen One' are initially still like a picture and parable to the disciples. Like a *Fata Morgana*, or mirage, on the heaven of the future the view finally appears of a still greater and more solemn reunion of Christ with His own in the future of the ages ...

Thus the *Love in the 'I'*, which carries in itself the guarantee of the eternal reunion, is the final, brightest of all the revelations of the 'I' of Christ in John's Gospel. Like a star raying forth it shines over the whole of this gospel, like the Star of Love (Venus Urania) itself, which, in the sign of the I-AM of Christ, governs in the Scales. From the creative revelation of this star in the primordial beginning of the Earth (♀ in ♉), right to its heavenly revelation in the 'I' of Christ (♀ in ♎), the rhythm of John's Gospel has led us, in order then to return to its point of departure. The love in the 'I', Venus Urania (♀ in ♎) holding the middle, governing the whole, shines over the whole of John's Gospel. And from here, when the Johannine 'I'-AM sayings find their conclusion in the Apocalypse, we are able deeply to lay hold of the keystone of the entire New Testament: 'I am [the 'I' is] the root and the offspring of David, the bright morning star' [Apoc./Rev. 22:16] ('I am' = ♎, the Morning Star = ♀). The Star of Love (♀) torn from Lucifer in his fall is become sacred again in Christ.

With this we stand before the actual star-Mystery of the 'I', to which the last, concluding chapter of this first part is devoted.

7.
The Star-Mystery of the Eternal Name
The Book of Life and the Book of Destiny

> Nevertheless do not rejoice in this, that the spirits are subject to you;
> but rejoice that your names are written in heaven.
> Luke 10:20

The Mystery of the Eternal Name

The Mystery of the Eternal Name, one of humanity's great primordial motifs in the Bible, runs through the whole Old and New Testaments, significantly uniting them both from the beginning of Genesis to the Apocalypse. In Genesis 1:1, the eternal Word of Creation designates and calls everything into existence, in order finally to reside with the power of the creative naming in the still paradisal humanity (Gen. 2:19f. RSV):

> So out of the ground the Lord God formed every beast of the field and every bird of the air, and brought them to the man to see what he would call them; and whatever the man called every living creature, that was its name. The man gave names to all cattle, and to the birds of the air, and to every beast of the field; but for the man there was not found a helper fit for him.

The Book of Revelation warningly tells of the heavenly *Book of Life* and the names of those who are written in the eternal Book of Life of the Lamb.

Between both revelations of naming, which stand as milestones grounded in eternity, there lies, reflecting the whole content of the Bible, a long pathway of humanity. We hear of the Fall of man and of the confusion of tongues with the building of the Tower of Babel (Gen. 11), where the Eternal Name itself and the power out of Eternity to give all things their names, was lost to human beings. Then we hear of the new revelation of the divine name when Moses called to be the leader of his people receives it from the Divine, from Yahweh Himself out of the Burning Bush: *Ejeh asher ejeh*, 'I-AM the

I-AM ... *that is My Name in [all] Eternity'*. For the first time in the history of the consciousness of mankind here the sacred *Mystery of the Eternal Name* is sacredly-significantly linked with *the Mystery of the 'I'*. In the one lies the revelation of the other. Then, this Mystery of the Eternal Name weaves powerfully through the Psalms, till it finds it future-carrying revelation in the words of the prophet Isaiah 43:1 (cf. also 40:26):

> But now thus says the Lord,
> he who created you, O Jacob,
> he who formed you, O Israel:
> 'Fear not, for I have redeemed you;
> I have called you by name, you are mine.'

What was lost and forgotten in the Fall of man is revealed anew in Christ, in John's Initiation and in John's Gospel: this is the transition from the Old to the New Testament. And so the eternal Creator-Word lives again at the beginning of John's Gospel: 'In the primordial beginning was the Word', or ('the Word already was', RNEB), with It the 'Mystery of the Eternal Name' as the 'power of the children of God', those who 'believe on His Name' (v. 12, as it is normally translated), that is, who sink the security of their heart into the Eternal Name, the Eternal 'I'. In these tremendous words at the beginning, the eternal, name-giving Creator-Word of Genesis Chapter 1 finds its New-Testament resurrection in Christ. And Isaiah's saying 43:1 finds its resurrection in John 10, in Christ's saying of the *Good Shepherd*; 'the sheep hear his voice, and he calls his own sheep [that is, those called to the 'I'] by name and leads them out'. Similarly, all the I-AM sayings of Christ, the appearance of Christ on the Earth itself, fulfil the revelation to Moses out of the Burning Bush, 'I-AM the I-AM'.

As a secret of meditation—initially indicated in Mark 11:22-26 [MG 275]—at the same time the 'power of prayer', the *Mystery of the Name* sounds in quite a specially significant manner right through the 'Farewell Discourses of Jesus', John 14–16 (John 14:13, 14:26, 15:7, 15:16, 16:23-28): 'If you ask anything of the Father, he will give it to you *in my name* [in the name of the 'I']. Hitherto you have asked nothing in my name; ask, and you will receive, that your joy may be full ... the hour is coming ... In that day you will ask in my name' [John 16:23-6].

The *Mystery of the Name* in John's Gospel finds its radiant climax in John 17, in the *great petition* of the 'High-Priestly Prayer' (NIV):

> I have revealed you to those whom you gave me out of the world... Holy Father, keep them in thy name ... I made known to them thy name, and I will make it known, that the love with which thou hast loved me may be in them, and I in them.

To these words of Christ are added John's saying at the end of Chapter 20: '... that by believing you may have life in his name'.

The Apocalypse of John

As a direct and manifest Johannine element this *name motif* lives ultimately in the *Apocalypse of John,* finding there its actual crowning conclusion. Here at the same time it links the beginning and ending of the Bible. It links the Mystery of the name-giving, eternal Creator-Word in the primordial beginning with the Mystery of the *Book of Life*, in which the Eternal Names are written. Whatever philological and theological research is able to tell or believes has to be assumed about the 'authorship' of John's Gospel and of the Apocalypse of John, the inner spiritual link between John's Gospel and the Apocalypse, the direct Johannine element in both of these books of mankind, becomes in the first instance clear through this great motif of the *Eternal Name* running through both books. The union of the Mysteries of the *Eternal Name* with that of the 'I' in the Apocalypse is completely, clearly revealed. The principal passages are:

> Rev. 2:17: To him who conquers I will give of the hidden manna, and I will give him a white stone, with a new name written on the stone which no one knows except him who receives it. [That is always the name 'I'.]

> Rev. 3:5: He that conquers shall be clad in white garments; and I will not blot his name out of the book of life; I will confess his name before my Father and before his angels.

> Rev. 3:12: He who conquers, I will make him a pillar in the temple of my God; never shall he go out of it, and I will write on him the name of the divine 'I', and the name of the new Jerusalem, the city of the divine 'I', which comes down from the divine 'I' out of heaven, and my own new name, the name of the 'I'.

> Rev. 5:1-5: And I saw in the right hand of him who was seated on the throne a scroll written within and on the back, sealed with seven seals...

and I wept much that no one was found worthy to open the scroll or to look into it. Then one of the elders said to me, 'Weep not; lo, the Lion of the tribe of Judah, the Root of David, has conquered, so that he can open the scroll and its seven seals.'

Rev. 13:8: ... whose name has not been written[41] before the foundation of the world in the book of life of the Lamb that was slain.

Rev. 14:6: Then I saw another angel [or 'the angel of the Countenance'] flying in midheaven, who had an eternal gospel to proclaim to those who dwell on earth, to every nation and tribe and tongue and people.

Rev. 17:8: The beast that you saw was, and is not, and is to ascend from the bottomless pit and go to perdition; and the dwellers on earth whose names have not been written in the book of life from the foundation of the world, will marvel to behold the beast [of the abyss] ...

Rev. 19: 12f.: [The 'White Rider'] ... and he has a name inscribed which no one knows but himself ... and the name by which he is called is The Word of God.

Rev. 20:12: And I saw the dead ... standing before the throne, and books were opened. Also another book was opened, which is the book of life. And the dead were judged by what was written in the books, by what they had done.

Rev. 21: 27 [about the 'New Jerusalem']: But nothing unclean shall enter it, nor any one who practices abomination or falsehood [cf. John 3:21], but only those who are written in the Lamb's book of life.

All these passages find their supplement and explanation through the significant passage Luke 10:20 that lets us gently surmise and as if from afar that the 'Mystery of the Eternal Name' touching on all the other passages is ultimately a *star-Mystery*: 'Nevertheless do not rejoice in this, that the spirits are subject to you; *but rejoice that your names are written in heaven.*'

True faith

The saying, spoken by Christ to the disciples, whom He wants to invest with full spiritual authority, closely encounters another important motif that also appears in many places in John's Gospel. To the truth implied in John 1:12, of the authentic 'belief in the Name' (= of the heart's security sunk in the Eternal Name, in the 'I') of the

The Star-Mystery of the Eternal Name 95

'children of God', there is opposed another, incorrect 'belief in the Name'.[42] Christ is uneasy about it; He repeatedly dismisses this as insufficient. Thus already at the beginning, John 2:23f., where Christ, Who sees into human hearts, cannot return the 'belief' or 'trust' induced in people merely through the sign, cannot with *His* trust and with *His* devotion return the devotion meant by the human hearts there.

Christ can only confirm the real activity of faith and security of the heart in the 'I' as *proceeding from 'I' to 'I'*. In the word 'I' itself lies the fact that it never has to do with an overwhelming of the inner realm, but only with what is received by the self in full inner freedom with all Christ's activity. Here we can compare some of the significant sayings of Novalis on the 'I': 'The "I" is choice and realizing the sphere of individual freedom and self-activity.' 'In the "I", in the *freedom-point*, we are in fact all completely identical'… I 'is the absolute comprehensive place, the central point.' 'In every moment, when we act freely, is such a triumph of the eternal "I" over the temporal …'.

Where Christ notices that the souls are certainly receptive for all sorts of magical influences, but the 'self' is still closed to the 'I' (the lower 'I' to the higher 'I'), He can not yet abide in the hearts of 'believers'. Consequently, His warning to the disciples, to the representatives of His work on Earth: 'Nevertheless do not rejoice in this, that the spirits are subject to you; but rejoice that your names are written in heaven.'

Earlier peoples knew, and so-called primitive people today know, of the 'Mystery of the Name' and its magical, enchanting effect.[43] In many cases it involves a final decadence of the primordial human forces indicated in the beginning of Genesis. We find ourselves on a higher niveau in early India, where the Veda is still full of the revelation of magical strength of the word and speech-sounds, of the 'mantram' and the effect of naming resting in it. Something of the original connection was known of the word and speech-sound with the creative primordial powers, of the 'naming' with the name of some thing or being. In early humanity there still lived a memory of the Mystery of the *original language*—it is mentioned significantly in the Bible, especially in Genesis [11:1]. And here not some original Sanskrit or some other predecessor of the 'early languages' is meant. The original language of the primordial human being is the receptive ability and expression of his being, which, from the effect of the Fall of man, was lost in the 'confusion of tongues'.

However, the magical intuition and magical receptivity in primeval times of the human race, progressively lost or fallen into decadence, was to become in Christ the free activity and receptivity of the

'I'. In the case of humanity's own *lost or forgotten Eternal Name*, Christ intends human beings to recall, and only the 'I' is able to hear this name in the interior of the inner space. Compare John 8:43: 'Why do you not understand what I say? It is because you cannot bear to hear my word.' It is similar in John 8:37, 'my word finds no place in you', οὐ χωρεῖ ἐν ὑμῖν, that is, 'finds no free space in you'. Similarly John 5:43; only the activity of the 'I', not the magical effect of naming, can be valid here.

It would have been easy for Christ magically to overwhelm the human soul. Then the Mystery of Golgotha would have remained of no avail. Humanity would never have achieved the fulfilment of the 'I', the surrender to the divine out of the freedom of the 'I'. This, Christ, the Representative of the true 'I', could never intend. Thus the sacrificial death on Golgotha became a necessity. Seen from the side of humanity, this sacrificial death appeared as the reaction of those estranged from the 'I', from the encounter with their true 'I'. Seen from the side of Christ it is the healing of the fallen 'I' through the divine 'I'. ('Only the Spear heals the wound which it inflicted'—explains Gurnemanz in Wagner's *Parsifal*.)

The above-mentioned 'believe in His name' (πιστεύειν εἰς τὸ ὄνομα αὐτοῦ) belongs to the most difficult to understand, but also most weighty and most significant sayings and leading motifs of John's Gospel. Only when we are able to link the Mystery of the 'naming' with the Mystery of the 'I', of 'belief', do we approach the Johannine meaning of these words. What is usually translated as 'to believe', the Greek πιστεύειν (*pisteuein*), is basically untranslatable. In its Johannine meaning it never signifies an acceptance by the understanding of something unproved, but a much deeper power of the heart and security of the heart. Already the sounds of the Greek πίστισ (*pistis*) 'faith' point to the German *fest* ('firm'). ['A safe stronghold our God is still', as Thomas Carlyle translates Luther's hymn *'Ein' feste Burg ist unser Gott'* (based on Psalm 46, 'God is our refuge and strength').] The picture of the *'festen Burg'* arises, or that other picture of Rudolf Steiner on the occasion of a significant moment for humanity of the 'laying the Foundation Stone in the heart' [the Christmas Conference of the refounding of the Anthroposophical Society, Dornach 1923]. Belief in the Johannine sense is not less, but more than a recognition by the understanding. It is only achieved when the recognition of the heart begins, becomes anchored in the heart, where it is recognized how [all] real knowledge ultimately is enclosed in the

The Star-Mystery of the Eternal Name

heart [is self-knowledge]. In its actual basic depths the heart is that which knows, indeed that which only really knows. This knowing, though, is covered over by that which the Indian called maya—the illusion of the sensory world. *'Glaube ist Empfindung des Wissens'*, 'Faith is the feeling of knowing' (*Fragments*, ed. Kamnizer 635) Novalis writes; and *'Glaube ist Empfindung des Erwachens und Wirkens und Sinnens in einer andern Welt,'* 'Faith is the feeling of waking up and doing things and thinking in another world' (*Fragments*, ed. Kamnizer 1757).

The Mystery of the Name

So much on the 'Mystery of Faith'. To approach the other Mystery, the *Mystery of the Name*, as it is formed in the whole of the Bible from the beginning of Genesis to the Apocalypse, we looked for the key to understand this Bible saying embracing the Mystery of the Name, especially the Johannine saying in the gospel and the Apocalypse—which here as elsewhere is the necessary supplement to the gospel. And the key was found in the words of Luke's Gospel, 10:20:

> Nevertheless do not rejoice in this, that the spirits are subject to you; but rejoice that your names are written in heaven.

The *Star-Mystery of the Eternal Name* shines before us as if from the distance. With it and in it lies the star-meaning of the words 'I and the Father are one' (John 10:30). Only when the star-dress of love—on which we continue to weave through the whole series of our repeated earth-lives—is really woven does the 'I' achieve in Christ its predestined authority, when, as in Christ, the innermost of the inner being with the starry-periphery of all the worlds—with the world of light of the Father—is closed in love, when it itself blooms into a new world star-circle. The simple expression of this relationship of the 'I' to the world star-circle, which so far was there only in Christ, the blueprint for the Earth, is the figure:

$$\odot$$

which, as is well-know, is at the same time the usual sign for the Sun, and thereby at the same time expresses the cosmic Sun of Christ. It also contains at the same time the star-Mystery of the Eternal Name. This relationship of the 'I'-middle point to the periphery of the cosmic star-circle, the world of light of the Father, is realized in Christ ('I and the Father are one'). And, as we shall see ever more clearly, it contains at the same time the 'Mystery of the Eternal Name'. It receives a still more tangible illumination through the fact of the birth-constellation of people, of the note on the birth horoscope by Rudolf Steiner in his *The Spiritual Guidance of the Individual and Humanity* [GA 15], where he says (Lecture 3; June 8, 1911):

> Other human beings are placed into their earthly existence through cosmic-spiritual laws, but these are then counteracted by those originating in the conditions of the Earth's evolution. In the case of Christ Jesus, however, the cosmic-spiritual powers alone remained active in him after the Baptism. The laws of the earth's evolution did not influence Him at all ... Christ always stood under the influence of the entire cosmos ... The events of these three years in Jesus' life were a continuous realization of His horoscope, for in every moment during those years there occurred what usually happens only at birth. This was possible because the entire body of the Nathan-Jesus had remained susceptible to the influence of the totality of the forces of the cosmic-spiritual hierarchies that guide our Earth ... The forces working in Christ Jesus were the cosmic forces coming from the Sun and the stars; they directed His body. The total essence of the cosmos, to which the Earth belongs, determined what Christ Jesus did.

To what is said here, Steiner then adds a very significant picture:

> Imagine every person at birth as a spherical mirror reflecting everything around it. Were we to trace the outlines of the images in the mirror with a pencil, we could then take the mirror and carry the picture it represents with us wherever we went. Just so, we carry a picture of the cosmos within us when we are born, and this *one* picture affects and influences us throughout our lives. [This fact touches on the fact, as Steiner had already showed, of the nature of the 'birth horoscope'.] Of course, we could also leave the mirror clean as it was originally, in which case it would reflect its surroundings wherever we took it, providing us with a complete picture of the world around us. This analogy explains how Christ was in the time between the Baptism in the Jordan and the Mystery of Golgotha. *What enters our earthly life only at our birth flowed into Christ Jesus at each moment of his life.* After the Mystery of Golgotha, what had streamed into Christ from the cosmos merged with the spiritual substance of the Earth, and it has been united with the spirit of the Earth ever since.

This is nothing other than the tangible cosmic meaning, the *star-meaning*, of Christ's saying, 'I and the Father are one' (John 10:30), which is expressed in the simple figure:

$$\odot$$

The periphery corresponds to 'world of Light of the Father', the cosmic star-circle; the 'I'-point in the middle signifies the experience of the Son. We can imagine this point individually shifted—mathematically there are endless possibilities of such shifts. In this shifting is expressed the individual destiny of birth, the *'karma'* that is expressed in the 'birth horoscope'. This contrasts with the exclusive 'birth horoscope' that 'in every moment realizes a new horoscope'. This, elevated over all earthly *karma*, is the relationship of Christ Jesus to the Father, to the essence of the cosmic star-circle. In the individual shifted picture the individual 'special constellations' make their presence felt as fate or destiny, as the necessity of destiny. The point in the middle expresses the *freedom of the 'I'* in the midst of the boundless world.

Only when this 'I' in the human being, through Christ blooms again in a new cosmic star-circle, in the 'transition from the Father to the Son', does the becoming-human 'I' reach its goal. All 'imitation of Christ' consists in the attempted approach to this harmony out of the 'I'. The Mystery of the 'I' has something to do with the centre; the inwardly linked Mystery of the name has something to do with the periphery, with the cosmic star-circle, with the harmonic context of centre and periphery. In this *losing, or at least forgetting of the Eternal Name* in the Fall of man, meaning that the human being has fallen out of this universal harmony with the whole cosmos, with the star-periphery of the worlds ('heaven', Luke 10:20), constitutes the name being 'wiped out—or appearing to be wiped out—of the Book of Life'. Forgetting is a losing consciousness of that which excludes itself as a 'losing the Eternal Name'.

Human Origins in the Spirit

Man was originally created in the image of God by the eternal Father in the realm of eternity. In every earthly name-giving—which is why it is mostly taken seriously—people even today feel somehow deep down something expressed in the *name* of this Mystery of the forgotten connection of the human being with the eternal and divine. It is lost to consciousness, yet they feel something of the fact that as human beings they are actually citizens of two worlds. With their earthly, bodily form they belong to the kingdom of the transitory; with their spiritual being, with their 'I', they belong to the eternal realm. The tragedy of this intimation, of the completely estranged human being, is comparable to those who have forgotten their name, who no longer know who they actually are, is movingly expressed—as frequently in the Psalms—in the Book of Job (21:17f. NIV):

> Yet how often is the lamp of the wicked [the godless,
> estranged from God], snuffed out?
> How often does calamity come upon them,
> the fate God allots in his anger?
> How often are they like straw before the wind,
> like chaff swept away by a gale?

It is the sinking into the earthly, into the 'death of matter'. In Christ, the eternal 'I', the Eternal Name, as it were, descends out of the eternal realm into the transitory realm, so that in union with Christ the 'children of God' (John 1:12) can re-find the Eternal Name or become conscious of the Name again. This is once again made possible for those 'who believe in His Name', who sink the security of their heart into the Eternal Name *Jesus Christ*, into the name 'I'.

The real *star-meaning* of this fact will be ever more clearly shown in what follows. Something of this star-meaning filled Saint-Martin (Louis Claude de Saint Martin, *Gott, Mensch und Welt*, freely tr. into Germ. by A.W. Sellin. Konstanz 1919, 160). First, with reference to the Hebrew name (Y(J)–H–V–H), whose earthly fulfilment is the name Jesus (J–S–V–S), he speaks of the *Name*, 'which comprehends in itself the life and the initial, primordial activity of everything that has existence, the Name, *through whose power the stars shine, the Earth brings forth fruit and the human being thinks.*'

First of all, it can be shown how the all-speaking star-Mystery of the name expressed in the simple figure:

$$\odot$$

is contained in the word *Name* itself, which in Greek (in the original text of John's Gospel) sounds ὄνομα (*ónoma*), in Latin *nomen*, in Indian (Sanskrit) *nāmari* (nominative *nāma*, originally, *nāmn*, that is, actually completely like the German '*Namen*'). The archetypal form of the word in that group of languages out of which also the inspiration for John's Gospel was received, the Indo-Germanic, is simply *n–m*.

Note: The consonants are spirit-decisive, in a certain way what remains throughout the historical changes; the vowels are the individual soul-expression and differentiation in the dialects in the word, for which reason, along with others, they were not written down in many ancient languages.

Linguistic research today, which is only concerned with pursuing the historical development of the various languages and comparing what has historically taken place, believes itself to be able to keep its methods pure if it disregards on principle all the questions of a spiritual experience of, and feeling for, the sounds. These questions do not belong to that sphere in which linguistic science is carried out today.[44] Consequently, these questions lie all the more in that sphere to which *John's Gospel as the primordial gospel of the word* itself belongs, that gospel which is completely born out of the essence of the archetypal word and archetypal musical sound. It is carried and filled by the Mysteries of the element of the word and the cosmic music of the sound-ether. In the empirical, factual realm of the spiritual meaning of sounds, of the spiritual experience and feeling for sounds, a real key is contained for the spiritual contexts of John's Gospel. The whole configuration of the sounds and words of John's Gospel is to all appearances tuned to these facts.[45]

The Polarity of M and N

A true insight into the words of wisdom 'As above, so below', the insight into the connection of everything earthly with the cosmic realm, also leads to a new understanding of the connection between all earthly sounds of speech and the musical element in speech with the cosmic archetypal harmony, the cosmic primordial musical sound and cosmic primordial word. Something like a *star-meaning of all speech-sounds and words* shines before us. In this sense, in his lecture-course *Eurythmy as Visible Speech* (GA 279. Lecture, Dornach, 8 July 1924), Rudolf Steiner aligns the consonants, or the twelve main ones, to the twelve signs of the zodiac. The vowels—the seven main vowels—are aligned to the spirit of the seven planets (☉ au, ♀ a ['ah'], ☿ i ['ee'], ☽ ai, ♂ a ['eh'], ♃ o ['oh'], ♄ u ['oo']). It initially depends on the fact as such, not on the details of this arrangement.

Both consonants contained in the word 'name' (*onoma*), etc. and the archetypal word *n–m* (the research of which we are looking at here) can be expressed in quite a simple observation, connected to the most natural and obvious one. These consonants stand near to the primordial musical sound; they, as the language of children shows, are archetypal sounds of all human speech. In the possibility of their long, dull continuous sounding, both sounds carry a certain vowel-element. They still stand, as it were, between vowels and consonants. (In the primordial Indo-Germanic language *m* and *n*, besides their consonantal quality, still possessed a vowel-significance.) Such a long-sounding *m*—as, for example, in the Indian *om*—can be compared to the dull sound of a bell dying away. Here we touch on an archetypal element of speech: *m* is the dull, lulling sound that is spoken to the greatest degree still with closed lips, standing closest to the word that is becoming mute.[46] Like *v* [Germ. *w*] (*v*, *u*) the creative, archetypal sound of becoming,[47] *m* is, as it were, the sound of dying, the zero-point of speech-sounds, in which we touch the innermost interior, the *sound of the middle*. Consequently, *m* in many languages is the initial sound of the word 'middle': Latin *medius*, Greek μέσος (*mesos*), Indian *madhyama*, Avstestan *madhöma*, etc. Otherwise in words, which express the relationship to the 'I': *mein* (Eng. mine), *mir* (to me), *mich* (me, accusative); Lat. *mihi*, *me*; Indian *mayam*, *me*; similar words in Greek, Hebrew and many other languages. When the mediating Indian submerges himself completely into the innermost interior, he speaks the sacred syllable *AUM, OM* with a long, deep resounding of the *m*.

If we go from the *m* as the sound of the middle, the 'I'-middle ('where the "I" always forms the middle'), then the *n* standing close to it can be felt as the sound of the periphery. In many words it seems to express that which flows away to the periphery in the distance, into the undefined (as *m* which, disappearing from the outer, consolidates within), one can think of 'end' (Sanskrit *anta*), 'infinite' (Sanskrit *ananta*), *Nacht* ('night'), *Nichts* ('nothing'), *nein* ('no') (here *n* in many words of the same meaning in other languages). The simple German word *nehmen* ('to take')—somewhat related to *Name* ('name') (with Wagner at one place: '*den Nahmen nim' ich von* dir', 'the name I take from you')—seems to speak of this, how something comes in from the periphery into the sphere of the 'I', is being taken in. In our basic figure:

⊙

we find the essence of *m* within, in the centre, the essence of *n* in the surrounding circle, in the periphery. The sign ⊙ stands there like a written symbol of the archetypal word *n–m*. If we take the sounds in their archetypal sense as words in their ultimate, highest and most sacred sense, then we see in the periphery, *n*, the cosmic star-circle, in the centre, in the *m*, the 'I', the 'Son', in Whom the world of Light of the Father is newly born and revealed.

With this, we have read the figure ☉, as it were, from the outside to the inside. This figure has formed itself as *n–m* into the archetypal word *Name* (name). Here we behold the Mystery of the Eternal Name in the context of the cosmic 'I'-middle and cosmic star-circle. We hear the Mystery sounding in the cosmic star-harmony. We can also read the sounds in reverse, from the inside towards the outside. Then there arises another archetypal word, *m–n*, the primordial root of the word *Mensch*, 'man'. This word 'man' is in Indian called *mānusha* or *mānushya*, from the root *man* (*m–n*) 'thinking' (cf. Lat. *mens*, 'mind, understanding'). In thinking, the human being gives all *things* their names; the 'I' connects with the periphery of the world. English retains the archetypal form, which also means 'male'. With the German *Mann*, the doubling of the *n* expresses the disturbance of the archetypal harmony of what is purely human, reinforcing the element lying towards the *n*-side, the sensory periphery. *M* is the softer sound, the somewhat cutting, penetrating *n* is the harder sound; *m* in a certain sense is a female sound,[48] *n* a masculine sound (cf. Indian *nr* (*nar*) 'man'). In *man* (the primordial root of the German *Mensch*), *m* and *n* are feminine and masculine—cf. Gen. 1:27, still in balance.

Thus the figure ☉ shows the Mystery of the name (*n–m*) inwardly connected with the Mystery of the human being (*man*, *m–n*). The name is originally in the periphery, written in the heavens (Luke 10:20), and flows from there into the 'I'. The reversal of this process (*m–n*) lies in the human being (*man*), who is a cognizing spiritual being (*man*, to think), who gives to all things their names—and originally out of the eternal primordial Word (Gen. 2:19). Rudolf Steiner speaks of the *star-meaning* of speech-sounds (*Eurythmy as Visible Speech*, lecture, Dornach, 8 July 1924; also discussed in the remarkable essay, Robert Völpel, 'Über die Laute M und N', *Gäa-Sophia* III, ii Völkekunde, Dornach 1929, 178-82). Steiner places the *m* to the spirit of the Waterman, the *n* to the spirit of the Fishes. [*Sefer Yetsirah* has M (*mem*) as the second of the three Mothers, representing Water, and N (*nun*, 'fish') under Scorpio once and later as Eagle—*Ed.*]

The Waterman points to the origin of the human being, to the spirit-etheric 'human being of the primordial beginnings'. The sign ≈ expresses visually the flowing wave; the double wavy line, which also in the round shape of the lips shows the inner connection with the essence of the *m*-sound (to which Steiner points as a quite tangible example of the 'esoteric script of the cosmos' in the first lecture-cycle, *At the Gates of Spiritual Science*. Stuttgart, 22 August–4 September 1906; GA 95). The Waterman triangle (♒ ♊ ♎, cf. the figures in 'The Figures of the Zodiac' and the chapter before the penultimate chapter) is the trigon of Matthew's Gospel: his, as we saw, is the 'gospel of the human being' (♒), as Mark's Gospel is the gospel of the Lion (♌), Luke's the gospel of the Bull (♉), and John the gospel of the Eagle (that then became ♏). In Figs. 1 & 3 on pages 334 and 336, the Matthew trigon appears significantly in the zenith with the elevated sign (♊): we think of the meaning already adopted by Plato of the Greek άνθρωπος (*anthropos*) 'human being': 'the one that looks up to the heights (the divine-spiritual)'. Concerning the relationship of this triangle to Uranus, *Uranós*—cf. Luke 10:20—see the chapter on the planets.

If, as Steiner shows in the above-cited source, we may relate *m* to the spirit of the Waterman (which besides ♄ is governed by Uranus), and *n* to the spirit of the Fishes (which besides ♃ is governed by Neptune), the star-meaning of the primordial root M–N, *man*, 'human being', at the same time points towards the origin of the spiritual human being beyond Saturn, to the origin in the *upper starry worlds* (in this sense, always *Uranós* in John's Gospel). We think here also of Novalis' saying in *Fragments* (ed. Kamnitzer 1320): 'Humanity is the higher meaning of our planet; the nerve that connects this member with the upper world [is] the eye, which he [the human being] lifts toward heaven.' In a deeply Johannine sense, the spiritual meaning of the word άνθρωπος (*anthropos*) 'man, the human being', is explained through this.[49]

In the original Greek text of John's Gospel this word άνθρωπος (*anthropos*) denotes the human being. But consequently the primordial root *man* (*m–n*) in the 'star-meaning' meant here is not foreign to John's Gospel. It can be found there (John 6:31, 49) in the word 'manna' (Gk. μάννα, Heb. mān): 'Your fathers ate manna in the wilderness/ desert.' This (atmospherical) manna is the last weak and decadent remains of the 'star-bread' of that time, of the spiritual nourishment, or provisions ('Grail nourishment', see MG 67), still received in earlier times of human consciousness and human Mysteries out of the etheric, the cosmos. It is now received through the power of Christ as new nourishment of life *in the 'I'*. 'I am [*the 'I' is*] the bread of life' is the great motif of John 6.

The 'manna' belongs to the descent of humanity. In it there appears, fallen and outwardly entombed, that which once was etheric, spiritual star-activity. Yet this *star-Mystery*, which at the same time is the human-Mystery, still lies in the speech-sounds of the word *manna*, which in its Hebrew form *mān* is identical with the primordial root of the German word *Mensch* and is retained in English. And this star-Mystery and human-Mystery lies over the whole of John 6, especially in the mention of the 'twelve baskets' in the narration of the Feeding of the Five Thousand (John 6:13). Already in the exposition on Mark's Gospel (MG 36f., 171), we recognized the *twelve heavenly powers*, a picture that embraces the whole human being. Thus the star-meaning of the root *m–n*, *man*, likewise the star-meaning of *Name* (name) with the root *n–m* (also contained in the Greek *ónoma*) and its reverse *m–n*, belongs to the motifs of John's Gospel.

Like the star-meaning of 'name', the star-meaning of the word 'man' and its primordial root *man* 'to think' have mostly been forgotten by humanity today. People no longer know how a *living thinking* of the spirit of the human being links once again with the spirit of the stellar widths, how such a thinking in reality is a creative unfolding of the 'I', a 'weaving of the star-dress of love'.

***

The motif *n–m* and its reversal *m–n* appears in John's Gospel not only in words that somehow link the star-Mystery of the *name* with that of the human being—in the Fig. ☉ the motif is expressed pictorially. But a series of other star-motifs join with this, whose connection with the one primordial motif is given quite clearly through both consonants.

The connection of the *n–m* in the German word '*Name*' and English 'name'—in the sense of entering or taking something in from the outside [sense-impressions, etc.] to the inside—with the Germ. *nehmen* has already been mentioned above. With the same vocalizing we find the motif in Greek νέμω (*nemo*), νέμειν (*nemein*) '*weiden*—to pasture', that is, a special case of *Nehmens*, 'taking', that exists between the cow and the grass that serves as its fodder, and the noun deriving from it νομή (*nomé*) Germ. '*Weide*'—'meadow, pasture'. This word becomes a star-motif of Christ in the chapter of the Good Shepherd and the Sheep. John 10:9: 'I am [the 'I' is] the door [to the spiritual world]; if anyone through me [through the door of the 'I'] seeks the [spiritual] entrance, will find salvation: he will go in and out and *find pasture* [νομὴν εὑρήσει].' All the ways of the Earth and of heaven—this is the meaning of this passage—are open to those who seek entrance from the 'I' and through the 'I'. From the earthly realm they will find the star-paths of the heavenly world, and from the star-realms once again find the way of the Earth and to the earthly realm. *On the great star-meadow, where the heavenly creatures find pasture*, such people will 'find pasture' who partake of the active heavenly forces, stimulating their own nature to unfold in the realm of these radiating forces. *Mysteries of the star-zodiac*, that are hidden behind the word *ónoma* 'name'—'rejoice that your names are written in heaven'—shine before us in the Johannine *nomé*, 'meadow, pasture'.

Nomé points to the root *n–m* and *ónoma* 'name'; the reverse of the same root, the human-star motif *m–n, man* contains in its second syllable an echo of that word which in the same context in the original text of John 10 is used of the 'Good Shepherd', the Greek word ποιμὴν (*poimen*). Something like 'creative unfolding of the human being' shines out of the speech-sounds suggesting a revealing of the spiritual meaning of the word *in this context*. And linking to this motif of the 'Shepherd of human beings' (*m–n*) in the same context with the name-motif (*n–m*): 'he calls his own sheep *by name* ... and the sheep follow him, for they know his voice' (John 9:3 & 4). The 'I' perceives the Eternal Name sounding out of the star-harmony of Christ, finds again access to the star-harmony, in which every individual human being sounds his 'individual primordial musical sound'. The 'Eternal Name' always referred to here is tuned to this 'harmony of the primordial musical sound', not any earthly alphabet although connections do exist. At the beginning reference was made to Is. 43:1:

> But now thus says the Lord,
> he who created you, O Jacob,
> he who formed you, O Israel:
> 'Fear not, for I have redeemed you;
> I have called you by name, you are mine.'

Dwellings and Abiding

The theme in the word νομή (*nomé*) in John 10 appears in reverse μονή (*moné*) in John 14:2 & 23: here the *m–n* appears again (the *n–m* as in *ónoma* and *nomé*). This word is translated as 'dwellings' (KJV/AV translates as 'mansions'): 'In my Father's house are many dwellings' (John 14:2). We intuit or recognize how the star-meaning of the one word leads to the meaning of the other. And the 'dwellings' referred to here are *star-dwellings*, cosmic star-locations, resting-places, stations of spiritual repose in cosmic star-regions. *Nomé* derives from *nemo, nemein* (to pasture); *moné* is derived from *meno, menein* (to remain, tarry awhile). Cf. 14:10, 'the Father who dwells in me [ἐν ἐμοὶ μένων; *en emoi menon*] does His works'. The mutual balance of the consonants (*n–m–m–n*) is especially characteristic in this passage. In this way the motif 'I and the Father are one', expressed in Christ's Sun-sign ☉, corresponds. The immediate living connection of the cosmic starry forces, which for earthly man are present only at the hour of birth, remain for Christ fully active in every moment of his earthly life.

Throughout the whole of John's Gospel μένω, μένειν (*meno, menein*) 'to remain, tarry awhile' is a significant word. Already in John 1:38 the two disciples of John [the Baptist] ask Jesus where He is staying (ποῦ μένεις). Rudolf Steiner points out (*The Spiritual Guidance of Man and Mankind*. GA 15) how in His whole earthly sojourn Christ Jesus did not take one step that would not have been in harmony with the whole starry cosmos. The otherwise everyday *menein*, with Christ always relating to the harmony of the stars (consequently, for this passage the meaningful indication from the viewpoint of this harmony, 'but it was the tenth hour'). In John 5:38 those are mentioned in whom the word of the Father does *not* dwell; in John 6:27 the food which remains for the life of future times (μένουσαν εἰς ζωὴν αἰώνιον). John 6:56, 'Who eats my flesh and drinks my blood remains [μένει, *menei*] remains in me and I in him'. In John 8:31f. *Christ* speaks: 'If you continue [ἐὰν ὑμεῖς μείνητε] in my word, you are truly my disciples, and you will know the truth, and the truth will make you free.'

Also in John 14:23ff. we see *moné* ('we will come to him and *make our home* with him', RSV) connected with *ónoma* 'name' and another *m–n* word that meaningfully fits in here (cf. *man* 'to think') with ὑπομνήσει (*hypo-mnesei* ['remind, recall'], cf. Lat. *memini*, 'I am being recalled') 'he will bring to your remembrance' [v. 26, RSV]: 'But the Counsellor/Comforter, the Holy Spirit, whom the Father will send in my name, he will teach you all things, and bring to your remembrance all that I have said to you.' In recollection, as in everything that now *abides* and *remains*, the 'I' is revealed, the eternal un-lost name.

The motif of *menein* ('remaining'), where Christ speaks to the disciples of the 'I' as the 'vine of the never extinguishable consciousness', completely shines over and sounds through the following chapter: 'He who abides in me, and I in him, he it is that bears much fruit' (John 15:5 RSV). 'As the Father has loved me, so have I loved you; abide in my love' (John 15:9 RSV). And in the final future vision of the Resurrection Chapter, John 21, this 'remaining' (*menein*) appears significantly connected with the disciple John's mysterious being: 'If it is my will that he [John] remain until I come [until the future of the 'I'], what is that to you [Peter]?' What is meant here is not a 'remaining' in the earthly body, as the disciples initially thought and is rejected by the evangelist (John 21:23), but a persistent conscious remaining in Christ's earthly-sphere, in the star-harmony of Christ that also gradually penetrates the sphere of the Earth. Already the name John (*Johannes*) with its (J) I-O-A points to the growing into the harmony of the stars of the great Sun-rhythm. In the Johannine wisdom, whether earthly embodied or not, from now on the uninterrupted, untainted stellar harmony governs, unlike other individual destinies, where intermittent harmonies of individualized horoscopes govern. More than anywhere else μένειν (*menein*) in this passage is a word of the stars.

Internalize

In John's Gospel νομή (*nomé*) stands with μονή (*moné*), νέμω (*nemo*) with μένω (*meno*), also the words νόμος (*nómos*) 'law', and μόνος (*mónos*) 'alone, sole'. Here too the motif n–m with its reversal m–n governs; here too the figure ⊙ shows the connection most clearly. Here too we see *n* as the periphery and *m* as the centre of the circle. That which actively streams from the cosmic sensory periphery towards the 'I'-middle point, so that in everything actively sent from the periphery (*n*) becomes what is passively received or suffered in the 'I' (*m*)—this principle is cosmic necessity, natural law, the outer law in general. And so in John's Gospel *nómos* always stands for the law of Moses (already John 1:17, then in John 7 and afterwards more frequently), the stony tablets, on whose dead, rigid letters the Jews cling. With this they always oppose the living word of Christ and His healing power of love. They remain with the Father's revelation of death; towards His living revelation they close themselves off ('no one comes to the Father, but by me'—by the 'I', John 14:6). Here there appears the 'transition from the Father to the Son' from what is past to what bears the future, from death to life, from the necessity of the law to freedom, from the 'divine wrath' to grace (χάρις). And this word χάρις (*charis*), in speech-sounds relates to words that signify 'free space' and similar things; in John's Gospel it is always clearly related to the experience of freedom in the 'I'. Grace (χάρις), which is given from above, is for human beings through Christ a possibility they develop out of the freedom in the 'I' to decide for the Good and Divine.

Thus νόμος (*nómos*) 'law', coming from outside (*n*), oppresses what is within (*m*). If the relationship is reversed and the 'I' within becomes aware of its sovereignty, then νόμος (*nómos*) changes into μόνος (*mónos*), 'the unique, the only [one]', occupying a class of its own with none above it. From this we best understand the Johannine μονογενὴς υἱος [Stephanus 1550: later texts have θεὸς] (right at the beginning, John 1:18) (*mono-genés hyiós*) the 'only-begotten, or once-born Son', that is, the one born out of Unity and in Unity, born in Eternity, whose Unity and Self-grounded existence reflects the essence of the Eternal. This 'all-oneness', not a luciferic isolation, really is All-Oneness. In the 'I' it embraces in love all earthly beings and all the stars, as the beautiful words of Novalis (Fragment 1254, ed. Kamnitzer) imply: 'We are alone with everything that we love.' (The Greek word μόνος *mónos* is related with the Indian *maunam* 'sacred/ holy silence', and *muni* 'the holy one'). In this sense, Christ says to His disciples, who leave Him in the lurch (John 16:32): 'The Scorpion's power of death (MG 314) scatters you now into separation, and you leave me alone; but *I am not alone*, for the Father is with me.' Where the 'I' in this cosmic, eternal sense is 'alone' (alone with the Father), there am I (there is the 'I') free and unconstricted. In this sense Christ is the *'only-begotten Son'*, *m o n o genés hyiós*. In this sense, when the others want to make Him an earthly king, He goes 'alone' (*mónos*) on the mountain (the spiritual ascent), and remains there transported from the crowds. Similarly, in the beginning of John 8, after the guilty accusers have disappeared, Christ remains alone (*mónos*), v. 9, with the woman.

In John 3:18 *monogenés* (motif *m–n*) is directly connected with the Mystery of the name (*ónoma*, motif *n–m*): 'he who does not believe [ὁ μὴ πιστεύων, see above]: is already judged, for he has not believed in the name of the only-begotten Son of God [ὅτι μὴ πεπίστευκεν εἰς τὸ ὄνομα τοῦ μονογενοῦς υἱοῦ τοῦ θεοῦ] he lacks the strength to sink the surety of his heart into the "I"'. Only by separating himself from the 'I' does the 'I' *'richet'*, judge, rectify.

Incorrect loneliness[50] is spoken about in John 12:24: It is as when 'a grain of wheat falls into the earth and dies, it remains alone …' (μόνος μένει *monos menei*). Yet the passage is remarkable through the way the two words containing the motif *m–n* stand adjacent. Christ speaks of the true loneliness especially where (John 17:3) He unites with His own in the most exalted divine love in the Great Intercession, or the

'High-Priestly Prayer': 'And this is eternal life, that they know Thee [Father] in the All-Unity of the never extinguishable consciousness resting in the Divine [τὸν μόνον ἀληθινὸν θεὸν ton m o n o n alethinón] and recognize as the Christ the Redeemer Jesus, born out of thy Star-radiance.' (The Greek of the original text ἀποστέιλλω (apo- s t e l l o) ['sent from'] has some kind of connection with the Latin *stella*, 'star').

The Amen-Amen sayings

We experience a final summary of the motifs of 'the name and the stars' and 'the human being and the stars' in the words that Christ always prefaced His teaching when in a festive consciousness He speaks of His 'I'-union with the cosmic star-circle of the Father, in the words that begin Christ's teaching of John 16, 'of the Good Shepherd and the sheep', especially where the star-motif n–m, m–n (in *nomé, poi m é n,* etc.) appears: in the word *Amen* (ἀμὴν ἀμὴν λέγω ὑμῖν, aman amen lego hymin*, usually translated 'Truly, truly, I say to you', or 'Verily, verily, I say unto you').[51] Already at the end of John 1, we find these significant words *Amen-Amen* where Christ announces to Nathaniel as the new, the unheard of thing, that from then on in the Son of man, *in the 'I'*, the portal to the world of the angels will be opened. With the same *Amen-Amen* He announces to Nicodemus the Mystery, for him unheard of, of the higher element of life in the birth from above (John 3:5). Especially characteristic is the *Amen-Amen* (John 5:19), where the union—one would like to say, the star-union—of the Son with the Father (the cosmic star-circle of the Father) is mentioned as the Mystery of His activity, the activity of the 'I'. Similarly John 5:24: for the 'believing' meant there is union with the stars in the Eternal Name. Other places are to be found in John 6, which is completely filled with star motifs of the 'bread of life' (vv. 26, 32). Then, the words of eternity that shocked the Jews so deeply (John 8:51, 58) are spoken out of the deepest union of the being of the Son with the Father. John 12:24, in the passage on the grain of wheat, the *Amen-Amen* links meaningfully to other words of the same motif (*monos menei*). Of highest significance, in the saying of John 16:23, Christ reveals the 'I'-magic of the Mystery of the name at work in prayer: 'Amen-Amen, I say to you [the 'I' says to you], if you ask anything of the Father, He will give it to you in my name [in the name of the 'I'].'

The magic of the divine name working in the 'I', in the power of prayer, in meditation, lives in Christ to a higher stage; earlier stages of human consciousness still dreamt the 'magic of the Name'. That in this old form which avoids ego-experience—as a mere 'sign-magic'—is always rejected by Christ. And so we find [Mark 11:20ff., also MG 269] this motif indicated for the first time in the above-mentioned places in John 14, 15 and 16 (esp. v. 23ff.). To the disciples Christ is emphatic that the most loving connections through the 'I' between people and the world, the loving embrace of the cosmic star-circle in the 'I' is the prerequisite of this 'I'-magic in prayer (consequently, the 'remain in the love of the "I"', John 15:7-10, consequently Mark 11:20-25). We can feel how all this is experienced out of the spirit of the sounds contained in the word *Amen* itself, how this word in its *M–N* motif proclaims the connection of the 'I' with the cosmic star-circle of the Father, as expressed in the figure ☉.

Sometimes it can appear to us as if in *Amen* the Eternal Name of the 'I' itself is somewhat indicated (although this Name can only be directly spiritually heard in the star-harmony itself, and cannot be expressed through the sounds of an earthly alphabet).[52] In the Apocalypse (Apoc./Rev. 3:14) the 'Amen' appears as a noun (otherwise used like an exclamation) as the divine 'I'-name, as the name of Christ: 'Thus speaks the Amen, the witness of the surety of the heart and of the never-extinguishable consciousness, the foundation stone of the divine creation ...'

Thus *Amen* as a word directly perceived out of the harmony of the stars actually belongs to the untranslatable words of John's Gospel. It is one of the oldest primordial words of all languages, and consequently to be understood completely out of the archetypal substance of language, out of the archetypal meaning of the sounds. Whereas the Indian mediation-word *Om* (*Aum*) that is most inwardly related only expresses entering the centre-point of the 'I', in *Amen* centre (*m*) and periphery (*n*), 'I'-centre point and cosmic star-circle, Son and Father, touch and connect. Like *Amen*, the Indian *Om* is a word of affirmation and confirmation of the divine confirmation, of divine positivity. Like the *Amen* in the Apocalypse (3:14), the *Om* finally becomes (initially only an interjection) in Yoga (with Patañjali) and in ancient sacred texts given directly as the name of the divine, the 'I'-revelation of the divine (*Ishvara*, emphasis on the I).

The word *Amen* stands before us like a decoding of the speech-sounds of the Mystery of the Sun-seal of Christ:

☉

and we recall the passage in John 6, where the Mystery of the 'Son of man' is mentioned, whom 'God the Father has sealed', that is, *to whom He has imprinted the seal of His Name*. Another significant place receives light from this, John 5:43: 'I am [the 'I' is] come in my Father's name, and you do not receive me [the 'I']; if another comes in the name of his separate nature [ἐν τῷ ὀνόματι τῷ ἰδίῳ], him you will receive.' Only in prayer, in devoted meditation, in meditative listening into the cosmic harmony, can this Name be actually perceived. The name *Jesus Christus* decoded in J–Ch (Germ. *Ich*, Eng. 'I') is as such initially only a product of earthly language, but can truly be taken up in meditation and experienced as archetypal language. It can lead far into the Mysteries indicated here and experiences of the cosmic harmony and of the cosmic word.

'Hitherto you have asked nothing in my name [in the name of the 'I']' Christ has to say to the disciples (John 16:24), who, despite all their long companionship with the Master, could not find the full spiritual connection with Him, and failed in their Initiation.

With all this, we now approach perhaps increasingly the true understanding of the first petition of the Lord's Prayer (Matt. 6:9), *'Hallowed be Thy Name'*. How many human beings already have a clear sense of what these words mean? Not that they can think nothing with it, but receiving them serenely can stimulate contemplation. These words contain a deepest Mystery concerning Christ, words in which the 'I' seeks and finds the harmony with the divine world of the Father. Through rightly understanding these words, every misuse of prayer, every deviation, will be held back through these words (Mark 11:24, 25 with John 15:7). These words cannot be comprehended through some sort of intellectual explanation or interpretation, but only through a path of devoted meditation one penetrates that sphere where the Eternal Name Itself sounds in the harmony of the stars.

Summary

In inner connection with the star-Mystery of the divine Name, the human being achieves the re-calling, forgotten in the Fall of man (and in forgetting, as it were lost), of *their own eternal Name*, as it sounds as a primordial sound in the cosmic harmony. Then, translating all this into the language of the Apocalypse, there stands *the name entered again into the Book of Life*. Then the human being becomes aware that this 'forgetting (or losing) of the name' actually has to do with *forgetting or losing an original and higher supersensory human member* itself, in order that there sounds ever again what is indicated in the first chapters of Genesis I (the creation, Paradise, the Fall of man), and then at certain prominent places in the Old Testament—the story of Moses, with Isaiah and other prophets, with the consecration of Solomon's Temple, in the Psalms, in the Book of Job. Everywhere there clearly appears the 'Mystery of the Name'. And this Mystery ultimately is a *star-Mystery*. It is still difficult to lead the mentality of today to this star-Mystery. In what follows, the attempt is made to approach an understanding from an initially perhaps surprising point of departure, at least to prepare an understanding perhaps lying in the near future.

The Birth-Horoscope and Astrology

In the present context, the subject often arises of the fact of the birth-horoscope and the way Rudolf Steiner in his book *The Spiritual Guidance of Man and Mankind* (GA 15) illuminates this fact. Many people today perhaps shun the spiritual viewpoints presented there, and yet do reckon with the fact of birth-horoscopes as a simple empirical experience, which everyone who is serious about it can make—at first with one close at hand, his/her own birth-horoscope. With the necessary will and self-knowledge, it is easy with the relevant information to learn to use the key, to take account of the purely astronomical realm. All sorts of reasons exist for avoiding such an experience—it is a matter of wanting or not wanting to do it; on the other hand, on this path there is no serious possibility of denying experienced facts when the will and self-knowledge are present. If the matter is properly conducted, the result will be correctly understood. The whole study, from the beginning of this book up to the present point, gives the possibility to see these facts not only empirically but also as understandable and obvious out of the spiritual context of the world (the cosmos of stars), the Earth and the human being.

Only *one* fact may at first glance disappoint or surprise some experts or observers of the birth-horoscope meant here and the normal methods of calculation. That is, in what is called the astrological realm, *the actual stars play no role at all*, if one takes the word *star* in its mostly established narrow meaning referred to here, of the realm lying beyond our solar and planetary system, of the 'upper star world' (i.e. essentially limited to the world of the fixed stars). The planets, Mercury, Venus, and so on, are in this sense still something bound to the Earth and the Sun, not yet actually 'stars'. We differentiate, that is, the 'world of the planets'—the world of our narrow solar system—from the actual 'world of the stars'.

In a usual horoscope we meet the planets as something essential. They do not belong, as we saw, to the actual 'world of the stars'. Furthermore, allowance is made, taking into account how these planets stand to certain signs of the zodiac. Because of their proximity to the Sun, they are not really companions of the fixed stars that are distant from the Sun. It is obvious that, at most, groups of fixed stars—what are called 'constellations'—are used (this, too, with a grain of salt) to fix the apparent place of a planet in the sky, that is, the *picture* that results from a certain earthly viewpoint. But all the same, with these pictures in the sky one does initially think of the fixed stars, with which we somehow orientate the planetary positions. If, then, the planets are not actual 'stars' in the true sense, one does have initially to reckon at least the signs of the zodiac, the actual star-world, as the other essential element of working out the horoscope.

At this point everything should be called up recalling what has already been said in the Introduction of this book about *signs and constellations*. The explanations given there, not repeated here, are essential to understand everything that follows. Especially important is to differentiate the *earthly zodiac*—as a rhythmical fact, taking place in time, reflected in the etheric periphery of the Earth—from the actual *star zodiac*. What is important is the orientation of the one zodiac to the other—the rhythms of the Earth's aura according to the zodiac, fixed-star pictures—has led to a naming. This, as a result of the actual shift of the spring equinox over the course of millennia, no longer corresponds to the actual places of orientation of the earthly rhythms in the sky, even if in a spiritual sense they remain correct.

Finally, important and remarkable is the fact that the correspondence of the earthly zodiac and the star zodiac, from sign and constellation, was at its most complete in the moment in time of the Mystery of Golgotha. This is a purely astronomical fact.

From the astronomical and mathematical viewpoint it should be added that, because the whole 'precession of the spring equinox' depends on a kind of spinning-movement of the Earth's axis, one can understand how the rhythms of the Earth and rhythmical fields of forces of the earthly zodiac participate in this movement of the Earth, that is, do not align to the fixed stars. The Sun-zodiac does orientate in a certain way to the fixed stars—one can consequently also call the star-zodiac the Sun-zodiac. The Earth's periphery, or Earth's zodiac, goes its own ways because of the cosmic dance-movement of the Earth. How significant that exactly at the hour of Golgotha it coincided with the Sun-circle!

The fact consequently exists that the zodiac, which, for example, at a birth-constellation—but also for any purely astronomical calculation—serving to indicate the planetary positions, is the earthly zodiac, not the star-zodiac. Expressed differently, it is the zodiac of the *signs*, and not the zodiac of the stellar *constellations*. And this, with a normal astronomical calculation is already the case, because the zodiac star-constellations vary in size; consequently, they also merge at their borders and the transitions and are not so easy to define exactly, whereas the zodiac of the signs is based on an exact division of the whole circle into twelve equal sections. Now, this could be correct and practical for the astronomical calculation, but for the spiritual observation, or the astrological calculation, it can nevertheless be wrong. But the facts that can be gained through an experience existing in this realm—or appearing at least initially to exist—shows that also for this spiritual observation, a proceeding from the *signs*, from the *earthly* ['*tropical'*] *zodiac* (leaving out of consideration the constellations) is the correct [choice]. It would then really be the case that with a usual astrological calculation *the actual stars play no role at all*.

The Fall of man

Do we not feel somehow mildly uncomfortable, that not merely somewhat in the realm of the feelings is [presented here], that some sort of background is demanded of a serious and justified thinking, that is, which points to a moment of knowledge? Are we not reminded today of an 'astrology without stars'—not in the somewhat questionable manner of today's 'psychology without the soul', or a 'Christology without the fact of the divinity of Christ', or the no-longer-far-distant 'theology without the fact of the divine'? Is not the adversary of mankind somewhere mixed up in this?

No doubt we have entered a realm here in which we encounter the adversary who has dragged down humanity in its Fall. Yet we can only overcome him when we meet him with a thinking that is also able to withstand his own. For we may never leave out of account a fact that as such really offers the experience, nor dismiss it out of apparently spiritual reasons. And the experience in the realm of the birth-calculation speaks for the reality and authority of the *signs*. Do we not recognize the adversary in this, not that this calculation would be false, but that it is correct? What does this mean? *The present calculation is not falsified by the adversary, but the underlying prerequisite fact forming it, [that is] the whole releasing of human nature out of the sublime star-context is objectively activated through him.*

In his ultimate origins the human being really belongs to the macrocosm, the actual star-world—recall the profound Greek myth of Uranos. The human being, at least in his conscious part, is torn out of this star context. Through the adversary, the Fall of man itself is revealed in the whole manner of thinking. Here in astrology we do not merely observe in an earthly manner but in a cosmic manner, [we find ourselves] as it were, closed within the boundaries of our narrow solar (or planetary) system. And so it appears we are 'controlled' through the planetary forces of this solar system.

With 'constellation' we are dealing with the fixed stars, with stellar worlds; but the 'sign' basically deals only with an earthly situation. If we describe the position of a planet according to one or other of the signs of the zodiac, we do not say how it stands to the fixed stars, but *how it stands to the Earth*, through which part of the Earth's periphery the rays of a planet are met in a specific moment. It is all really related only to the Earth. And the destiny of a human being—right through the whole earthly life created by him/herself—the *karma*, as it is also called with an Indian word (*karma* means 'deed', 'self-caused')—works itself out from the primordial Fall of mankind right into the present. This *karma*, which is always somehow something that releases and separates the human being out of the divine of the entire cosmos (in the 'scattering into loneliness', as it is named in John's Gospel [16:32]), is expressed precisely in that constellation, which, as something lying only between the planets and the earthly periphery, no longer has anything to do with the actual star-world.

John 8 and earthly karma

In John's Gospel this *'karma'*, this account of the sins of humanity, appears most significantly in John 8, where Christ writes in the Earth the obligations of the woman taken in adultery. The whole context is full of earthly Mysteries. This episode seriously and insistently expresses what the human being has become through his connection with the Earth. We can look at all this from many different viewpoints.

We can also ask, what planetary constellation expresses the woman's disposition? What did she herself weave through the deeds of her earlier earthly lives and then brought into this life, that karmic disposition which led her to stray, so that because of it she should now be stoned?[53] We will discuss the debt, the obligations, as revealed here as essentially expressed in the rays of those two planets, which as 'love' and 'death' find their main expression as planets of destiny in Venus and Mars. The Greek word ἁμαρτρία (*hamartia*) stands here in the Greek original text [John 8:11, usually translated 'sin'] for 'karmic debt' has a purely linguistic connection with *Mars*. It is thereby essential which sign these planets stood at the hour of birth, that is, not how they stood to the one or other fixed star, but *how they stood to the Earth*. And—besides many other viewpoints that still exist here—one can understand also from *this* viewpoint, why Christ *writes into the Earth* the cosmic account of debts. The determining thing here is how certain planetary rays encounter the Earth, not the worlds of the stars. Perhaps, in contemplating this episode (John 8), we can also arrive precisely at a *Johannine concept of the difference between signs and constellation*.

But does everything in the human being and human destiny consequently really lie within that which forms the context of the planets of our solar system with regard to the Earth? Has the Fall of mankind, has the might of the adversary in this Fall (in the 'Fall of man', *Sündenfall* [literally 'Fall into/of sin']), torn the human being out of the exalted cosmic contexts, completely alienating him from the upper star worlds (*Uranós*), where the Greek myth sought the deeper origin of the human being? We already feel, in asking all this, how closely and directly the problem—initially seemingly distant—hangs together *with that of losing or forgetting the Eternal Name*. This indeed appears as the losing or forgetting of one's own higher, cosmic, human member. This member is to be incorporated into the Divinity of the star-worlds, *that human member, which we regain through Christ*. In the same chapter, John 8, which begins with the narration of the woman taken in adultery, Christ says to the Jews (John 8:23): 'You are from below [actually: from the beings of the lower world], I am from above [from the beings of the upper world]; you are of this world, I am not of this world.' And in the conversation with Nicodemus (John 3:13), Christ speaks directly of Himself as the One Who descended from heaven (from the upper world of the stars), (ὁ ἐκ τοῦ οὐρανοῦ καταβάς), and states the Mystery of birth from above, out of the upper world, as the prerequisite for entering into the divine realm of the heavens (John 3:3-5). The original text of John's Gospel has here (v. 13) the same word *Uranós* (as the being of the upper world of stars) that we know from the Greek myth.⁵⁴ Christ appeals to the human being to recall his lost and forgotten cosmic origin, his origin in the stars; He gives the human being the possibility to unite with this *star-origin in the world of the Eternal Name.*

In his book *Theosophy*, Rudolf Steiner also describes the highest of these spiritual regions (beyond Saturn) as a *World of Eternal Names*, through which human beings progress in the 'life between death and a new birth'. (These are the same regions to which, in the lecture-cycle mentioned below, the various spiritual planetary and stellar spheres are related.) The *World of Eternal Names* as the actual spiritual world of the stars, the world of the starry constellations, lies—as something lost or forgotten—high over that of the earthly-human contexts of destiny. These are expressed in that which lies between the planets of our solar system and the signs of the earthly zodiac. And yet it is that in which the true human essence—and thereby also that true astrology, not only the variety limited to earthly *karma*—finds its true and actual fulfilment. It is the *Book of Life*, mentioned in the Apocalypse of John (cf. the passages mentioned at the beginning of this chapter), the Book of Life in which our Eternal Names are written (cf. also Luke 10:20), where it sounds in the stellar harmony. Like this 'Book of Life' in the upper star-world, in the world of the stellar constellations, is the other book, the *'Book of Destiny'*, as we can call it with reference to Rev. 20:12, written in that world that lies between the destiny-planets and the Earth, the earthly 'signs', the earthly zodiac. It is the book in which the karmic debts of the adulteress are entered—and for this reason Christ also 'wrote into the Earth'. At the end of this episode, by raising her to herself again, her name appears shining in the Book of Life.

From here we understand perhaps better what Rudolf Steiner in *The Spiritual Guidance of Man and Mankind* (GA 15) says about the birth-horoscope. He touches on a point we do not find indicated in any of the usual presentations of astrological matters, how the configuration of the human brain exactly corresponds to the heavenly constellations, as it appears for this place of birth at this hour, or in this moment of birth:

> If we photographed a person's brain at the moment of birth and took a picture of the sky directly above his or her birthplace, the two pictures would be alike. The stars in the photograph of the sky would be arranged

in the same way as certain parts of the brain in the other picture. Thus, our brain is really a picture of the heavens, and we each have a different picture depending on where and when we were born. This indicates that we are born out of the entire universe.

Facing the earthly ascendant (the rising 'sign' of the hour of birth), the whole firmament is placed as a more comprehensive, more heavenly picture of the moment of birth.

Without disregarding the experience which initially orders the earthly connections of the destiny of a human being, his *'karma'* or 'Book of Destiny', with the earthly 'sign', we nevertheless feel how something of the 'secret of the Eternal Name' that is written in the Book of Life lights up before us in that actual, comprehensive heavenly picture indicated by Rudolf Steiner in the above-mentioned book. This secret, or Mystery, of the heavenly human member, forgotten by man and which consequently has been lost, at the same time still belongs to him in a higher sense. It waits for the re-unification of the lower members that have been ripped away through human *karma* and have been caught in the earthly planetary connections. Then we will understand Steiner's advice and stimuli not as if we should simply put the zodiac constellation in place of the sign, in order to achieve the correct calculation of a birth-constellation. (In the Introduction, it was shown how especially in lecture-cycle *Christ and the Spiritual World*, Leipzig 1913 [GA 149], Rudolf Steiner leads us to the profound spiritual backgrounds of the difference between sign and constellation of the earth-zodiac and the star-zodiac.) But we will also begin to understand how above this world of the earthly sign and its planetary earthly connections of destiny, the other much higher world of the star-constellations, the actual star-world, exists as the world of the Eternal Name and the world of Eternal Freedom, whereas the world lying between the earthly sign and the planets is that world of the karmic, self-occasioned bonds of destiny.[55]

In that world of the Eternal Name and of the Eternal Freedom, human beings originated with their true, heavenly being; there as in seed-form the primordial basis of this higher human being rests, which, as it were, is the upper, lost and forgotten essential part of the human being. In forgetting the Eternal Name there lies the losing of his own higher being. But in the world of the eternal stars, the fixed stars, the forgotten Eternal Name is written, with which Christ, who descended out of these worlds, re-unites us (John 3:13). In weaving the 'star-dress of love', the most inner interior is lovingly joined again with the cosmic star periphery, just as the figure:

$$\odot$$

that closes in itself the Mystery of the spiritual being of the Sun always indicated to us, the higher Christ-'I' is enclosed in the human being, as John's Gospel tells. That astrology which only looks at the connections of destiny, the links of the planetary influences with the earthly element, with the signs of the earthly zodiac, remains fixed with the 'astral' human element as the epitome of his harmonious or disharmonious psychological tensions that manifest in earthly destiny. It does indeed know that the 'house-builder', the actual human self, the 'I', is not contained in this building of houses that is contained in the 'birth-horoscope' that it makes. The whole of astrology, justified within its own realm, remains an 'astrology of the astral element', which in a certain sense, of course, is the meaning of its name.

John's Gospel and the stars

Only an astrology that recognizes again the contexts of the human being with the whole starry cosmos, with the upper world of the stars, would be an astrology of the 'I'. John's Gospel leads us to this astrology of the 'I' as a higher, Johannine, Christened astrology, if we correctly understand the Mystery of the 'I' in connection with the star-Mystery of the Eternal Name. Already the whole rhythm of John's Gospel that initially follows the rhythm of the great cosmic [Platonic] year—as described in the Introduction—points to such a context.

With the course of the Sun and the course of the year viewed from the Earth that forms the basis of Mark's Gospel, we find ourselves in the earthly zodiac. But when we look towards the great cosmic year, at the precession of the spring, or vernal, equinox taking place over thousands of years, which affects the whole displacement of sign and constellation, we find ourselves in the Sun-zodiac. This zodiac, important for the Sun itself, is always the *star-zodiac*. This star-zodiac affects the earthly realm, in the displacement of the spring equinox itself, in giving the different stamps to the various cultural epochs and periods of the Earth. The earthly [zodiac] signs remain the earthly signs. But by their standing in different ages of earthly development in the different star-constellations and being irradiated from various star-regions, they manifest ever again in different ways. Ever-new revelations of the development of the human 'I' link to this variety of cultural epochs relating to the star-zodiac. John's Gospel itself prophetically points to this in its first chapters following the great cosmic star-rhythm. The future Mystery of the 'I', the whole future development of the 'I', is cosmically connected with the Mysteries of the star-zodiac reaching far beyond the earthy planets and earthly zodiac. Here at this point, beholding the actual star-zodiac—always indicated by Rudolf Steiner—becomes decisive and revealing. Everything that concerns the 'I' as the human member that is for the future and which only exists today in seed-form, belongs to a higher world than the earthly zodiac and the planetary connections of destiny, pointing us to the real worlds of the stars.

In this sense, John's Gospel is the first gospel of the 'I', the actual, the true star-gospel, whereas we can understand Mark's Gospel still out of the context of the Earth-zodiac and of the annual earthly rhythm. In John's Gospel we find the higher, the Christ-penetrated astrology of the future, which is something other than the making of birth-horoscopes. Several things in the more *esoteric* realm of astrology today, especially its taking into account the world beyond Saturn, Uranus, etc. already points in this direction. Here we can only point towards the task, the problem itself, which is a deeply Johannine, deeply Christian issue. At the cross of Golgotha, in the hour of birth of the 'I' and of human freedom there was ultimately also the hour of birth of a new astrology, even if the old, planetary connections of destiny from the past are still active for a long time. Only to the degree that human beings become sovereign in the 'I', when they take on the heritage of their freedom in the 'I', does this new Christ-penetrated astrology slowly gain reality. Therein, too, the transition from the Father to the Son takes place, from the necessity (*νόμος*) to freedom. If the old starry contexts were active according to destiny from outside, now the star-world newly blossoms out of the inner centre, out of the freedom of the 'I'. The Star-Mystery has become Earth-Mystery, 'I'-Mystery on Golgotha.

The path to this new stellar 'I'-Mystery penetrated by Christ is none other than the path of John's Gospel. The early Egyptians already knew in their Mysteries how the secret of all deeply understood astrology is a secret of the music of the spheres (cf. Friedrich Creuzer, *Symbolik und Mythologie der alten Völker*, Bk. II, p. 170f.), having to do with a listening into the cosmic music and star-harmony. John's Gospel has led us from the signs of the earth-zodiac, to the upper star-world, to the actual star-constellations. We should not remain fixed with these star-constellations, star-*pictures*, if we intend rightly to comprehend John's Gospel. This spirit of John's Gospel (as we saw earlier) has been received out of the cosmic primordial Word and harmony, the cosmic star-harmony. In meditative immersion within these harmonies lies the path on which the deeper understanding of this gospel can be opened up in its inner being, resting on cosmic music. In this cosmic music all earthly material, astronomical concepts that repeatedly so easily lead one astray, are overcome. Here the starry worlds become a sounding harmony of the stars in which we hear our own individual archetypal musical sound, and with it our own Eternal Name. In this Eternal Name sounding again in the star-harmonies the Mystery of the 'I' is revealed to us out of the region of the Johannine cosmic primordial Word. The Johannine Christ-penetrated astrology founded on cosmic music and the harmony of the stars is the astrology of the 'I'.

PART TWO

FROM THE RIDDLE OF THE STARS TO THE RIDDLE OF THE EARTH: THE RHYTHMIC STRUCTURE OF JOHN'S GOSPEL IN DETAIL

I. THE DESCENT OF CHRIST
(John 1–5)

1. The Word in the Primordial Beginning
(John 1:1-18)

The cosmic rhythm going through all the chapters of Mark's Gospel corresponds to the course of the Sun through the year. The rhythm of John's Gospel in its first chapters corresponds to that of the great World-Year [the 'Platonic Year'] (see Part One, Chapter 4). That is, we do not step from the sunrise towards the heavenly heights, but descend downwards through the dark heavenly signs. If we were to orientate the rhythm of both gospels according to the construction of the human form (MG 27ff.), then we would say, in Mark's Gospel the rhythm leads from the head (♈) downwards, in John's Gospel from the feet (♓) upwards.

In Mark's Gospel the rising of the Christ-Sun in the Jordan-Baptism (♓) is preceded by the two dark signs of the Baptist John (♑ ♒), the two 'Elijah-John signs', like a 'Prologue' from below. John's Gospel with the initially reversed direction of the movement of its rhythm can have a Prologue only coming from above. Mark's Gospel has a Prologue concerning John from below; John's Gospel has a Prologue concerning Christ from above. This also corresponds to the nature of the 'Christ gospel'. In the Prologue to John's Gospel, we are not led into the dark regions of loneliness of soul and abandonment of the 'I' (♑ ♒), as with the Baptist John in Mark's Gospel. We are led into the sphere of light of the cosmic 'I', into the Christ-sphere of the cosmic Primordial Word and cosmic Primordial Light, into the *world of the Eternal Name* (see Part One, Chapter 7). This region of the cosmic Word corresponds in the heavenly zodiac to the *sign of the Word* (♉). In it and the sign of the Incarnation adjoining below, the entrance into the earthly realm (♈)—'and the Word became flesh' (John 1:14)—we have to seek the Prologue of John 1, whose cosmic situation corresponds to that of Mark 1 (♓–♍).

If we ascribe the beginning of John's Gospel: 'In the primordial beginning the Word [already] was' to the *sign of the Word* (♉), to that sign which in Mark's Gospel was always simply aligned to the word 'word' (MG 109), then we shall immediately recall how, for the Mystery-recollections of all peoples, this sign of the word, the Bull, is at the same time the *sign of the Earth's Primordial beginning* as revealed in spiritual research (more details in R. Steiner, *The Spiritual Hierarchies and their Reflection in the Physical World*, Düsseldorf, 12-18 April 1909 [GA 110]). In Ancient Indian *ga* (root *gā*), linguistically related to German *Kuh*, 'cow', means at the same time *Erde*, 'Earth' (Greek *γῆ, ge*, Gaia), and the ancient Egyptians recognized an earthly cow as an earthly revelation of Isis.

This tradition passed down in the early Mysteries, still recognized in all languages, and developed by Rudolf Steiner (see above), we can also see in one of the three cosmic crosses, in the one lying diagonally (see the figure). Its four points representing the four elements and the four kinds of ether, at the same time are those of the four evangelists (see Part One, Chap. 5).

Occult cosmogony adds here the aspect of the four great stages of the Earth's evolution in its cosmic becoming ('Ancient Saturn, Ancient Sun, Ancient Moon, and the Earth', (MG 84f.). With the Lion, with the sign of the element of fire and of the warmth-ether that here in the primordial beginning of Old Saturn ignited the whole system (today's solar system of Sun and planets), we experience the cosmic sacrificial fire and cosmic primordial fire. In this sacrificial fire, in the fiery Lion, which is indeed the sign of the heart, the Heart of the World begins, as it were, to pulse. Here too, at the end of Saturn-evolution, it stopped pulsing. Here, moreover, with the Scorpion-Eagle, with the Johannine sign of the sound-ether and of cosmic music, we experience how the coming out of the long 'cosmic sleep' (*Pralaya*) the re-awakened cosmic system (the solar system—as understood in Steiner's *Occult/ Esoteric Science*; we are dealing here with early incarnations of the Earth) took place in the Primordial Sun-sign (the 'Ancient Sun'). We pass over from the reflected appearance of life of Saturn-existence to real life.

Like the transition that took place from the 'cosmic Saturn-day' to 'cosmic Sun-day'—that transition which in its earthly reflection became the dispute over the Sabbath of the Pharisees, in the gospel such a significant motif—here in the 'Sun-Eagle' the 'Sun life' really originates (cf. MG 29f., 40, 116, 183f., etc.). The same sign, which became thereby the 'Scorpion', also received the sting of death. Taking all this with the often described events of John's initiation (the changing back of the Scorpion into the Eagle (MG 29f., 122),[56] we can understand how far the Eagle stands over the cosmic depths and world-wielding Prologue of John's Gospel.

- With the *Bull*, as the sign of the Word and of earthly beginnings, equally the *Eagle* stands as the actual Johannine sign.
- With the primordial beginning of Ancient Saturn we experience the *Lion*;
- with the primordial Sun-existence we experience the *Eagle-Scorpion*;
- with 'Ancient Moon' (this expression is already found in *Heinrich von Ofterdingen* by Novalis), with the stage prior to Earth-existence, we experience the *Waterman*, the etheric-astral 'human being of the primordial beginning'. On this 'Waterman corner' of the cosmic cross, we find Matthew's Gospel as the 'gospel of the human being' (Part One, Chapter 5), and with the Scorpion-Eagle we find John's Gospel. The 'Ancient Moon-existence' is not yet physical like the earthly conditions of today. Then everything still lay in the element of the etheric, watery, ether-light belonging to the Waterman.
- With the Bull, the fourth corner of the cosmic cross of the gospels, we find with the 'life-ether', the highest ether, at the same time the solid earthly element as the lowest of the elements. Here the Earth and the human being first become physical. Here first, after the 'Ancient Moon

evolution' has run its course, and after a 'cosmic sleep', the Earth stage gradually emerges. In this context, the *Bull is the sign of the beginning of the Earth.*

To the sign of the sound-ether and cosmic music (Scorpion-Eagle), the beginning of the Earth comes in the *Bull* as the actual *sign of the Word.* Everything that lives in the Prologue to John's Gospel 'In the beginning was the Word', and in the connection of both signs (Bull and Scorpion-Eagle), we feel here behind the secret of creation of the beginning of the Earth, pointing to the deepest Christ-sphere: there *stands the Mystery of the primordial Sun-existence.*

- In the 'primordial beginning of Ancient Saturn' (♌) there arises in the cosmic sacrificial fire and the cosmic primordial fire the first (warmth-etheric) seed stages of the human 'physical body'.
- In the 'primordial beginning of Ancient Sun' (Eagle-♏), at the same time as the first outline of the 'etheric', the 'life-body', there arises the primordial seed of the living element that human beings share with the plants.
- In the 'primordial beginning of Ancient Moon' (♒) in the 'astral body' the first seed of the light of consciousness arises, which the human being shares with the animal kingdom (the 'astral' is experienced as 'inner light').
- Finally, in the 'primordial beginning of the Earth' (♉), this physical-etheric-astral human vessel, along with the simultaneous solidification of the physical element to real solid earthly matter (♉), receives from the creative beings (the 'Spirits of Form') the imprint of the *ego, the 'I'*. In this the human being first wakes up to human self-consciousness. The consciousness in the astral realm was still only one of the feelings, not yet self-conscious.

Here we find the context expressed in the occult language, again in the plain, Johannine language of the gospel, when we recall what was developed earlier (Part One, Chapter 5) in this regard, referring to the language of fairytales.

- The primordial situation on Ancient Saturn of the physical element in the human being appears then simply as the *'body'*.
- To it comes the Sun-filled etheric (the 'Sun-dress' of the fairytale [Allerleirauh]), the *'life'*,
- in the lunar astral (in the 'Moon-dress' of the fairytale) the *'light'*.
- And the earthly 'I' was completed in *love* (in the 'starry-dress' of the fairytale), of which Novalis says: 'Love is the goal of world-history' (he means the whole evolution of the Earth), 'the Amen of the universe'.

As *body, life, light* and *love* the fourfold human being and the fourfold world-becoming appear in Johannine language:

- 'In the primordial beginning was the Word', of which later: 'and the Word became flesh' …
- 'in him was life' …
- 'and the life was the light of men.'
- Love, as we saw, becomes real only at the end of things, when the darkness has comprehended the light. It could not do this at the beginning of things, and it still experiences difficulty today. The motif 'the light shines in the darkness, but the darkness has not comprehended it' [RSV, equivalent here to Luther's translation] is an overarching motif of John's Gospel. The crisis of humanity that erupts in Chapters 6 to 10 of John's Gospel, leading on to the event of Golgotha, is devastatingly revealed. The whole triune structure of this chapter of John's Gospel can be seen:

    A. the Mystery of Christ's descent,
    B. the crisis of mankind,
    C. the awaking of the disciples of Christ and the inner joining with the disciples (in the 'Chapters on the Disciples'), already illuminated through the Prologue to John's Gospel (cf. especially Part One, Chapters 4 & 6), how the beginning of this descent, how then vv. 10 & 11 ('… and the world knew him not') speak of the 'crisis', following ('but as many as received him…') the 'coming out' of those chosen.

When we notice how the heartbeat governs and rules everything bodily, how the heart is also the most inner [awareness], that 'which first lives and is the last to die' (called the *primum vivens ultimum moriens* in the Middle Ages), then it is understandable here how we place:

- the ♌, the sign of the heart, with regard to the corporeal part and its primordial constitution,
- the ♏–Eagle to the source of life,
- the ♒ to the light of the astral,
- the ♉ to the love that is developed in the earthly-'I'.

Here, as everywhere, we may add the planets to the signs of the zodiac. At the beginning of that stage of evolution where love is developed in the earthly-'I'—which is precisely 'earthly development'—we can write the sign of the Bull. This recalls the earlier chapter on the planets (Part One, Chapters 2 & 3). In this sign Venus (♀), the Star of Love, governs as creative love—on the other side, in the sign of ♎, Venus Urania rules as heavenly love. Thus, from the aspect of the planets,

Venus (♀) stands over the ♉, the sign of the Word and of the Earth's primordial beginning. In his *Divine Comedy*, Dante calls her *love in the primordial beginning, 'il primo Amore'*—divine Love revealed in the creation. In one of his paintings of the fullness of light of the Obergadin, Segantini expressively names her as 'the love at the primordial fountain of life'. Both revelations of Venus are divine. In the ♉ she 'holds sway over world-becoming', creative 'love in the primordial beginning'. In ♎ she is the 'heavenly love' (Venus Urania), the redeeming love which leads back to the primordial source of being (cf. Novalis, *Hymns to the Night*: 'then came eternal Love's redeeming hand—and he slept.').

For this point, lines of communication reach to Luke's Gospel, everywhere intimately linked to John's Gospel. Luke's Gospel is indeed in a special sense aligned to the sign of the Bull, as John's to the Scorpion-Eagle. As we saw, Luke's Gospel is above all the earthly gospel, belonging to the maidenly and motherly life-ether. Consequently, the earthly secrets of the feminine and maternal play a special role, the stories of the birth and Christmas. ♀ in ♉ relates to the inward and loving side of this gospel.

***

The two shining signs over the entrance to John's Gospel, the Bull (♉)—the word—and the Ram (♈), the 'Word becoming flesh', were in the early Mysteries still in a special sense *signs of light*, signs of the revelation of primordial Light. These contexts can be followed right into language. The word *go* in Vedic Sanskrit means, besides *cattle, bull, cow* and *earth*, in the plural also *rays of light*; words which express the cow's horn or the ram's horn that at the same time signify the ray of light. One notices the relationship of the Latin *cornu* 'horn', of the Indian *kirana* (emphasis on the first syllable) 'beam of light' and of the Hebrew *queren*, which mean both.

This also solves the riddle of the ram's horns on Michelangelo's sculpture of Moses. They are an Imagination of the aura of light and of the impulse of light of the ego-thinking inspired by the Ram, the bright forces of the head. Already taken purely outwardly, the Ram and the Bull are the *signs of the rising light* in the rhythm of the year. The Ram (the 'Easter Lamb') is the sign of spring, the Bull the sign of the light, increasing ever more strongly in the fullness of budding natural life (in May in the Northern Hemisphere). If we look from the sign to the constellation (the difference is explained in the Introduction), then the Bull with the stars Aldebaran, the Pleiades and the shining triangle, the Hyades, reveal the highest abundance of light among all the starry constellations of the heavenly zodiac.

In the flowering of the Mysteries of the ancient Egyptian cultural epoch, the Sun shone at the spring equinox in the starry constellation of the Bull. The 'earthly Ram' lay then in the heavenly Bull, as today it lies in the 'heavenly Fishes'. (On that account, the sacred Bull in the Isis-Venus culture [♀ in ♉] of Ancient Egypt and its Mysteries, its deep insight into the secrets of the Earth and the 'primordial beginnings of the Earth'.) The same signs, which in the rhythm of the year accompany the rise of the light each year, stand in John's Gospel over the rise of the Light of the World.

Thus above all the *Bull*, as the *sign of the word*, is at the same time a *sign of light*. We may recall how in ancient languages, especially in Vedic Sanskrit, numerous words exist which at the same time express an appearance of light (or colour) and a phenomenon of sound. What later is a revelation of light, was originally a revelation of sound. This is particularly clear with certain primordial words for *light* and the *Sun*; *swar* in Old Indian is one such word, *surya*, from which Germ. *Sonne*, Eng. 'Sun' are derived. In the Avesta (in the original Persian of Zarathustra) the word is *hvar*. An older form of this (also meaning 'Sonne', 'Sun') is the word *hvan*, genitive *hvöng*.[57] This again corresponds to the Indian word *svan* 'to sound', Lat. *sonare*, whereas *svar* as a verb in Indian means 'to shine'; *r* is the vibrating consonant of light; *n* with its possibility of continuing the sound, the sounding consonant. In this sense the German word *Sonne*, preserving a Teutonic primordial experience, still as a sounding word, recalls times when the revelation of the sunlight was still experienced as sounding (cf. Goethe's *Faust*, 'Prologue in Heaven'. Raphael: 'The sun makes music as of old / Amid the rival spheres of Heaven …').

The sign of the Bull standing over the entrance to John's Gospel links:

- the *revelation of light* with
- the *revelation of the word* and
- the *revelation of sound.*

Moreover, if we take the word in the Greek for the word 'word', λόγος (*lógos*), and simply try to experience the sounds, it does not belong to the sounding words but absolutely to the words of light. It stands in quite a different sequence of development from the German word *Wort* ('word'). With *'Wort'* we experience the *becoming (Werden)* ('all things were *made [geworden]* out of the same' or 'through him'); the Indian *vrl*, 'being, becoming, become' points in the same direction, cf. *vrdh*, 'to grow, flourish, develop'. The *v* alone in all these words is the 'primordial sound' [cf. the author's article 'Let there be light' in *The Source of Speech*, TL 2020, 154-80], *r* the vibrating movement, *l* the arrival into form—similar to the sounds in the Latin *verbum*, 'word'. The Indians also knew the *creative primordial word*, vāc nominative vāk (= Lat. *vox*, *vocis*, 'voice'), the connection of the primordial sounds with the palatal-gutteral, creative sound *c (k)*, the 'Bull sound' (ȣ) and initial sound of *Kuh* and cow (as *g* in Indian *go*).

The Greek word λόγος *(lógos)*, the 'Logos', that also appears in John's Gospel, stands in the same sequence of development to which the German word *'Licht'* and English 'light' belong.[58] Certainly, logos initially and in the first place means 'word, speech, conversation', and is used especially in John's' Gospel incontestably with this meaning. But at the same time it means *'Vernunft'*, 'reason'; *'Überlegung'*,'reflection, consideration', expressing everything connected to the word *'logisch'*, 'logical', that which in thinking is clearly discernible in a light, bright consciousness.

The word λόγος *(lógos)* 'word' at the beginning of John's Gospel, like the Bull-sign to which it belongs, even links the *element of light* to the *word element* and the *sound element.* It does not only listen into the depths of the *cosmic Word*, but raises us at the same time to the *heights of the cosmic Light*. It speaks of the *revelation of Christ* at the beginning; this not only of a *revelation of the creative, primordial cosmic Word*, but at the same time is such of the clear *primordial Light of worlds* and *bright, divine primordial thoughts*. The 'I'-gospel tells us nothing other than the Christ is revealed in light and in a shining consciousness.

We find ourselves in that sphere to which the word (usually translated as 'truth') ἀλήθεια *(aletheia)* points (see Part One, Chapter 6), which, anchored in the World-'I', could hold itself before the Light of the World as the *never extinguishing consciousness*. John's Gospel itself links the Being of this consciousness with the light. John 1:9, mistranslated by Luther,[59] who used the Latin Vulgate, and the AV/KJV ('That was the true Light, which lighteth every man that cometh into the world'), means more correctly: 'For the light of the never-extinguishing consciousness (the eternal light in the 'I', *lux perpetua*), which enlightens everyone, was about to come into the world'. This *world of Eternal Light* is also the previously characterized (Part One, Chapter 7) 'world of the Eternal Name' and its stellar revelation. In this sense the beginning of John's Gospel speaks significantly of those 'who believe in his name' as children of God, that is, *they sink the certainty of their hearts into the eternal 'I' revealed in the Light of the World.*

The original text also points to the secret of the *cosmic primordial light*. The word for *light* in the Greek φῶς *(phos)*, which again has a quite different sequence of development than that belonging to the German word *Licht (lux)*, English 'light'. This word is related to *logos*, or to the words for light based on the Latin *dies*, 'day' (this, like many names of the divine in ancient languages, leads back to the old Indo-Aryan root for light *di*). *Phos*, though, lies in a still higher, supersensory sphere, approaching the primordial sound and primordial word, and relates to *phoné* 'voice' as does the corresponding Indian word *bhas* 'lighten' to *bhan* 'sound, speak'. In the sounds of φῶς there still lies something of the primordial word and primordial sound that has become light. It is not yet our light of day, which is lit with warming flames of heat. But when we meet it in the Johannine sphere, it enables us to think of the word formed from it, *phosphorus*, white phosphorus that shines with a *cold flame*. In Greek φωσφορός (phosphoros) is the Morning Star, Venus, whose light in the early Mysteries right into Buddhism was felt as the highest super-earthly revelations of light. We may also recall what was said in Günther Wachsmuth's book (*The Etheric Forces*, Book I) about the *cold light*, the 'cold flame'. It is a revelation of etheric light, belonging to a *higher*, element of life-ether and sound-ether (the 'Tree of Life' in Paradise, lost to humanity.) [See the essay on 'The Tree of Life' in *From the Mysteries*, TL 2020, 202ff., esp. 218]. Rudolf Steiner's [4th] Mystery Drama mentions the 'cold light of cosmic fields of ice' [Scene 4]. And something of this element of Isis lives in the cosmic heights of the words of the Prologue to John's Gospel, which stands in the sign of the word of the Bull, governed by Isis-Venus.

'In him [the eternal cosmic Word] was life'. The 'Word' meant here is no everyday, earthly word. With the secrets of the primordial light and of the magical-creative, forming and governing of the sound-ether, the 'Word' still carries in itself the life-ether, the highest ether (as also the sign of the word ♉ is a sign of the life-ether; see the Appendix). With 'the word became flesh', with the appearance of Christ on the Earth, this lost element of life in Paradise enters again into the earthly world.

From this aspect, let us look again at the *L* in *Logos*, or on that fourfold Johannine *L* in German *Leib, Leben, Licht, Liebe* (English: 'body, life, light, love') that lives as *that creative light unfolding in life*. Universal life ('*All-Leben*'), creatively unfolding is expressed in the sound L.

We think of the German '*All*' ('the universe') and the names for God in Hebrew, El, Eloah, Elohim, and of what Steiner says in the *Speech and Drama* lecture-course concerning L: 'When you feel L correctly, you feel that it would be well to be yourself; you swim in the element of life.'

'All things were made through him, and without him was not anything made that was made.' Here too we can notice how certain main motifs running through the whole Bible return in John's Gospel, here, as it were, assembled at the Christ middle-point, freshly illuminated in the Light of Christ. Thus there lives in the 'I-AM' sayings of John's Gospel as the immediate revelation of Christ, the divine 'I-AM the I-AM' revealed to Moses in the Burning Thornbush. In the 'Good Shepherd, who calls his sheep by name' (John 10) there lives again the saying in Isaiah 43, 'I have called you by your name, you are mine' and with it the great name-motif of the Bible (Part One, Chapter 7). And in the *creating life* (the life-ether) and *the magic-fashioning and ordering power of the sound-ether* bearing in itself the *cosmic Word* in the Prologue to John's Gospel, there lives again the *Words of the Creator* (Genesis 1) that spoke here in the primordial beginning, 'Let there be Light' calling all things into existence, giving them their names. With the motif of the creative Word there is linked the name-motif as again in John's Gospel. (In the gospel it is especially the case in 1:12, where it is said 'those who believed in his name', who sink the certainty of their hearts into the Eternal Name of the 'I'.) The whole world into which the Prologue of John's Gospel places us, the sublime kingdom of the creative cosmic Word, is that which earlier (Part One, Chapter 7) we called the 'world of the Eternal Name'. Out of this *world of the Eternal Name* Christ now descends into earthly existence: 'and the word became flesh'.

It is the world to which human beings belong with the higher part of their being, today only present as a seed, with their being changed through the 'I', *new born out of the 'I'* (to speak with John: with the 'not of blood, nor of the will of the flesh nor of the will of man, but of the divine', 1:13), with what are called the *higher trinity* of the human being (manas, buddhi and atmā). The trinity of vowels in the Greek form of the name John (MG 46) point to this trinity. John is that one who again lives consciously in the world of the Eternal Name, and speaks creating in it and out of it.

In Him lived, as in no other 'higher human being', the 'power that may speak creatively, because in silence it could create itself' (words from Rudolf Steiner's Mystery Drama, *The Guardian of the Threshold*). Consequently, the writer, the inspirer of John's Gospel, wants to announce with such a primordial force of the Word, standing unique in the literature of the world, the Mysteries of the *creative cosmic Word in the primordial beginning*. Having himself undergone the path of initiation led by Christ, he can awaken in himself this power of the Word, the eternal Cosmic Word. In the schooling and testing, the silent treading the way right through, he knew how to find the *Word* (in the sense meant here).

At this point where everywhere the communication lines are drawn to Mark's Gospel (MG 220f., etc.), we may recall the often presented *picture of the silent invalid*, who then matured through incredible crises, tests and temptations to *become John*. He finds the initiation that the others fail to achieve. This picture of the *silent invalid* we think we have found again in the *invalid* in the chapter on Lazarus (John 11:1). We can recall especially the moment when the hitherto *silent one*, from the moment of witnessing the wakening of the son of the widow of Nain (if we may followed the legends from this point on) into ever deeper silence, falling in ever more critical illness *gains the word*. He becomes the spokesman in that moment when another, who speaks too soon, lost the word (MG 210ff.). This moment when the one hitherto always silent speaks for the first time, is also clearly emphasized in the gospel. In this *finding of the Word*, this accomplishment on the path of initiation *the full power of the Word*, lay and lies the power to express the Mysteries of the creative Word in such a way as they are expressed in the Prologue to John's Gospel. Many mystics and Gnostics have written about the 'Logos'. That which lends force to the words of the Prologue to John's Gospel, unique in all literature, is that we sense how these words here are written out of the *full inner power of the cosmic Word*, out of a full power that in the whole history of humanity was there *once only*.

We recognized in the passage of Mark's Gospel, in which *the one becoming John finds the Word*, lay at that time *in the sign of the word, the Bull* (MG 210f.). It is in the same sign we find the revelation of the Word at the beginning of John's Gospel. Making this link can spread light over the deeper context of the gospel in the history of humanity.

To the Christ-Mystery of the eternal Cosmic Word and the divine Creator-Word is added significantly the Mystery of John as the Mystery of the human being. In this Mystery, the cosmic word, the *lost word* (as it was called in the Mysteries of humanity, see Part One, Chapter 7) could live again. In the way in which this fact as a fact of initiation could take place in the disciple John is at the same time a fact of the great pre-Christian Mysteries, including that of the Baptist John. The exposition of Mark's Gospel has shown how the inner connection of both facts presents the actual *Mystery of John* (MG 45ff. etc.). At this point, let us look initially only at how the Prologue to John's Gospel presents the divinity in Christ facing the fact of the human initiate; the Mystery of Christ of the eternal cosmic Word ('In the primordial beginning was the word ...' 1:1-5) faces the Mystery of John ('There was[60] a man sent from God ...' 1:6ff.). It faces in both directions, firstly (expressly) where John the Baptist is spoken of, then (if only in a veiled hint) the disciple John (1:12f.). It need be no cause of wonder that he is only hinted at, not expressly named, since it is well-known that nowhere in John's Gospel is the disciple John named, but always only in veiled hints.

The personal side of the great disciple and writer of the gospel (even if not in fact the writer himself, cf. John 19:35, 21:24, 25) steps back completely in John's Gospel. But in actual fact the divine sonship, mentioned in 1:12 ('children of God') only of John, during the life of Christ Jesus, and also only of the other disciples after the resurrection, will actually be achieved by others. Notice, for example, the writer of Mark's Gospel also bears the name of John, becoming a 'John' through initiation. That is, what is said from 1:12 onwards, applied initially in the first place to the disciple John as the one advancing before the others in initiation. This becomes most clear in 1:14, 'and we saw the glory of his revelation [*doxa*]'. This is not something general, unclear, but relates most correctly and quite directly to the beholding of the solar splendour of Christ in the *Transfiguration on the Mount* (Mark 9). It could be said with that event narrated of Mark's Gospel (MG 203), but not expressly narrated in John's Gospel, that the 'solar splendour of the Transfiguration' is poured out as a substance over the whole of John's Gospel.

Only three disciples are here with Christ on the 'Mount'—Peter, James and John—because in their whole *being* they are connected to the Mystery of the event. In *consciousness*, as we saw, only John experiences it as a real revelation; the others (as the evangelist expresses quite clearly) are so deeply transported through beholding the glory of the event that they cannot hold the 'fullness of the Appearance' in their consciousness; they do not penetrate to beholding the *revelation* (and this essentially lies in the concept *doxa*). Sharing in *being* is something different than sharing in *consciousness* (James does manage; MG 201). Thus the sentence 'and we beheld the splendour of his revelation' in the sense of full consciousness only applies to John, and it can be seen how the writer of the gospel here speaks about himself. He experiences the revelation of the 'only begotten' (born in the unity of the 'I') Son 'full of grace and truth', that is, in the full clarity of consciousness of the cosmic light (this is *a-letheia* 'truth'), which out of the inner freedom can open to the divine (χάρισ *charis* 'grace' has like χαρά *chará* 'joy' in John's Gospel always to do with this inner experience of freedom).

How Christ arrives out of the *world of the Eternal Name*, lies in initiation experience in the name *John* that leads back to it again. Thus a *motif of the stars* lies in what is said of John (1:6): he was 'sent from God' (ἀπεσταλμένος παρὰ θεοῦ): ἀποστέολλειν (*apostellein*) 'to send' has somehow to be related to Lat. *stella* 'star'; here it points to stellar contexts, to the radiant starry emanation of the cosmic light, of being bound within the stellar harmony. Christ, the Light of the Cosmic Ego, stands in the centre of the circle [cf. Part One, Chapter 7] of the great initiates of humanity who form the periphery of the circle. In India they are called 'Bodhisattvas', in the Apocalypse the '24 elders'. Of these the last and pre-eminent in the time directly before the appearance of Christ is John the Baptist.

2.
The Meeting at the Jordan
(John 1:19-51)

In the Prologue of John's Gospel, the *Bull* points to the revelation of the eternal cosmic Word in the primordial beginning of the Earth; the Ram points to the 'Word becoming flesh', the entrance of the divine Logos into earthly incarnation. In the meeting of Christ Jesus with John the Baptist at the Jordan (John 1:19ff.), we arrive at the situation we know from Mark's Gospel. It is cosmically orientated to the *constellation of the Fishes*, or in the zodiac axis Fishes–Virgin (the sign of the Fishes was then cosmically orientated to the constellation of the Fishes; today it is orientated to the constellation of the Waterman).

This does not say something or other about the time of year in which the meeting took place. That this basically cannot be the meaning of the whole arrangement of the gospel events to the individual heavenly signs was already clearly explained in the book on Mark's Gospel (MG 21ff.). And in John's Gospel such a view would really have no place at all, because the rhythm here does not initially follow the course of the year, but the reverse direction of movement, that of the great [Platonic] cosmic year. Thus in the first chapters of John—which in a special sense are Mystery Chapters—there is far rather something to discover. There is also an arrangement of the contents to the divisions of time—resulting out of the precession of the spring equinox—to the great cosmic year, to the great cultural epochs of humanity.

Thus we can see the sign of the Bull at the entrance [to the gospel], governed by Isis-Venus, pointing not only to the primordial beginning of the Earth, but in a certain sense also to that age of the Bull of the ancient Egyptian Mysteries, significant for the Christ-events of the gospel. The gospel itself (Matt. 2:15) even emphasizes the inner relationship. And the sign of the Ram following it, of the earthly incarnation of Christ, gives us a glimpse of the Graeco-Latin cultural epoch governed by the Mars-sign of the Ram, in which the earthly incarnation of Christ actually took place.

In this sense the sign and the *constellation of the Fishes* (MG 64ff.) standing over the meeting at the Jordan points to our cultural epoch today, as that in which the revelation of Christ in the etheric is to be expected. Astronomically the transition of the spring equinox from the constellation of the Ram to that of the Fishes already took place in the Turning Point of Time, at the moment of the Mystery of Golgotha (some people place the moment already some decades earlier). We find ourselves in the *meeting at the Jordan* at the threshold of that epoch, *which actually receives its spiritual signature through the constellation of the Fishes*. For this reason in early Christian times, when people still felt this cosmic context, the fish was always symbolically used relating to Christ and the cross of Golgotha. Not only because the initial letters of 'Ἰησοῦς Χριστός, Θεοῦ Υἱός, Σωτήρ (Iēsous Christos, Theou Yios, Sōtēr— Jesus Christ God's Son Saviour) renders the Greek word ἰχθύς (ichthys), 'fish', the symbol of the fish linked to Christ, but because there was still a sense for this cosmic context, the fish-rune resulting out of this name for Christ was felt to be significant.

In Mark's Gospel we found the constellation of the Fishes—at that time it coincided with the sign of the Fishes—over the Jordan Baptism of Christ, over the miracle of the Feeding, and over the Transfiguration of Christ on the Mount—wherever the divine life of Christ is sacrificed into the Earth. In John's Gospel we will meet it especially as the sign of the foot-washing (John 13, then as well as with these other events connected with the etheric sign of the Virgin), we will meet it already as the sign of the 'last anointing', when Mary Magdalene anoints the feet of Christ Jesus. Deepest devotional submission of the heavenly to the Earth, a heavenly life that annihilates itself, giving itself completely to the earthly, sacrificing itself into earthly existence, is the heavenly meaning of this sign—which, as in the heavenly script, we can see in the peaceful darkness of the strange constellation of the Fishes, with its few stars.

The death of Christ, the dying of the God into the Earth, does not happen first on Golgotha but it already begins at the Jordan, in order to achieve a still higher stage in the Transfiguration (Mark 9) (MG 192ff.). Then words full of significance sounded just as at the Baptism, out of the *world of the Eternal Name*: 'You are my beloved Son …' (Mark 1:11, 9:7). In the episode of the meeting [at the Baptism] in John's Gospel this occurrence [dying into the Earth] already lies in the past. In a deeper and more intimate, still in an esoteric sense, the Fishes like the Scorpion and Archer are a death-sign; especially in the beginning of John 13 this is strongly expressed. (In astrology, the sign of the Fishes is inwardly—not outwardly—related to the 'twelfth house', as to the house of earthly constraint and of 'difficult destiny'.)

In the Jordan-event, in the sign of the *Fishes*—one also recalls the Greek ἰχθύς (*ichthys*)—the 'I' of Christ, selfless in the earthly realm, is revealed, that Self whose innermost Being is complete selflessness. The Baptism of all baptisms takes place here. In the light of the highest consciousness, the *Name of all names*, the Name of the Son of the Sun, is united to the one who becomes the bearer of the Eternal Name: J–Ch (Jesus Christ).

The Baptist

The *selflessness of the will* in Christ—here too is revealed the heavenly meaning of the sign of the Fishes—meets in John the Baptist the *selflessness of knowledge*: 'I am not the Christ' (John 1:20). We have briefly to consider what these words contain. The last and highest pre-Christian initiate is the first and only one who *completely out of himself* recognizes Christ. All the people, even the disciples, do *not* recognize Christ; even Peter's confession (Mark 8:29) is not a full, final knowledge (MG 311ff.); the disciple [Lazarus-]John becomes the one who recognizes Christ only because the Elijah-being of the Baptist sacrifices himself into him, *allowing him to become John*.[61] John the Baptist is the first and only one who, out of his own illumination, recognizes Christ in the selflessness of His being ('the Lamb of God'). John the Baptist recognizes the subsequent *bearer* of the Christ. From the primordial cosmic beginning John was united in the stellar harmony (MG 64f.); he is the one *sent* from this stellar harmony into humanity—mentioned at the end of the previous chapter. Every lesser [initiate] ennobled with a part of this starry-grace, out of overconfidence could have made himself out to be the Christ. Yet John the Baptist possesses the humility of knowledge: 'I am not the Christ.'

We should be able to feel in this, that under the given circumstances it was also somehow difficult for that great initiate to reach that apparently negative aspect of this knowledge. It was something great and unique, to express it in this humility and selflessness. In John the Baptist, directly before Christ, the pre-Christian Mystery-initiation has its final and highest pinnacle. In him at the same time it breaks off the tip of its own pinnacle, struggles through to the highest and most difficult of all conquests, in order completely to sacrifice itself, its own being, to offer the summary of all the pre-Christian Mystery-substance into the sphere of the Christian-Johannine initiation. This is now about to begin for the world, *in order, through this its sacrifice, to enable the becoming of the great Christian initiates, of the disciples of John.*

This selfless Mystery-sacrifice of John the Baptist also stands in the sign of the Fishes, revealing the heavenly meaning of this sign. For this reason, too, with inner consistency he denies the question whether he is Elijah (John 1:21), because the being of Elijah in him had already begun to sacrifice itself into the sphere of Christ. Perhaps it is a living fact that the being of the great preparer and forerunner of Christ, the being of Elijah in him, was never fully in his consciousness; only Christ Himself has the knowledge about him and relates this knowledge to the disciples (Matt. 11:14; Matt. 17: 12, 13; Mark 9:13; Luke 7:27; cf. also Luke 1:17). The highest expression of selflessness and self-emptying of the greatest pre-Christian initiate in the gospel is found in the words of the Baptist (John 1:27): 'the thongs of whose sandals I am not worthy to untie'. Here too the zodiac-sign of the Fishes is revealed (the *feet*, on the human body; [MG 66]).

***

In the first chapters of John's Gospel we see Christ, before, as it were, stepping on to the lower floor of fallen humanity—this first happens towards the fifth, sixth and seventh chapters. He first worked through a series of Mystery-spheres lying over these lower-lying human spheres; gradually He completed his *descent into humanity*. The first and highest of all Mystery-meetings took place with the Baptist John, who carried in himself the last substance and quintessence of the pre-Christian initiation. This meeting is not to be thought *only* as spiritual; it must have been a quite physical meeting. But everything in the outer narration speaks *at the same time* as a picture for spiritual events. This spiritual side is expressed in the zodiac-sign of the Fishes. This is revealed especially in looking at Mark's Gospel, from which we here proceed everywhere.

Out of the obscure regions of the Goat and the Waterman, the region of soul-loneliness and 'I'-abandonment, turning aloft to the cosmic light, John the Baptist meets the Sun-Being Christ in the sign of the great transition from the darkness to the light, in the *sign of the Fishes*. Out of the cosmic environment, turning Himself downwards out of the region of light of the Bull-Ram, Christ Himself descends into the earthly plane. In the sign of the Fishes the Prologue of Mark's Gospel meets that of John's Gospel. The ruler in the sign of the Fishes is not the Sun itself—this sign is precisely that of the highest self-emptying of the Sun-being, His divesting of Himself for the Earth, in sacrifice to the earthly sphere. But the ruling planet Jupiter in the sign of the Fishes points to that sphere of 'Ancient Sun', to which originally Christ's spiritual Being was united. (See the chapter on the planets, Part One, Chapters 2 & 3.) At the same time, it is the planet that has to do with everything concerning the descent into the earthly sphere, the investing of the earthly-physical garment. Over the meeting at the Jordan and the Baptism in the Jordan, as then over the Transfiguration of Christ on the Mount (in John's Gospel not expressly narrated) there shines the *Mystery of the Ancient Sun* as the 'Sun-Splendour of Christ' (MG 195).

The Disciples

To the meeting with the Mystery-sphere of the Baptist John, the last great pre-Christian initiate, there follows the *meeting* with those who henceforth are called as disciples of Christ to become the bearers of the new, the Christian-Johannine initiation. In the earlier initiation *one stands over the earthly sphere*; for the new Christian initiation *one inclines in sympathy* towards the earthly, to receive, penetrate, change and transfigure the earthly sphere—that is the essence. For this reason, this new Christian initiation as such stands spiritually in the sign of the Fishes—perhaps more correctly, it can be seen how the three signs of the Johannine triangle, Fishes, Crab and Scorpion-Eagle, relate to Christian initiation. This is also expressed by Rudolf Steiner (*Excursus on the Gospel According to St Mark.* GA 124. Berlin. Jan. 1911). Steiner ascribes the initiation of John the Baptist, the 'baptism of water by John', spiritually to the sign of the Waterman; it was a Waterman-initiation. The 'Waterman' is the spiritual-etheric, primordial human being; those being baptized experienced in the immersion in the waters of the Jordan this, their spiritual-etheric prototype.

To this etheric experience of the 'Fishes', those pictures in the narrative of the calling of the first disciples in Mark (1:16ff.) and the other 'synoptics' (especially Matthew 4:18ff, cf. also the beginning of Luke 5) are related to fishermen, fishing boats, fishing nets and draughts of fishes. Here, as in many other cases, John's Gospel, which approaches nearer to the outer historical facts of the events (MG 21, 70), relates nothing of fishing boats and fishing nets. It allows more the fact to appear, that Christ seeks the first disciples out of the Mystery-sphere of an earlier initiation, that initiation which now through Him will be led out if its old forms into the new, Christian-Johannine form, governed by the spirit of the sign of the Fishes.

That the first disciple—called to discipleship—upon whom the eye of Christ alighted, was the later disciple John, cannot 'exactly be proved' from the words of John's Gospel. But according to John 1:35 with 1:40 it is probable. It corresponds to the fact that the spiritual author, or inspirer, of John's Gospel never names himself in it. He always steps back in his person. It belongs to the most significant connections of the gospel, that, similar to the beginning, the following narration of John the Baptist in John 1 also turns immediately to him who then later becomes the disciple John. For his original name is not *John*—this has always been emphasized here (MG 46f.)—he is not originally *called* John, but he *becomes* it.

Who was he, then, who was the first [disciple] with Andrew to meet Christ here at the Jordan? Was he 'Lazarus'? (cf. on this question MG 49ff.). Here it is increasingly shown, how 'Lazarus', too, is not a 'name' in the usual sense, but contains an indication to the Mystery of the 'invalid' touched on in John 11:1, already referred to in the exposition of Mark's Gospel. He who meets us in John 1:35, 40 without being named, is initially—regardless what he may have been called hitherto—in the spiritual sense is really the 'nameless disciple', who first receives his true *name* through the Johannine-initiation. His Mystery-sphere, then, with which Christ comes into contact here at the Jordan, was that of the 'son of the widow'—consequently his later 'awakening' through the power of Elijah-John (further details on the Mystery-sphere, MG 273ff.). At the Jordan, in his meeting with John the Baptist, whose disciple he appears to have been for a while, he meets the sphere that completes his own being. This is the sphere of Elijah-John, which opens up for him through Christ into an increasingly alive, future-bearing sense.

With him, named before Peter, is Andrew, who later signifies for the Eastern Church what Peter does for the Western Church (MG 71f.]. Andrew and Peter belong, as does Phillip, to the Mystery-sphere of the lands east of the Jordan (John 1:44). In this area many forces were still alive of old, atavistic clairvoyance; the 'holy Mother of Asia' was still to be felt in the whole atmosphere of the land. It is significant, that the meeting between Christ Jesus and John the Baptist also takes place in the land east of the Jordan. Only later does the Baptist, inwardly facing death, moving towards the experience of dying, lead the pull of the soul towards Ænon, from the east to the west (John 3:23).

In this lies a secret, how the Mystery-sphere of the Baptist John as that of the *Waterman*—where the dark Saturn (see the chapters on the planets Part One, 2 & 3) is linked with the secrets of the light of Uranus, of the upper starry heavens—faces the spiritual sphere of Peter as that of the dark Goat, governed alone by Saturn (MG 198f., 309f.). (More exactly, the sphere of the Baptist is Ram + Waterman, that of Peter, the Goat alone.) This sphere [of the Goat] is the sphere of the *old* initiation, in which the 'enlightenment', the spiritual awakening of the Buddha took place (MG 225f.). The Goat, the sign of the 'bringer of light' (Lucifer) is also the sphere for the enlightenment of the Buddha. (Buddha's initiation takes place in the nocturnal sign of the Goat; the Christian-Johannine initiation in the counter-sign of the Crab ♋, which with the Fishes ♓ and the Scorpion ♏ together form the Johannine triangle. See Part One, Chapter 5.)

A direct indication to this enlightenment-sphere of the Buddha, already emphasized by Rudolf Steiner, is contained at the end of John 1 in the story of Nathanael and the fig tree. The fig tree is a symbol of Buddha's enlightenment (MG 262ff. cf. the author's *From Buddha to Christ*. 4ff.). The sphere of Nathanael is the last of the Mystery-spheres with which Christ comes into contact in John 1 in a significant and future-bearing manner. Nathanael re-appears in the story of the resurrection (John 21:2). That he was a named member of the group of Twelve, and would be named here with another name than otherwise (cf. the names, Mark 3:16-19) is not very probable. Rather, he appears as a member of that esoteric group to whom, apart from the later disciple John, Nicodemus and Joseph of Arimathea belong. Like Mary Magdalene and her sister Martha, Nathanael is one of those persons who takes a spiritually intimate part in the whole Christ-event of those 'three years' (cf. John 19:38, 39), without being a member of the Twelve, a direct bearer of the young Church. The disciples of the group of Twelve were appointed to work more outwardly, these other persons more esoterically, inwardly. The later disciple John was the only one who in a complete manner combined in himself both sides of the work.

The scene with Nathanael (John 1:46-51) is thoroughly remarkable, in that Christ Jesus speaks the language of the Mysteries to someone whom He recognizes as a member of a specific group (for details, see Rudolf Steiner's first lecture-cycle on John's Gospel. Hamburg 1908. GA 103). This is a significant motif we shall meet later in John's Gospel, with Nicodemus in John 3 and with the Samaritan woman in John 4. When Buddha under the fig tree found 'enlightenment', the spiritual beings, the heavenly hierarchies, inclined once more towards the human being, in order, with the disappearing old-clairvoyant vision, increasingly to withdraw from him [see the author's 'Buddha's Passing' in *From the Mysteries*, TL 185-201]. It was the last 'experience of the higher worlds' of the pre-Christian times of humanity's descent, carrying the greatness of the primordial world.

Christ points out to Nathanael, experienced in the Buddha-Mysteries, that now the time had come when a newly opened-up clairvoyant eye of humanity will behold the angels ascending and descending on the 'heavenly ladder' of Jacob's stellar dream, through the 'open door' of heaven (John 10:9, Rev. 3:8). Earlier beholding will be transformed into an 'I'-conscious beholding. In this new beholding, in the consciousness advancing from the experience of the Father to the experience of the Son in the ego, the 'I', the new higher human being, the 'Son of Man' (John 1:51) is revealed. We recognize here the decisive 'I'-motif of John 1 (Part One, Chapter 6).

***

The ego-motif in the sign of the Fishes now becomes, at it were, the birth-sign—commencing with the Mystery of Golgotha—the heavenly 'ascendant' of the new stage of birth of the planet Earth, the new Christ-era. To the Fishes is united the counter-sign of the Virgin standing there as the 'descendant' in a world-horoscope, a motif of the etheric. Already in the exposition of Mark's Gospel (MG 67), this 'etheric side' of the Jordan-event was mentioned. Moreover, as with Mark's Gospel, with John's Gospel we have always to keep in mind the whole respective axis of the zodiac, connecting sign and counter-sign. We pointed to a significant passage in Steiner's lecture-cycle on John's Gospel (Kassel. GA 112, Lecture 10). We see there the 'Mystery of the Virgin' gently entering into the Jordan-event. The earlier Mystery of Isis, of the 'Virgin with the sheaf' (MG 102, etc.), the bread of life and the cup of life, now becomes in the Christian events the Mystery of Mary, Virgin and Mother.

Maidenly, virginal forces of the cosmic life-ether, which once like stellar provisions for the way were received out of cosmic distances, are now revealed in the *'I'-sphere of the Son of Man*. Such a new revelation of cosmic virginity already lay in Luke's Gospel relating the birth of Jesus, the birth of the son of the child-like mother who died early. Over this whole Christmas story of the birth lies the enchantment of the childlike and etheric virginal quality, which is already peculiar to the birth-story of the Bodhisattva who became the Buddha, the son of Māyā. Something like cosmic virginity out of the world of Christ is bestowed on the one, who, in innocent unconsciousness, is about to enter the earthly events to become the mother of the future bearer of Christ. And something of the influence of the same cosmic virginal forces sinks down, if we follow Rudolf Steiner's indications, with the descent of Christ, that is, with the event of the Jordan, on to the other mother. She becomes the foster-mother after the early death of the first, childlike mother, of him who now carries the bodily sheath of the son of the childlike mother.[62]

The Mystery not expressed in words in John 1 lies within the constellation of this chapter (♓–♍) and also with the sign of the Fishes, linked to the counter-sign of the Virgin: in the widest possible context—the *power of the higher life-ether* lost to the human being through the Fall of man in Paradise—this is the meaning of the commandment not to eat of the Tree of Life, Gen. 3:22-24. In the descent of Christ out of the higher worlds this higher life-ether is now newly bestowed on humanity, and produced henceforth in the 'I', received in the 'I' ('I am the Bread of Life').[63] The motif of the Jordan Baptism is linked with that of the miracle of the Feeding (Mark 6), standing in the same constellation.

With this we touch at the end of John 1 the Mystery-sphere of mother and virgin, which in the now following Chapter 3, is furthermore important in the *Marriage in Cana*.

3.
The Marriage-Miracle in Cana
(John 2)

Courage! for life is striding
To endless life along;
The sense in love abiding,
Grows clearer and more strong.
One day the stars, down dripping,
Shall flow in golden wine:
We, of that nectar sipping,
As living stars will shine.

Novalis, from *Hymns to the Night* (tr. George MacDonald)

The progress of the rhythmic movement corresponding to the great cosmic year, which hitherto showed itself, leads over from the constellation ♓–♍ in which John 1 ended, to the constellation, or zodiac axis, ♒–♌. Linking with the Fishes, the first zodiac sign in the cosmic rhythm (not the rhythm of the year) leading downwards to the dark zodiac signs would be the Waterman, the second of these signs. The great motif of this chapter clearly and obviously points to this: 'Christ changes the water of the impersonal etheric into the wine of the personal, ego-penetrated principle.' The motif of John the Baptist already contained in the Gospels of Matthew and Mark, 'I baptize you with water, but he will baptize you with the Holy Spirit and with fire' [Matt. 3:11, cf. Mark 1:8] points in the same direction; in the exposition of Mark's Gospel it was linked with this constellation and the 'Marriage in Cana' (MG 31f., 62). The 'water of the etheric' as the element of the impersonal-etheric 'human being of the primordial beginnings' still living over the Earth, corresponds to the 'air sign' and light-ether sign of the Waterman. The fiery power of the Sun-blood—revealing itself in the wine—of the blood in general, corresponds to the fire-sign of the Lion standing opposite on the axis of the zodiac. In the blood the warmth element, the ego-strength and heart-strength, is kindled, ultimately also the power of 'Spirit-man' penetrated by the ego, the 'I', and changed by the 'I', the physical body renewed right into the blood, 'Spirit-man' (atma).

We found the Mystery of John's baptism by water everywhere deeply linked to the sign of the Waterman. The person immersed in the waters of the Jordan beheld life's etheric panorama of destiny—Rudolf Steiner frequently speaks of this. It was similar to that experienced today by a drowning person, or someone who is suffering a heavy fall, feeling death approaching. The immersed person felt he was transported into the regions of light of the spiritual-etheric primordial human being, in the Uranus-region of the Waterman. The *Mysteries of the baptism* and its bright, cosmic-etheric 'primordial waters'—pictured in and comparable to the 'waters of birth'—stand over the chapter on the Marriage in Cana in John's Gospel. Here the 'water jars' mentioned (John 2:6 & 7) are nothing other than baptism pitchers; the Jewish 'ceremonial washing' mentioned is nothing other than a baptism ritual, though here a Mystery-rite, not the daily ritual.

In John's Gospel in general, ever again the initially given motifs of a chapter work into the following chapter; they sound on and are worked further. So here, the 'motif of baptism' from John 1 works on in John 2, in the chapter on the Marriage in Cana. All this lies in the sign of the Waterman. John 2 helps us to look up to the one side of the etheric human origins in the bright region of Uranus, the 'cosmic, primordial water'. What was noted earlier (in the chapters on the planets, Part One, 2 & 3) corresponds to the 'etheric-astral' side, that is, the *starry nature* of this sign.[64]

Everywhere in John's Gospel the especially important and emphasized opposite pairing of sign and counter-sign, in this case of *Waterman* and *Lion*, is clearly discerned. These first 'Mystery Chapters' of John's Gospel (see Part One, 4 & 6) are not only concerned with retrospective views of the primordial past, but at the same time with significant glimpses into the future of humanity. John 2, the 'Marriage in Cana', presents not only a 'traditional marriage', but is in the most eminent sense such a 'Mystery Chapter'. Thus the future, to which John 1 with its constellation of the Fishes points is today the age of the Fishes; it has already become the present. John 2 with its constellation ♒–♌ points to a future that today is still future. As will be shown, depending on the viewpoint from which we begin, a future is either earlier or later. Here lies the significance of the fact that in the initial 'Mystery Chapters' of John's Gospel, the cosmic rhythm follows that of the great cosmic year. We are shown here in tremendous prophetic glimpses how through Christ the primordial past of humanity is carried over into the near and far future, indeed into the farthest future of mankind. This viewpoint is significant at least until John 4.

At this point it is important to look at a fact, which in his first lecture-cycle on John's Gospel [Hamburg 1908. GA 103] Rudolf Steiner indicates at the end of Lectures 4 and 10. He says how already the words 'on the third day', with which John 2 commences, point to Mystery-contexts; these words belong to the language of the Mysteries. 'For the person engaged in initiation,' says Steiner (Lecture 4), 'one truth after the other was revealed day by day. An important truth, for example, was always revealed on the third day.' At another place (Lecture 10) he speaks of most significant connections with cosmic events to this experience of initiation taking place on certain days. With this phrase—'on the third day'—the writer of John's Gospel points to the fact that it 'not only has to do with a real experience, but at the same time of a great, tremendous prophecy. This marriage expresses the great marriage of humanity, which in initiation is shown on the third day'.

On the *first* day, he continues, specific Mysteries of the past were revealed. These took place at the transition to the beginning of the then current 'fourth cultural epoch' (to use the historical terms of anthroposophy for post-Atlantean times). On the *second* day specific processes took place of a then future, which today is already the present or [more recent] past (transition of the fourth to the fifth cultural epoch). On the *third* day, events that still today lie in the future, which with the transition of the present fifth into the following sixth cultural period, in the time of 'Manas-culture', are to do with developing 'Spirit-self'.

Here, simply out of spiritual research, without expressly mentioning the cosmic rhythm of the zodiac signs, what Steiner says on the meaning and contexts of John 2 coincides in a remarkable way with what the cosmic rhythm of the heavenly script reveals for this chapter. For as the sign ♓ points to the 'fifth post-Atlantean cultural period' of today as the 'age of the Fishes', the sign ♒ standing over John 2 points to the *sixth cultural period* as the *age of the Waterman, or Aquarius*, still lying before us.

So a double aspect is possible:

- Firstly, the anthroposophical aspect of 'cultural epochs', that only fully and completely carries the signature of a specific sign when the spring equinox standing in the middle of the respective constellation has already been crossed. In this sense, it would concern a future of millennia, with the 'age of the Waterman/ Aquarius' as the actual 'sixth cultural epoch' (the number 'six' of the water jars appears to point to this).
- Or, secondly, the purely astronomical aspect, simply regarding when the spring equinox in the constellation of the Fishes where it is still found today, passes over into that of the Waterman—as the transition from the Ram to the Fishes was the hour of the Mystery of Golgotha. This example already shows that here too it concerns not only something 'merely astronomical', but at the same time something spiritually significant in the most eminent sense.

In this sense, the opening of the 'age of Aquarius/ Waterman' is today no longer an extraordinarily distant future, in about 150 years time [written in 1930]. (A precise formulation is not possible, simply because the boundaries of the constellations are not uniform and specific, unlike the 'sign' mathematically measured as precisely 30°.) Thus the sign of the Waterman, governed by the planets Saturn-*Uranus* (Part One, Chapters 2, 3) is already spiritually felt long before the actual entrance of the 'sixth cultural period', as it were, casting its shadow before. Today that is already the case. Stellar forces ('forces of Uranus') are already to be increasingly felt in the earthly realm, as the Apocalypse also teaches. The time is not so far off when humanity will experience something of the tremendous forces of change and metamorphosis: the miracles and crises of transformation of the 'Marriage in Cana', of the great Marriage of Humanity.

***

This already touches on a further significant motif, speaking to us in the 'Marriage in Cana'—the motif of the 'changing of water into wine', of *change* in general. The *Lion* in the constellation ♒–♌ speaks—apart from everything else that is has to say—also of the *alchemical secret* of the 'red lion', which dogs our steps in the 'occult figures' of the early Rosicrucians.[65] From the 'changing of water into wine' at the Marriage in Cana (John 2) to the wound in the side of the Crucified made by Longinus, from which streamed water and blood (John 19:34), the *motif of the alchemical transformation of the Earth* runs like a red thread through John's Gospel. We feel how the 'motif of water and wine' is most

The Marriage-Miracle in Cana 151

inwardly related to that of 'water and blood'—we meet this initially in the story of Moses and the 'plagues of Egypt' and finally in the Apocalypse—as in the *blood* (to that in the plant realm there corresponds again the 'sun-blood of the grape' as also the red sap of the rose) is expressed a *secret of the 'I' working in the physical realm*. In so far as it really is about processes of alchemical transformation of substance, we touch here on a secret, which for now will have to remain such. Several things, we feel, lie here between the words of the evangelist, which today we cannot yet decode, we are not able clearly to solve.

The 'changing of water into wine'—when we understand it not only subjectively[66]—shocks our consciousness today as apparently 'according to natural science, impossible'; with the flowing of 'blood and water' out of the wound in the side we feel today, on the contrary, as 'nothing special', although the evangelist speaks of this event as of a miracle (John 19:35). In both cases the solution of the problem must somehow lie *behind the words* of the evangelist, or between them; both cases must point in a very similar, uniform direction. Only in both cases, as regards the external words we can*not* understand the gospel. Not because we do not possess an organ for this more outer side of the event—to the question, what did actually happen in Cana, purely outwardly?—but because the hidden problems of earthly alchemy hidden here have not been fully investigated touching on spiritual alchemical questions, and because from this spiritual side the possibility exists some day also to approach the earthly side of the problem. Here too, where these problems are aired in writings of previous centuries, to which today we no longer posses the key, it happens that in so far as we are dealing with genuine accounts, in many cases with references to the Bible, especially John's Gospel and the 'Marriage in Cana', the decisive thing of the event is always presented in the picture of the marriage, the *chymical wedding*.[67]

***

Let us return to the 'Marriage in Cana'. We have already touched on the fact that it has to do not only with a 'normal marriage', but with Mystery-processes and a Mystery-context. It probably took place in Galilee, far from Jerusalem and Jewish 'high esotericism'. We are led in John's Gospel to a group of simple, straight-forward people, but yet a 'Mystery-group', a group of people who in their way, in a freer, more universally human manner than would have been possible in Jerusalem, cherished certain cults and traditions connected to the spirit of the early pre-Christian Mysteries.

In the event in Cana, too, we see how everywhere in the first five 'Mystery-Chapters' of John's Gospel, Christ goes through a certain 'Mystery-sphere', and here, as also in the other Mystery-spheres, Christ and His ego-message meet a much higher degree of understanding that later from Jerusalem, where Christ descends into the general, lower sphere of humanity. When it concerns these 'Mystery-spheres', the understanding for Christ and His message meets certain limits. It bumps against certain difficulties in human consciousness and the 'consciousness of the Mysteries' among those concerned. For assessing the whole 'Mystery-events' and the 'Mystery-sphere' in which they play, the fact is also not without significance that Cana in Galilee lies close to Mount Tabor, the 'Mount of the Transfiguration'. Something of the 'Sun-splendour of the Transfiguration', about which we said that it flowed like a substance over the whole of John's Gospel [MG 205] is especially clearly to be felt in the events of Cana. Here as in the Transfiguration the 'change', the 'transubstantiation of the Earth', meets us in illuminating pictures. And this illumination can also be felt in the Uranus-Saturn constellation ♒–♌ of this chapter, facing the Saturn-Moon constellation of the following chapter ♑–♋ something much more obscure and dark.

There in Cana in Galilee, as in other Mystery-groups, people sought the experiences of a higher consciousness, a higher enthusiasm, a higher ecstasy. And all this appears here, as in other pre-Christian Mystery-groups, only attainable when the connection with the physical world was loosened, when on that account, also on the other side, all ego-like, personal qualities—which the human being always wants to press down into the physical sphere—are eliminated as completely as possible. Wine, too; alcohol has to a certain degree this effect, which is what it is about here. Only the striven for and aimed for enthusiasm—everything in the Greek Mystery-sphere connected to the name *Dionysus*—is basically not a 'higher', but actually a lower consciousness, a pushed down, a damped down, a dreamy-nebulous consciousness. Compare here the real dreaming-condition in sleep. Here in erasing the awake-consciousness, the 'I' is pulled out, and the astral body pulled out with the 'I' connects more closely with the etheric environment, if the condition of sleep goes over into a more dreaming consciousness. With the advancing loosening of the etheric body—as it was also produced through John's baptism by water—ever higher, supersensory conditions of consciousness appear. Here the 'inner starry world' of the astral body (♒) begins to shine.

Thus, the human *physical body* and *'I'* (the 'I' linked to the physical body), appears to belong more to the awake condition and awake consciousness; the loosened or lightened *ether-body* in union with the astral body appears aligned more to a 'higher' (*cum grano salis*, 'with a grain of salt'), a dreamlike, supersensory consciousness aligned to its super-earthly blessedness, transports and ecstasies. If we would translate all these anthroposophical, technical terms into simple, human terms, then there offers itself—as Steiner suggests in his lecture-cycle on John's Gospel—the well-known verse by Goethe:

> *Vom Vater hab ich die Statur,*   From father I got my physique,
> *Des Lebens ernstes Führen,*   and my earnest nature;
> *Von Mütterchen die Frohnatur*   from my dear mother my happy nature
> *Und Lust zu fabulieren.*   and joy in the imagination.

What lies, in the sense meant here, between the physical (the outer 'physique') and the 'I' (that has the 'earnest nature' in hand), was called in the Mysteries the *Father*. The other side, that of the maternal side, of the *Mother*, lying more in the realm of inwardness, the imagination, of dream and inspiration, the connection of the 'astral' with the 'etheric' (loosened or lightened from the physical). This was felt as the actual *element of magic*. All magic, all enchantment has something to do with this maternal-feminine element. And with it again *love*, linked to the age-old connections of the blood, as it was experienced in those Mysteries. Compare the saying from Novalis: 'Love is the basis for the possibility of magic. The effect of love is magical.'[68]

In this magical contact with the female-maternal of the world people experience something of the 'higher element of life', of the *Tree of Life*. Concerning this, the teaching of the ethers, the higher kinds of ether of the 'eternal Feminine', the sound-ether and life-ether, contain an indication (see Part One, Chapter 5). The *Tree of Life* was experienced as the feminine-maternal (in the ether-body and astral body); the *Tree of Knowledge*, that had become the 'Tree of Death', was associated with the element of the Father (in connection with the physical body and the 'I').

Thus we find the 'magical element of the Mother' from the oldest pre-Christian Mysteries right into later times, in the Egyptian Isis-Mysteries, in Indian Yoga, and in the Irish-Hibernian Mysteries—from which such a significant, powerfully developed echo towards the magical and musical side lives in Wagner's *Tristan and Isolde*. In a most revealing manner, also for understanding the gospel—or receiving elucidation from understanding the gospel—the *magical motif of the Mother* is found in such passages as [I, 1]:

Isolde: *Wohin, Mutter,*	On whom, mother,
vergabst du die Macht,	Bestowed you the might
Über Meer un Sturm zu gebieten?	To command the storm and the ocean?

and [I, 3]:

Brangäne: *Kennst du der Mutter*	Have you forgot
Künste nicht? ...	Your mother's art? ...
Für Weh' und Wunden	For pain and wounds
Balsam hier ...	A balm is here ...

Right into the Christian gospel, right into John's Gospel in particular, we find this *magical motif of the Mother*. Rudolf Steiner shows how it plays a significant role in the Marriage in Cana. Christ Himself turns to the maternal strengths: 'Woman, what is working between you and me?' (as v. 4 should be properly translated); 'my hour' (the hour of the 'I') 'is not yet come', that is, the hour of mankind, the cosmic moment is not yet arrived when, out of the 'I' alone, there can be developed what hitherto was received out of feminine-maternal magic. The 'strengths of the Mother' which hitherto were at work, are now to find the transition to the *strength of the 'I'*, as revealed in Christ—this is the significant meaning of this passage.

From this point we also understand what kind of difficulties the members of that Mystery-group made for the revelatory influence of Christ in the 'Marriage in Cana'. A removal of the Father element (everything that played between the 'I' and the physical body) and a uniting alone to the 'maternal' (with that from the astral tending toward the etheric) was present there as the watchword, the motto, as in all early Mysteries. This fundamental law (as Steiner goes on to show) lives in the famous motif of the Greek story of Oedipus, of 'slaying the Father and marrying the Mother'. All conscious wakefulness—the 'I' working into the physical realm, the 'Father'—had to be omitted, as it were 'slain', when access was sought to what was felt as the higher Mystery-experiences, as higher enthusiasm and blessedness.

A Dionysian element, the wine of life of a higher enthusiasm, an ecstasy beyond all the ties and narrowness of the personal existence, was felt, wanting to bless the soul.

Christ now appears, in order to introduce the 'I' once more in its full power, lost through the Fall of mankind, in order to show human beings that the true 'I' in this relationship works differently. The lower personal self may always show itself as a hindrance for the higher life, the experience of the Mysteries. The true 'I', however, makes possible the 'higher life' only in awake-consciousness. What was otherwise achieved only through a damping and a befogging of consciousness, precisely through the power that awakens the 'I' to its full power, is the true wine of life bequeathed to mankind. Through the power of the Father, the water of the etheric-maternal is changed into the higher Wine of Life (♒–♌).

What did human beings still caught in the old Mystery-views have to fear? Nothing other than that, through such a receiving of the 'I' in the sphere of higher experience, from which hitherto it was strictly excluded, the temple of the physical body would have been devastated, destroyed. The earthly temple of the body would not have been able to withstand the force of those higher experiences. And Christ replies: 'Destroy this temple of the physical body, and I will raise it again in three days'—this body is meant, as John's Gospel itself expressly says in v. 21—'or, if you destroy it yourselves, I [*the I*] will raise it again in three days' (John 1:19). In the lower self, drawn down by the adversary in the Fall of man into the astral sphere, the forces of destruction are at work. The followers of those Mystery-views rightfully feared them, for drawn into the experience of the Mysteries they would in fact work destructively.

However, the forces working destructively in the ego-like astral realm are restored through the higher forces that humanity lost in the Fall of man. They are restored through Christ again in their full power. The *forces of resurrection* work constructively in the true 'I' on that which has been dismantled, indeed destroyed by the [lower] astral element. These ego-forces are aligned to the physical sphere, to that portion that humanity lost in the Fall, to the supersensory, higher physical body carrying in itself the pure 'crystal forces of the cosmos'. This is the resurrection body, about which Rudolf Steiner spoke in detail in the lecture-cycle *From Jesus to Christ*, Karlsruhe, 5-14 October 1911 [GA 131].

Steiner also points to the relationship of these forces *reconstituted by the 'I'*, to what is called in alchemy the transparent, crystalline 'stone of the wise, the philosopher's stone' (ibid., Lecture 6).[69] For the essence of this body he himself uses the expression 'phantom'. The decaying portion in the body is inherited from the Fall of man; the new, higher, non-decaying portion of the 'phantom forces' is inherited from that portion which in the Resurrection was raised out of the grave of Golgotha. The *Temple building of the New Jerusalem* already takes its beginning from this moment, at first invisibly. In that Temple, the human being connected to the resurrection forces of Christ is called to become a living pillar (Rev. 3:12). With this, the human being, penetrated from his 'I' with these higher physical forces of the resurrection body, has become 'Spirit-man', has developed the Spirit-man (Atma) in himself. These are, again related to the zodiac, the forces of the ♌ (MG 34 below), those forces of the Lion which spiritualize, 'fire-through' and 'Sun-through' the earthly-physical element right into the blood that leads the 'baptism of water of the etheric' into the fire-blood baptism of the 'I'.

In this way, with the motif 'out of the "I" the new higher wine of life, the new higher blood of life' in the 'Marriage in Cana', there appears at the same time the resurrection-motif of the renewing of the temple—'out of the strengths of the "I" the new, the higher Temple of life, the Resurrection-Body', which meets us again at the end of John's Gospel. Significantly, the beginning and end of the gospel meet precisely in the motif of change in the Marriage in Cana. We can imagine why this first of the 'seven signs' is presented as the foundation stone, the basic principle ($\dot{\alpha}\rho\chi\dot{\eta}$) of all the 'signs' performed by Christ in John's Gospel (John 2:11), as those events which above all 'revealed his glory [$\delta\dot{o}\xi\alpha$]'.

Moreover, from all this we understand why the event of the 'Cleansing of the Temple' in John's Gospel, which otherwise frequently keeps historically true to the temporal contexts of what is narrated, does not correspond to that of the other gospels. Purely externally the Cleansing of the Temple historically could not have corresponded to this early date. From Mark's Gospel we know that it was the essential cause of the earthly death of Christ (MG 246ff.). The report in John's Gospel appears more like a spiritual vision, placing itself before those who, in view of the events in Cana on the fate of the temple of the body, had to tremble. Not for nothing does John's Gospel itself relate everything expressly to the fates of the physical body (John 2:21). And the thought of cleansing (purification) of the physical body, which has to precede the revelation of the 'I', is heard in the narration of John's Gospel.

A most significant motif expressed in the constellation of John 2 is this, that stellar forces (forces of the starry heavens, Uranos; see Part One, Chapters 2 & 3) hitherto experienced in the region of the ♒, in the etheric-astral maternal element, henceforth through the fiery strength of ♌ are drawn down into the 'I', are experienced in the 'I'. Uranus-power, stellar life, has become on a higher level the *power of the Sun* and the *life of the Sun in the heart* (cf. the passages from Steiner's Berlin lecture-cycle of 1913 [5 Nov. 1912–1 April 1913, GA 141] in Part One, 2 & 3).

> One day the stars, down dripping,
> Shall flow in golden wine:
> We, of that nectar sipping,
> As living stars will shine.

***

We cannot conclude this exposition of the 'Marriage in Cana' without recalling what was given at the beginning as a glimpse of the 'sixth cultural epoch', the age of Uranus-Waterman. We glance towards Eastern Europe, where, as many believe, this human experience of the future in a prophetic manner is initially announced. The 'soul of the East' initially appears to give an idea of these Mysteries of humanity's future.

The final chapter of Book 7 of Dostoyevsky's *The Brothers Karamazov* carries the title 'Cana of Galilee'.[70] The narration concerns the passing of an old priest-monk, loved and honoured by many, of the *starets* (senior [most advanced in spiritual wisdom and love]) Zossima. Alyosha, a young man, especially deeply mourns the one who has died. He finds he is the last of the visitors at the bier. Many details are described, right to the *smell of decay* coming from the coffin—several things remind one here of the Mysteries of the Lazarus-Chapter in John's Gospel. A churchman reads at the coffin words from John's Gospel. Alyosha listening, faintly weak and exhausted, falls into a kind of slumber. The words of John's Gospel reach his ear: 'On the third day there was a marriage at Cana in Galilee, and the mother of Jesus was there; Jesus also was invited to the marriage, with his disciples.' All sorts of memories of life crisscross through Alyosha's dreaming consciousness: 'When the wine failed, the mother of Jesus said to him,

"They have no wine."' The young dreamer becomes conscious how much he always loved this passage. 'It was not men's grief, but their joy Christ visited ... He who loves men loves their gladness, too ...'

And further we hear the words:

> And Jesus said to her, 'O woman, what is happening between you and me? Mine hour is not yet come.' His mother said to the servants, 'Do whatever he tells you.' ... Jesus said to them, 'Fill the jars with water.' And they filled them up to the brim. He said unto them, 'Now draw some out, and take it to the steward of the feast.' So they took it. When the steward of the feast had tasted the water now become wine, and did not know where it came from (though the servants who had drawn the water knew), the steward of the feast called the bridegroom, and said to him, 'Every man serves the good wine first; and when men have drunk freely, then the poor wine; but you have kept the good wine until now.'

Evermore lifelike, as in a clairvoyant dream, the picture of the wedding appears before the soul of the young man. It appears as if there is no longer a coffin, the corpse has become alive again and approaches him with shining eyes. 'Is he too invited to the wedding ...'? And the dead man, the resurrected one, speaks to the dreamer of the new wine of life, of the wine of the new, the great joy—and of the many guests who await the new wine, from the governor of the feast, from the bridegroom and the bride. Into eternity ever-new guests will be invited. All the feelings in the dreamer reach the highest tension, then he wakes up and sees the coffin before him, hears again the measured reading of the gospel by the churchman. But now he no longer listens to the words. Once more, he looks in quiet emotion on the dead man, then, no longer able to bear the enclosed space, he feels the urge to get out.

> His soul, overflowing with rapture, yearned for freedom, space, openness. The vault of heaven, full of soft shining stars, stretched vast and fathomless above him. The Milky Way ran in two pale streams from the zenith to the horizon. The fresh, motionless, still night enfolded the earth. The white towers and golden domes of the cathedral gleamed out against the sapphire sky. The gorgeous autumn flowers, in their beds round the house, were slumbering till morning. The silence of earth seemed to melt into the silence of the heavens. *The Mystery of earth was one with the Mystery of the stars ....*

Overcome by a deep emotion, Alyosha suddenly throws himself on the ground, sprinkling the earth with tears.

> What was he weeping over? Oh! In his rapture he was weeping even over those stars, which were shining to him from the abyss of space, and he was not ashamed of that ecstasy. There seems to be threads from all those innumerable worlds of God, linking his soul to them, and his whole heart was trembling all over in contact with other worlds. He longed to forgive every one and for everything, and to beg forgiveness. Oh, not for himself, but for all men, for all and for everything ... But with every instant he felt clearly and, as it were, tangibly, that something firm and unshakable as that vault of heaven had entered into his soul ... He had fallen on the earth a weak lad, but he rose up a resolute champion, and he knew and felt it suddenly at the very moment of his ecstasy. And never, never, all his life long, could Alyosha forget that moment.

***

A new light flows from the cited words of the Russian poet on to Rudolf Steiner's revelation, how for the clairvoyant eye, the Earth, receiving the blood from the wounds of the Crucified, begins to shine again as a star amongst stars. The blood out of the wound in the side of the Crucified connects again with the miracle of Cana, with the wine transformed from the water. Christ renews the wine of the higher life out of the *spring of living water*; the stellar source of eternal life is renewed in the 'I', which is the *vine of the never extinguished consciousness* (John 15:1). Uranos, the starry heavens, becomes the higher Sun in the heart.

> One day the stars, down dripping,
> Shall flow in golden wine:
> We, of that nectar sipping,
> As living stars will shine.

4.
The Conversation with Nicodemus (John 3)

We recognized the first five chapters of John's Gospel as 'Mystery Chapters', with their rhythm following that of the great cosmic year that progresses by descending through the dark signs of the zodiac. We saw Christ encountering different Mystery-spheres, playing their part in His progress through these Mystery-spheres before He enters the ground of lower, fallen humanity, round about Chapters 6 and 7. Most of these early chapters—especially Chapters 2, 3 and 4 of John's Gospel—and their constellation are based on the contrast of old and new, pre-Christian and Christian initiation. Yet this contrast is viewed from ever-different aspects. To this the ever-different constellation corresponds.

In John 1, Christ, descending out of cosmic heights, meets the one [the Baptist] who completely understands Him, who is himself completely committed to world-becoming, given himself for the immediate realizing of the new, the unfolding. In John 2, the 'Marriage in Cana' meets this with something like a glimpse of the future, with a view of a perhaps not-so-distant future. On the other side we encounter here powers of the past that do not yet *completely* understand Christ and the new that He brings, that are still shocked about it, are astonished. But it is initially a joyful surprise; the people get to know a new joy and blessedness in Christ. It is truly possible that here we step into a Mystery-community separate from Jewish prejudice and blood relations, that which already brings a relatively extensive understanding for the new. Here everything still plays out in a very exalted sphere, not far from Mount Tabor, the Mount of the Transfiguration. And finally, the way the 'bridegroom' is spoken of (John 2:9), even though initially it is the bridegroom of this wedding, yet still allows us most strongly to look towards Christ as the actual 'bridegroom' of the 'chymical wedding' and the great marriage of humanity of the future (as portrayed in the Apocalypse). All this is a most exalted Mystery-experience. In Dostoyevsky we hear this motif sounding, and in John's Gospel itself it is taken up (John 3:29) when John the Baptist speaks the significant words of the bride and bridegroom and of the 'friend of the Bridegroom'. It is characteristic for the whole style and construction of John's Gospel that a motif in some way sounds first, then in what follows is repeatedly taken up and further developed.

The sublime spiritual sphere in which John 2 moves corresponds to the constellation in which it lies. Here the principle of the old initiation stands in the Saturn-sign of the Waterman, in which at the same time the star-Mystery of Uranus, the higher world of the stars shines in; and for the new that Christ brings, for the 'new wine of life' there is the exalted Sun-sign of the Lion. The highest star-Mysteries, married to the Sun of Christ, form the spiritual background of this chapter.

In John 3 the narrative moves out of the constellation of Waterman–Lion to the constellation Goat–Crab (John 3:30 contains the clearest of all indications). After the Waterman, the sign of bright etheric experience and stellar experiences—also revealed in the 'baptism by water'—there follows the sign of the Goat governed alone by Saturn. The Goat is the sign of soul-loneliness, of 'I'-darkness and 'I'-solitude, in which John the Baptist raises the call to change one's thinking, whereas others here hold fast to the 'meaning of the old'; Herod with obscure 'self-will' remains standing in this sign. The dark Saturn-sign of the Goat in the gospel especially expresses everything that in the Jewish nature and in Pharisaism especially oppose the Light-impulses and Ego-impulses of Christ.

In Nicodemus there stands before us an erudite representative of the Hebrew world and of Jewish Pharisaism, a profound initiate who knew about Jewish esotericism. Already the name Nicodemus—'conqueror of the folk', that probably means the overcomer of the folk-soul, of one-sided racial qualities—indicates that, although a Jew, he had raised himself beyond narrow Jewish racial prejudices. Spiritually seen he was a leader of his people to a higher humanity. Every word at the beginning of this chapter—as in the gospel generally—is significant, especially the word ἄνθρωπος 'human being, man' as the first, and not least, of the predicates for Nicodemus. He was a *true human being*, a front-line fighter for true humanity against the narrowness in Jewish nature. That he belonged to the Pharisee community should not mislead us. In the gospel we normally look too one-sidedly at the indeed very strongly emphasized negative stance of Pharisaism, how rigid and loveless many of its representatives were with their stubborn clinging to the national racial prejudices. We should not forget the seriousness of spiritual striving, as it was normal in those groups. Probably he only seldom and periodically attained to such heights of spiritual striving, a spiritual life of high-tension as was seen around the Turning Point of Time in Palestine, or in Buddha's time in Ancient India. This seriousness of spiritual striving Nicodemus shared with the other Pharisees; he was before them in humanness, in humanity, as a *human being* (ἄνθρωπος). And he was a member of the ruling council of the temple (ἄρχων, Archon) among the Jews, with the same degree and profession as that disciple who then became the disciple John (MG 265f.). We can well imagine that the two were linked in esoteric life, that they had mutual Mystery-connections.

It has already been emphasized by Rudolf Steiner that an esoteric experience of Nicodemus, no normal 'conversation on the physical plane', forms the content of John 3. He points out that the words 'he came to Jesus *by night*' has so to be understood, pointing to a 'night experience', that is, a night-time meditative experience, a nocturnal spiritual vision. The nocturnal sign of the Goat above all points to this sphere of spiritual experience. Therein stands, amongst other events, *Buddha's enlightenment* under the sacred fig tree (MG 315), which likewise was such a 'night-time experience'. This great pre-Christian Mystery-experience recalls Christ meeting Nathanael (John 1:48). Nathanael, too, seems to have belonged to those esoteric groups in which, in addition to the later disciple John and his sisters, we find Nicodemus and Joseph of Arimathea.

In this pre-Christian Mystery-life it was fundamental that illumination took place 'during the night', in extinguishing the day-time consciousness. In the nocturnal state of consciousness the highest things were penetrated. Nicodemus apparently belonged to those who, in the spiritual vicinity of Christ within humanity, already felt an inkling while He was still active within the various Mystery-spheres. That spiritually tremendous things took place at the Jordan and also at Cana in Galilee, even if hidden from the eyes of lower humanity, was intuited by Nicodemus in his own spiritual, meditative life. In a kind of nocturnal illumination in Capricorn, in the Goat, similar to that of Buddha or Nathanael—with this we do not need to place Nathanael on the Mystery-heights of the Buddha—he knew about such events.

And it urged him deeply to learn more about the Mystery of His Being, Who in the Baptism in the Jordan had entered the earthly sphere and the sphere of humanity.

In this conversation by night, narrated in John 3, it also initially appears as though Nicodemus is slow on the uptake, as though he were unable to grasp the Mysteries of Christ. Because of the backwardness of his consciousness hanging on to what is old, and the hardened and undeveloped organs of knowledge, it is as though Christ regarded him as hopeless and dismissed him. We may not take this *too much* as something merely negative. We have to remember, that this is no usual meeting or conversation on the physical plane. Nicodemus *experiences all this in spiritual vision, in his own spirit-vision*. This spirit-vision, this strength of meditation can lead him to such a spiritual meeting with Christ—Whom he has not yet met in the physical world—that in this spiritual meeting he *gains an objective, correct picture of Christ*. We have to be clear what degree of spiritual concentration and self-knowledge belongs in meditation in order to gain such an objective picture of the other higher Being. Particularly when that other Being has to say something devastating to one's own self, to such a degree as happened to Nicodemus. A different, narrower person would perhaps have had some kind of 'wonderful' and blessed experience of Christ in his meditative dreams; Nicodemus experiences in spiritual reality Christ's being in rigorous austerity. Without indulgence, He taught how little he, Nicodemus, as representative of the old, was in the position to lay hold of the unprecedented new and tremendous thing that is to come in Christ. Is it not similar to those dreams when asked by the teacher during a lesson at school we are unable to give the answer, and some other pupil gets up and victoriously gives the right answer? Do not both, our own shameful ignorance and the shaming correct answer the other supplies, originate out of the same consciousness of the dreamer ...? (A similar experience is presented in Strindberg's *A Dream Play* [1902], in the middle of Act 2.)

So with John 3 we can feel that elevated Mystery-experiences are narrated, spiritual experiences that few of the then contemporaries could have had to such an elevated level, and least of all other normal Pharisees. Nicodemus had to raise himself high above his own Pharisaism to arrive at such a spiritual view of Christ's being, spiritually to receive such a teaching, even if the content of the teaching was basically devastating for him and his whole spiritual height as a Pharisee.

This one viewpoint faces another, precisely that negative aspect that Nicodemus in the spiritual conversation, the Mystery-conversation, has to experience with Christ. We would say a perceptible retrogressive step is here present, as seen against that Mystery-experience at Cana in Galilee. There a relatively extensive understanding was shown for the new that was to come in Christ, for there up in Galilee people were furthest removed from national narrowness, furthest open to the comprehensively human that was to come with Christ. They were simple, straightforward people at Cana in Galilee, upon whom some sort of 'representative of Jewish high-grade esotericism' would perhaps with a certain arrogance have looked down. And yet these simple, straightforward people at Cana in Galilee in their Mystery-groups would have felt much of what the developed Jewish esotericist was not able to understand. There we experienced in stellar light, the light-filled revelation of the sign of the Waterman, here the dark loneliness of the mountain Goat.

What did Nicodemus not understand of the Mysteries of Christ—if these Mysteries of Christ and his own non-comprehension did spiritually take place in his own consciousness, in his lonely nocturnal meditation? At Cana in Galilee you had the 'Mother', there, where 'weddings take place', the Mysteries of birth were known, the 'Eternal Feminine' and the feminine-maternal (in the spiritual sense). People were only alarmed about the 'Father', about the way Christ brought the connection of the physical with the 'I' into this Mystery-experience. It was something otherwise avoided as a bringer of death. He brought the *Father* into that Mystery-experience, which hitherto only presented the Mysteries devoted to the *Mother*. But on the other side, there lay in the 'Mother' something again of the *receptive* side, that allowed those Galileans to a certain degree to understand the *Mysteries of the Father* placed before them in Christ and the 'Mysteries of the bridegroom'.

As a member of Judaism and its esotericism Nicodemus still knew of the *Mysteries of the Father*. We find generally—with a significant exception still to be mentioned—the essence of the pre-Christian Mysteries is mainly of the *Mother*, governed by the principle of the maternal and Eternal Feminine. It is precisely Hebraism, which in its Yahweh-impulse, the Father-impulse, venerated the Father-God, the great I-AM, the 'I' in its connection with the Mysteries of the physical world and of the blood. The difficulty of the older Judaism did not lie as with these Galileans, who only knew of the 'Mother'; to them the 'Father' was strange. But the 'Father' was hardened and killed for Judaism, so that it itself became death. In actual Jewish esotericism the experience of the Father was only known as the experience of death. For this reason the Sabbath was hallowed, the day of Saturn, the day of death, on which not even the sick could be healed. You were not allowed to draw people away from the grip of death, because it would have offended the Fatherly majesty of death. In the dark Saturn-sign of the Goat, the special sign of Hebraism, all this spiritual revelation is at home.

Through Christ, as Rudolf Steiner has expressively shown (*The Gospel of St John*, Cassel, 7 July 1909. GA 112), the experience of death is changed into the spiritual Father-experience. The Jews experienced the opposite at that time, the Father as death, that is, only as death. To them the once living revelation of the forces of the Father had become rigid and dead. What did Christ, as bearer of the forces of the Son revealing Himself in meditation, say to Nicodemus? Of what does He have to remind him? Not of the Mystery of the Father, but of the *Mother-Mystery* of the world, not of the revelation of death, but of those of *birth*, of life, of the Eternal Feminine and the Eternal Maternal, as now through the 'I'-experience of Christ and of the experience of the Son they can be there in a new, heightened meaning.

Facing Christ, the bringer of the 'I', it was not enough that Nicodemus senses the magic in the sign performed by Christ, that he is especially receptive to this magical effecting of miraculous signs (John 3:2). For those who 'believe on His name' only because of the signs, Christ is not yet able to open the heart (cf. John 2:23-25). There lies Nicodemus' difficulty. He felt the magic of the 'Name'; his 'I' does not yet enable him to open to the Christ-Mystery of the Eternal Name, which with the Baptism in the Jordan descended to humanity. Consequently, he could not yet understand the Mystery of the 'new birth', which is a birth *from above* (this is the literal sense of the Greek ἄνωθεν, that AV/KJV and others translate as 'again'), a birth out of the *stellar world of the Eternal Name*. Only through the gate of death, as an earthly reincarnation, could he imagine such a new birth (John 3:4). But he cannot find it as a fact.

Christ, however, does not mean *this* rebirth at all, which would imply an ageing and dying of the physical body; he means another birth out of the secret forces of the 'I', out of the forces of the Son. This birth can take place at any moment if the human 'I' with the 'forces from above', lost in the Fall of man, through Christ are implanted anew. In its lost full power the 'I' implanted through Christ creates a new connection also with the forces of the 'Mother', the Eternal Feminine, with the life-element 'from above' of the 'higher kinds of ether' (life-ether and sound-ether), that have frequently been mentioned (Part One, Chapter 5, etc.). We find them again as the 'water of life' and the 'wind of life' (John 3:5). Rudolf Steiner points out that to translate the Greek πνεῦμά (*pneuma*) as 'spirit' here is too abstract; really the element of the air, wind and breath (expressly mentioned in v. 8) is to be thought. Only we must not think of 'wind' and 'air' as too physical but initially raise them into the 'etheric' realm. The picture of the water of life, or 'living water', is used everywhere in the gospel itself (cf. John 4 & 7:38) for the 'higher ether of life'.

With this higher 'water of life' is linked the higher 'wind of life'. Not as the necessity of earthly birth with its pains and 'travail' is this higher birth-experience, but in the freedom of the 'I', in the sighing of the wind that blows down from above, out of cosmic heights: 'The wind blows where it pleases. You hear its sound, but you cannot tell where it comes from or where it is going. So it is with everyone born of the Spirit' (John 3:8). In a wonderful manner we are allowed especially here to feel in the revelatory cosmic-symphonic language of John's Gospel that in the cosmic wind, as in the blowing earthly wind, we perceive the Mystery of the cosmic music. This, though, is at the same time the secret of the sound-ether in the world. As in the 'water of life' of John's Gospel, the Mystery of the life-ether is hidden in the wind of life of the magical sound-ether.

The early Indians still lived deeply into this secret of the cosmic music and sound-ether, into the wind's breath and the breath of life. Their practice of Yoga was completely built on this *Mystery of the wind's breath* and of the cosmic music, of the sound-ether in the breath.[71] In the depths of life, in the 'lower human being', the Indian yogi through control of the breath awoke the mysterious 'snake' (*Kundalini Shakti*). There sleeping below as the blind force of the human being in the 'unknowing', is caught in the darkness of the urges, appetites and passions. However, as the 'knowing snake', awakening and rising up as the healing force of life and love, it becomes the bringer of the inner freedom through the light of redemptive knowledge.

Right into the Moses-Mysteries, right into the snake-magic before the Egyptian pharaoh and the 'raising up of the snake in the wilderness' (John 3:14 with Numbers 21:8) these Yoga-secrets are evident, which in Ancient India have their classic place. What then out of the centre of life, out of the depths of the subconscious was raised up, that this Christ now effects out of the strength of the 'I', in the light of the higher consciousness? Out of the strength of the 'I' and in the freedom of the 'I' the higher life-element (life-ether and sound-ether; in Johannine terms—water of life and wind of life) is now received *as in a new birth received from above*. This is then the *raising of the Son of Man* (see Part One, Chapter 6), the unfolding of the seed of the 'I' and higher revelation of the 'I' of the human being, to replace the 'raising of the snake' out of the forces of the subconscious centre of life still practised in the pre-Christian Mysteries (John 3:14). Here the higher Mysteries of birth and Mysteries of the 'Eternal Feminine' govern, as they are now evident in Christ.

The sign of the Crab (♋) standing with the Goat (♑) over this whole chapter of John's Gospel was always bound with these secrets of birth, of the feminine and maternal, especially the mother's breast (MG 31, etc.). Already the 'creation of Eve out of Adam's rib' (Gen. 2:22) points to this sign, in which one can see 'both ribs' or parts of the ribcage. Amongst the 'twelve senses', the sign of the Crab ♋ (in which one can also find the shape of the human ear) is connected to the sense of hearing, the sense of sound. We recognize how the 'higher birth' out of the sound-ether forces of the 'wind of life' unites both aspects of this sign. Nicodemus' difficulty is that he remains stationary in the sign of the Goat; he cannot reach the forces of the higher elements of life and of birth from the Crab.

In the Christian-Johannine initiation (MG 238ff.) the Crab is the sign of the transformation of the physical, of transubstantiation and higher alchemy, the new birth even of the physical out of the forces of the 'I'. Twins, Crab and Lion stand over this initiation. The same three signs appear again in John's Gospel in the three 'Mystery-Chapters', which especially take up the contrast of the old and the new initiation (Chapters 2, 3 and 4) as *upper counter-signs*. The primary signs, as otherwise in John's Gospel, are the lower, dark signs, that is, with these three chapters: Waterman, Goat and Archer. In Chapter 2 on the 'Marriage in Cana', which concerns the contrast of 'water and wine', baptism by water and baptism by fire, the effect of the ether and the effect of the 'I', the Waterman appears as the opposite sign of the Lion. In Chapter 3 on Nicodemus, it has to do with the contrast of the Father-force still revealing itself in death and the maternal strength working in the 'rebirth from above' of the upper life-element. There the Saturnian Father-sign of the Goat appears as the dark contrast to the bright Moon-maternal sign of the Crab. Here the contrast between the old and of the new initiation in the zodiac axis Goat–Crab is revealed.

Rays of Uranus, the light-ether forces of the upper stellar world, as we saw, unite in the sign of the Waterman (John 2) with the influence of Saturn. For this reason everything appeared there, with the marriage in Cana, in a brighter element. These rays do not reach the dark Saturn-sphere of the Goat, in which Nicodemus, the Jewish esotericist, finds himself at home. The higher star-Mysteries, *the Mysteries of Uranus*, remain closed to the old Judaism and its Saturn-impulse. We recall (Part One, Chapters 2 & 3), as we do *Uranus, uranós* in the Ancient Mysteries was a name for the *upper stellar sphere*, the actual starry world lying beyond the system of seven planets, beyond Saturn. Out of this *uranós* (the word finds its same meaning in John's Gospel), this realm of the upper stellar world, this 'world of the Eternal Name', Christ descended to the Earth (John 3:13). And humanity, who has forgotten its Eternal Name written in the stars (Luke 10:20), has lost its connection with the upper stellar world (Part One, Chapter 7). Humanity, in such an advanced esotericist as Nicodemus was, no longer suspects this secret of the name of Christ, is no longer able 'to believe on this Name', because the stellar harmony of the Eternal Name no longer echoes in the heart. Christ's words refer to this in the conversation with Nicodemus (John 3:12): 'I have spoken to you of earthly things and you do not believe; how then will you believe if I speak of heavenly things?'

As with earthly birth and the giving of an earthly name, the heavenly birth Christ refers to here, the 'birth from above', is connected to rediscovering, or recalling, the Eternal Name. This Name shines in the 'Book of Life', in the stellar script of the Book of Life, which is mentioned in the Apocalypse (on all this, see Part One, Chapter 7). In the other case, the correcting entries in the 'Book of Destiny' stand confirmed.[72]

In the Eternal Name of the Son, in the 'I' itself, there lies the correcting power (John 3:18). The 'I' itself chooses between light and darkness, separating itself, when it chooses darkness, from the light (John 3:19). As the Light of the World, for the healing of the world, the Son is sent from the Father out of the world of light into the earthly world (John 3:17), and only the darkness that does not want to comprehend the light utters its own verdict, extinquishes itself from the *Book of Life*, from the world of the Eternal Name. In the conversation at night,

Nicodemus receives this teaching of Christ in a sublime Mystery-language that he as an initiate understands.

***

For Nicodemus some things remain as not understood. In John the Baptist there lives the full understanding of the meaning of the new initiation (John 3:23ff.). What once was working out of the sign of the Goat, he, the Baptist, has tirelessly sacrificed to the new that is to come in the sign of the Crab. The saying, 'He must increase, but I must decrease' (John 3:30) expresses most completely the meaning of the constellation ♑–♋ standing over the whole chapter.[73] Initially it relates to the relationship of the Baptist to Christ; it also corresponds to both Johns. In the Goat stands the—now superseded—initiation of the old, pre-Christian John; in the Crab the new, Christian initiation is fulfilled. In this saying [John 3:30] the turning point of St. John's-tide (midsummer) during the course of the year becomes a picture of the watershed of John in world-history.

The question can be raised, only as a 'hypothesis', whether, following Steiner's spiritual research, we take Nicodemus' conversation as a nocturnal meditation-experience. Then the whole picture of the Baptist in the process of complete sacrifice towards the new unfolding of Christ's world—unaffected by the objective reality of the events related in this section of the gospel—can also be understood as a picture arising in the mediation of Nicodemus. In beholding the figure of John the Baptist, Nicodemus finds the answer to the doubting questions that hitherto had made him restless. The gospel narration itself (John 7:50, 19:39) indeed supplies evidence how Nicodemus increasingly connects himself to and grows into the sphere of Christ.

5.
The Samaritan Woman at the Well
(John 4:1-42)

By the well, the ancient pool,
Where Abraham his cattle brought,
By the pail whose rim so cool
Once the holy lips have sought;
By the living waters vernal
Springing from that sacred place,
Sending through the world eternal
Clear abounding flow of grace—

Goethe, *Faust* II. Act 5 (tr. Philip Wayne).

With these words put into the 'Mulier Samaritana', the Samaritan woman of John 4, at the final apotheosis of his *Faust*, Part 2, Goethe points to the background of the Mysteries to John, Chapter 4:1-42, which allows precisely this to appear as the 'Mystery Chapter' before all the others. To the first Mystery encounters of Christ at the River Jordan (John 1), a second at Cana in Galilee (John 2) follows, then a third (only playing in the spiritual sphere) in the 'conversation with Nicodemus' (John 3). In John 4 we see how the way leads Christ Jesus to one of the towns where ancient heathen Mystery traditions, even if in a late decadent form, are still linked with recollections of ancient Hebraism. The conversation carried out with the Samaritan woman is such a Mystery-encounter of Christ *before* He enters the lower spheres of humanity. As in John's Gospel in general, the fact that many things point to an actual scene—one thinks of the lad sent into the town to buy provisions (v. 8), and similar little touches—as really occurring in the outer life of Christ Jesus as He travelled with His disciples and so on, does not exclude this aspect of the Mysteries. To those who can read between the lines here, in all the simple devotion of the outer narration, the background of cosmic depths is revealed, particularly for this chapter.

The 'cosmic rhythm' of the gospel illuminates the situation here too most clearly. The direction of the 'great cosmic year' following the Goat, to which it arrived in John 3, has to lead on to the *Archer*. To this dark sign the bright counter-sign of the *Twins* is aligned in the heights; this is the sign of the Holy Mount and the initiation-impulse given on it (MG 86). We do in fact also find in this constellation ♐–Ⅱ the decisive key to the problem of John 4. The Archer indicates the freshly springing source of life in Christ (John 4:14; MG 128, 339f.); the elevated sign of the Twins indicates the 'Holy Mount' (MG 86ff.) and the 'worship on this mountain' (John 4:20f.) indicates everything that has flowed as great spiritual impulses into humanity. Historically, recalling everything that has gone before, this exalted sign of the Holy Mount Ⅱ links to that epoch of humanity when the spring equinox was in the constellation of the Twins, with the Ancient Persian 'cultural epoch', to that (prehistoric) age of the great initiate of humanity Zarathustra, or Zoroaster. This figure is not the later inspirer of the Avesta documents, but the primordial Zarathustra whom Plutarch mentions, the 'magician Zoroaster' who lived 5,000 years before the Trojan War, that is 6,000 BCE.[74]

The Zarathustra who in the later Avesta presents us [the original] Zarathustra's teaching of duality, the great teaching of light and darkness, good and evil is anchored in the innermost being of the Twins. As this exposition proceeds, it will become ever clearer how precisely looking into Zarathustra, his primordial Mystery-impulse and primordial-Twins impulse throws light on the questions of John 4 (with the 'Samaritan Woman at the Well' the primordial Mystery-impulse is involved; with the story of the centurion's son the ethical Twins-motif of the cosmic polarity takes the foreground).

It is not that the Samaritan woman, with whom Christ Jesus enters into conversation in John 4, would be an actual priestess of Zarathustra. We find ourselves in Samaria, at the borders of Palestine, in the region of that mountain-cult and its Mysteries which already in Old-Testament times played a significant role. Ancient heathen-Chaldean Mysteries of Istar-Astarte-Astaroth—Isis in her later Chaldean form—with her world of pictures of a decadent, old clairvoyance affects Hebraism. To the Hebrews the commandment was given: 'Thou shalt not make unto thee any graven image, or any likeness of any thing that is in heaven above, or that is in the earth beneath, or that is in the water under the earth' [Ex. 19:4]; you should find the divine in the 'I' alone. The 'mount of worship and of offering', the cosmic revelation of the divine, placed itself against the 'temple in Jerusalem' (John 4:20). But the Chaldean Mysteries operating there, like the Hebrew Mysteries of Moses themselves (H. Beckh, 'Zarathustra' in *From the Mysteries*, TL 92ff.) also lead back ultimately to Zarathustra of the primordial times. And between Moses and his 'tablets of commandments' and the first Zarathustra and his moral commandments there exists a secret, as it were, an underground spiritual connection. Zarathustra—the first Zarathustra—is the great inspirer of all the great post-Atlantean pre-Christian Mysteries, at the same time the great prophetic proclaimer of Christ. And we shall see how his impulses, which point towards the whole constellation standing over John 4, are recognizable in a particular way in individual motifs within this chapter.

It is not a normal 'woman of the people', but the hierophant of a decadent Mystery-centre, in whose tradition, however, still some perceptible impulse pointing to Zarathustra stands before us in the Samaritan woman of John 4. And something of the mood of the 'great midday of Zarathustra'—as this 'great midday' still lived in the dream-visions of Friedrich Nietzsche (cf. Beckh, 'Zarathustra', in *From the Mysteries*, TL 68ff.)—lies over the whole chapter. With Zarathustra this 'great midday' signifies the cosmic midday-hour and decisive cosmic hour (the 'great verdict'). In a New Year lecture (Dornach, 31 Dec. 1915. GA 165) Rudolf Steiner has shown how such an hour of decision comes for human consciousness in a certain millennial rhythm, for the stellar consciousness of humanity. An ancient stellar revelation in human consciousness as it lived 6,000 years before the Turning Point of Time in the Mystery-impulses of Zarathustra, will appear again 6,000 after the Turning Point of Time in the 'I' on a higher level, renewed through the Christ-impulse. The Sun that stood in the 'great midday of Zarathustra' in the constellation of the Twins at the spring equinox will then be in the constellation of the Archer. Thus the constellation standing over John 4, ♐–Ⅱ, is also that of *the great midday*, of the cosmic midday-hour. Not for nothing, as we saw, does the 'cosmic rhythm' of John 1 (the 'Mystery-Chapter') follow the great cosmic year. We recognized in the constellation of John 1, even more in John 2, a great cosmic prophecy. This prophecy increases to its highest and most exalted height in John 4. All the secrets of the great cosmic year, with the renewal of Mystery-impulses of the primordial past through the Christ-impulse, shine to us in the light of the 'great midday', to which the ♊—or the constellation ♐–♊—point.

The rhythm of the course of the year has its greater reflection in that of the great cosmic year; it has its smaller reflection in the course of the day (MG 24, 25ff.). The ♊, which in the cosmic year signifies the 'great midday of Zarathustra', as the sign leading to the summer solstice, is also the 'midday-hour of the year' (the beginning of the decline of the year standing in the sign of the Crab actually falls today in the sign of the Twins). And in the same way this sign in the rhythm of the day signifies the midday hour.

***

We are told about this midday hour right at the beginning of the chapter (John 4:6), where it says how Jesus, tired from the journey, rested at the well, 'and it was about the sixth hour'. When we bear in mind how the Hebrews reckoned the hours beginning from sunrise—that probably means, with the hour of sunrise at the equinox, beginning at 6 o'clock in the morning—we easily see that it really is the hot midday hour (noon) in which Christ Jesus sat thirsty on the edge of the well. It is the same hour that meets us again with the Crucifixion (Mark 16:33). The cosmic significance of the constellation ♐–♊ is then clear. Between these two signs in the course of the day lies the Mystery of midday and midnight, and in the course of the year lies the Mystery of the summer heights and the winter depths. And likewise in the rhythm of the great cosmic year, the Mystery of the cosmic stellar hour governs these initial chapters of John's Gospel. The primordial impulse of the Mysteries is given (♊), and that other hour, when it was renewed on the Cross (♐). The 'great midday of Zarathustra' is on the one side, the Mystery of Golgotha on the other side.

Out of the constellation Fishes–Virgin in John 1, the rhythm of the great cosmic year leads in John 2 to the constellation Waterman–Lion, with John 3 to the constellation Goat–Crab. In John 4 the constellation Archer–Twins logically follows. Here we enter the 'Cross of the Etheric', into the 'Christ-cross' of the middle, from which we took our beginning with the meeting at the Jordan (♓–♍). We could also view this cross as the great hour of the birth on the Earth, the hour of the birth of the 'I', which took place on Golgotha, prepared in the Jordan-event.

What regarding the hour of birth in a horoscope is called the 'ascendants' (the ascending signs) and the 'descendants' (the descending signs), appear with this cross as the constellation Fishes–Virgin, whereas with the constellation Archer–Twins we behold the *heavenly middle* and the *heavenly depths*, what are called *Medium Coeli and Imum Coeli*. (The figure on page 335 shows all this in full clarity.)

We know the Twins already out of the exposition of Mark's Gospel, that elevated sign of the Holy Mount and the 'great midday', as the sign of the great zenith of the heavens. It is the cosmic stellar hour of the great initiation-impulse of the original Zarathustra, who then inspired not only the Persian culture but directly or indirectly also the Egyptian and its Mysteries of Isis, the Chaldean, and the Hebrew cultures.

If we look first at Hebraism, we find its great patriarch Abraham, as he wanders out of *Ur of the Chaldees*, the land of old, primordial star-wisdom (Gen. 11:31). He is still united with the clairvoyant consciousness of the original stellar homeland, still receives prophecies of the divine out of this stellar primordial consciousness. What was more a beholding of the outer starry heavens becomes with the Egyptians more deeply interiorized. We see them meet (Gen. 12:10ff.). Behind this Chaldean wisdom and behind the Egyptian wisdom and its Mysteries of Isis stand once again the stellar primordial wisdom of Zarathustra.

With Abraham what was still a living union with spiritual worlds, with the spirit of the starry worlds, becomes dream-experience with Jacob, his great successor. Sleeping under the glittering starry heavens, in dream Jacob still sees the angels, the beings of the heavenly hierarchies, ascending and descending on the great ladder of heaven (Gen. 28:10ff.). Only later does he meet them also when awake (Gen. 32). Of his twelve sons only Joseph retains this gift of a dreaming clairvoyance, and is consequently shunned by his brother as a 'dreamer' and receives hostility. It was precisely the impulse, the task of development for the Hebrew world, to dissolve this old clairvoyance and dreaming experience of pictures and consequently build up the awake consciousness of the understanding and the 'I'-consciousness. In this sense Moses, who himself still possessed clairvoyant-magical gifts, carried Zarathustra-impulses and Zarathustra-forces in himself, becoming the leader of his people towards [preparing for] the 'I'.

Not without deep meaning does John 4 speak to us of *Jacob's well*. The picture of the depths of the well of old clairvoyant knowledge, ancient dreamlike picture vision arises before us—the depths of the well in which the dreamer sinks, which in the pictorial language of our fairytales plays several roles, where the poor girl wakes up to find herself in a sun-drenched meadow full of flowers ... [the Grimms' fairytale 'Mother Holle']. The whole location where the meeting takes place in John's Gospel is deeply significant. When we hear of the field that Jacob gave to his son Joseph (John 4:5), given as he was dying as a legacy (Gen. 48:22), this leads us to think of all that as a spiritual inheritance passing on from Abraham through Jacob to his descendants, to 'Joseph the dreamer'. And as behind the later wisdom of Moses, there rises here too behind Abraham and his homeland *Ur of the Chaldees*, the centre for ancient star-wisdom, the great figure of Zarathustra, the primordial inspirer of all the later Mysteries, also the Egyptian Mysteries of Isis, whose decadent, fallen form comes to meet us in the later cults of the 'high places' of Istar-Astarte-Astaroth on the borderlands of Palestine.

In the glow of the midday-hour that reflects something of the hour of the 'great midday of Zarathustra', of the heavenly Twins, lie all these primordial memories of the fallen, abandoned Mystery-centres into which John 4 takes us. They are no longer preserved in the clarity of consciousness. But as we still hear as in a not-too-distant past, out of confused remnants of old forms of consciousness, here and there the sleeper in the high cornfield in the hot glow of midday experiences the eldritch, nightmarish figure of the 'midday woman' who oppressed him with her painful questions, with obscure riddling questions about space and time, life and death. This dream experience of the 'midday woman' and her painful questions relates to the great Sphinx-experiences of the Ancient Egyptian Mysteries. And what then was still spiritually present of those decaying Mystery-centres also relates to what had been earlier. Thus, those past shadows of Mystery glory still hover over the abandoned place.

The name *Sychar* itself—as the town of Samaria is called in John's Gospel where the meeting takes place—appears to mean something like the *choked spring*, the *dried up well* (cf. Wilhelm Gesenius, *Hebräisches Handwörterbuch*, 538, under s-k-r.). We think of the great *fountain of life*, from which in Paradise the four rivers flowed, the four ethers' streams of the world that carried the life of the primordial age, which then as a result of the Fall of humanity, increasingly dried up and choked from their separation from the divine primordial source. From this stream Zarathustra could still renew the forces of the ancient Mystery-experience, which then in Egypt and Chaldea blossomed in new splendour. Abraham, the patriarch of the Hebrew people, brought with him yet another reflection of this splendour out of his Chaldean primordial home to the new homeland. This last living connection with the ancient source of life had already become dreamy in Jacob and Joseph.

In the nocturnal depths of the well the source of life since then is closed. Only with effort, with 'scoops, dippers and ladles' can it still be reached. And we will have to watch for this 'motif of vessels for drawing' in John's Gospel. It appears first with the sacramental water-jugs in the marriage of Cana (John 2:6). A further allusion is contained in John 3:34, where John the Baptist says that 'God gives the spirit not by measure'. In the lecture-cycle on John's Gospel, Rudolf Steiner shows how it points to the difference between the old and the new spirituality. In ancient times—especially the Indian ritual texts give eloquent evidence of this—everything was ordered by certain laws of the mantram (that means, the sounds and syllables of the words and the whole sound connections) and metre; the lawfulness of number revealed in the element of sound of the words still works in a magical, 'mantric' manner. In the living word found again in Christ it does not depend in the same way on number and measure, on the outer 'vessels for drawing' of the mantram. Here the free creative power in the 'I' is decisive. Here the laws are livingly created in the 'I'.

We meet the same motif again in John 4. The woman of Samaria knows not otherwise than with the old, traditional 'vessels' of earlier spirituality one draws with great effort the subsiding remains out of the depths of the well that was once the source of life (John 4:11). And Christ speaks to her of the *new source of life* that springs afresh and freely out of the innermost zero-point, the 'I'. The old source of life, which once was a mighty stream, then flowed ever more scantily, increasingly choked and dried up, whereas the Mystery of the new source of life is this: Out of every humble, hardly visible and perceptible beginning it flows ever wider and mightier into the future of mankind. John 4:13, 14: 'Everyone who drinks this water will be thirsty again, but whoever drinks the water I give him [that the 'I' gives him] will never thirst. Indeed, the water I give him will become in him a spring of water welling up to eternal life' (in the 'life of eternities', the 'future cycles of time'). We called the great motif of John 4, 'Out of the "I" the new source of life, the new stream of Paradise' (Part One, Chapter 6).

But why, when *He* is the bringer of the new source of life, does Christ speak to the Samaritan woman, 'Will you give me a drink?' (John 4:7)? Here lies one of the most significant and profound of all the Mysteries of John's Gospel, whose interpretation we do not want to rush through with a simplification, viewing the things from the outside. Jesus of Nazareth, tired and thirsty from the journey, asking the woman for a drink, as Buddha sick unto death on his final wandering on Earth asks his favourite disciple Ananda. Certainly, the event could have happened like that, seen purely externally. And it could also be natural to say: Well, when (v. 14) Christ speaks of the water of life, of 'a spring of water welling up to eternal life', He of course no longer means normal water, here He takes it spiritually; but what the Samaritan woman means and what initially forms the point of departure of the whole dialogue, is still only normal water, H_2O. But with this the actual depths, the true backgrounds of John 4 are not reached. Nothing is more clear, and in the following exposition it will become even more clear, than that Christ and the Samaritan woman in John 4 from the beginning speak together in 'Mystery-language'. It is similar, as we found in a scene of Mark's Gospel (Mark 7:25-29, & also 27-28), where Christ also speaks with a hierophant of a decadent Mystery-centre (MG 160f.—the suggested context for Mark 7 of the sphere of Herodias (MG 159) does not come into question with John 4).

As a result of clairvoyant research, Rudolf Steiner once related how already before the Jordan event, Jesus of Nazareth on his wanderings came into the orbit of many fallen Mystery-centres and experienced spiritually significant things there; in the spiritual atmosphere he beheld the whole past of these centres and the whole abyss of their later decline. In this way Christ Jesus also in John 4 immediately sees at what centre He finds Himself and who the woman is whom He has before Him. In the midst of everything decadent surrounding Him there, He sees nevertheless the once great spiritual past, how something of the clairvoyant eye is still present, that it perceptibly and invisibly-visibly weaves about the place. And the dialogue for both concerns not only normal water, but everything that lies between the distant primordial past of humanity and the distant future of humanity. Already everything we found of indications of the Hebrew past, of Jacob, Joseph, of 'drawing vessels', and so on, points in this direction.

But if it just has to do here with a 'Mystery-conversation', the question remains: Why does Christ speak to the Samaritan woman, 'Will you give me a drink?' (John 4:7)? Why does he, the bringer of the new source of life, demand the drawing of refreshment out of the old, exhausted source? The woman herself feels the request as something very unusual, to her, initially incomprehensible (v. 9)—an attitude, which would indeed be meaningless if it would only have had to do with a normal drink of water. It is unusual because, seeing a representative of Judaism in Him Who asks, she is used to an arrogant passing by of everything that comes from Samaria, though perhaps still (in the spiritual sense) something 'can be fetched' (v. 9, 'For the Jews do not associate with Samaritans'). And we see the disciples of the Lord consequently take offence at what takes place here between Christ and the Samaritan woman (v. 33ff.). We are not to take this simply as mere arrogance, but have to understand that the spiritual impulse to be developed by the Jews lay in fact in a completely different, in a fully opposite direction from this half-heathen cult of 'high places'. Their way was a completely *inner* concern, to develop spirit-strength out of the 'I'. Precisely for this reason their race was intended to prepare the bodily vessel for Christ, the living bearer of the new 'I'.

And yet it belongs once again to the negative side of Pharisaism in their certain spiritual self-sufficiency: standing aloof from what one receives as spiritual gifts, forgetting all longing after higher things, all *longing for the lost source of life*. But what would be true humanity without this longing? As it is true, that everything to do today with human longing is connected to the Fall of humanity, the other aspect is also true, that a longing exists without which the human being could never experience himself again in the heights of his lost origin. Through Christ, the star of love and longing has become sacred again (Part One, end of Chapter 6). There lies something of greatness in the ancient 'heathendom' that it kept for itself this longing which Judaism prematurely negated.[75]

An inkling of the deep connections governing John 4 lies in the verse of Angelus Silesius:

Gott selber klaget Durst: ach, dass du ihn so kränkest	[God himself complains of thirst; alas, that you insult Him thus,
Und nicht wie jenes Weib, die Samaritin, tränkest.	Unlike that woman of Samaria who gives Him a drink!]

The God in Christ was raised above all human thirst, because He was one with the source of life. But the decisive thing regarding the real fact of Christ does not lie in this, but in the fact that the divine love unites precisely with human longing, that God takes on Himself the human condition, that includes the sufferings of humanity, takes on Himself the infirmities of humanity, the craving of humanity. Buddha taught people the renunciation of *thirst* (*Trischnā*), the longing of desire. *Christ on the cross takes all the thirst, all the longing of humanity on to Himself.* In the words from the cross—reported precisely in this gospel (John 19:28)—'I thirst', there sounds spiritually all the longing and thirst of the whole of humanity into the starry spaces. Not *what* these words mean—Rudolf Steiner in conversation once told the writer of this work—'but we should ask what it means *that* they were spoken at all'.

Not without significance also for the viewpoint of the 'cosmic rhythm', is the fact that both sayings concerning thirst—the word from the cross and the request in John 4:7—or the passage in the gospel where they are found, both stand in the same heavenly sign, in the death-sign of the Archer, to which the constellation of John 4 like that of Golgotha belongs, which is the sign of the new source of life springing from the death on Golgotha. One of the most intimate Mysteries of John's Gospel is revealed here. And through this direct connection with the constellation of Golgotha, John 4 appears as the most profound and significant of the 'Mystery-Chapters' forming the entry to John's Gospel.

***

Christ looks differently at the secrets of the fallen and abandoned Mystery-centres and their choked and almost dried-up source of life. He is no mere representative of Hebraism and Pharisaism—this already lies in the direction and explanation of the request, John 4:7. Open to his spiritual eye is the one-time greatness of the primordial times, the richness of its spiritual revelations. What was once present in Zarathustra and in his announcement of humanity's worth, what lived in the Isis-Mysteries of Egypt and in the star-wisdom of Chaldea, lives for Christ not only as something past. Because He carries in Himself the eternal and eternally renewing, eternal rejuvenating source of life, He sees this past as a renewing factor for the future. Christ appeared on the Earth not in order to replace some elapsed 'heathen' teachings and religions with a new 'Christian' version, but as the *re-enlivener of the dying Earth-existence* to renew the life of the Earth itself out of the source of the cosmos.

In the Blood (*in dem Blute*) that flowed from the wounds of the Crucified, cosmic star life shone on the Earth. The new source of life itself, the new stream of Paradise sprang from the cross of Golgotha. (MG 340 shows how an inkling of this is contained within the ritual of the Catholic Church.) Everything great that was and is on the Earth, everything carrying eternal value in itself, finds its renewal in this stream out of eternal sources. It is a secret of all the blossoming (*Blüte*), all prime of life, that this most transitory [phenomenon] on Earth can be understood, not out of the earthly and transitory, but only out of the eternal, out of the shining-in of a spiritual, starlight. The saying of Novalis points in this direction: 'The plant world is the mid-day nap of the spiritual realm' (*Fragments.* Ed. Kamnitzer. 652). All the blossoming of the Ancient Mysteries was also shone over by this eternal light; it carried eternal worth in itself. What this eternal worth carried in itself is not abolished through Christianity; it finds its renewal here precisely out of the eternal source of life. What treasures of higher spirituality in the Ancient Mysteries were once present, what through a running-dry of the life-stream in the descent of humanity was increasingly used up, would have been lost forever had not a new impulse arrived. In Christ it finds this new impulse, renewal *out of the source of the eternal 'I'*.

This renewal, however, is no mere repetition of the past. What went before is now reborn out of the 'I'. It appears out of a new, higher stage of consciousness born of the 'I'. The subsiding of the old source of life finally disappeared at the zero-point; out of this zero-point of the 'I', the new flowed in, as an ever-widening stream for the future. The disciple John went through that zero-point of the 'I', that 'eye of the needle' of consciousness. In going through shocking, deeply moving experiences of death, he found the new source of life, the *way of life* (MG 325). We can well imagine how everything to which he alludes precisely in the first, the Mystery-Chapters of his gospel, is deeply connected to what he lived through and beheld in the sleep of death at Bethany.

***

So Christ asks for the drink out of the subsiding source of life (John 4:7), also because He recognizes the worth of the earlier time, because He wants to give to the hierophant of the fallen Mystery-centre the new teaching of the value of this source from a primeval age and the possibility of its renewal out of eternal sources. At this point, however, we have to keep the whole overpowering drama, the whole Mystery-drama of John 4 well in mind. How Christ speaks to the woman of the source of life, which in an ever-widening stream will flow into the life of the future, the aeons (the 'future cycles of time') (John 4:14), causes a wonderful change in the soul of the woman (we recall here the change in an apparently similar case, though indeed quite different, already alluded to—Mark 7:28f., MG 161).

Forgotten original memories and original prophecies of the Ancient Mysteries rise up in the consciousness of the hierophant. Does there not flow, did there not flow through the Ancient Mysteries—of which she felt she was a last remaining Guardian, as she still felt herself—the stream of a great prophecy, which leads right back to Zarathustra, the great Zarathustra, whose shadow we, as it were, feel in the harsh shining of the hot midday Sun, in the hour of the 'great midday' (John 4:6) still hovering over the abandoned Mystery-centre?

Here is here this not precisely the point where in the narration of John 4 the felt connection between the decaying Mystery-centre and the primordial memories of Zarathustra is being revealed? Was not the renewal of the old source of life through the event of Christ out of the source of the eternal 'I' precisely prophesied by Zarathustra? Indeed, was there not precisely in the impulse of Zarathustra an encompassing of all this? What lies in the middle of the elevated sign of midday and the death-sign of Golgotha? Did we not see rising up from the beginning in the Mystery-conversation of Christ with the Samaritan woman at the well the whole Zarathustra-Mystery and Christ-Mystery of these constellations?

In the ancient Avesta the great Christ-prophecy of Zarathustra is handed down in the following way [the original text of the Avesta can be found in H. Beckh, 'Zarathustra', Eng. tr. in *From the Mysteries*. TL 2020, 116].

> The mighty, the kingly prophecy-carrying Sun-ether-aura,
> the divinely created, we venerate in prayer,
> who will go on to the most victorious of the saviours and to the others,
> his apostles,
> who move the world onwards,
> who lets the world overcome age and death, decay and putrefaction,
> who helps her [the world] towards eternal life, towards eternal increase,
> to free-will ['to govern the will'],
> when the dead rise again, when the living Vanquisher of Death will come,
> and through the *will* the world is brought forwards.

This incomparable prophecy of Christ leading back in a grandiose manner to Zarathustra, in the clarity of its indications for the Christ-event, the resurrection of the dead, the Christ-message of the 'I' and of the free will, went through the Ancient Mysteries. The Samaritan hierophant, who at the well entered into the Mystery-conversation with Christ, knew the spirit of this prediction—whether she knew the actual words or not. She was still somehow moved, when she herself mentions the Christ-prophecy (John 4:25). For her, the 'worshipper on the mountain' (John 4:20) and guardian of the primordial heathen Mystery-tradition certainly there lived not only the narrow Jewish Messianic expectation in such a prophecy, but still something of the wider cosmic view of the 'sacred mount of Zarathustra'. Yet she does not know, does not yet see, that He in whom the prophecies of the Ancient Mysteries are fulfilled, and to Whom they point, *Christ* stands before her. Yet she already has an intimation of the Mystery of the new source of life, and asks to drink from it. Also in her, the guardian of the ancient, drying-up source of life and source of the Mysteries *thirst* stirs, the great longing of humanity for the *Water of Life*, where she no longer needs the ancient drawing vessels that have long shown themselves to be redundant ... What has Christ, the bringer of the new source of life, to reply to her? In what does the Mystery of the new source of life consist?

Already from what was said above regarding the *zero-point of the 'I'* as the origin of the new source of life there lies an indication of the secret. The entry to it can be found, not with passive soul-forces; not alone through the art of 'measure, number and weight' [cf. Wisdom 11:20], as it governed in the spirituality that has gone, can the new source of life be achieved, but only *in the free creative power of the 'I'*; it can be found through the *will in the 'I'*.

We recall what has been said about the *magic of the Mother* with the marriage of Cana, of the whole Mystery-contrast of *Father* and *Mother*. We met there the feminine, receptive nature of the maternal element as the active soul-force that had the upper hand over the ego-like, masculine element. The influence of Christ in that Mystery-group produced such amazement because He introduced the ego-filled masculine element even into the physical realm, in a new manner, taking hold and changing. Where in the early Mysteries the *Mother* carried weight, the Christ-Ego led the *Son* again to the *Father*. What in ancient Hebraism was still evident of the Father-principle—as we saw with Nicodemus—was in a state of inanimate numbness. So essentially all the pre-Christian Mysteries were carried by the impulses of the *Mother*. Was there no exception? Only the one that we already know— with *Zarathustra*. In the later Egyptian Mysteries of Isis, in everything to do with Egypt generally, we find the decisive force in the maternal, Eternal Feminine. The impulse of Zarathustra was decisively *male*, will-filled. The active-magical will-impulse, to change the Earth, leading to positive work on the earth, as we know it in the great prophecy, is the Mystery-principle of Zarathustra. Still the actual *birth hour of the Mystery of the Earth* had not yet arrived, that first came in Christ. More than any other great pre-Christian Mystery-impulse that of Zarathustra with the 'I'-Mystery is bound to the Mystery of the free-will of the 'I'.

With the German poet Novalis, moved throughout by Johannine depths, we find the saying: '*pure will-strength*, without all the weight of refined feeling, is that wherewith we are able to live and work. It is the *male element*; without it you are not a man. Through it we are and become healthy ... Thus health of the body and of the soul work together ... when *pure, solid, eternal strength of will* is there.'

With these words, nothing more fine and impressive can be said about what signifies Man in the Mystery-sense, which here at the same time is the *Johannine sense*. With the marriage of Cana the story is in a significant Mystery-sense of the *Mother* (John 2); in the Mystery-conversation of John 4, it is of the *Man*. It is certainly a Mystery-conversation, not a mere enquiry after private relationships, from the way Christ answers the hierophant and leader of the old Mystery-source. At her request for the water of the new source of life, His answer makes understandable everything that preceded it: 'Go, call your *husband* (Germ. *Mann*) and come back.' As a usual priest of Istar-Astarte, the hierophant from Samaria could not understand the Mystery-sense of these words. But we saw how precisely over *this*—even if decadent—Mystery-centre there still lies the recollections of the great impulse of Zarathustra, the primordial initiator of the early Mysteries. Here for what He means, Christ can expect to be understood. 'If you really desire to drink out of the new source of life'—that is what Christ wants with these words to say to the Samaritan woman—'and if there is still only a weak shimmer in your soul from the great Zarathustra whose name is still shining over your decadent Mystery-centre, then you have to know out of what strength alone you can find the source of life, then you have to know that this strength is the *creative will in the 'I'*, that it is the *Man* in your soul.'

In all this there does not lie some way-out, arbitrary and subjective interpretation of the gospel context, but something that has existed for a long time among free spirits with insight. Such a free spirit strongly connected to the ego-filled male quality in the soul lived in the Middle Ages (thirteenth century), in the German mystic Meister Eckhart, who found words about the *will*.

As long as this will remains untouched by all creatures and everything created, *so long is it free*. If this will even for a moment looks away from itself and from everything that has been created, and turns back to its origin, then it stands in its right, free way and is free; in this one moment all lost time is retrieved.

In his 'Sermon of the Faithful Servant' (Matt. 25:14ff.), Eckhart touches on John 4, the episode of the Samaritan woman at the well. There, far removed from all one-sided mysticism indulging only in inner visions, he reveals a profound understanding of the gospel, resting on tangible spiritual knowledge. He says:

Nowhere does God give Himself openly and without restraint to the soul, *unless it brings the male element into the soul—its free-will*. 'Woman,' says our Lord, 'you are right: you have had five husbands (John 4:18) who are dead!' Who were the five men [/husbands]? The five senses! With these she has sinned, therefore they are dead. 'And the man you now have is not your husband!' This was her *free-will*, which did not belong to her, because it was bound in deadly sins and she had no power over it—'what one can't lay hold of does not belong to one'; it belongs more to him who has the power.

Thus far Meister Eckhart. He correctly recognizes the decisive conversion that through the conversation with Christ enters the soul of the woman, when (relating to John 4:28f.) she 'suddenly filled with God, overflows and bubbles over with the fullness of God. See,' Eckhart continues, 'this happened to her, when she let out *her Man [husband] ... her free-will*.'

In so far as 'Mystery language' is really spoken in John 4, at this point it is revealed the most clearly. We can take what Meister Eckhart says about the 'five husbands' (John 4:18) as the 'exact solution' of the problem of this passage in the gospel. It is confirmed through looking at the cosmic constellation of the chapter (♐-Ⅱ). The effect of the Fall of man causes the sublimity of the Zarathustra-impulse and the impulse of Hermes-Mercury of Ⅱ (Part One, Chapters 2 & 3) to be intellectually doubted—which we also find in the disciple Thomas, the 'Twin'; in the death sign of ♐ the 'mind-soul' or 'intellectual soul' (MG 33) is revealed, a thinking based on the 'five senses'.[76] Through Christ the negative effect of this constellation is turned into something positive: the primordial Mystery-impulse (Ⅱ) is re-enlivened; out of death itself (♐ as the sign of Golgotha) the new source of life springs. (Rudolf

Steiner gives in his teaching of the 'twelve moods' to ♃ in ♐ the words: '*Im Sterben erreift das Weltenwalten*',' In dying the cosmic-governing powers mature.')

In an impressive intensification, the dramatic construction of John 4 in the conversation with Christ allows us ever more deeply to experience how the presentiment of the Mystery of the Christ-ego comes to life ever more deeply in the Samaritan woman; an ever-deeper change takes hold of her whole being. The first request regarding the Water of Life was followed by the allusion to the *man* in the soul, the lost *will in the 'I'*. This answer of Christ awoke in her the presentiment of His prophetic spiritual greatness; the presentiment consolidated to a new question; the Zarathustra prediction of the great prophecy pressed on her lips, till in a final dramatic intensification the point is reached where, linking to this prophecy, Christ can reply (4:26), 'I who speak to you am he'. In the Greek stands only ἐγώ εἰμι, 'I am', the meaning in the ultimate fine-tuning of this untranslatable passage (see Part One, Chapter 6, p. 85) is: 'I am the "I"; out of me speaks the "I", that makes our conversation have value.' What in the mighty words of the great prophecy of Zarathustra lives as a promise, a hope, a thought, has now been revealed to the woman in its essential reality. Not only in all this has she received a magical impression of the tremendous greatness of Christ, but *she has found in it her own 'I'*.

And now the experience also takes objective effect further afield. Not only through the enthusiastic report of the hierophant are the people won, but in their own 'I' they experience the revelation of Christ's 'I' (4:42). The divine Name sounds reflected in their hearts. It is the effect that always matters to Christ, and which is so seldom achieved (cf. John 2:23-25, and Part One, Chapter 7).

In the face of the denials of all the people, the denials even of his own disciples—who precisely with certain difficulties for their understanding coming to the light of day (John 4: 31-38) already softly announced and as if from a distance—in the face of the whole tragedy of mankind, which then in the following chapters of John's Gospel is increasingly shockingly revealed, in the experience of Samaria there lies something positive, affirmative, the greatest of all successes (if one may use here an expression of daily life), that reached the 'I' of Christ, walking amongst humanity, and otherwise everywhere rejected. On the free mountain-top, in cast-off Samaria, one still understands what in the lowlands of humanity is no longer understood.

On the peak of the Sacred Mount, over which the light of the heavenly Twins shines, the Zarathustra prophecy, *the Christ-impulse as the fulfilment of all religions* and their Mysteries has been mightily revealed. All customary contrasts of heathendom, Judaism, Christianity—as people understand them in some kind of limited confession or opinion in doctrine—retreat before the greatness of this revelation. In the light of Christ holding sway 'in widths of space and depths of time' the words contain deeper meaning. Here the greatness of 'heathendom' where one 'worships on the mountain' (John 4:20), that is, where one conceives the revelation of the divine in the cosmos, in the widths of the world; the greatness of Judaism where the divine is experienced in the one-sided closed-off inwardness—for which the 'temple of Jerusalem' is the sublime symbol. On the free height of the mountain, the heathen worshipper experiences 'the divine world-creating breath'; in the temple of Jerusalem—in this lay the advance of the Hebrew influence (John 4:22)—one strives in devotion towards the awake 'I'-consciousness.[77]

But both, Christ tells the woman of Samaria, are only a preparation, both will find each other and will appear on a higher level in the true revelation of the Christ's 'I' (v. 21-23): 'Believe me, woman, a time is coming when you will worship the Father neither on this mountain nor in Jerusalem … The hour of the "I" is coming, and is already here, when the true, awake worshippers will worship the Father in the *spirit* of the living breath and *in the truth* of the never extinguishing light of consciousness; for the Father seeks such to worship him. The Godhead is living breath; and those who want to approach it, have to do so in the spirit of the life-creating breath and in the wakefulness of the never extinguishing consciousness.'

6.
The Healing of the Nobleman's Son
(John 4:43-54)

Following the episode with the Samaritan woman, John 4 ends with the healing of the Nobleman's Son in Capernaum. For a view clinging to the externals, a connection of the gospel to the cosmic rhythm is incomprehensible. Viewing it out of the constellation, however, it is immediately comprehensible. Regarding the cosmic rhythm is a major gain; connections of the gospel which otherwise could remain incomprehensible become clear.

- The deeper aspect, out of the constellation of the chapter (♒–♌) could lead us out of the apparent riddle in John 2 of the link between the miracle of the Wedding at Cana and the motif of the Cleansing of the Temple and the Destruction of the Temple.
- Likewise in John 3 the connection of the episode of John the Baptist at the end with the apparently far-removed conversation with Nicodemus at the beginning became completely clear out of the constellation (♑–♋).
- And it is no different here in John 4 with the episode of the Samaritan woman; it ends apparently completely differently with the healing of the Nobleman's Son. Also for this episode the decisive aspect, as for that of the Samaritan woman at the well, is contained in the constellation (♐–♊).

As the sign of Zarathustra, the elevated sign of the Twins met us already in the first part of the chapter. It has to do here not only with the chronological point of view, that the era of Zarathustra—the primordial Zarathustra referred to by Plutarch—is characterized through the vernal equinox of the Sun in the constellation of the Twins, but with the fact already touched on likewise in John 4. That is, Zarathustra's impulse with his teaching of good and evil, light and darkness is also spiritually a 'Twins-impulse'; his teaching is a 'Twins-teaching'. The previous primordial Indian epoch (the age of the Crab) was still completely given over to the divine primordial Unity, whereas Zarathustra in the age of the Twins turned the gaze towards Duality, the cosmic opposition. Zarathustra initially conveyed the moral problem to a massive extent to humanity.

The 'seven signs' of Christ in John's Gospel are:

1. the miracle of the Marriage at Cana (Chapter 2);
2. the healing of the Nobleman's Son (Chapter 4);
3. the healing of the Invalid at Bethesda (Chapter 5);
4. the miracle of the Feeding of the Five Thousand (Chapter 6);
5. the Walking on the Sea (Chapter 6);
6. the healing of the Man Born Blind (Chapter 9);
7. the Raising of Lazarus (Chapter 11).

Rudolf Steiner first suggested the seven signs are inwardly connected with the seven sacraments, and these again with the seven great 'post-Atlantean cultural epochs' of humanity. The relationship, for example, of the first of these signs, of the miracle of transformation performed by Christ at the Marriage at Cana, to the sacramental realm of baptism in John's Gospel, is itself obvious when we know that the reference there to 'cleansing' (Gk. *katharismos*) signifies a kind of baptism ceremony. It is not different when the 'motif of baptism', initially sounding with John's Baptism by water in John 1, then meets us in John 2. Even the constellation (♒) points towards it. Furthermore, in recognizing the relationship existing between water in general, the 'waters of the Jordan' in a special sense, with the essence of the 'etheric', and in recalling the whole role that the watery element plays physiologically with birth, then one will also understand how the early human culture following the Atlantic Deluge—the first 'primordial Indian' epoch—still included a certain gaze up to the paradisal primordial past of the human being when everything still existed more in the etheric realm.

In this sense, Novalis speaks in *The Novices at Sais*,[78] of etheric primordial waters:

> In the golden age, we lived like these waves; in brightly coloured clouds, in those swimming oceans and primordial wellsprings of all life on earth, in perpetual frolic, the races of man loved and begot one another, and were visited by the children of heaven; until finally, in that event that sacred tradition terms the Great Flood, this flourishing world

perished; the earth was laid low by an inimical being, leaving behind a few human stragglers marooned on the craggy mountaintops of a strange new world.

Like the sacrament of baptism for the newly born, the first post-Atlantean cultural epoch contains the relationship to the etheric-maternal element of the 'primordial water', and we find both sounding again in the events of Cana and in the whole Mystery-sphere there. The inner allocation to what then in the 'second post-Atlantean cultural epoch', the age of Zarathustra, in that era when the human being managed for the first time fully consciously to face the cosmic opposition of good and evil, light and darkness, has then that sacrament which follows baptism in the later years of development of the young person. As baptism links to birth and childhood, the sacrament of confirmation is linked with youth, with that age when the young person in puberty becomes more aware of the contrast of the genders, at the same time, moreover, of certain moral problems and demands, of the contrast of good and evil. This aspect leads us at the same time closer to the spiritual background of the second of the seven signs, of the healing of the Nobleman's Son at Capernaum narrated at the end of John 4.

We clearly understand from this how far the constellation ♊–♐ also governs the ending of John 4. In the Twins the differentiating knowledge of good and evil, light and darkness was originally given as a divine impulse. Through the earth-forces of the understanding (♐) all this was pulled into the lower, earthly-human sphere. The adverse mights, Lucifer and Ahriman, now approach the human being. The 'heavenly Twins' (♊) have now become the duality of the adverse mights. In the age of puberty, when also the intellect, thinking to understand, ripens in the human soul, that which in the entire cultural development of humanity in the age of Zarathustra was experienced in a special manner, is, at it were, [also] undergone in the development of the individual life.

This takes place not always without inner and outer difficulties, crises and conflicts. The balance both of body and soul through these crises of development, is to an enhanced degree endangered and threatened. This at the same time points to the riddle of the illness of the nobleman's son and his healing through Christ. A crisis of the years of development has brought the lad into a flaming, feverish condition. The 'cosmic contrasts' have made themselves felt. The narration allows us to see that the lad is deeply bound to his father through the power of blood connections. Christ knows this and initially calls the father to account for his 'weakness of faith', as a weakness of the 'will in the "I"', that he calls on foreign help, expects a healing from external magic, when the inner magic of the 'I' would affect the balance of the cosmic contrasts.

It is one of the ever-recurring motifs of John's Gospel—the way from father to son out of the might of the 'I' is found so difficult. Here John 4:50 points—gently, as in such cases—to the change in the soul of the father, which is aroused through the 'I' of Christ. In the *will* the paternal 'I' is awoken. It is not *only* the magical word of Christ that performs the healing. With the first signs, the miracle of transformation in Cana, the strength of the mother intimately participates; here with the healing of the nobleman's son the strength of the father participates. Both signs are intimately connected, which is also indicated through the nearness of the places (4:46). As in John 2 the Mysteries of the female and of the mother stand in the background; with John 4 there stand those of the male and of the father. Already here—as with the Samaritan woman at the well—the *will in the 'I'* proclaims itself as the ultimate ground of what works the healing, and therewith at the same time we find already the motif of the following chapter.

7.
The Invalid of Bethesda
(John 5)

In John 4, we heard significantly of the motif that we could name *the will in the 'I'*.

In this the male aspect in the soul is revealed, that 'element of the male' which already for Novalis is the *pure strength of will*. That which contrasts with the masculine in the soul is already revealed in the Marriage at Cana. It is that which governs between the 'I' and the physical aspect of the human being, the Father-principle, and the feminine-maternal that is more inwardly evident.

This *will in the 'I'* is that which Christ admonishingly recalls to the Samaritan woman who requests the water of the *new source of life*. He challenges her: 'Go, call your *man/husband*.' This power of *will in the 'I'*, which at the same time appears as the *primordial power of faith* in the human being, Christ seeks to awaken in the father of the sick lad. Initially the father expects help only from without, from the personality of the stranger. And we saw how alongside what Christ effects, already something of that power of faith and strength of will is in the father, allowing the healing of the fever to take place for the lad who finds himself in a crisis of development. It is the *strength of the father*, strengthened through the power of Christ, through which the son is helped here. In the miracle of transformation at Cana, the *strength of the mother* appears as the active agent, strengthened in a certain way through the power of Christ.

For the whole structure of John's Gospel, always recalling certain musical and symphonic facts and laws, it was frequently informative for us to recognize how a motif first sounding in one chapter appears in the following, decisively determining the content. Thus the content of John 5 is determined through the motif of the *will in the 'I'* in close connection with the *motif of healing* that initially appears at the end of John 4. Here too we strongly experience the *masculine element in the soul* as that which manifests directly between the 'I' and the physical plane. The *will in the 'I'*, in the 'I' of the sick person himself, appears here as that which ultimately performs the healing. Here it is no longer the strength of the father, who through Christ is called to help his son, but the strength in himself; the actual 'miracle' or 'sign' just appears as simply the way this strength through Christ awakens, called through the *word of Christ*. Earlier (Part One, Chapter 6) we called this motif 'the renewed health out of the "I"'.

The story of the healing of John 5, purely outwardly, ends closely very much like the other gospels (especially the healing of the paralytic, Mark 2). The *cosmic rhythm* allows us clearly to recognize everywhere in Mark's Gospel how here through the healing power of the living divine word (♉) the active power of darkness and illness active in the death-sign (♏) is overcome. All these healings of illness lie clearly on the zodiac-axis of the sign of the word (♉) and of the death sign (♏). And the often provoked response of the Pharisees to such healings, especially when taking place on the Sabbath (cf. Mark 3), the whole resulting *clash of Christ with the Pharisees*, lies in the polarity of both signs. The living, healing word of Christ (♉), as we saw, is always set against the rigid and dead leaven of Judaism (♏).

Thus, John 5 ends after the Sabbath healing with the dispute of Christ with the Jews. This too stands in the living might (♉) opposite the death might (♏). Precisely with John 5 the constellation is given, as was already given through Mark's Gospel. The rhythm of John's Gospel itself logically leads to this zodiacal axis and its own direction of movement—it follows the constellation ♐–♊ in John 4, when we follow the direction of the great cosmic year further downwards into the constellation ♏–♉ in John 5. The dark, critical death-sign ♏ is, with the main emphasis in John's Gospel on the lower dark signs, here the one primarily emphasized. This also corresponds to the recognized fact that the crisis of humanity indicated with this sign is formed through the essential content of the five following chapters of John's Gospel. We are aware everywhere how the specific motifs of a chapter or gospel-passage are already indicated in that which immediately precedes it, how a certain inner connection links the individual chapters that then is also expressed in the 'cosmic rhythm'.

***

In this way, John 5 forms the transition from the first chapters, the *Mystery-Chapters*, to the later ones, which we increasingly recognize as the *Chapters on the Crisis of Humanity*, or for short we could call them the 'Chapters on Humanity'. Is there more to be discovered in the content of John 5, recognizable in its connection with the 'Mystery-Chapters'?

One such clear Mystery-motif already lies in the Pool of Bethesda itself and the enlivening, healing power of its waters. In a Christmas lecture Rudolf Steiner refers to the legend of the seed of the lost Tree of Life in Paradise. Out of this seed planted by [Adam's third son] Seth on Adam's grave, a tree grew from whose wood various things were formed, finally the cross of Golgotha. The powerful magic rod of Moses was cut out of this wood that still carried the strength of the Tree of Life. And it was built into one of the great pillars in Solomon's Temple, the same pillar that for a special reason was sunk in the Pool of Bethesda. Thus something of the healing forces of the Tree of Life was at work in its waters. (Albert Steffen has uniquely worked this motif into the first scene of his drama *Hiram and Solomon*, already referred to more than once in the exposition on Mark's Gospel.)

What have we to imagine with these 'healing forces of the Tree of Life'? Nothing other than the forces of the higher ethers, especially of the life-ether, that ether that we already know from John 3 as the 'Water of Life'; the 'motif of the Water of Life', which in John 4 appears significantly and from there influences John 5, where the water of Bethesda contains something of this Water of Life (the 'old source of life', as we shall see). With these 'forces of the Tree of Life' humanity in its still more etheric, its 'Paradisal condition' was still actively linked, still a part of the divine life, before the 'expulsion' effected by the 'Fall of man'. What caused this expulsion?

In the 'Tree of Knowledge', as the Imagination of the Bible says in its eloquent clarity, in the premature eating of the fruits of the Tree of Knowledge lies the cause that the Tree of Life was lost. Something bringing death lies in the 'knowledge' which estranged the human being from his Paradisal innocence, separating him from the childhood-forces of germinating life. In the flaming, feverish illness of the nobleman's son of Capernaum, too, this 'knowledge of good and evil' takes effect as it approaches the young person in the crisis of growing up, when he in a certain individual way experiences the 'Fall' of the human race. Yet the same forces and struggle allow him also to mature from childhood to manhood; they bring not only external maturity but they also mature the 'man in the soul', the *will in the 'I'*.

- In the higher kinds of ether live the *forces of the Tree of Life* (life-ether and sound-ether) the Eternal Feminine and the feminine-maternal.
- In the lower kinds of ether ('knowledge' is ignited with the essence of the forces of light), in the light-ether and warmth-ether, live the *forces of the Tree of Knowledge* of the Eternal Masculine.

In bringing death the forces of knowledge at the same time ripen the 'I', initially as the *lower* 'I', estranged from the divine. Only from the divine can it be raised again to the higher 'I'. How Christ does this forms the content of John's Gospel, initially in its first five chapters, the 'Mystery-Chapters'.

Thus, in the waters of the Pool of Bethesda initially there sounds again the 'motif of the old source of life' from the previous chapter, that source of life still connected to the stream of Paradise. Who were the sick people who could find healing in these waters? Apparently those who still retained something of the old forces, or a receptivity to the angelic forces of the infancy of mankind. This receptivity still enabled a certain access to this 'old source of life', in which something was still at work of the powers of the prelapsarian life.

John 5:5 speaks of these forces, where it speaks of the angel who at specific times—in a specific rhythm—moves the water of the pool, thereby conveying its healing effects. We may not reject this—philologically contested—text if we don't want to lose a necessary key that explains the whole chapter. What we call in a more abstract language the 'etheric formative forces', appears with elemental, clairvoyant sight that deals with realities, as the 'world of the angels'.

Why could the thirty-eight-year-old invalid, as narrated in John 5, no longer find the healing in the miracle-working water? Is it not more than strange that he attempted for so long and that every time another went before? Even if we could take all this really still literally as outer occurrences, is it not a picture of something spiritual? Who, spiritually speaking, is this 'other', who always pushes himself before us, the other who is basically ourselves, who as the picture of our personal being is often such an unwanted companion? (A modern dramatist called it the '*Spiegelmenschen*', 'mirror man' [by Franz Werfel. 1920].) The thirty-eight-year-old invalid was already too deeply embedded into his personality, too much entangled in the expulsion from the divine source of life resulting from the Fall of humankind, for help to come from what was still left over from this divine source of life.

Did he for this reason stand, or does he stand, in our human-moral judgment lower than the others who could still find healing in the water? Would such a judgment correspond in the eyes of John or Christ? The opposite is correct. To develop the 'I' was and is the meaning of the Earth and of humanity, willed by the gods. Novalis in his *Fragments* speaks of the 'task, the "I"'. What as the gift of the gods, however, he should have received at the right time, the human being received *prematurely* through powers of the adversary. The gift of the 'I' shows itself as a double-edged weapon, which as the 'lower "I"'— that is, estranged from the will of the gods—hits and wounds the person himself through the soul-element right into the body. The lower 'I' surrenders the person, the bearer, to the powers of sickness and death.

Not to extinguish the divine gift of the human 'I', but to return it to the divine will *in the human being*, is the meaning of the Christ-Event and the human task. '*Die Wunde heilt der Speer nur, der sie schlug*', 'The wound is only healed by the Spear that inflicted the wound itself'— this saying expressing the Mystery of the 'I' in Wagner's *Parsifal* libretto throws light on the Mysteries of John 5.

Because he had *too much* of the ego, in the sense of ego-development, because he was an *advanced* human being, this ill person could no longer find healing through the etheric, angelic forces of the water. Not from the old forces, but consequently only *from the ego* could help come: 'The wound is only healed by the Spear that inflicted the wound itself.' The *will in the 'I'*, that *pure strength of will* of which Novalis speaks, is the 'element of the man' through which we are and through which we become healthy. This heals the illness caused through the turbidity of the 'I'.

For this reason this *will in the 'I'* is also the point at which Christ finds the possibility to engage helpfully, when He asks this sick man, '*Do you want to get well?*' Not some kind of magical healing from outside is His intention; Christ wants to awaken the *will in the 'I'*, the 'strength in himself'.

As in another case, which we know from Mark's Gospel (MG 158ff.), Christ awakens the right *word in the 'I'*, here in John 5 He awakens the right *will*. This *will in the 'I'*, this strength 'in himself' with the healing of the sick man is the actual effective thing.

We should consider what forces of the will are demanded in the sick person, who throughout thirty-eight years did not lose his courage and hope to become healthy. Despite uninterrupted, persistent disappointments he repeatedly attempted to reach the health-giving water. Feeling the divine in bodily health, with all the forces of longing, with all fervour of soul he strove for and desired this health. Impressing on ourselves the whole picture of this sick person in a living way, we recognize, it was basically *in him*, this will, that then actually made him healthy. But the curse of humanity weighed on this will; it was like a spell, as in an enchantment. And only Christ, the divine blueprint of the human Ego-being itself and unfallen human nature was able to lift the spell. It was as with the Samaritan woman at the well, to whom Christ said [John 4:18], 'The man you now have is not your husband'. Meister Eckhart explains this:

> This was her *free-will*, which did not belong to her, because it was bound in deadly sins and she had no power over it—what one can't lay hold of does not belong to one; it belongs more to him who has the power.

***

Only John 5 allows us into the full depths of *human illness*, and to experience in human illness the depths of the *Fall of man*. Only now do we touch completely and painfully the world of the senses—which in the 'five covered colonnades' of this place of healing (John 5:2) as in a picture is placed before us—whereas in the previous Mystery-Chapters we still lived as in an elevated light, breathed in a rarefied air not yet fully in contact with the general suffering of humanity. The atmosphere of John 5—we feel it immediately—is another; over it lies as a heavy, stifling vapour all the infirmities of humanity. In the greatest of all contrasts this chapter has led us to the governing constellation, the zodiacal axis ♏–♉. In one of these signs, in ♉, we are again close to the 'word in the primordial beginning', which also here reveals its divine awakening power, awakening the healing will in the human 'I'. In the other sign (♏) the whole depth of the Fall of man, we experience the whole critical seriousness of the human sickness and the powers of death at work in it.

Moreover, for the whole argument that now follows, concerning healing on the Sabbath, for the whole dispute between Christ and the Jews (John 5:16ff.), this, as we have seen, is characteristic of this constellation ♏–♉. The living element of the divine word (♉) in Christ and his healing force of love (♀) stands facing the stubborn adherence to the dead letter of the law, the powers of death (♏) and its dark demon (♂) of Judaism. Behind the dead letters of the tablets of stone of the law, Christ still sees the living revelation of the divine given to Moses in the words on Sinai, to which the Jewish Pharisaism no longer penetrated (John 5:45-47, and I Cor. 10:4). The opposition of the power of death (♏) and the power of life (♉) governs here also between *writing* and *word* (5:47): 'But since you do not believe what he [Moses] *wrote* [no longer take the writing livingly to heart], how are you going to take my *words* livingly to heart?'

In all this the great *crisis of humanity* is at work, which then forms the content of the following chapters (John 6–10), already entering as the *sign of this crisis*, as that which we have always recognized as the ♏ (MG 116ff., 178ff., 303ff.); it already stands over John 5. As almost everywhere in John's Gospel, the leading motif of a chapter or section is indicated in what precedes it. And so we find already at the end of John 5, in the dispute of Christ with the Jews, ever and again the words κρίνειν *(krinein),* 'to divide, to judge' and κρίσις *(krisis)* 'division, verdict' (5:22, 24, 27, 30, alongside many other expressions in the Bible taken from earthly legal procedure).

For knowledge of the spiritual background of this whole argument, as the whole *crisis* presented in the following chapters of John's Gospel, what is important in Christ's answer is the first sentence placed before the Jews, on justification for healing on the Sabbath (5:17). AV/KJV translates, 'My Father worketh hitherto, and I work'. The sense is: In the now concluded past the work of the Father was revealed in the necessity of the law's obligations; from now on, however, from the present and into the future, *the 'I' works* revealing itself in creative freedom. In this revelation of the 'I' the *transition from Father to Son* take place as the transition from death to life (John 5:24), from necessity to freedom, from law to grace. A basic motif of John's Gospel is already contained in the opening words (John 1:17): 'The law was given through Moses; *grace* and *truth* [that is, the *inner freedom in the light of the inextinguishable consciousness*] came through Jesus Christ.'

This working of the hitherto hidden strength out of the living 'I' in the light of the clear, cosmic truth stands only in its beginning; in the future it will be ever more mightily revealed to those called to the 'I' (that is, 'his own', John 1:11, 12); 'For the Father loves the Son, and shows him all things that he himself is doing; and greater things than these he will show him, that you may marvel' (John 5:20). The *love in the primordial beginning* ('Il primo Amore') wanted this advance to the 'I', in which the creature develops itself towards creative freedom. The way the love of the Father to the Son is revealed in pure earthly, human relationships, can be seen and recognized as the earthly expression and at the same time as a significant picture of what in the Johannine sense, in the cosmic depths of John's Gospel, is the *love of the Father to the Son*, cf., also John 3:35: 'The Father loves the Son, and has given all things into his hand.'

(In a remarkable article 'Twilight of the Gods and Resurrection', included as an Appendix in Hermann Beckh, *The* Parsifal-*Christ-Experience in Wagner's Music Drama* [Anastasi 2014; TL forthcoming], Emil Bock shows how the Johannine motif of 'love of the Father to the Son' plays a decisive role also in Wagner—*The Ring, Tristan and Isolde, Mastersingers* and *Parsifal*. And here it is recognizable how this transition first takes place in the Christian Mystery; wherever it remains incomplete the tragedy of humanity is revealed.)

In the 'transition to the Son', in the 'I'-experience, the meaning of the Father-creation, the *will of the Father* is completed. The division of spirits, the crisis, does not lie between *Father* and *Son*; it is revealed in humanity, where the human aspect closes against this transition from Father to Son in the 'I'. Here the 'I' becomes the crisis for humanity, leads to the decisive point where the spirits divide, where it has to be shown whether the meaning of humanity is taken hold of or is rejected by the soul, John 5:22f.: 'For the Father judges no one, but has given all judgment to the Son, that all may honour the Son, even as they honour the Father.' Some judgmental forcing is not carried out, but the darkness in the 'I' closes itself off from the light in the 'I' (John 3:19). This is the essence of the 'verdict', the 'crisis'.

So seriously does John 5 reveal the contrast of the power of life ($\aries$) and of the power of death ($\scorpio$), of the *power of life* that, once again, wants to call the human being to freedom and the fullness of power of the individual 'I'. Out of the re-awakened might of this 'I', the sickness of sin and with it the sickness of the body itself is healed. The *power of death* closes off this life-awakening and healing-bringing breakthrough of the 'I'. Those who, placed in the choice between Life and Death, obligation and freedom, choose death, want to remain standing with the stiff law of compulsion of the power of death that they had hitherto chosen. In the way *how* the Sabbath, the day of Saturn, the *death-day* with the Jews is kept sacred, everything finds its religious-cultic expression. (Concerning the deeper spiritual background for all this, see MG 83f.)

The appearance of Christ on Earth is the hour of world-destiny. Those in the grave of the earthly element, the souls imprisoned in physical corporeality, perceive the voice of the Spirit (John 5:25-29). The soul follows the call to Life out of the freedom of the 'I', to which it can raise itself only *in the light of consciousness*, in that light to which it can only open to itself, if it penetrates through its deeds of darkness surrounding it, that the web the darkness has woven around itself: 'the light shines in the darkness, but the darkness has not comprehended it' [John 1:5].

Innermost Mysteries of the effect of deeds of soul and spirit, of *karma* are in John 5:28 & 29 (also John 3:17-21) spoken by Christ, the 'Lord of *karma*'. Only the self-created, self-spun darkness in the heart can see to it that the *light-rays of the spiritual world* do not reach the heart, that the voice of Christ in the heart does not resound. In this *resounding in the heart* the Mystery of 'faith' lies determined. The Mysteries of the *Book of Destiny (karma)* and of the *Book of Life*, in which the *Eternal Names* are written (Part One, Chapter 7) shine in it. From here we understand John 3:18, where the Mystery of the *crisis*, of the 'verdict' sounds for the first time: 'He that believes on him is not condemned, but whoever does not believe *stands condemned already*, because he has not believed in the name of God's only begotten Son. And this is the verdict: Light has come into the world, but men loved darkness more than the light, because their deeds burdened their destiny.'

The Greek word πονηρός, is mostly translated as 'evil', from πόνος (*ponos*) 'load, burden'; it actually means 'loading, burdening' and expresses the karmic burdening, oppressing, darkening of human action. Thus it appears that the 'motif of crisis' is initially struck in John 3, significantly again at the end of John 5, in order from there to throw a decisive light on the whole following section of John's Gospel (Chapters 6–10).

II. The Crisis
(John 6–10)

But this is the divorce and the verdict, that the light is come into the world, but men loved darkness more than the light because their deeds are burdening their destiny.

John 3:19

1. Essence, Cause & Outbreak of the Crisis
Feeding of the Five Thousand and Storm on the Lake
(John 6 & 7)

The cosmic rhythm, as it was shown for the first five chapters of John's Gospel, corresponding to the great cosmic year from the Fishes (or the constellation Fishes–Virgin) in the first chapter (preceded, like a Prelude, by the Bull, the 'sign of the word', and the sign of the Ram, of the earthly incarnation of Christ), in a descending direction passes through the five lower, dark zodiac signs. Yet with this the corresponding upper counter-sign is also always accented. The movement is led down to the death-sign Scorpion (or the constellation Scorpion–Bull) in John 5, in which is narrated the healing of the invalid at Bethesda and the conflict of Christ with the Jews because of healing on the Sabbath. Here the pending crisis is announced.

The rhythm would now continue in John 6 leading to the sign of the *Scales*. This sign, we know from Mark's Gospel, has to do with the struggle for inner balance, as narrated in the stories and pictures of the voyage and Storm on the Lake and of the fear of the disciples, then in the picture of this Storm on the Lake and storm in the soul brought to rest by the *I-AM* of Christ walking over the waves. From what has

Essence, Cause and Outbreak of the Crisis 201

already resulted from Mark's Gospel concerning the connection of certain words in the gospel with the cosmic sign, we know that this great *I-AM* of Christ is precisely the gospel-word corresponding to the sign of the *Scales* (MG 109).

In fact, we also find in John 7 this alignment to the sign of the Scales, as should be demonstrated if shown to be justified. The whole direction of movement hitherto of the observed rhythm of John's Gospel would similarly correspond to Mark 6:47-51—the story of the Storm on the Lake with the I-AM of Christ Walking on the Waves (John 6:16-21). Yet this story is preceded by another, which likewise corresponds in Mark's Gospel, the narration of the wonderful *Feeding of the Five Thousand* with five loaves and two fishes, whereby twelve baskets of broken pieces remain over. This story in Mark's Gospel is so aligned to the constellation Fishes–Virgin that, because the whole event is a spiritual experience at night, one pointing to the future of mankind—to that of today, the 'age of the Fishes'—the sign of the Fishes appears the one primarily emphasized (MG 142–49). Only with the 'Feeding of the Four Thousand' (Mark 8:1-9), to be thought of as a daytime experience—not told in John's Gospel—do we find primarily emphasized the sign for the Bread of Life, the Virgin.

What was found in Mark's Gospel when applied to John 7 purely externally would lead initially to the constellation Fishes–Virgin, leading over to the story of the Storm on the Lake to that of the Scales (or of the Ram–Scales). The hitherto clearly demonstrable continuity of the rhythm would thereby be broken. If we read a little further in John 7, we encounter that great dispute of Christ with the Jews, in the middle of which stands the frequently repeated, strongly underlined saying of Christ, 'I am the bread of life'. This is actively contrasted with the saying of the Jews, 'Our forefathers ate the manna in the wilderness' (John 6:31).

Of this saying, 'I am the bread of life', we already know from Mark's Gospel that it is aligned to the spiritual meaning of the sign of the Virgin, forming with the 'Fishes' the 'Last-Supper constellation'. This stands initially over the parable of the Sower and the Seed (Mark 4), then over the Feeding, finally over Christ's great Last Supper. If we, then, would think of the end of John 7 especially in the sign of the Virgin, we would feel that the rhythm of this chapter beginning in the constellation Fishes–Virgin, after it has moved on in the middle to the Scales (or the constellation Ram–Scales), would return at the end to the Virgin (or the Last-Supper constellation of Fishes–Virgin).

In all this, as will soon be shown more clearly, there lies something corresponding to the facts, at least something partly correct that does bring us nearer to solve the problem. The corresponding viewpoint is only found when, seeking the rhythm of the whole, we recognize how John 7 may not at all be viewed on its own. It forms a unity with the following chapters, up to Chapter 10. The content of this section John 6–10 already appears announced at the end of John 5, the crisis of mankind. We see Christ amidst His adversaries; the I-AM of Christ is affirmed in the middle between the powers of the adversaries to the right and to the left (this viewpoint is first indicated in MG 319ff., mentioning John 6–10). Here, too, there are certain ever-recurring words of the gospel that clearly point to this connection of the individual chapters. Everything recalls the scene, 'But passing through the midst of them he went away' (Luke 4:30). The passages (John 6:15, 7:30, 7:44, 8:59, 10:39) have already been introduced here in Part One, Chapter 4. One important passage at the end of John 8 agrees with Luke 4:30 ('passing through the midst of them he went away')—according at least to one of the existing sources, literally (διελθὼν διὰ μέσου αὐτῶν).

From what has been said earlier, we know the essence of the 'crisis' (κρίσις), of the 'verdict' meant by Christ, that in Christ the lost 'I' and blueprint of humanity has appeared amongst people. To the humanity who has fallen to the power of darkness, who cannot bear the light of this 'I', there takes place what is presented in John 3:19 (discussed in the previous chapter) as the essence of this crisis, the nature of this 'verdict': 'And this is the verdict: Light has come into the world, but men loved darkness more than the light, because their deeds were burdening' ('burdening their destiny', cf. the remarks towards the end of the chapter on Nicodemus, p. 169, and the end of the Bethesda chapter, p. 192f.).

To the spiritual nature of this crisis, however, this 'verdict' through the I-AM of Christ effecting the 'division of spirits', corresponds in the cosmic rhythm of the gospel to the sign of the great Christ I-AM, the *sign of the Scales*. Here we can definitely recall how also in a quite earthly meaning the *Scales* is a *sign of judgment*, of earthly justice. It otherwise appears as a correct description, that the figure holding the 'scales of justice' is usually portrayed as blind, whereas in the Christ-'I' the *cosmic light* is revealed. Already at the end of the first announcement of 'crisis' in John 5—see especially 5:31 & 32, where it is claimed that the 'testimony of a second witness' is valid as a true witness—containing the words of Christ Himself, a clear allusion is made to earthly justice and earthly judicial procedure. And in the midst of the actual 'Chapters of Crisis' (John 6–10) the same thing clearly emerges, especially with the judgment scene in John 8 and the ensuing justification of Christ (8:13-18, esp. v. 17: 'In your law it is written that the testimony of two men is true'). The end of John 9 and the words of Nicodemus (John 7:51) should also be mentioned in this connection. In the context of the cosmic rhythm, everywhere we shall clearly meet this 'motif of earthly justice'.

After everything already said on these things in the exposition of Mark's Gospel—see especially the Gethsemane Chapter (MG 297f. & 300f.)—which is like an introduction to the present book, it should be clear that everywhere the concern is not with astronomical things, but in understanding the sign of the Scales in a purely spiritual sense. Already in earlier ages, and with earlier peoples the earthly 'scales of justice' has at the same time been a picture of the cosmic scales of justice, the expression of the universal judgment. This is felt or recognized as an expression for that which takes place in the spiritual worlds— the last decision on the destiny of souls in world events. In this sense in the *Book of the Dead*, the ancient Egyptians already picture the great judgment scene where the one who has died is led before Osiris, the divine judge in the underworld, where the heart of the one who has died is weighed on the scales of the world. Two deities, Horus and Anubis, hold the scales, whilst Hermes-Thoth (the word causing us to recall the 'Mystery of death', in Egyptian it initially means 'hand') as the divine 'scribe of the judgment' watches the swing of the scales. In his weighing pans the heart of the human being and the feather of truth are balanced against each other, and the result is written on his writing tablet [Heinrich Karl Brugsch. *Religion und Mythologie der alten Ägypter*. General Books 2012. 465]. Here in Egypt the divine world-judge Osiris is portrayed in medieval Christian images as the 'world-judge Jesus Christ' with the scales of justice.

Such visions of earlier human consciousness gain a special interest when we meet echoes of this Egyptian picture-world in more modern times, as in the Scandinavian 'Dream Song' of Olaf Åsteson (see Rudolf Steiner. Lecture, Berlin. 7 Jan. 1913. GA 158 [also R. Steiner. Lecture, Dornach 31 Dec. 1914. GA 275]). Here we hear of the youthful dreamer who, in the Christmas Holy Nights, having fallen asleep at the church door, in clairvoyant dream-pictures accompanies departed souls on their paths of destiny in spirit-land (*Brooksvalin*). There he experiences amongst other things the *judgment scene with the scales* recalling very much the Egyptian 'Book of the Dead'. Christ as world-judge and the Christian *Archangel Michael* appear in a role recalling the Egyptian Hermes-Thoth:

> In majesty Michael stood there and weighed the human souls on his Scales weighing sins, and the world-judge Jesus Christ stood in judgment, in Brooksvalin, where souls stand under world-judgment.

Several verses end with the words: 'The tongue/ finger of the Scales spoke, and world-truth sounds in Spirit-Land.' In Egypt the 'world-judgment' does not appear as here as an event in the far future, but as the end of the individual earthly life.

This also leads to a closer understanding of Chapters 6 to 10 of John's Gospel. Compare the words of Christ, already encountered, in John 5:25, 29: 'Truly, truly, I say to you, the hour is coming, and now is, when the dead will hear the voice of the Son of God, and those who hear will live ... and come forth, those who have done good, to the resurrection of life, and those who have done evil, to the resurrection of judgment.' This is in a certain sense through the 'I' of Christ *placed in the midst of the physical, earthly life*, what otherwise in people's imagination will so easily be associated one-sidedly only with a distant cosmic-future. The *division of spirits* (crisis) brought about through the Christ-'I' in the midst of the earthly world appears like a grandiose reflection of the *world-judgment*. We have an intimation how this crisis, this division of the spirits is an *eternal cosmic fact*, connected to the innermost essential core of humanity, with the 'I'. This as the true 'I'-bearer of humanity in Jesus of Nazareth who at that time walked over the Earth of Palestine, is also revealing itself in the course of earthly time.

***

The motif of Michael with the Scales, met in the 'Dream Song' of Olaf Åsteson, is widespread in the Christian Middle Ages. It is found both in numerous paintings, and in architecture and sculpture. In the town Michelstadt in Odenwald [S. Hesse, Germany] there is a 'Michael well', in which Michael is depicted with the Scales of Justice in his hand. This Scales of Michael, the Scales under whose sign also John 6–10 is to be thought, the *cosmic* Scales, is the *spiritual* Scales. It is really there to show how, in order to conceive the spiritual nature of this cosmic Scales, it is not necessary to direct the gaze into the widths of the fixed stars. In the rhythm of the year this span of time simply appears when in the autumn equinox day and night become momentarily equal, held in balance in the Scales, that is, the season of Michaelmas as the 'sign of the Scales'. One might seek to fix this sign of the Scales (that is, where the Sun stands during the whole season), to fix it astronomically according to the great heavenly clock of the starry heavens. But as a consequence of the 'precession of the spring equinox' (and thereby all the other points in the course of the year) in the greater time-context, one does not meet today the stars of the constellation of the Scales, but those of the constellation of the Virgin.

However, at that time close to when the Mystery of Golgotha took place, especially in the time when Christ walked the Earth, the sign of the Scales (that is, the time at the beginning of autumn when the days and nights enter into the balance of the Scales) really *did* lie in the constellation of the Scales. This constellation with its three characteristic stars looks like scales with its beam held from above to below. It is, just in this earthly time of Christ, as if the 'heavenly script' wanted to express something of what was happening on the Earth, as if it was somehow written in the stars that heavenly events and earthly events at that time stood in a special relationship. Here, however, initially and further on we shall keep in mind not this aspect of the 'heavenly script', but the simple astronomical fact that the earthly Scales and the heavenly Scales coincided at that time, as far as such a coinciding is possible. (The constellation of the Scales as an especially small constellation takes up a smaller space than the sign of the Scales—like all the other signs, it remains in all cases the same, a twelfth of the whole circle, 30°.)

It was already pointed out in the exposition on Mark's Gospel, that the 'cosmic rhythm' discussed therein was not intended to date some earthly event or other according to the time of year. The only concern was to see how the great pictures of the gospel narrative, arranged by the evangelist in a series of [zodiac] signs corresponding to the yearly rhythm, could possibly correspond to the specific outer events in the individual case, but did not have to do so. Only in the individual case—so it was said—can any given sign, out of the rhythm of the narrative, once, as an exception, also contain an indication of the time of the event. To understand or want to interpret the 'cosmic rhythm' as a whole from this viewpoint would lead to misunderstandings. What is said in this sense for Mark's Gospel is even more valid for John's Gospel, which does not follow the yearly rhythm at all. Here too only in individual cases could such a relationship exist.

Such a case is shown precisely in the sign of the Scales. John 7, when the 'crisis', that great conflict of humanity spiritually standing under the sign of the Scales, fully bursts out for the first time, contains a reference to the time (7:2): the 'feast of Tabernacles (σκηνοπηγία) was at hand'. The time of this feast falls today and probably also at that time during the last days of September, the beginning of Michaelmas in the Christian calendar, that is, really in the time when the Sun in its annual circuit stands in the sign of the Scales. During the time Christ walked the Earth, it is the sign that oriented to that constellation which according to its appearance is called the Scales.

Thus the Scales also stands as the outer heavenly sign over those events that in the middle of John's Gospel are presented as the great conflict of humanity, the crisis of mankind. This does not apply to the whole content of John 5. The time given at John 6:4 ('The Jewish Passover Feast was near'), if we take the reference to the festival in connection with the sign of the Ram, drawing the 'Easter lamb' into the considerations, this points to the sign following the Ram, that is, the Fishes, to the story of the Feeding narrated there, now often presented, to which it relates spiritually. How this relationship to the sign of the Fishes in the narrated story of the Feeding at the beginning of John 6, or how the constellation Fishes–Virgin aligns to that of the spirituality of the Scales governing the whole character of John 6 to 10 shall be discussed in what follows.

Balancing Opposite Forces

In the first part of this book (Part One, Chapter 4) it was already shown how for the present passage of the gospel it depends on recognizing that the decisive thing is not only the Scales as the sign of the I-AM of Christ, but the characteristic quality is how Christ here passes in the middle right through between the fiendish opposites—'but passing through the midst of them he went away' (Luke 4:30, John 8:59). He, as it were, holding the Scales, passes between the two adverse powers threatening humanity to right and left. A continuous conflict of the Christ-'I' with the two adverse powers takes place in this chapter. Only then do we livingly lay hold of the rhythmical meaning of the whole, by recognizing how the *Scales* govern as the spiritual sign of these chapters (6–10) of John's Gospel. It is not simply in repose, but *to be thought of, as it were, oscillating, fluctuating hither and thither, always touching the two other signs*. These are its previous upper, brighter sign

(♍) and the following lower, darker sign (♏). With these two signs it also stands cosmogonically in a particular relationship; at one time in world-history it had to produce the balance between their contrasts (MG 123).

It is not whether in the spirit both of these other signs themselves were to incorporate the adverse powers. This is out of the question especially with the Virgin, concerning whose original pure, divine meaning above all the event of Christ's Last Supper teaches us. But it depends on seeing how with both signs there lies a specific point of attack for the adverse powers. Christ, the Light of the World, stands with His I-AM carrying the lost 'I' of humanity, as it were, in the middle. In Him the great I-AM, which is the never extinguishable light of consciousness, has placed Itself in the midst of mankind. The tremendous saying of Christ, *'I am the light of the world'* (John 8:12) allows the governing motif of the whole section of the gospel to light up for us. This great I-AM of Christ as the true Light of the World stands here always in the middle between the powers of Light and of Darkness.

- On the one side is the bright sign of the *Virgin*, to whom amongst the human senses the sense of sight, the earthly light of the eyes is allocated. When light in the earthly sphere becomes superficial, it becomes 'deceptive apparent light'.
- On the other side lies the dark sign of the *Scorpion*, the sign of the dark, consciousness-darkening power of death (MG 116ff., 178ff., 303ff.). This power petrifies and numbs the human heart; it wants to pull the human soul into the darkening of matter. It is the power of death that darkens and extinguishes the human 'I'.

This power of darkness reaches its climax in the effect on the human heart in the section under discussion of John's Gospel where the Jews lift up stones against Christ (John 8:59, 10:31). In this darkening of the 'I' and extinguishing of the 'I' the ahrimanic adversary is at work.

But also the bright, and in its origin divine, sign of the Virgin offers a point of attack for the 'I'-hostile powers of the adversary. From the dark sign (♏) proceeds the darkening and *extinguishing* of the 'I'; from the bright sign proceeds the *dazzling deception* that wants to place a deceptive apparent-'I' in place of the true 'I'. In this deception, in the production of this deceptive apparent-'I', the luciferic power is at work. With this, too, Christ, the Light of the Word, the carrier and bringer of the true 'I', has to come to terms.

The activity of this luciferic adversary appears really clearly in John's Gospel. In John 6:15 we are told that those who experience the miracle of the Feeding of the Five Thousand—at this moment it does not matter whether they participated externally or whether it was but a spiritual experience—want to make Christ Jesus an earthly king (in the sense of the Jewish Messianic hope). Here, too, Christ has to withdraw from their hands, just as He did when they wanted to seize Him or stone him (Luke 4:9): 'But passing through the midst of them, he went away.' What is the deeper sense of earthly kingship? Basically, that this 'I' in its sovereignty is taken as an outer picture by those whose human ego has not yet awoken to its full power, not yet conscious of the 'I' in its full power as their true inner kingship.

All historically fully justified, external human kingship acts out a part of the 'education of the human race'. It appears in the history of the Indian people, but especially clearly in that of the Hebrews. The Hebrew people through its spiritual leaders, especially through Moses, is given the task to develop the 'I'-impulse of Yahweh ('I AM the I AM' [or better 'I AM He who causes to be']) in their own inner being, to make no external image or likeness from what is then experienced only in the holy of holies within the human being. This commandment not only applies to idolatry but also to a false earthly kingship. Later the clouded clarity of the Jews 'I'-impulse wrested only reluctantly from the then leader of the people, Samuel, the concession of this outer kingship [I Sam. 8].

In the narration of John's Gospel we see how the original pure spiritual hopes for the Jewish Messiah were deflected into a false earthly direction. The whole crisis of the disciples, especially the betrayal of Judas and the denial of Peter is linked to this deflection, with this whispering of the luciferic adversary (MG 367f., 369f.). And John 6:60-71, pointing so clearly to this 'crisis of the disciples', shows how initially it affected the wider circle of disciples, till finally also the smaller group, the Twelve, appear threatened by the crisis.

The crisis of the disciples as the inner preparation of the crisis of humanity—bursting out in John 7—forms the actual content of John 6. And what at the end comes to the light of day as a darkening of consciousness of many disciples of the wider circle (John 6:66), appears but as the darkening, ahrimanic effect of what as a luciferic error is narrated already in the beginning of the chapter, at the end of the story of the Feeding (John 6:15). We only correctly understand the contexts of the gospel when we take note of such moments in its composition.

Indeed, we only find the actual key to John 6 when we recognize—already known from Mark 6—how the story of the Feeding of the Five Thousand is not at all told for its own sake. The higher 'synopsis' or overview of the gospels results only when we notice precisely what in the narration of the one gospel distinguishes it from that of another. In John 6 (compare with Mark 6), this is the incorrect reaction of those who are touched by that experience expressed in the effort to make Christ Jesus an earthly king conveyed in John 6:15.

The Feeding of the Five Thousand

The explanation of the 'miracle of the Feeding of the Five Thousand' was already given in the exposition of Mark's Gospel (MG 32f., 35f., 145ff.). From the aspect of John's Gospel, it appears significant here to point out how the 'five loaves' of this Feeding symbolize the five lower, dark powers (from the Scorpion downwards) of the realm of the human will. This is particularly significant for the whole composition of John's Gospel. After passing in the first five chapters of John's Gospel in descent through those five lower, dark powers in their corresponding heavenly signs (from the Fishes to the Scorpion), all five appear as in a cosmic summary in the story of the Feeding in John 6. All the contents and pictures of the first five chapters (compare the account in the previous section) can be so understood that—apart from what they otherwise signify—they contain an indication concerning the future of humanity and future human strengths. What special content there is in the first five 'Mystery-Chapters' of John's Gospel, becomes the experience of the disciples in what is narrated as the great Feeding of the Five Thousand in John 6 (as also in Mark 6).

Christ brings to the group of human beings gathered around him as disciples—in an extended sense—that world of the higher formative forces, in particular of the life-ether. This had become increasingly lost in the effects of the 'Fall of man', though in the Mysteries for a time the initiates kept the connection, or attempted to maintain it. The forces of the stars were received again in the earthly world, now in the 'I'. That is the meaning of the great 'experience of Feeding'. It is the 'cosmic chalice experience', at the same time also the 'Grail experience' of humanity. We stand before a future vision of humanity of a tremendous nature, as Rudolf Steiner has shown (MG 181ff.).

Voyage on the Lake

As in Mark 6, the story of the Storm on the Lake follows the Feeding in John 6. The connection with the inner difficulties and crises of the group of disciples was already discussed in the exposition on Mark's Gospel (MG 141ff., 189ff.). As we saw, the story of the Storm on the Lake and the fear of the disciples in Mark always stands in the constellation Ram–Scales. Initially (Mark 4) the Scales, later (Mark 6) the Ram—as the sign of carrying over the night-experience to the 'secure solid land' of day-consciousness—is the sign primarily emphasized. Initially, in the story of the Sower and the parable of the Grain of Corn, what is experienced is what awakens the inner unrest in the hearts of the disciples. Later, it is what is experienced in the 'Miracle of the Feeding', in the nocturnal feeding-event. And in John's Gospel the experience is set in the spirituality of the Scales sign. Connections in language, as that of *Wage* and *wagen* [the 'scales' and 'to dare'], *wagen* and *Woge* ['to dare' and the 'wave'], *wogen* and *Wage* ['to undulate' and the 'scales'] one can inwardly feel, can be recognized as deep revelations of the genius of language. The story of the Storm on the Lake in John 7 contains the clearest indication of the beginning of the crisis of the disciples, in which the general crisis of mankind (John 7ff.) is prepared.

The Scales and Christ

With the sign of the Scales governing the whole section of the gospel (John 6–10), to which it spiritually belongs, this story stands at the focus of John 7 and the group of disciples (suggested in John 7:60-71). And we will then directly feel in the narration of the Feeding the clearly present relationship to the Last-Supper constellation; in John's Gospel the sign of the Virgin is more emphasized ('I am the bread of life'). It is like an oscillation of the Scales upwards. The influence of the death-power of the Scorpion is felt like a tipping of the Scales downwards.

Not merely the Scales as such, *but the sign of the Scales, as it stands in the middle between the bright, upper sign of the Virgin and the lower dark sign of the Scorpion, gives to the middle section of John's Gospel (John 6–10) its spiritual signature.*

As the Christ-'I', or ego of Christ, between above and below, between the adversaries to the right and to the left, the Scales holds the balance in the middle. This forms the actual tremendous content of this section of the gospel. In this 'holding the balance, the scales' (this in the Michaelic sense is the 'scales of justice') consists the actual 'division of spirits' (this is the literal meaning of the word *crisis*), the actual 'verdict', which in this chapter of John's Gospel is repeatedly mentioned.

From these contents of John's Gospel, of the 'crisis' brought out through the sovereign, victorious, onward-striding 'I' of Christ placing Itself amongst humanity, between the adversaries, our gaze rises to the tremendous Imagination of mankind: here is the innermost meaning of the development of the Earth precisely as the very kernel turns itself in this present age towards the self-conscious soul of humanity. This is artistically encapsulated in the great sculpture carved out of wood that was originally intended for the interior of the first Goetheanum [Rudolf Steiner's working centre], destroyed by fire [1922/3]. The sculpture was saved before it was installed and today is housed in the second Goetheanum, CH-Dornach. 'The Representative of Humanity' between *Lucifer* and *Ahriman*, striding out in a sublime gesture, bringing both adversaries to ruin not through outer force, by judging or reproving, but only streaming out divine love. Yet you can see how, met by the rays of this love, Lucifer in the heights breaks his own wings, as, from the same love, Ahriman in the depths fetters himself in the Earth with golden chains of light.

Verbal explanations cannot exhaust the cosmically profound, universal meaning of this great world-Imagination, now re-found in the picture that John 6–10 places before us. Christ reinstates the lost human 'I' and human prototype; in the midst between the adversaries from above and from below, to left and to right, He proceeds in sublime, divine tranquillity between the efforts to set up a false earthly kingship of the one and the stoning of the other. In this attitude, as it were, in the middle, He holds the *balance*, the *Scales*, that becomes in this decisive cosmic hour *scales of judgment*, a division of the spirits, the crisis of humanity.

Thus we also find in the cosmic rhythm of John's Gospel, corresponding to the great Imagination of humanity, the picture of the heavenly script in the cosmic sign of the Scales. As the sign of the great I-AM, it holds the middle between the sign of light of the Virgin and the dark sign of the death-power of the Scorpion. The Scales, as the *sign of the I-AM*, the seventh of the twelve sacred heavenly signs, is at the same time the *sign of humanity*, of the human archetype. The other heavenly signs govern other 'hierarchies'; the Scales orients itself to the hierarchy on the point of becoming, still today incomplete, the *hierarchy of human beings,* in the sense of Genesis 1:27, created after the divine image, in the likeness of the divine. (On the meaning of this 'fourth hierarchy' and the nature of the divine human archetype, see the author's 'Genesis' in *From the Mysteries*, TL 2020, 21f., esp. 22). We recognize ever more clearly, more deeply, how after the first five 'Mystery-Chapters' of John's Gospel, the five following are 'Chapters of Crisis', in the most eminent sense *Chapters on Humanity*.

The Great Dispute

The chapter of John's Gospel giving an account of the characteristic 'oscillation of the scales', the whole conflict of the sign of the Scales with the upper sign (♍), then again with the lower sign (♏), becomes particularly clear when at the end of the chapter, after the narration of the Storm on the Lake and of the Walking of Christ on the Waves ('I AM: fear not!'), in the following proclamation of the bread of life again the sign of the Virgin (as also at the beginning of the chapter) appears equally emphasized. In this great dispute, the ever-repeated saying of Christ, 'I am the bread of life' ('The I-AM is the bread of life') resolves the innermost divine meaning of the sign of the Virgin. On the other hand, in the way in which the Jews cling ever again to the past, 'Our forefathers ate the manna in the wilderness' (John 6:31), in the way they still want to take the etheric life-nourishment from outside as a phenomenon of nature, not out of the 'I' grown to its full power, lies the error.

The occasion given for the great dispute is a scene that is told in John's Gospel following the episode of the Storm on the Lake, and has much in common with the story of the Feeding (6:21). It has to do with the fact that the people—essentially as we can gather from John 6:60, the members of the wider circle—see Christ Jesus where, according to the purely physical context of the event, he cannot be met. It is similar with the Storm on the Lake concerning an appearance of Christ in the supersensory, etheric realm, with the story of the Feeding and other etheric actions of Christ. Those coming from Tiberias were convinced before their journey, that Jesus was not voyaging with the disciples. (Between Tiberias and Capernaum, the disciples experience the Storm on the Lake with Christ Walking on the Waves.) In addition, there was no ship that could have taken Him. Nevertheless, they find Him after their crossing in Capernaum, that is, we are here dealing again with an experience in the supersensory-etheric sphere, a sign of the spiritual power of Christ. Here too, it is once again a case of Christ feeling a 'faith' of the people as intractable, when this 'faith' only through an outer magic is quenched through some kind of 'sign', when the action does not proceed from 'I' to 'I'. What the people should grasp, and first the disciples, is that which lies in the word 'I am the bread of life'—that is, 'in the "I" itself all the etheric activities of life can from now on be experienced'—this is precisely what they are not able to grasp. They still hang on to the traditional notions out of the old Mysteries of humanity, according to which the strength of the life-ether, of the heavenly 'bread of life', whose bearer was experienced as the heavenly 'Virgin with the sheaf' from outside, as it were, from the cosmic periphery, is initially experienced still from the stellar periphery, later still from the etheric surroundings of the Earth.

The Indians called this etheric stellar influence the 'heavenly soma', also 'the honey of the heavenly wilderness', recalling the nourishment of John the Baptist. Later the Indians still experienced the soma in the etheric world of the plant that bears its name. The final decadent manifestation of the old etheric heavenly forces is in the Old-Testament story of the etheric-atmospheric phenomenon that as 'manna' was served as food to the Hebrews in the desert. In its name (Heb. *man*) this manna signifies all the stellar Mysteries of the human being (*man, manes*), as discussed in the chapter on the 'Eternal Name' (Part One, Chapter 7).

The whole depiction as given in the Old Testament of this manna, then decaying on the Earth, expresses with eloquent clarity how it has to do here with a final product of the decadence of an old etheric splendour. The strengths of the Mysteries of the old 'bread of the stars' and 'heavenly bread' are dwindling; in the future it will no longer serve as nourishment for humanity. These strengths will be lost to humanity forever, unless they are able freshly to enliven the awoken 'I' to its full strength. Not out of itself would the 'I', fallen into unconsciousness and darkening, be able to find this full strength. Only the Deed of Christ has created the possibility, that the connection to the lost 'I' and therewith access to the source of life can be found once again.

This is not grasped by those who, out of Christ's saying, 'I am [the I-AM is] the bread of life', can do nothing other than only once again to request, 'Lord, give us this bread always'. These people always expect only from outside what they should find from within themselves, out of the strength of the awoken divine 'I'. In all animation Christ can say of Himself (6:35), 'I am the bread of life; he who comes to me shall not hunger, and he who believes in me shall never thirst'. But in this lies the meaning: 'The "I" is the bread of life. Whoever comes to the "I" will not hunger; and who takes the "I" into his heart, he will no longer thirst'. In a sublime sense the Mysteries of body and blood appear here as the most inner *Grail-Mystery of the 'I' awoken in Christ* (6:53ff.). The living, bright primordial substance of the flesh and blood darkened in the sinful human body and penetrated with the forces of death can be called into life afresh, to its 'I' awoken to its full power, out of the strength in Christ.

We can have an inkling how hard it was for the disciples to grasp this saying of Christ (6:60), for that time unheard of, how for them the meaning of such words indeed appeared truly unbearable (the Greek word σκληρός *skleros* 'hard'—one thinks of 'scleroticize'—expresses clearly the ahrimanic hardening of the human being, that locks the living meaning in Christ's saying). The whole vexation of humanity (6:61) awakens with the words of Christ. Precisely here we clearly recognize how the whole crisis of humanity—it enters here initially as the crisis of the disciples, of the larger group, later also the smaller group of disciples—according to its most inner being is a *crisis of the 'I', the ego*. It brings human beings to hopeless despair, when they feel, as it happens here through Christ called to the full power of their 'I', to full responsibility, they fail. And we can appreciate how that which initially is revealed as the crisis of the disciples, soon breaks out as the greater conflict of humanity.

***

We could experience in John 6, in connection with the 'Last-Supper events' of the miracle of the Feeding of the Five Thousand and Christ's saying 'I am the bread of life', how the first difficulty (perhaps already announced in John 4:27ff.) arises both in the extended group and in the smaller group of disciples. John 7 shows how the crisis of the disciples advances to become the crisis of humanity. This crisis of humanity, already experienced in the beginning of John 5, now breaks out in full.

We see Christ, Whom we initially saw only at work in certain Mystery-groups and Mystery-contexts, almost hesitating to take the fateful step of difficulty and decision that He now undertakes. He knows exactly how the re-appearing 'I' in its divinity has inevitably to call up conflict in human souls. And consequently

He answers His brothers—they are actually his step-brothers who urge Him to show Himself to the people at the feast—'My time has not yet come, but your time is always here' [John 7:6], that is, 'the time of the "I", the world-hour of the "I", is not yet arrived; it is still the time of the human being moulded through the adversary, the time of denying the "I", the darkening of the "I", the world-hour of Lucifer and Ahriman'. When He does in fact go up to Jerusalem, He remains initially in private [7:10]. It is as if we experience here especially clearly how Christ, as Steiner once said, could take no other step than out of the lawfulness of the stars in the cosmos, out of the cosmic rhythm of world-events. Only when He recognizes that now, as it were, the cosmic stellar moment has come, does He speak publicly before the people. The time of year chosen by Him for this, equivalent to our Michaelmas to which that feast of the Jews is connected, as was shown, stands with the sign of the Scales of the I-AM, the sign of world-crisis.

Motifs from John 5 work into the conflict breaking out in John 7, through linking the healing on the Sabbath to the flared-up dispute. Essentially it has to do with experiencing this chapter as a whole, to perceive, as it were, the world-symphonic viewpoints governing everywhere in John's Gospel. In it we see, or perhaps rather hear, how in shrill discords, in shocking disharmonies, the hitherto only prepared conflict now breaks out into a full drama. Everything reaches us like a wild, chaotic weaving of different voices talking past each other, till in the midst of the wild, wrong notes there sounds ever again the sublime saying of Christ, carried by the cosmic harmony.

That saying itself releases from the astonishing confession from the myrmidons of the Pharisees, who are sent out to trap Christ Jesus, 'No man ever spoke like this man!' (7:46). 'But no one laid hands on him, because his hour had not yet come' (7:30, 44). The split lies not only between Christ and the Jews, between the divine and the 'I' darkened by the adversary, but separate groups of people are themselves gripped by the split (7:43)—darkness rages against darkness.

The people look to Christ for the very adversary who darkens consciousness for them (7:20)! And Christ tells them precisely the deepest reason for their split: 'Where I am you cannot come' (7:34), that is, where the 'I' is, you are just unable to find access. And the conflict will get ever more acute, the misunderstandings of people ever more hopeless.

Living Water

In inner connection with the great motif of the previous chapter, 'I am the bread of life', there now stands Christ's saying, in which we can glimpse the climax, the actual 'I'-motif of John 7 (Part One, Chapter 6). This saying He himself first speaks at that moment when the whole feast reaches its climax: 'He who believes in me, as the scripture has said, out of his heart shall flow rivers of living water' (7:38).

'I am the bread of life' has to with the whole Mystery of *body and blood in the 'I' and out of the strength of the 'I'*. Here the human creature facing the divine creator is, as it were, the receiver. With what Christ now speaks (7:38), the 'I' is not concerned with what it receives or retains for itself. It takes the great stream of cosmic life not only for itself, but it gives it again; it becomes a point of transmission for this stream of life. From here, it wants to bestow blessing in all directions, pouring this out on all creatures. The human body, whose innermost 'I' can come into contact again with the forces of the stars, will be streamed through by etheric forces. This pours out as a fresher stream of life dispensing blessing and healing everywhere. Right through every chapter of John's Gospel, stage by stage we see the magic of the 'I' proclaimed by Christ striding ever higher, so that it thereby contains ever again a new piece of the human future.

Nicodemus

In the midst of the wild conflict of voices—ever and again drowning the sublimity of Christ's words—as it reaches our ears in John 7, the one person who perceives, or at least intuits, the true Mysteries of the 'I' is Nicodemus, who once had that significant discussion with Christ in meditative nocturnal experience. He is the only one amongst the Pharisees who challenges their inner old-fashioned attitudes, who feels the unreliability of everything past, all the old Mystery-traditions and wisdom of the schools, is impotent to grasp the new and future-bearing impulse that now in Christ has been placed amongst the people.

- Not for nothing is the Mystery of the crisis, of 'judgment' that has now come over humanity, conveyed through Christ precisely to Nicodemus in his meditation-experience (John 3:19). He is the one who in deep

meditation has taken in something of the significance of the 'great decision' now taking place, the crisis of humanity.
- Not for nothing does the gospel of John, by naming Nicodemus (John 7:50) especially here recall the nocturnal meditation-experience, his spiritual encounter then with Christ. And so in this critical hour he alone warningly holds up to the other Pharisees the 'seriousness of the scales of judgment', that forbids judging a man before he has been examined and charged with his deed.

2.
The Woman caught in Adultery and Stoning
(John 8)

In John 7 we experience the full outbreak and in John 8 something like the climax of this crisis of humanity that has been conjured up through the Christ-'I' placed amongst humanity and its adversary. The description of the great conflict becomes increasingly dramatically acute. The *motif of judgment* in the sign of the Scales appears initially as a spiritual picture and its spiritual process in the *words* of Christ Jesus. John 8 goes over to what always takes place to present this dramatic picture of an earthly scene of judgment. The motif of the whole section of the gospel (Chapters 6–10): Christ, the Representative of Humanity between the adversaries, the I-AM of Christ, Who carries the fullness of the Light of the World in Himself (John 8:12) between the earthly power of light and the power of darkness, the Scales of Judgment, the just balance between the Virgin and the Scorpion, [all this] appears here in John 8 in dramatic pictures.

Higher critics of the gospel text question the origin of the whole introductory episode of John 8:1-11, 'Christ and the woman taken in adultery'. It is as if that power, which in the tremendous pictures of John 8 is brought into the light, itself turns against these pictures. (One finds the questionable passage, especially in editions of the Greek text, only in the section of 'Notes', the important passages even in the 'Further Notes'.) To understand the whole context, a spiritual consideration precisely of this passage of the gospel cannot be renounced. It originates from the most genuine spiritual Inspiration, grasped with most sure Intuition the innermost leading and governing motif of the whole section of the gospel, presented to us in a grandiose picture in Imaginative clarity. For the dramatic composition of the whole chapter, indeed of the entire section of the gospel (Chapters 6–10), this introductory episode of John 8 gives the actual key. That which in a certain sense (cf. John 3:19) governs this passage, indeed the whole of John's Gospel, working initially and directly right into John 9, this great I-AM saying of Christ, 'I am the light of the world; he who follows me will not walk in darkness, but will have the light of life'

(John 8:12), receives the full effect of its full dramatic inner strength just through the way it appears at the close of the episode of 'Christ and the woman taken in adultery'. Whoever has but a faint sense for the Mysteries of the symphonic and dramatic composition of the gospels, will not want to place this motif 'I am the light of the world' without more ado at the beginning of the chapter.

Judgment and Crisis

The whole *motif of the scales of judgment*, so decisive for these Chapters of Crisis (6–10), contains now in John 8, firstly through the full dramatic clarity and visibility that in the pictures of the earthly scene of judgment are directly presented, how Christ judges differently from human judges. The meaning of the 'judging' here, released through the 'I' in the sign of the cosmic scales in the I-AM—notice the *ich* ['I'] in the German word *richten* ['to judge']—is different from what people associate with earthly judging. Thus are solved, too, all apparent contradictions between the different 'words for judging' out of the mouth of Christ in John's Gospel.

So, when it says (3:17), 'For God sent the Son into the world, not to condemn the world, but that the world might be saved through him', and then once again (5:22), 'The Father judges no one, but has given all judgment to the Son'. Or in John 8:15, 'You judge according to the flesh, I judge no one' and immediately after, 'Yet even if I do judge, my judgment is true;[79] for it is not I alone that judge, but I and the Father who sent me. It is written in your law that the testimony of two men is true'. 'I have much to say about you and much to judge' (8:26). 'For judgment I came into this world' (9:39). 'Now is the judgment of this world' (12:31). The word in the original text, usually translated 'to judge', is everywhere the Greek κρίνειν (krinein), from which is derived the noun κρίσις (krisis), that is also always used here in the meaning of the original text ('crisis').

κρίνειν means, literally 'to divide', and κρίσις, the 'crisis', the 'verdict' is actually the 'division of spirits', that comes to effect through the 'I', the Christ-'I' of the middle. The 'division of spirits' in John's Gospel is most clearly spoken in John 12:31, 'Now is the judgment of this world, now shall the ruler of this world be cast out'. But precisely because this 'verdict', this division of the spirits through the 'I', uses the freedom of the human being, it does not come about through a judicial coercive force. The German word *'richten'* ['judge'], in which the Intuition of the genius of language has included the word *'ich'* ['I'], can be felt to render really expressively what John's Gospel understands with κρίνειν and κρίσις (crisis).

Christ—this is the thought—judges indeed differently from human beings, than an earthly judge. The 'I' judges differently from the coercive force of the adversaries who want to suppress the 'I'. And all this is presented in John's Gospel not in conceptual abstractions, but is dramatically and pictorially visible in the scene of judgment where we see Christ in the middle between the judging, damning Pharisees and the young woman accused of adultery. Here Christ shows the human beings who cannot fathom Him, cannot fathom the 'I', through the living deed, *how He judges*, how the 'I' decides.

People have always pointed to the wonderful mildness that is revealed in the way, as at the end of this scene, after the accusers convicted by their own conscience have crept away, Christ turns to the woman. To His question, 'Woman, where are they? Has no one condemned you?' she answers, 'No one, Lord'. He says, 'Neither do I condemn you [*so the 'I' also leaves you free*]; go, and do not sin again.' Only more lies in the words than at first glance.

Precisely when we look in this way at the divine mildness of Christ, Who does not judge as human beings, Who does not condemn, but Who raises the accused, lifts her again to the height of her lost 'I', to that 'I' that leaves human beings free and makes them free, allowing them to breathe freely again in the light of the world, then it could be obvious that for our part we look with the right feeling at the dark, loveless accusers, the 'self-righteous, hypocritical Pharisees', those who support themselves on the rigid letters of dead legal words, who raise stones against their fellow sister. And it is certainly true that no one has found harder words against Pharisaism, against all dark, sanctimonious clericalism than Christ Jesus. Indeed, we may probably say, that amongst all earthly-human manifestations of the might of darkness, of the dark adversary, He was disgusted by *this* most of all. John, who is the furthest advanced above this dark Pharisaism, himself places this motif, the least of all these judging words of Christ (cf. Matt. 23:13ff., Luke 11:39ff.), in the foreground. He lets the facts in the effective scene of John 8 speak for themselves.

It corresponds to the Johannine attitude when we leave the words of judgment on the Scribes and Pharisees to Christ Himself. We all so easily repress in ourselves rising feelings of judgment also against the earthly judge; then the deep, moving pictures of John 8 themselves offer us the key to understand the problem.

Stoning

Significantly, over the entrance and exit of John 8 stands the *motif of stoning*. At the beginning it is the adulteress whom the Pharisees want to stone according to the Law of Moses, and at the end they lift up stones against Christ Jesus Himself. So tremendous in this section of John's Gospel is the dramatic intensification.

Let us take the whole motif of 'stoning' and stoning out of the deeper, cosmic backgrounds out of the 'cosmic rhythm'. Externally seen the Pharisees lift stones against their fellow sister, and finally against Christ Jesus Himself. Seen more from within, the event appears differently. The more we endeavour to see with the loving eyes of Christ Himself into all their judging strictness at the Mystery of the event, we recognize that the stone the Pharisees raise here is actually on their own hearts. It is the 'stiffening' and hardening of their hearts that makes them lift the stone against their fellow sister, and against Christ Jesus Himself. The pressure of the law written on tablets of stone, whose original divinely alive meaning they no longer grasp, weighs on their hearts. They no longer know how to release themselves and their fellow human beings from the deadly pressure of these tablets.

The motif of stoning, and in it the *Mystery of the stone itself*, lies over the whole of John 8. What is this Mystery of the stone? Can we get deeper to the bottom of it in the cosmic light, in the light of the world, that radiates so mightily out of John's Gospel itself? Who, in the light that Rudolf Steiner has lit in anthroposophic spirit-knowledge, is able to see into, will intuitively recognize, how in the stone, in everything mineral, still the final condensation of the primordial spiritual substance, of the divine primordial light is contained, how that which we experience in the visible-tangible 'material', is actually the negative of the spiritual primordial reality, the *shadow of the light* (cf. Part One, Chapter 6). Ahriman, the power of darkness, has brought about in human consciousness the whole contradictory notion of the nature of matter. He has darkened the primordial consciousness into what today we call our consciousness. This whole 'darkening of the primordial consciousness' in *the becoming of the stone*, of the mineralizing of the Earth, lies precisely in the context of the becoming of the human 'I' that happened prematurely with the 'Fall of man'. Novalis speaks of this in his story *The Novices of Sais*: 'May not Nature have been turned to stone by the gaze of God? Or for sheer terror at the advent of man? ...'[80] In the 'Mystery of the "I"', of the relationship of the human 'I' to the divine 'I' that stands over this whole section of John's Gospel (Chapters 6–10), the riddle of the stone also lies hidden, which in John 8 (as also later) plays a role in the motif of stoning and of 'hardening of the heart'.

In the realm of the stone, Rudolf Steiner always emphasized, in the mineral element of the Earth, the power of darkness, Ahriman, is the legitimate lord. Evil—i.e. what works against development—first exists where this petrifying might, which, enchanting archetypal light into dark earthly substance, does not contain itself within its legitimate realm. It penetrates where the progressive world-will always wanted to ray in the world-light, the world of truth, and where through Christ's sacrificial Deed it can shine again. This is where 'the Earth has remained Sun' in the human heart.[81]

Since one of the two adversaries [Lucifer] in the 'Fall of man' put the deceptive apparent light and apparent 'I' in the place of the true, divine, archetypal light, the true 'I', meant that the other adversary, the Lord of Darkness, was able to darken the light of the heart for human beings. This brought the heart into rigidity and petrification, subjected it, as it were, to the laws of the stone. Consequently, the stony tablets of the Law weigh so heavily on the hearts of those who raise stones against their fellow sister. Through the rigid and petrified penetration of the power of darkness, as through an evil magic or curse, love in their heart has died to such a shocking degree.

Where, however, between both adversaries does the cosmic light of Christ stand? Do we not find also for this sublime Mystery, for the Christ-Mystery, a picture in the realm of nature? Does not a manifestation in the realm of the minerals exist, in which we could sense the primordial Mystery of the light of all earthly material? We all know this manifestation of the mineral, the *crystal*, which, as it were, still speaks to us of its origin in the light.

Crystals

Already the wonderful word *crystal*, which in its original significance speaks to us of the phenomenon of ice, of the ice-crystal and snow-crystal, but also signifies the mineral crystal, especially the mountain crystal—does it not appear to us through its sounds to speak of Mysteries of Christ and miracles of Christ, of primordial Mysteries, recalling to us much that links in Ancient Egypt to the name *Isis*? The ice-crystal of the snowflake tells us of the mother of material, Isis.[82] These crystals, when enlivened in the 'I', become Mysteries of Christ. Mysteries of Christ appear before the soul in the miracle of the world of crystals. Are there not *in the crystal* somehow indicated *cosmic Mysteries of light and cosmic Mysteries of the stars, which become in Christ Mysteries of the Earth*?

Christ, the bearer of the cosmic 'I', who speaks of Himself: 'I am the light of the world' (John 8:12)—has He not bound Himself deeply with the Mysteries of earthly matter, in which the purity of the cosmic light shines enchanting into the darkness? Has He, Who in His innermost Being is spiritual Sunlight, Himself chosen the Earth as his Body, in order to redeem her from the curse of her darkening, the spell of her enchantment, in order Himself to lead her again to become a spiritual Sun? Indeed, Christ, the Light of the World, *stands in truth between the Stone and the Light*, the two poles of cosmic becoming; He stands where we in the realm of nature and her pictorial script find the *crystal*. He is utterly founded on inner connections, on the Mystery of the world itself, to have pointed to the connections of the sounds of the words *crystal* and *Christ*, although we know very well the different origins and derivations of both words.

As the crystal stands in the realm of natural manifestation, *Christ* stands in His earthly manifestation in the realm of the spiritual becoming *between the Stone and the Light*. All the Mysteries of John 8 could lead us in the light of this fact to a deep understanding. The divine 'I', that out of the purity of the cosmic light that formed all things in the primordial light of creation, has within it clothed Itself with an earthly Body—It could grow out of those forces which through the human 'ego'-darkening have brought about this earthly ego. In Christ the divine 'ego', or 'I', has the power, again to release the spell of enchantment through the earthly apparent-'I' to raise the human 'I' again to its divine origin. For this reason it allows us to experience in a tremendous manner, and at the same time in the double manner, John 8: the *judging might* of the divine ego in Christ.

> [i] On this one occasion facing the earthly judges, to whom Christ only said the word ('Let him who is without sin among you be the first throw a stone at her' [John 8:7]), resulted that they themselves speak the verdict, converted by the voice of their conscience; they slink away silent and beaten. The picture of the wooden sculpture of the Christ-group in CH-Dornach, the 'Representative of Mankind' between the two adversaries who judge themselves, appears again profoundly before the soul.

[ii] But towards the woman, the young adulteress—whose 'I' is bound by the deadly sin, held under the spell of un-freedom—the judging power of the divine 'I' in Christ works in such a way that it allows the fallen one to hold her head again freely towards the Light of the Word, in which also her own higher 'I' originates. Christ, the bearer of the divine 'I', indeed judges differently from human judges. They always want to raise stones against their fellow sister, only want to lynch and stone. *The Pharisees want to execute (hinrichten); Christ raises (richtet auf)*—this is what speaks to us so tremendously, so upliftingly about this episode in John 8.

Virgin and Scorpion

Christ between the Stone and the Light, where the crystal stands in the realm of nature—could we perhaps discover this great motif of John 8 in the cosmic script? As we saw, over the whole section of the gospel (Chapters 6–10) stands the *Scales* as the sign of the divine I-AM, between the bright sign of the *Virgin*, where a point of attack is sought in the case of the deviation of the luciferic tempter, and the dark sign of death of the *Scorpion*, where a point of attack is offered in the case of the deviation of the ahrimanic tempter.

Are not the Pharisaic accusers also seduced by the deceptive apparent light of the one tempter, fallen to the power of darkness? Had not the exposition of Mark's Gospel, as also within John's Gospel that of Chapter 5, shown how all the tragedy of the Jewish people and its Pharisaism is connected with the Scorpion's power of death? From there everything proceeds which brought the divine primordial light into the darkening, rigidity and petrification, which even opens the area of the light of the human heart to the penetration of those darkening and petrifying powers.

And does there not lie in the same corner, in the realm of the Scorpion's sting of death that point where the young adulteress fell into sin, into aberration? (MG 29f.). At no other place in these whole chapters [6-10] is it clearer than here, how we always have before us the judging *Scales of the Christ-'I'* in the midst between the Virgin and the Scorpion's sign of death. The power (♏) that brings the human soul into temptation, into darkening of consciousness, into crisis, becomes revealed in this Johannine chapter from ever-new aspects. From earlier (MG 122f., 276ff.), we recall how the sign of the Scorpion (♏) actually came about from the deadly arrow of the Archer wounding the Virgin. The Scales, dividing and protecting, placed itself between

Scorpion and Virgin. Not astronomical but spiritual backgrounds of world-events are indicated, which are connected with the effects on the human constitution by the Fall of human nature and on the nature of the world.

And in the case of the young adulteress of John 8, earthly virginity (♍) is wounded through the Scorpion's power of death (♏). But the I-AM of Christ in the sign of the Scales appears judging, yet with Christ that means: giving direction, raising, raising up to the light in the middle. The great motif of John 8 is *Christ between Stone and Light*, between the darkening and the petrifying power of death (♏) and the spiritual power of light (♍). It appears like this: Christ, overcoming the power of sin (♏), which robs the human soul of virginity, leads the soul again to the heights of light, from whose virginity it bestows itself ever afresh in a higher, spiritual sense—as John in his Initiation had experienced the soul's becoming virgin again through overcoming the Scorpion's sting of death (MG 122f., 276ff.).

The Woman, Johannine Initiation and the Magdalene

Here the whole introductory episode of John 8, and with it the meaning of the sign of the Virgin, which appears in a new light with the Scorpion, and the Scales holding the balance in the middle over the whole passage. The I-AM of Christ draws the fallen one out of the depths of sin and darkness of death up to the heights of cosmic light, bestowing on her in the spiritual sense a new higher virginity (♍). The woman experienced something deeply overwhelming her whole soul, something burning, or, as it were, melting, transforming her whole being, who in this destiny-laden manner was allowed to meet the Christ. She experienced a completely new birth out of the heights of cosmic light, a new existence had opened up from this hour onwards.

With reference to the exposition on Mark's Gospel (MG 122f., 227ff.), it has already been mentioned how the meaning of this spiritual becoming-virgin-again is deeply connected with the Mysteries of the Johannine Initiation. Unlike Mark's Gospel, where the Johannine Initiation is an insight that can be gained, it does not form the primary content in John's Gospel, which is more a pure gospel of Christ and gospel of humanity. Initiation is only dealt with in passing. Only occasionally is the initiation of the disciples and the destiny of the disciples directly touched on in John's Gospel. Only the Farewell-Chapters following the raising of Lazarus and again the two final, Resurrection-Chapters (see Part One, Chapter 4) are in the actual sense 'Chapters on the Disciples'. The disciples' motif otherwise plays a certain role only under different motifs. After the calling of the disciples in John 1 and occasionally sounding in John 2, 3 and 4, initially significantly sounding again in John 6, it quietly chimes in. Out of the crisis of the remaining disciples, we can increasingly sense that the becoming of the disciple John, the gradual completion of his initiation, is now emphasized. Not, as with Mark, as the focus, but only as on a distant background we see all this shifted to John. Not once is the disciple (John) named; in John's Gospel, John himself completely steps back with his whole personality behind the narrated events.

Only quite softly and as if from a distance, by looking up at the same time to the cosmic constellation, in the 'motif of becoming-virgin-again' we sense how in John 8 it meets us at the same time as a motif of Johannine Initiation. Certainly, the episode at the beginning of John 8 might remind us of the 'sinner' in Luke 7, who, to the annoyance and envy of the Pharisees, is also held aloft by Christ, of that story which again stands in such an obvious relationship to that other one in Mark 14 and in John 12 where the one-time sinner like a priest performs on Christ Himself a sacramental deed. How far the whole incident and context alongside the absolutely possible, indeed probable, outer actuality also has it spiritual significance, how it intimately relates to the initiation-experiences of John himself, whose own spiritual experiences—his whole inner advance from the curse of Cain on mankind to a new virginity, reflected in the experience of the sister-soul—all this is discussed in the detailed presentation of Mark's Gospel (MG 284ff.). There, moreover, the purely outer circumstances are indicated, how it comes between the various 'Magdalene stories' and the three 'wakings from the dead' in the gospel. When we look from here once more to John 8, we can become aware how—indeed already purely externally—we are approaching the third of these awakenings, the one immediately decisive for the initiation of John, the 'raising of Lazarus' (John 11).

Not for outer reasons does the 'Magdalene story', as it is told at the beginning of John 8, have to relate to the earthly figure of Mary Magdalene. If this story also in the strongest and most living manner awakes the impression of outer actuality, appearing as a picture true to life, as an encounter of Christ with humanity that really did happen, this still in no way says that this woman was the later Mary Magdalene. Indeed, this cannot for a moment be taken here as probable.

More important for the manner of contemplation is another point of view. As is frequently the case with the narration of the gospel, this whole episode, apart from its possible outer actuality, can be seen as a *picture for a specific spiritual event*, for specific spiritual processes. Only then do we arrive, in a purely spiritual sense, at the sphere of Mary Magdalene and with her approach the initiation of John. Then it can be said, what Christ then did and brought about for the young adulteress placed precisely in the middle of the 'Chapters of Crisis' can be seen as a picture for that which took place at that time in the soul of John himself as he goes towards his initiation, regaining his inner virginity, and what then takes place in the spiritual experience of the sister-soul, in what is reflected as the 'Magdalene-experience' raised up to the 'Mary-experience'.

Writing in the Earth

With His finger Christ twice *writes in the earth* (John 8:6 & 8). It is one of the most significant features of the episode at the beginning of John 8. The natural thought[83] that he *writes the obligations of the adulteress in the Earth*, is confirmed by Rudolf Steiner in his lecture-courses on John's Gospel. In this writing into the Earth of the account of destiny and account of debts we touch on a Johannine motif, which later in the Apocalypse appears as the *Book of Destiny* (to be distinguished from the *Book of Life*). It is the same as what the Indian calls *karma* (*karma*, 'deed', i.e., self-motivated, from *kr* '*creare*' 'to do, to make'). Steiner emphasizes that Christ had reasons not yet publicly to confide the fact of *karma* and rebirth. Only by looking into the 'repeated earthly life' can the Mystery of the spiritual effect of deeds, '*karma*', be rightly understood. (For the way He speaks on this to His disciples, see the beginning of John 9, Matthew 17:11-13 and other gospel passages.) Christ did not give a theoretical teaching on '*karma*', Steiner emphasizes, but in the way He writes the account of obligations of the adulteress into the Earth, He objectively states the fact of the law of *karma*. With this, Christ says to the people, no other verdict on this woman is necessary, because indeed her obligations are anyhow written in the 'Book of Destiny', if one may use the Johannine expression.

The circumstance is especially significant how Christ writes into the Earth what is recorded of the account of debts into the spiritual book of obligations to the world, in the Book of Destiny of the woman (her '*karma*'). He *writes in the Earth, and precisely in the Earth* which He Himself had chosen as his Body, with which He Himself is united, is about to unite ever more. Christ, who is offering Himself to the Earth and earthly humanity, takes the *debt of humanity on to Himself*; not in the sense that the personal balance of deeds thereby would become meaningless, but in the sense that some *karma* or other, some deed or other, can no longer weigh down, no longer hinder human beings from holding their heads up again to the spiritual light, to feel accepted again in freedom in the kingdom of human spiritual activity. (On this important issue, see Steiner's last lecture-cycle before the Great War, *Christ and the Human Soul*. Norrköping. 12-16 July 1914. GA 155.) In the episode with the adulteress this raising again to the heights of spiritual light ('I am the light of the world …') and the original virginity of the human essence is very expressively revealed.

That Christ writes the woman's obligations *into the Earth*, can be understood in an even deeper sense precisely as the facts of *karma* in the light of the three cosmic signs governing the whole section of the gospel, when we add to the aspects of the zodiac signs the already-discussed planetary influences (see Part One, Chapters 3 & 4). The I-AM of Christ in the sign of the Scales between the Scorpion and the Virgin corresponds, as we have seen, to the great motif of *Christ between Stone and Light*. The contrast is between the earthly darkening and hardening and the heavenly origin of light, of virginity (virginity in the spiritual sense is in itself heavenly, which through the hardening, darkening forces of the Earth is wounded and destroyed). All *karma*, all karmic effects of deeds is connected in a certain sense with the whole manner how through the Fall of man the Earth has fallen out of the whole connected life of the cosmos, become hardened in itself and fixed. The 'Fall of man' in this sense really is a *fall*, a falling out of the heights into the depths of matter, into earthly darkening.

From the aspect of the planets, the lowering, degrading forces lie in that which Mars in Scorpion does, whereas as long as heavenly virginity exists, the spiritual essence of Venus was united with Mercury in the sign of the Virgin. Only with the division that occurred in the Fall of man, in the 'Fall of Lucifer', does Venus approach the Earth. Venus, the heavenly gemstone, was once the homeland of Lucifer. Before his Fall, Lucifer was an angel radiating light in divine magnificence. In his Fall the crown [Venus], drops from the fallen heavenly leader and was placed by Christ in the Scales, which henceforth is the 'house' of Venus in her heavenly revelation as *Venus Urania*.

Mercury, however, remained in the house of the Virgin. (The widespread practice of mutually exchanging [the names] of Mercury and Venus in Middle-Age astrology not only serves to make occult things obscure for the profane mind, but is connected with the primordial Mysteries touched on above.)

Where heavenly virginity is re-won in the Johannine sense everywhere meant here, Mercury and Venus are spiritually united again in the sign of the Virgin. One thinks of the Mystery of the word 'hermaphrodite' (*Hermes = Mercury, Aphrodite = Venus*), when it is not a physical abnormality but in the higher spiritual sense that it also possesses, taken in the sense of the spiritual primordial fact touched on by Christ in Mark 10:6—cf. also Mark 12:25—in connection with Genesis 1:27 (MG 215ff.).

Seen from the earthly aspect, that is, from the circumstances that entered through the *karma* of the Fall of man, Venus—precisely as Venus Urania—stands as the heavenly redeemed Love, in the sign of the Scales. The young adulteress, who through an aberration in love—♂ in ♏—fell into the obligation of sin, is through the divine love of Christ—♀ in ♎—raised again to the original source of light of the heavenly virginity (primordial union of ♀ and ☿ in ♍). We recall the revelation of Venus Urania, ♀ in ♎, with the Storm on the Lake (John 6), where Christ's divine being of Love with the tranquillity of the eternal I-AM in the sign of ♎ brings the Storm on the Lake and the storm in the soul to peace.

How far Mars in the Scorpion, which for the sin of the adulteress was the ruling might, also appears sounding out of the word ἁμαρτία (*hamartia*—'sin, debt, obligation') of the Greek original—the quality of Mars is heard; it is linked to Mars—(in the episode at the beginning, initially it appears in certain derivations, in John 8:21ff. frequently in the quoted form). Cosmically seen, *harmartia*, the debt of the woman, seems to be the daemonic effects of Mars. Venus, wounded through Mars in the Scorpion would be the kind of astrological expression for that which in John 8 stands before us as the spiritual constellation. And that Christ writes the obligations of the woman, this cosmic influence of Mars *in the Earth*, can be significant for us in the light of the first part of this book, discussed under 'Signs and Constellations'. Everywhere, where it has to do with *karma*, the working of destiny and the 'Book of Destiny', initially the *sign* appears, i.e. the *relationship of the planets to the Earth* and to the earthly zodiac is important. And only where *karma* is overcome, where the region of the 'Eternal Name' that is entered into the 'Book of Life' is achieved, does the actual world of the stars come into consideration.

Through the daemonic effect of Mars the soul is estranged from this region, exiled into the darkness of Earth and dependency on the Earth, weighed down with an entry in the 'Book of Destiny'. Only when the obligation in the Book of Destiny is wiped out, can the forgotten name standing in the Book of Life light up again in the starry script. A time will come when people will understand how we are led through John's Gospel into the depths of a new, 'Christened' astrology. And it will be recognized how far precisely John 8 contains significant signposts in this direction.

***

To the Jews all this is an annoyance and a foolishness. They do not see the light of the divine Ground of the World standing behind Christ, the world of light of the Father, speaking and revealing itself through Him. The power of death has bound them to the earthly element and estranged them from their cosmic origins. Christ has to say to them: 'You are from below, I am from above; you are of this world, I am not of this world' [John 8: 23]. The ultimate foundations for this saying are Mysteries of the stars. Here, too, we recognize the Mars-power in the Scorpion as the power that has estranged the earthly human from the cosmic context. 'Everyone who sins is a slave to sin (*hamartia*)' (John 8:34), falls before the coercing power of Mars, whereas the One working out of the powers of the light of the upper world, Christ, knowing Himself one with the divine Father as the light-filled cosmic ground, places the *Mystery of freedom* before human beings: 'If you hold to my teaching, you are really my disciples. Then you will know the truth [ἀλήθεια *a-letheia* the world of the clear, light-filled, unquenchable consciousness, see Part One, 6] and the truth will set you free ... if the Son sets you free, you will be free indeed' [John 8:31, 36]. As the decisive 'I'-motif of John 8, besides the one 'out of the divine "I" the regained higher virginity', the other appears here: '*out of the "I" and in the "I" the true freedom*'. Christ speaks here of freedom, which is the actual fulfilment of the human being. This freedom which is not arbitrary, or a whim, but especially a working in union with the divine cosmic Ground, a working in the divine ('I am the light of the world'), that is, a working from above, whereas daemonic compulsions lay hold of the human being from below. The purely cognitive development of this Johannine thought is contained in Rudolf Steiner's *The Philosophy of Freedom*.

The human soul, fettered by these coercive powers, caught and darkened in the errors of sin, can no longer penetrate the world of light of the Father, the light of divine truth out of which Christ works; the soul is consequently no longer able to find the way from the Father to the Son, to gain freedom in the 'I'. The world of the dark adversary obtrudes before the world of the light. Ahriman, as is revealed with arresting clarity with the Jewish Pharisees in John 8, has taken over the place of the divine Father, as he takes that place today for anyone who can only understand the world as the working together of dead, natural necessities and the coercive powers given through nature.

Towards the end of the chapter, ever more grandiose, ever more deeply moving, the picture is fashioned of Christ as the divine Representative of Humanity between the adversaries. The climax comes when Christ has to say to the Jews (John 8:44 NIV): 'You belong to your father, the devil [Ahriman] and you want to carry out your father's desire. He was a murderer from the beginning, not holding to the truth [in the light of cosmic clarity], for there is no truth in him. When he lies, he speaks his native language, for he is a liar and the father of lies.' More than any other, the phrase concerning freedom in the 'I' awakens wild, confusing conflict in the human soul darkened by the adversary. Like a picture of the world-judgment itself, the great entrance appears in John 8 arising out of the judgment scene at the beginning and linking everywhere to its motifs of earthly verdict-making (John 8:13-18). Increasingly dramatic, increasingly disturbing it narrows to a point, until the Jews, no longer recognizing the eternal Father in the light of the world, raise up stones against Christ-Jesus because of the saying that wells up out of the depths of the eternal 'I', 'Before Abraham was, I am'. This chapter, over whose whole content there lies the Mystery of the stone, begins and ends with stoning. 'And he passed through the midst of them and went away.'

3.
The Healing of the Man born Blind
(John 9)

For the 'cosmic symphonic' style and structure of John's Gospel, where everywhere some motif characteristically works on and sounds on in the ensuing chapter, the transition from John 8 to John 9 appears especially significant. The great saying of Christ, 'I am the light of the world', in John 8, in the middle of the whole section of the gospel, indeed of the whole Gospel of St John, that which in Chap. 8 can be felt as a potent ending to the episode of 'The Woman taken in Adultery' lights up mightily in John 9. In Christ's healing of 'The Man born Blind' it comes, as it were, to effect; out of the depths of the cosmic light the might of the divine 'I' is revealed in the darkness of Earth.

The cosmic aspect of this section of the gospel, the Scales as the sign of the cosmic-'I' between earthly light (♍) and earthly darkness (♏), becomes especially clearer with this saying of Christ, 'I am the light of the world', and with the healing of the blind man proceeding out of the spirit of this saying. We glimpse the *Scales* between these two signs oscillating hither and thither in all sorts of tensions. Among the human senses the sense of sight, we recall, is to be found in the *Virgin* (MG 32, 176f.). This is the great motif of John 9: the *Scales* of the I-AM of Christ between the power of light of earthly eyesight (♍), and the power of darkness that closes the earthly eyes (the physical as well as the spiritual) in blindness (♏)—Christ out of the depths of the cosmic light in the full power of the divine 'I' bestows earthly eyesight on the man born blind. We will recognize the inner harmony of the gospel, how also in Mark's Gospel with the healing of the blind man narrated there (Mark 8:22-26), the cosmic rhythm leads to the Scales (MG 176).

In John's Gospel, to all this comes the aspect of the 'I'-crisis, the 'division of spirits'. In the ordering, straightening sign of the Scales, the I-AM of Christ occasions the division between the one born blind and the Pharisees. The one born blind, the 'blind seer', is open for the spiritual light and consequently through Christ is awoken to earthly sight. The Pharisees, the 'sighted people who are blind', in their spiritually bright presumption have nevertheless lost the truthfulness of the flowing, spiritual beholding out of the forces of the heart (John 9:39): 'For judgment I came into this world, that those who do not see may see, and that those who see may become blind'—that is, it becomes obvious they are blind. In this respect, one can compare the other healing of the blind man in Mark 10:46ff. (MG 238f.).

It was pointed out earlier (MG 20f.) how convincingly the narration here of John 9 in its eloquent vitality awakens the impression of outer actuality, the whole way things happened at that time in Palestine. Notice in the narration, for example, especially the way the neighbours and the parents of the blind man are introduced (John 9:8, 18-23), all the confused, chaotic voices reaching us in this chapter. Truly, a dramatist wrote John, Chapter 9, who like no other knew how to listen and thereby also lay hold of what was happening on the surface of the earthly and historical scene. Consequently, whatever else may happen, we may not surrender this aspect of the outer actuality for John 9.

What can especially strike one with the narration of this chapter, is the frequent repetition of motifs, how Christ Jesus *by applying earthly substance mixed with His own spittle* opens the eyes of the blind man, bestowing thus his eyesight. The narration returns ever again to this (John 9:6, 11, 14, 15), until the man healed of blindness, repeatedly questioned about it, is finally unwilling and refuses to repeat the story yet again (9:27). Concerning the Mystery of the event, an explanation is found in Rudolf Steiner, *The Gospel of St John* (Lecture 7. Hamburg. 26 May 1908. GA 103). Steiner declares:

> There are, however, in the world great and mighty Mysteries which mankind is not yet entitled to know. Human beings of the present day, even though they may be sufficiently developed, are not yet strong enough to go through the great Mysteries. They can know of them, they can understand them when they are able to experience them spiritually; but our present humanity, so deeply immersed in matter, is not yet capable of converting them into their physical expression.

In this connection Steiner points in particular to the *Mystery of the corpse and of decay.* Spiritual vision can notice on the corpse something like a shining of spiritual light. In the gathering of matter in the process of birth the opposite occurs, that at the same time in the spiritual world a consciousness there dies away. Here a lighting up, yonder a dying of spiritual consciousness in a becoming of earthly consciousness and earthly corporeality.

> In the rushing together of substance to form a human physical body can be seen, in a certain sense, the dying of a spiritual consciousness;

while on the other hand, at the moment of decomposition or of the burning of the physical body, when the parts disintegrate and dissolve, the opposite actually becomes manifest in the spiritual world, that is, the awakening of a spiritual consciousness occurs. Physical dissolution is spiritual birth. Consequently, all processes of decay and dissolution mean something more to the occultist than just decay and dissolution. A churchyard, spiritually observed, where physical bodies are in the process of dissolution, is the scene of remarkable processes, the continuous flashing up and glistening of spiritual birth—I am now speaking of what is taking place spiritually in the churchyard itself apart from the human beings there.[84]

Let us imagine, for example, that a person were to give himself up physically to a certain training—naturally no one would recommend this, for the present physical body could not possibly endure it—to a schooling in which he would train his body to breathe in putrefied air for a certain prescribed period of time with the conscious intent of taking in the spiritual processes which have just been described. If he does this in the proper way, then in his following incarnations—it cannot be done in one—he can be incarnated with that force which offers restorative and health-giving impulses. *Breathing the air of death* belongs to a schooling that gradually gives strength to the spittle, when mixed with the ordinary earth, to become the healing substance that Christ rubbed upon the eyes of the blind man. This Mystery through which a person consumes, eats or inhales death, by which he acquires the power to heal, is the Mystery to which the writer of John's Gospel refers when he describes such signs as the healing of the man born blind.

Concerning the writer of John's Gospel himself, Steiner says: 'There was such a person who was thoroughly initiated into this Mystery about which we must try to acquire an understanding.'

Here, touching on the Mysteries of death and of decay that Rudolf Steiner connects with the healing of the blind man, we can look from the aspect of the cosmic sign standing over the whole section. We can, for example, recall the decay, with rotting vegetable substances going right into the physical side, at times as far as blinding lustre of intensifying phosphorescing light-phenomena, and from here to sense the mysterious relationship lying between the dark depths of death of the Earth (♏) and the realm of light of the phosphorus-Lucifer (♍), and we can sense how here too power lies in Christ's 'I' in the middle (♎) to unite the two kingdoms, out of the earthy depths to conjure up the

Mystery-source of light. The whole original relationship, here often mentioned, of the two signs (♍ and ♏, MG 123) is shifted into a new light.

In John 9, in the Healing of the Man Born Blind, there is revealed the *magic of the 'I'* shown by Christ advancing from chapter to chapter to ever-higher levels. We can lay hold of the leading motif of John 9 as 'new eyesight, out of the "I" and through earthly materiality transformed by the "I"' (Part One, Chapter 6). In the cited lecture Steiner emphasizes that only in the future of humanity the ego has to arrive at a new strength and fullness of power, so that it can change earthly material so far, beginning with its own corporality, that out of the Earth thus changed active healing forces are released as far as restoring eyesight. Not for nothing does Christ speak in the teaching of John 6 concerning the Last-Supper Mystery of 'flesh and blood of the "I"', remaining for the disciples so obscure and offensive.

In this are contained deepest Mysteries of cosmic alchemy, Mysteries of renewal and spiritualizing of all bodily substances—and furthermore of the whole earthly materiality—from the 'I'. John's Gospel—that has gradually to become more known—is entirely written out of these Mysteries. This cosmic alchemy reaches its climax with that event we are approaching more closely—to which also the events already presented, initially almost unnoticed yet finally leading to ever-more clarity—with the *raising of Lazarus*, in which the initiation-secret of John's Gospel is revealed most directly. How uniquely we feel there, too, the secret of death and decay (John 11:39). What Rudolf Steiner conveys regarding the healing of the blind man will be an essential key to understand it.

Metamorphosis through Christ

A significant inner thread is spun from the 'episode with the adulteress' in John 8—where, initially as from a distance, we can sense a connection to the secrets of the one becoming John—via the Healing of the Blind Man in John 9 to the Raising of Lazarus—and with this to the initiation of John himself in John 11. How the content of John 10 is inserted in all this has yet to be presented. The motif 'I am the light of the world' works over from John 8 into John 9, similarly the motif of *karma*, the motif of 'the Book of Destiny' and with it that of the Earth and the Mysteries of the Earth. The event of Christ writing the obligations of the adulteress into the Earth can only be understood out of the depths of relevant knowledge of *karma*—always with the knowledge of repeated earthly lives. Similarly, at the beginning of John 9 the question of the disciples, 'Who sinned, this man or his parents, that he was born blind?' is a question that has indeed no meaning unless the fact of repeated earthly lives were presupposed. And in John 8, what Christ does there was a moment to recognize beyond the Indian teaching of *karma* that which leads deeply into the earthly Mysteries of Christ. So, in the entry to John 9, the answer Christ gives to the question of the disciples points in a quite different, future direction. The Samaritan woman at the well, the invalid of Bethesda, the adulteress raised by Christ out of the depths of her fall, and now the man born blind, they all experience with Christ the revelation of the divine, the *miracle of the 'I'*, and they are raised through it to a new stage of being and consciousness.

A most significant *motif* working over from John 8 to John 9 is that *of the Earth and her metamorphosis through Christ*. Christ, in *writing* the *karma* of the adulteress *into the Earth*—into the Earth into which He sacrifices Himself, that He chooses for His Body—the Earth is no longer only the cause of the darkening of consciousness and the darkening of dark obligations of destiny, the sum of everything that alienated the soul from the cosmic light and the spiritual light, but the Earth herself becomes released and is gradually given back to the spiritual light. And because Christ takes upon Himself all earthly darkening, the soul of the woman is released from this darkness, she can freely breathe again in the light. Likewise in John 9 the Earth is no longer only the bowels of the power of death which overshadows the eye with blindness, but as Christ, with the light drawn out of cosmic depths, with His 'I' shines and transfigures the substance of the Earth; she first absorbs again the power of light in herself which then activates the healing of the blindness of closed eyes.

Change in John and the Disciples

After the outer actuality of the narrated events in John 9 are sufficiently emphasized, we may conclude by indicating the aspect already mentioned in the exposition of Mark's Gospel (MG 175ff.). In the picture of the Healing of the Blind Man, regardless of the outer reality of the event, certain spiritual events of the initiation of the disciples are also mentioned. Christ endeavours to strip away the spiritual blindness from the eyes of the disciples. If, alongside John, in Mark's Gospel Peter stands in a certain way in the foreground, then we have to think most strongly with the account in John's Gospel of the disciple John himself. He was *not* the one born blind—this must be said most clearly—yet the narration that is given of the Healing of the One Born Blind through Christ is intimately connected with the way the narration of the adulteress, too, in John 8 points to certain spiritual processes and inner transformations in John's consciousness. We approach ever more closely to the great fact that the 'raising of Lazarus' forms the spiritual centre of John's Gospel.

Rudolf Steiner has shown how in this 'raising of Lazarus' an initiation-deed of Christ is to be recognized. In this deed the last of the 'seven signs' of Christ in John's Gospel (listed on p. 188) there appears the last and highest revelation of the 'magic of the "I"'—apart from the resurrection of Christ Himself. In what Christ performs on Lazarus-John, there lies at the same time the transference, or part of the transference, of that which hitherto was revealed predominantly with Christ on to a suitable human vessel prepared through Christ Himself. The divine 'I', that in Christ descended to the Earth, should in future increasingly become the new member of mankind, in which human beings first find their true fulfilment intended by the divine powers.

Consequently, everything that would be received concerning this revelation of the 'magic of the "I"' of John's Gospel is incomplete, unless—and this now takes place in John 10—the *way* from Christ would be shown, on which the divine full power of this 'I' can be achieved by the human soul in the future. To everything that was hitherto revealed concerning the *nature of this 'I'*, the *way to find this 'I'* has to be added. And what in John 10 still remains theoretical teaching—in this lies the further advance presented in the transition from John 10 to John 11—in the 'raising of Lazarus' through Christ this is presented as a deed.

4.
The Good Shepherd
(John 10)

Externally speaking, the content of John 10 is initially heard by him who has just been healed from blindness. He heard that judging, straightening saying of Christ, the saying (John 9:39) through which the whole event of the Healing of the Blind Man is so clearly inserted into the 'crisis of the 'I' of Chapters 6–10, leading to the judging of the *Scales*, 'I am [the 'I' is] come into this world, that those who do not see may see, and those who see may become blind'. It is a significant event bound up with the Turning Point of Time and the Turning Point of the World, the great crisis of mankind, placed completely openly before the world. Christ teaches on the *way*, on the *path*, to a knowledge of the higher world and to *finding the 'I'*, proclaiming quite openly to humanity, just as the unheard of, destiny-laden deed of the 'raising of Lazarus' then takes place before the world in the presence of many. We know, and in John 12 it is clearly expressed, that this was a main contributing cause why 'the Jews' decide on the death of Christ Jesus.

For the whole pre-Christian world and its Mysteries, it was unheard of to place the secret of the path of the Mysteries so openly before the world. Formerly only in strict seclusion should these things be heard by those chosen and inwardly prepared for this proclamation. So it was above all in the country that looks back on the oldest spiritual culture of humanity,[85] that country in which since ancient times a knowledge of the path of the Mysteries and a practice of this path in *Yoga* was available. The whole cultural life in a certain way bore the impression of these Mysteries; the knowledge concerning the secrets of this path (Yoga teaching) and the practical exercise of this path (practice of Yoga) was protected as a sanctuary.[86] Only in small, closed groups was Yoga practised, only in them could the actual secret of Yoga teaching be experienced. Although later much was written and reached the public, yet the most inner secret, the decisive point upon which it all depended, was always kept secret. Only a few teachers experienced this secret quite personally. Only Buddha placed the essentials of the path before groups of human beings in his 'Eightfold Path', inwardly entirely based on Yoga teaching, yet in a relatively already very abstract form aiming at the 'zero-point of consciousness'.

In this context, Buddha appears as a forerunner of Christ. The actual practice of the Path nevertheless remained in a reduced form for those connected to the Buddhist religious orders.

Similar to the Indians is the context in Ancient Egypt, where secrets similar to Yoga of the temple sleep and the temple Mysteries were meticulously protected by the priests, until in later times they fell increasingly into decadence. The 'raising, or awakening, of Lazarus' contains several moments that point to a connection with these Ancient Egyptian secrets.

In a quite different sense than the Ancient Indian Yoga-teaching, even than the Buddhist Path, *Christ's proclamation of the Way* ('I am the way', John 14:6, and in addition the words of John 10) bear a purely human and comprehensively human character. This is so, even if on the other hand the content of this proclamation is a matter of the human future and initially actually directly achieved in practice only in the initiation of John, the only disciple initiated by Christ Himself. By placing the Mystery openly before the world—as then happened especially through the raising of Lazarus—Christ knows He completely seals His own death. He thereby makes the 'Mystery of Golgotha' unavoidable, and consequently it has a deeper meaning. All this He expressed for the first time with full clarity precisely in John 10; He knows that His hour (cf. John 7:30) is now come, 'For this reason the Father loves me, because I lay down my life, that I may take it again. No one takes it from me, but I lay it down of my own accord. I have power to lay it down, and I have power to take it again; this charge I have received from my Father' (John 10:17, 18). And once again His words awaken only discord, the inner division amongst the Jews (John 10:19), which brings the crisis to a focus: from now on it is the fully acute conflict within mankind that has broken out.

In John 10, Christ stands there before us, where He proclams that initiation path which then is realized in the raising of Lazarus, wholly as the self-sacrificed victim. For this reason just from this chapter onwards, the wonderful tenderness and inwardness of the language, which stands in strange contrast to the severity of the previous language conjuring up the dramatic conflict, the crisis—probably the climax is John 8:44, the beginnings go back to John 5 (cf. 8:42). First it was intended, and this was the command of the higher, divine love, to place the 'I' amongst humanity initially without regard, indeed apparently without compassion. The 'I' lost for humanity, incomprehensible to humanity, awakened confused division in the heart and thus conjured up the conflict, the crisis. But with this awakening of the crisis, Christ could not remain stationary.

From the aspect of the divine, 'the one step drew the other after'. Christ showed the path to the 'I' that at first remained incomprehensible, by sacrificing His own life, and showed them in such a way that in the initiation of John He gave the great example for the finding of this path. Finally, in the Mystery of Golgotha, in the way He sacrificed Himself into the Earth and humanity He created the possibility for the substance of the Earth and the substance of humanity—that had been hitherto completely darkened, unable to take up the divine 'I'—to be penetrated again with spiritual forces of light and in this way the substance could gradually become again a suitable vessel to receive the divine 'I'.

Thus the language of John's Gospel takes on that wonderful inwardness, especially where Christ as the 'Good Shepherd' shows the *way* towards the 'I', in which is revealed the divine cosmic love that sacrifices itself. All the star-Mysteries of the Eternal Name—touched on in the first part of this book—the 'I'-fulfilment of the human being, begin to shine in this proclamation of the Good Shepherd, about Whom it says 'and he calls his own sheep by name and leads them out', recalling Isaiah 43:1, 'I have called you by name, you are mine' (you take part in the divine 'I'). This inwardness of language is distinguished very characteristically from the language common in the Indian Yoga-documents, which are either completely abstract or tell us with every step that we do not belong to the chosen ones, that the actual secret despite all the words spent on it, basically is not allowed to be experienced. You are ultimately to feel with this, as a human being, that you are 'taken for a ride'. Again, in Middle-Age alchemical and similar writings such a manner of expression [that the secret is incommunicable] was much favoured.

Yoga and the Tree of Life

We cannot enter here into the details of the Indian Yoga-teaching and the differences from that of the Christian path of knowledge. To understand John 10 only the directly essential things should be underlined. At the centre of Indian Yoga stands a Mystery that we also find in Egypt as the Mystery of Isis and Osiris (cf. MG 215ff.), that ultimately appears in its actual world-historical fulfilment in the

Christian-Johannine event, when under the cross Christ unites the disciple with the Mother—as far we are able to raise ourselves to a spiritual understanding of this event (John 19:26, 27). Now the Indian awakes the power (*Shakti, Kundalini*) that the world reveres as the Eternal Feminine, in the subconscious depths of life, in order to lead her above, where she then in the head, in the sphere of cognitive consciousness, finds union with the 'divine Lord' (*Shiva*).

The Indian wants to raise the forces of the Tree of Life to the Tree of Knowledge—as we could say using an understandable pictorial expression out of the whole spiritual background of the present work. Rudolf Steiner has suggested—and the most exemplary Yoga-documents, especially the Yoga-Sutra of the Patañjali, yield the same thing—that also for the Indian Yoga-exercises the actual aim was the *development of the 'I'*, not only in the sense how—for us, too, today—the higher 'I', the higher Self, the 'I'-fulfilment is still a matter of the future, but in the sense for the normal 'I' as the thinking self-consciousness of what is already present today. Out of an earlier, more dreaming consciousness—and so with that human consciousness gifted with atavistic clairvoyant forces—the Indian was to strive to achieve a more conscious level of clear, thinking self-consciousness. Consequently, also for Patañjali, for the most noble, prodigious Indian Yoga, there is such characteristic distain for those clairvoyant, mystical and magic forces that today have such an attractive force as the occult and sensational side of Indian Yoga for many—they have to be overcome if the fulfilment of consciousness in the 'I', the actual aim of Yoga, is to be achieved.

What for the pre-Christian Indian was at least a preparatory *aim* of the path of knowledge, is today the point of departure with the Christian, Western path. The early Indian could live on the 'forces of the Tree of Life', still existing even if diminishing in pre-Christian times. At the Turning Point of Time the capital of these forces had essentially been used up in the West. Certain late remnants Christ Himself extinguished in a significantly fateful world-hour (cf. on Mark 11:13ff. and on the secret of the 'cursing of the fig tree, MG 269ff.). To want to proceed from such still remaining remnants today would not be in the sense of a spiritual advance. The Christian way does not proceed from the depths of the centre of life, but from the heights of clear thinking consciousness, that is, from that which today as 'I' is already available, in order to lead up to the higher stages of the divine 'I'. This way does not lead forces of the Tree of Life up to the Tree of Knowledge, but it is enabled and in the overcoming of death through Christ it wills to bring the Tree of Life to a new germination—or *'Ausgrünen'*, 'greening out', as Jacob Böhme says. Out of the withered wood of the cross on Golgotha the Tree of Life sprouted afresh.[87]

Access to the Indian practice of Yoga lies through the 'hidden door' (*brahmadvara*) in the depths of the life-centre, where for a clairvoyant view the organ of the 'four-petalled lotus-flower' is found.[88] Access to the Christian path through the *open door* of a clear-thinking self-consciousness, proceeds from that which we today already have as an 'I' in ourselves. In this sense Christ, the 'Good Shepherd' and Leader of souls speaks to 'his own': '*I am the door*' (John 10:9). That is, the I-AM, the 'I', as it lies in clear thinking consciousness, is now the door, through which the way to the higher divine 'I'-fulfilment leads, to the 'starry pastures' (νομή, *nomé*) the 'World of the Eternal Name' that the earthly side of the human being forgot.

Here too the Christ-'I' speaks in the *Scales*, in the sign holding consciousness in balance that is closely connected to the counter-sign, the Ram, the sign of the powers of conscious thinking of the head. Where the human being, quite naturally, has the sign of the Ram between the eyebrows, early clairvoyant vision found, and still finds today, the 'two-petalled lotus-flower' at the level of the eyes. At this place, to the sign of the Ram, Rudolf Steiner aligns one of the 'twelve senses', the 'sense of the "I"', MG 32.[89] From here we can also understand the 'sheep' of John 10, who feel in themselves the forces of the cognitive head (forces of the Ram) aligned to the impulses of the Christ-'I'.

It is worth noting, and it can appear to us as a presentiment of the Christian experience, that in later Indian Yoga a sect existed that for their exercises took the point of departure not from the 'four-petalled lotus-flower' in the depths, but from the two-petalled with the 'I'-centre at the level of the eyes. This was the sect that for their central meditation took the 'Sun verse' of the Rig Veda:

> The Light awakening Love of the enlivening Sun-being, of the divine, let us receive in meditation; it develops in us thinking filled with devotion.

And ultimately the union of *Shiva* and *Shakti* (in Christian terms, 'of the disciple and of the mother') was felt not, like the others in the thinking head, but in the heart, where it was also found in the Christian path [more details in the cited articles on Yoga in *Collected Articles*. TL forthcoming (2022)].

The sayings of Christ, 'I am the Door' and 'I am the Good Shepherd' thus achieve a certain meaning for knowledge, through which they are clearly and meaningfully placed into the whole 'I'-motifs of John's Gospel. Christ, the Light of the World, during a time when only this path is still legitimate, teaches the path of clear thinking leading to the fulfilment of the 'I'. Others who place themselves before this entrance door, blocking the way because they want to keep the soul in a darkening of consciousness, wanting to detain it with ancient forces that have become decadent, are 'thieves and robbers of the "I"' (John 10:8), and the sheep, the 'I'-people, rightly carrying the sign of the Ram on their heads, who hear the voice of Christ, will not follow such leaders—who still play a role today. They alone find the way to the height of the true 'I', and the 'Guardian of the Threshold' will allow them to pass (John 10:3).

Thieves and Robbers

Christ, the Good Shepherd, sacrifices Himself into the Earth, dies into the earthly realm, so that human beings can live again in the spirit, can find the way to the divine 'I'. That is the meaning of the words, 'The good shepherd lays down his life for the sheep' (John 10:11). Against him stand the 'thieves and robbers of the "I"', the *wolf*, who lies in wait for the sheep, those called to the 'I', to lead them to darkening of consciousness, seeking to lead them away from the path of the 'I'. The most terrible representatives of such dark Mystery-paths, Herod and Herodias, appear in the story of Mark's Gospel. They are not named in John's Gospel, yet they are meant in the first instance when the 'wolf' is mentioned. The story of Herod and Herodias shows how the 'wolf' mostly watches for the disciples of Christ called to the 'I'. To them he seeks first to cloud and darken the consciousness, in order most effectively to attack and extinguish Christ's earthly work. Right into the wording, it is interesting the way *how* John's Gospel speaks of the hostile effects of the wolf against Christ, of the robbers and murderers of the 'I' (10:12): he 'snatches the sheep and scatters them', that is, isolates them, in separation from the divine life of Christ. The word in the original text here and at the end of John 16:32, where Christ points prophetically to the flight of the disciples in Gethsemane, the Greek σκορπίζειν (*skorpizein*), clearly sounding reminiscent of the Scorpion, the consciousness darkening power of death (MG 313ff.). Christ speaks in John 10 not merely theoretically and abstractly of some kind of possible danger, but to what tragically the disciples actually do succumb. He sees beforehand this tragic end of the disciples' initiation, and consequently He nevertheless does everything in order to create in the *initiation of the one* the basis for the later earthly work.

Thus we recognize also in the description of the path of Christ in John 10, proceeding from the 'I' and leading to the higher 'I' of the 'Good Shepherd', what is appropriate, most progressive for the time. We recognize the true *middle way*, how here the I-AM of Christ holds the middle in the *Scales*, whereas those who now still want to detain the past that was once justified, deviate from the 'I', falling into the ego-extinguishing consciousness-darkening (♏) of Ahriman. Here too the Scales of the I-AM of Christ stands between the sign of light (♍) and the sign of darkness (♏): whoever today follows the deceptive apparent light of the one tempter experiences the consciousness darkening of the other, as Peter has to experience in a tragic manner (MG 189ff.). Thus this dark path leads 'from Lucifer to Ahriman', whereas the 'I'-path of the middle is the way of Christ.

This way of Christ leads to the finding of the higher divine 'I' of humanity that had become lost. The 'I', out of whose full power Christ speaks; to whose heights of light He allows the human being to look up in the proclamation of the path, knowing Himself one with the cosmic Light of the divine Father-ground: 'I and the Father are one' (John 10:30). We see in John's Gospel, how precisely this saying of Christ drives the conflict to the extreme, bringing to a dramatic conclusion the whole section of the gospel presenting the 'I'-crisis. There sounded, like a tranquil transition movement, in an inner heartfelt mood, Christ's proclamation of the Good Shepherd and the sheep who follow Him; in human hearts darkened by Ahriman it awakens only wild division, driving it to its peak (10:19).

Those themselves possessed by the adversary, who have lost their divine 'I', see the adversary in Him Who speaks to them out of the divine consciousness (John 10:20, cf. 8:48). John 10:22-24:

> It was the feast of the Dedication at Jerusalem; it was winter, and Jesus was walking in the temple, in the portico of Solomon. So the Jews gathered round him and said to him, 'How long will you keep us in suspense? If you are the Christ, tell us plainly.'

We feel that it is not only winter outside, but as those who so speak to Christ, who soon lift up stones against Him, themselves bear winter in their hearts. This recalls to us how already in Mark's Gospel what was said about winter and of the 'flight in winter' (Mark 13:18), contains an indication of the power of death of the Scorpion (MG 317f.). The Scorpion is the sign that introduces the wintery half of the year. And in the Gospels of Mark and John it appears everywhere as the power producing the darkening of consciousness in the human heart. The Greek word (*skorpizein*) used in John's Gospel for this confusion of consciousness (Luther translates: '*Zerstreuung*', 'dissipation' [John 16:32, '*ihr zerstreut werdet*', most English translations have 'you will be scattered']), clearly resembles *Scorpion* in sound, as we have seen.

In a deeply shocking manner there appears at the end once more the *motif of stoning* (10:31) framing the whole section of the gospel, triggered through the saying of Christ, 'I and the Father are one'. Once again the Jews take up stones against the Representative of the divine 'I', Who speaks to them out of this divinity of the 'I'. Only he who, like Christ, also beholds the counter-divine of the fallen human being when striding right through the middle of the two adversaries, can behold this divinity of the innermost kernel in truthfulness and may speak of it. The drama of the whole crisis-filled section of the gospel increasingly intensifies to the heights, till Christ finally hurls back to the Jews the words of the Psalm (82:6), 'You are gods' (10:34: 'Jesus answered them, Is it not written in your law, I said, you are gods?'). The Psalm contains a serious postscript (Ps. 82:6-7. RSV):

> I say, 'You are gods,
> sons of the Most High, all of you;
> nevertheless you shall die like men,
> and fall like any prince.'

Unlike people who perhaps here and there in frivolous, presumptuous philosophizing, without taking themselves quite seriously, speak of their own divinity or that of their works, Christ speak here out of the depths of the divine, cosmic Father-ground Itself, of the human 'I' predetermined in the divine will of the Creator. Only through this 'I' does the human being become the crown of creation, as Genesis 1:27 means it: 'So God created man in his own image, in the image of God [the divine 'I'] he created him; male-female he created them.' In a certain sense, the Creator Beings wanted to create beyond themselves, by intending to fashion in the spiritual human being the 'Hierarchy of Freedom'. Cosmic beings in their creative spiritual thinking, conceived human beings that in freedom could decide for the Divine, in freedom could also shut themselves off from the Divine.

Through the temptation of the adversary, permitted by the Divine for the sake of human freedom, the human being fell into sin, into separation; he was estranged from the Divine, lost the divine 'I'. The Fall was so deep that the fallen human being could so little bear anything in all the world as the gaze of the divine 'I'. The human being is brought through nothing else to such a confused conflict than when, in that cosmic solemnity which happens through Christ, this divinity of the forgotten 'I' speaks to him. To seek for the Divine somewhere outside and worship it, this was always easily won for human beings as the history of all religions and Churches confirm. To depend on one's own responsibility, on one's own standing in and being anchored in the Ground of the World, to depend on the Divinity hidden in the deepest depths of the human being, *on the 'I'* in the true and ultimate meaning—this was and is for human beings, as they have become through the Fall of humanity, always the most deadly dread.

No one has presented this more shockingly than John the evangelist in Chapter 10. '… the Father is in me and I am in the Father' is here Christ's last word (10:39). 'Again they tried to arrest him, but he escaped from their hands …'

III. THE RAISING OF LAZARUS
(John 11 and 12)

(NB This whole section should be compared with MG 208-81, esp. 238-81.)

1. The Invalid
(John 11:1–6)

Outwardly and inwardly John 11 stands in the middle-point of the whole; we meet therein the innermost part of the content of Christ's activity forming John's Gospel. In what preceded, the depicted crisis of the disciples expanded to the crisis of humanity. In this crisis the revealed inability of human darkness to lay hold of the light of the divine 'I' brings to a head Christ's decision, with divine necessity, to sacrifice Himself into the dying, darkened substance of the Earth and of humanity. Through this sacrifice, He will inject into this substance the *seed of light* (cf. John 12:24), into the darkness the *tincture of the light*—to use the Rosicrucian, alchemical expression of earlier centuries employed by Jakob Böhme—in order that humanity can again become a vessel to perceive the divine 'I' in itself.

It lies, however, in the nature of the Mystery of Golgotha, that it could be effective *not as a merely natural event*. It turns to the *consciousness* of human beings, wanting to come to life in the human 'I'. Consequently, Christ's unending care over the choice and preparation of the group of disciples; they were initially to offer their human vessel for the divine event. And from the story of Mark's Gospel we know this spiritual preparation, this 'initiation' of the group of disciples was a disappointment. With the Mystery of Golgotha, the disciples, in the first place Peter, the 'rock of the church' (MG 189ff., 197ff.), failed precisely to understand Christ's tremendous sacrifice of death and His decision to die. What the actual meaning and essential content of the whole 'initiation' was to have been—precisely this remained incomprehensible.

Thus, the whole future of the Earth and of humanity hung there, depending on Christ still managing out of the collapse of the initiation of the group of disciples at least to save the *initiation of the one*, in which the Mystery of Golgotha lived consciously. In his consciousness it could, as it were, be saved, to be there for the future of the Earth and of humanity. As the one who took cognisance of and collaborated in the Mystery of Golgotha (MG 282f.), to this one disciple above all it was allotted to ray forth his spiritual help to the other disciples, who during the earthly life of Christ Jesus denied Him. In this way they could later understand what initially was not understood, and were able to let their work flow with the work of Christ on the Earth.

So the 'disciple who stood under the cross' himself, the one who *knows this Mystery* has to come to the Mystery of Golgotha, as the only one called and in the position to point humanity the way to its future out of Golgotha. With this is indicated the actual secret of the 'Johannine Initiation' as well as of the event told in the mid-point of John's Gospel. Right through unspeakable, super-human difficulties and crises, which this disciple still had to undergo—the initiation-story of Mark's Gospel gives tidings, about which in our earlier exposition we sought to awaken a concept—on the path of this unique initiation in world-history performed by Christ Himself, the consciousness had to be created, or be formed, for him to be in the position to recognize and take in the greatness of the Mystery of Death. The more the others failed, the more everything depended on the spiritual awakening of this one disciple. Through Rudolf Steiner we know in what context the events portrayed in John 11 stand with this inner and outer becoming of the disciple of Christ.

In this we recognize the actual Christian Initiation-Mystery was completed in John Chapter 11. Through this and what follows, the inwardly related Chapter 12, the five of what we called 'Mystery-Chapters' (Part One, Chapter 4) become complete in the seven. Moreover, the 'Chapters on Humanity', John 6–10, through the two Passion Chapters, the 'Chapters on the Disciples', John 13–17, are also supplemented to seven. We see precisely with these two middle Chapters, John 11 and 12, rays emanating in all directions. They are also inwardly closely connected to the following 'Chapters on the Disciples'; with these two 'Passion Chapters' they stand significantly parallel; with the two 'Resurrection Chapters' they stand more than ever in an inner connection. For the crisis of mankind portrayed in Chapters 6–10, the events in Bethany form the actual climax (John 11:46-57). Already in the words at the beginning of John's Gospel (John 1:12, 13) we find the first indication of the secret of Bethany (John 11).

The first 'Mystery-Chapters' (John 1–5) contain specific meetings of Christ with various representatives of the earlier pre-Christian initiation and its Mysteries. Thus in those events related in John 11 as the 'raising of Lazarus' out of the sleep of the grave of Bethany, the new *Christian* Mystery takes place, resting on the awakening of the 'I'-forces (John 10, 'I am the door'). In his two lecture-cycles on John's Gospel, as initially in his book *Christianity as Mystical Fact* (GA 8), Rudolf Steiner shows how Christ Jesus, with what here happens through Him, is outwardly still served by certain forms of the earlier pre-Christian initiation, the Egyptian and its closely-related Indian Yoga initiation. There the candidate for initiation was sent into a three-day, death-like sleep, during which the secrets of the supersensory world were impressed in pictures on the forms of his fine etheric body, as it were, imprinted. In this sense, Rudolf Steiner shows, the 'raising of Lazarus' reveals the transition from the earlier pre-Christian to the new Christian Initiation.

To all this we would not have had the key, had it not been handed us through Rudolf Steiner. Of the future-carrying significance of what we have received from him, and thereby the enormous debt of gratitude it carries, humanity in the midst of the civilization of today is not yet aware. With each attempt to approach consciously and consciously to lead to the sphere of Johannine-Christian Mysteries, the duty also exists to call into consciousness Rudolf Steiner's deed—without which the actual meaning of the Christ-Event, the Deed of Christ would fall asleep in the consciousness of mankind.

It is nevertheless to keep at a distance the misunderstanding as if somehow it has to do here with taking over dogmas. Here, too, Steiner—and this appeared especially clearly with the previously-mentioned 'Last Address' [Michaelmas Eve, 28 Sept. 1924, in GA 238 and MG Appendix 4]—has spoken in such a way on the Lazarus-Mystery and the questions regarding John, that he turned towards the striving for knowledge in people, to their will freely to test the communications, to use what was offered as a key to knowledge, also to use such a key for knowledge.

In the present work lies the attempt in such a way to employ what Steiner has given; it lies already in that which in the presentation on Mark's Gospel could be said on the Mystery of John (MG 45ff., 48ff., 122ff., 208ff., 238ff.). Intellectual 'evidences and proofs'—with which in such cases we do *not* have to do—want to force the understanding to accept a statement or other, whereas the essence of a *key to the Mysteries*—which is what we have been given by Steiner—consists in leaving the soul free, that it remains to the active soul-forces to work further on the matters, to test the worth of knowledge of what has been communicated. Only such a 'key' is not beneficial when it falls into the hands of those who take everything again 'dogmatically', who are themselves forced and want to force other people. This attitude of mind, still widely prevailing both within and without theology, stands in contradiction to that of John's Gospel. There, through the whole work of *knowledge of the truth in the light-filled consciousness (aletheia)*, Christ wanted to lead to freedom, to the 'I'.

***

Once again, not as 'proof', but yet as an indication of a direction of inner search for how with our thinking we can approach the Mystery of John—on the one hand the *Mystery of both Johns* (MG 45-53), and on the other hand the *Mystery of Lazarus*—out of the whole construction, the whole composition of John's Gospel, there lies the following advice given by Rudolf Steiner in his lecture-course. There we find at the end of the first half of the gospel (John 10:41) in a way summarizing what has gone before—a reference to the witness of John the Baptist— reminding us how right at the beginning of the first section of the gospel (John 1:6ff.) the name John appears significant. The Baptist is meant here—the disciple is never mentioned by name in John's Gospel.

Reference is made to the witness of this *disciple* (that is, the disciple John) as the 'disciple whom the Lord loved' at the end of the second half of the gospel, the end of the whole work (John 21:20, 24). Steiner revealingly shows how, not without deep meaning and significance at the beginning of this second half of the gospel (John 11:3), we hear of a—or we may say, of *the*—disciple 'whom Jesus loved' (for it is only the one, cf. MG 218f.), and how there the secret of this disciple is linked with the name Lazarus.

The symmetry shown here by Rudolf Steiner between the beginning and the ending of the first, the beginning and ending of the second half of the gospel, and the connection of this symmetry with the Mystery of John, of this Mystery again with the secret of the 'disciple whom Jesus loved', is obvious. Always in the gospel this 'love' is used in an exceptionally deep, fully important Mystery sense, and where it is otherwise found, also in other gospels (cf. Mark 10:21)—only a few passages come into question—it everywhere suggests a connection with the Mystery of John (MG 218f.).

So, the first section of John's Gospel (Chapters 1–10) would point to the witness of John the *Baptist* (whose spirituality later increasingly passes over to the disciples), with the second section (Chapters 11–21) to the witness of the John the *disciple*. The story told at the beginning of the second half, the 'raising of Lazarus', would then, as it were, contain an indication of the secret of the event through which the strength of this witness of John would be awoken in the disciple through the deed of Christ. To an enhanced degree we are aware of the chief emphasis of the passage at the beginning of this section, where it says that Jesus loved Lazarus and also *his two sisters*—the spiritual connection of his own two sisters with the Mystery-experience of the disciple already emerged everywhere previously.

Right into the language the two halves of the gospel are indeed very different. Over Christ's revelation of the 'I' and the 'I'-crisis in the first half still lies something of the judging seriousness and severity that was peculiar to the sermon of the Baptist John, the 'voice in the loneliness'. From John 10 onward we perceive ever more of that wonderful, lovely tenderness and inwardness in Christ's language, which then spreads with increasing light over what follows. In the first half we experience in the 'I' of Christ still the judging which effects the division of the spirits, in the second wholly the One who lovingly sacrifices Himself. The first half is still concerned with the division (crisis), the second with the higher connection.

Thus, in the first half of the gospel—for the 'Christian' level in the full, highest sense of all only begins with the Mystery of Golgotha itself—there is still in a certain sense a 'pre-Christian element' (for this reason we also find the indication to the witness of the Baptist at the end of this section). Only from John 11 onwards the way the great Christ-Event is told carries fully and entirely the stamp of the disciple of Christ as such. It is not whether this disciple would not be the writer or the inspirer of the whole gospel according to John. But with the experience of his initiation onwards, he is inwardly connected in a completely different manner with what he experienced before he was the disciple of Christ. The earlier part he experienced directly, the later part in a manner of spiritual retrospect, intimately connected with the 'witness of John the Baptist'—that from now on lives in himself in a more spiritual manner.

***

After all this, will we then say that in the beginning of John 11 the name Lazarus should be the disciple John? Already from the earlier presentation developed about this, it arises that we are not actually able to speak in this form over this middle section of John's Gospel, nor for that matter over the controlling connections between the gospels of Mark and of John. And *Lazarus*, too, as we always saw, is not in the usual sense a 'name', is not the actual name of the personality as really that of the 'nameless disciple' from the beginning, whose Mystery (cf. John 1:40 and what was said earlier on this) runs through the whole of John's Gospel. It is not the same, as with John the Baptist at the beginning of John's Gospel [John 1:6] 'his name [ónoma] was John' (ὄνομα αὐτῷ Ἰωάννης), than mentioning something about a 'chronically ailing man', an 'invalid', in John 11, that his name was Lazarus. The word *name* (ónoma) is significantly and indicatively missing (most versions translate here contrary to the original text; RSV is an exception: 'Now a certain man was ill, Lazarus of Bethany, the village of Mary and her sister Martha.'). A *name* is precisely here significantly and indicatively missing. A *name* does not stand before us in 'Lazarus', but a *picture*, that we saw everywhere intimately bound to the Mystery of the one becoming John (MG 155ff., 319ff., 327ff.). Not the true name of the richly mysterious personality who stands in the mid-point of John's Gospel speaks to us in the word *Lazarus*, but the fact of his being an *invalid* presents itself everywhere like an external counter-picture of those processes pointing within, appearing as the crisis of consciousness of the one becoming John.

In this illness leading to death, or hard by the border of death, in this *Lazarus-experience* the mysterious ripening of the disciple of Christ, accompanied and overcome by Christ Himself with such frightful care, the blooming of the Johannine spirituality present in the pre-Christian Mystery-meaning reaches to a new Christianized level. *In the dying of Lazarus there takes place the becoming of the new, the Christian John, the Johannine being* (similarly expressed in Part One, Chapter 6).

Also that *John* is not a name in the normal sense but a higher Mystery grade, that one is not simply called 'John', but *becomes John*, that an initiation-Mystery which at the same time is *Mystery of the cosmic rhythm*, lies in this name, was underlined with emphasis earlier (MG 45–53, etc.) Only through the whole penetration and overcoming of all the different crises of development experienced in the name *Lazarus* does the one becoming the disciple of Christ find in his consciousness the point when the name *John* shines before him in the eternal stellar script, where he perceives his Mystery-name as spoken to him out of the *world of the Eternal Name*, where he finds it as his *Eternal Name* written in the *Book of Life* (see the account in the first part of this book, Part One, Chapter 7). In John's Gospel itself he remains to the end the *nameless disciple*, the 'disciple whom the Lord loved'.

Thus Lazarus, the ailing invalid, had to die, so that John the disciple of Christ, could appear ever coming into existence. He who was raised as the initiated disciple of Christ out of the grave of Bethany was another person from the one who previously lay closed in the sleep of death, even though he still bore in himself in the moment of resurrection the picture of the one-time invalid, of Lazarus. Lazarus, the invalid, is as different from John, the disciple of Christ, as the chrysalis of the caterpillar is from the butterfly freed to the light.

In Mark's Gospel the events leading to the initiation of the disciple of Christ, as it were, lit from its *conscious side*, presented from the aspect of Johannine consciousness. John's Gospel allows us, as it were, to catch a glimpse of the process of the *Mystery of the Earth*, which *as an initiation deed is performed through Christ*. The peculiarity of both gospels is expressed in this characteristic difference, the points of view. If we were able to bring home to ourselves in our exposition of Mark's Gospel the experiences of consciousness of the one becoming John in the crises of his initiation, then John's Gospel answers the question that could arise. From Mark's Gospel we can read what the events signify for John's consciousness; John's Gospel as the actual gospel of Christ (MG 51) tells us, *what it means for Christ Himself*, how it adds into the tremendous Christ-event told in this gospel. The initiation of the disciple of Christ is told in John's Gospel as a Deed of Christ, not only as an experience of John.

***

The sickness of Lazarus, involving his whole suffering and death, relates to the suffering and death of Christ Himself. *This sickness of Lazarus is the outer, earthly counter-picture of the spiritual becoming of John*. At the same time it expresses the *synthesis of Mark's Gospel and John's Gospel*. This tremendous, closing motif of the gospel story livingly expresses the *cosmic rhythm* of both gospels:

- (1) Previously (John 6–10) the cosmic rhythm of John's Gospel reaching the Scales, the sign of Christ's I-AM, as it were achieves its decisive turning point. The rhythm in the Lazarus story of John 11 now turns downwards, towards the dark part of the zodiac (♏ ♐ ♑ ♒).
- (2) These signs, as will be shown in detail, are the counter-signs of those heavenly signs through which in the rhythm of Mark's Gospel the consciousness of the one becoming John, going towards his initiation is led upwards (♉ ♊ ♋ ♌). This is clearly seen from the exposition of Mark's Gospel (MG 231ff.)

The corresponding things in John's Gospel—Chapter 11, from the burial to the raising of Lazarus—will be summarized in what follows.

We recall the cosmic rhythm of Mark's Gospel. On the third of the three rounds or 'octaves', after the Transfiguration of Christ on the Mount, the rhythm (for the third time) enters into the sign of the word, of the Bull from Mark 9 and 10. The experiences of the Johannine consciousness stand increasingly in the foreground. That is, from now on the gospel narration gains an especially deep meaning. A special light pours over all the gospel connections when we take into account the inner relationship of the gospel pictures that pass by us in a colourful sequence. They are initiation-experiences of the consciousness of the one becoming John.

Everything still standing under the sign of the word, of the Bull, appears like a *preparation* for the actual initiation-experience. For once—and this is the positive side of the Johannine experiences of this section of the gospel—we saw how here John (that always means the one becoming John), the one who hitherto was silent, 'finds the word'. He becomes the spokesman, whereas another one who talks too early 'lost the word' (MG 210). The living power of the word (♉)—and this can be found especially in the beginning of Mark 10—in the consciousness of the one becoming John now wins the ultimate victory. He triumphs over the power of death working from ♏, the lower sensuality. In him the creative power of love (♀ in ♉) now overcomes for good the dark daemonic power of Mars poisoning the life of love (♂ in ♏). John—the becoming Johannine consciousness—recovers the inner virginity of his being (♏ changes into ♍, cf. what was indicated to John 8).

Facing these positive experiences and achievement standing in the constellations ♉–♏ the section contains attacks and crises, which the becoming consciousness of John has to withstand before the actual finding of initiation. They are expressed in Mark's Gospel especially in that 'episode of the rich young man' (Mark 10:17ff.), of whom it is said that Jesus loved him (10:21) and who nevertheless, because he is not yet able to do the last thing, is dismissed by Christ. It is not as though it should be said John—or 'Lazarus'—would have been that 'rich young man', but in the picture of the youth there arises before the spiritual eye of the one becoming the disciple of Christ (who is still 'nameless') certain inner difficulties, that he has still to undergo, certain crises of consciousness that he has still to withstand (cf. the explicit description MG 210ff.). In these last initiation crises of the one becoming John the power of death is still active (♏), which, in so far as it appears as lower sensuality, has already been overcome, but still appears as the adversary, when it concerns the one becoming the disciple of Christ finding in 'going through the eye of the needle' the 'narrow gate' of the zero-point of consciousness, the zero-point of the 'I' in consciousness—the path of life and of the future in Christ, now to let go once and for all everything of the past, even everything spiritual that has been carried over: this is the 'testing of the rich young man' meant here.

As the outer counter-picture of those inner difficulties and crises in John's Gospel there is the *sickness of Lazarus*, and we can well understand why over the entrance of John 11 ('Now a certain man was ill, Lazarus of Bethany ...') it stands for our observations in the sign of the Scorpion. It is the sign incidentally also known as the *sign of John* belonging to the 'Johannine triangle', and from the 'esoteric corner' of this triangle (MG 363) it is the sign that connects the deepest depths and the highest heights, revealed on the one hand as the power of death in illness and sickness but on the other hand again as the metamorphosis of the 'Sun-Eagle'. This swings up to the cosmic heights of the origins of life and regained by the disciple John becomes the sign of the evangelist John and as such stands already over the entrance of John's Gospel.

As the ♉ points towards the *victory* of inner consciousness of the becoming disciple of Christ, the counter-sign of ♏ points to the outer and inner sickness of him who still has to wrestle for the victory. Of this sickness, reminding us immediately in the context of John 11 of the becoming disciple of Christ, old legends prophesy as we frequently thought in the exposition on Mark's Gospel (MG 49f., 119f., 181f., 222, 273ff.). These indicate, following the narration of the gospel, the moment when the sickness of Lazarus in which the Johannine initiation experience begins, comes to its first outbreak, when Lazarus becomes the sick, silent disciple. It is not that such legends in themselves should be regarded with a special value for knowledge, were they to be mentioned, but because of their content covering what the spiritual research finds independently from all 'legends' and other outer documents, independent also from the written gospel, and what on the other hand with more intimate reading can be found between the lines of the gospel. When this is found it pours out a wonderful light over the connections and contexts of the gospel. We are reminded how, besides the initiation story of Mark's Gospel and the Lazarus story of John's Gospel, also of the sections of Luke's Gospel (7 and 16) and how especially the story of the Magdalene of the gospel (initially Luke 7, with the echo of John 8) are woven together. Also the 'healing of the blind man' of John's Gospel (cf. the echoes of John 9:3 and 11:4) places itself into the context of this 'Lazarus-event'.

2.
The Grave of Bethany
(John 11:7ff.)

From the sign of the word, the Bull, in which the one becoming John finds the word, the cosmic rhythm in Mark's Gospel leads to the exalted sign of the *Twins*, the sign of the Sacred Mount and of Initiation. Here too we find in the initiation of John, in the consciousness of the one becoming John, the decisive beginning of the initiation-experiences. This exalted sign of the Twins stands over the episode of the 'sons of Zebedee', Mark 10:35ff. In the Johannine initiation-experience, we recall, the 'Mount of the Transfiguration' appears again in spiritual review. The whole spiritual picture of the Transfiguration—Christ between Moses and Elijah, James and John with Moses and Elijah—already in Mark 9 as also in John's inspiration could be recognized as something deeply inspirational (MG 196). For Christ Himself this 'Transfiguration on the Mount' already signifies the beginning of His death, of dying into the Earth, of the Mystery of Golgotha. Consequently, over the beginning of this process stands the Archer, the sign of the revelation of death. Over the whole Transfiguration the same four signs stand as over Golgotha.

The one becoming John takes deep into his consciousness this revelation of death. Now in the elevated sign ♊, in the sign of the Sacred Mount, he spiritually looks in retrospect at the experience of the Transfiguration. If from this spiritual experience we seek the outer counter-picture in the Lazarus-events of John's Gospel, we come from the exalted sign of the Twins again to the counter-sign, to the death-sign of the Archer in the depths. From illness (♏) the experience of Lazarus has been led to death, to earthly dying (John 11:13 & 14), to an event at least hard by the borders of death. Precisely where the consciousness of John spiritually beholds the heights of light of the Mount of Transfiguration (♊), for the outer sight the outer counter-picture (♐) is the Lazarus event of earthly death.

It is deeply significant how the whole rhythmical signs of the Mystery of Golgotha, of Christ's death and Christ's resurrection (♐ ♑ ♒ ♓) return, or already announce themselves in the events of Lazarus. For outwardly and inwardly the Christ-Event takes into itself this Lazarus-experience, inwardly and outwardly reproducing it. The Johannine path of initiation—and that is the concern here—is absolutely and in every respect an 'imitation of Christ'. The spiritual beholding of the Mystery of Golgotha that takes place in the upper, the bright counter-signs (♊ ♋ ♌), is the one, spiritual side of the experience of initiation. But, right into the physical body, *as far as this lies within human possibilities*, the one becoming the disciple of Christ in these three (or three and a half) days of sleep of the grave of Bethany also relives the Christ-Event. *He experiences in his own body*, while his consciousness tarries in cosmic heights (♊ ♋ ♌), *the Mysteries of death and the grave* (♐ ♑ ♒).

There, in the death-depths of the Archer, he encounters the source of life; from here springs the new Paradisal stream of the Christ-future of humanity. The sign of a turning-point of the Goat, the dark Saturn-sign, follows the Archer; the counter-sign of the Crab, of the turning-point in the heights, following the exalted sign of the Twins, marks at the same time the beginning of the descent. We recall how here above, from the spiritual aspect of consciousness, the Johannine Initiation is completed, which is characteristic of this initiation. Yet it finds its completion not in the spiritual mountain-heights, but in the descent to the lowliness of humanity. Precisely the Crab is also the Moon-Earth sign; here is experienced and manifested the secret of matter, the Mystery of the Earth, the secret of metamorphosis, the transformation of the Earth. The fact that in earlier, pre-Christian Mysteries it did not yet reach to this point belongs to the nature of the Christian, Johannine Initiation. In the Crab, connected to the Sun-sign of the Lion (the 'red Lion'), the *alchemical Mystery* of this Christian-Johannine Initiation is expressed (MG 280f.).

The earlier initiation ended in the Goat; the new initiation ends in the Crab. The polarity ♑–♋ standing over John 3 led us significantly to see the contrast of the earlier with the new initiation. We glimpse this measuring itself of the one against the other. This now belongs to the Mysteries of John 11. In his consciousness the disciple becoming John experiences in the heights of cosmic light the secret of the changed Earth, of the virginally bright Earth of light (to ♋ the musical key of A-major belongs, the key [in Wagner's *Lohengrin*] of the shining Grail in distant cosmic heights). Its earthly part is led through deepest darkness of Earth, through the darkest depths of the grave. *In the darkest depths of Earth* and Saturn depths of the cosmic events *the transition takes place* from the earlier (♑) *to the new initiation* (♋). This is the meaning of the dark Saturn-sign of the Goat in the Lazarus-events of John 11. In this dark Saturn-sign ♑, in the counter-sign of the Crab, the Johannine Initiation initially touches the alchemical depths of the secret of the Earth at that point where the consciousness of the one becoming John experiences the Moon-sign (♋), the star-secret of the transformation of the Earth.

In all this, we know from the earlier exposition, how the two signs ♑ and ♒ summarize the spiritual secret of the being *John* (the 'Elijah-John' being). These two signs of the dark keys traverse the Lazarus-events of John 11; *the Mystery of Lazarus combines at the same time with the Mystery of John*. In the initiation accompanied by Christ now approaching its completion, the entity of the nameless disciple, who as Lazarus is led right through the experience of the grave, takes on here the spiritual essence of John. Hitherto, already increasingly in contact with this spiritual essence, finally and mostly in the Transfiguration (Mark 9:4, 5, 196f.), now in the depths of his being he identifies with him.

The deepest Mysteries are linked with the sign ♒ standing over this and the previous chapter. We know this sign as that of the depths of the grave, such as the etheric experiences of the Baptism in the Jordan. We would find in this sign John's baptism by water, later the burial of John, and finally the burial of Christ Himself. From the planetary aspect, we know that this sign ♒ is no mere dark sign of Saturn, as the ♑ is, but a Saturn-Uranus sign, in which the dark side of the depths of the Earth are illuminated towards the star-side, the bright etheric region of Uranus. We found with this sign the star-origins of the still etheric 'human being of the primordial beginning'. As the 'sign of the human being', in the group of four evangelists it points to Matthew's Gospel. And so in a special sense we experience with this sign ♒ on the one side the Mystery of the grave, the depths of the grave, on the other side the Mystery of the world of the stars, the Mystery of Uranus. Something of Goethe's *'Stille/ Ruh'n oben die Sterne,/ Und unten die Gräber*—Tranquil, the stars rest above, and below the graves' ['*Symbolum: Des Maurers Wandeln es gleicht dem Leben*'] speaks to us out of the Mystery of this sign ♒.

Moreover, this Uranus-sign of the Waterman standing over the grave of Bethany, is the lower counter-sign of the Lion that we found in the trinity of signs. In this sign, from the aspect of the experience in consciousness, the Johannine initiation is completed. The ♏ is inwardly connected with the ♉, the ♐ with the ♊, the ♑ with the ♋; so is the ♒ inwardly connected with the ♌ that we already know from the miracle of the Marriage at Cana: the starry world shining now as the inner Sun.

> One day the stars, down dripping,
> Shall flow in golden wine [Novalis],

we recognized as the secret of this constellation. Because he experienced so deeply this secret in the sleep of death in Bethany, which at the same time was a sublime clairvoyant awakening, the disciple of Christ as the inspirer of John's Gospel could place the miracle of Cana so profoundly and significantly before us. In this Uranus-sign of the Waterman, which is the sign of the human being, and this constellation ♒–♌, which is also that of the miracle of Cana, *Star-Mystery* and *Earth-Mystery* meet at the most intimate level. And it is the experience of the slumber in the grave of Bethany, in which this encounter of Star-Mystery and Earth-Mystery directly takes place. Here the Sun shines, that is at home in the Lion, for the disciple of Christ now in the depths of the Earth, here it rises in his own heart, here he experiences in this star-world become inner Sun the meaning of the Mystery of Golgotha, the meaning of mankind, the meaning of the Earth ...

He experienced all this in going right through the innermost 'I'-zero-point of consciousness. This ego-zero-point of consciousness is the 'narrow door', through which the 'path of life' leads (Matt. 7:14), the 'narrow door', which was always meant in the presentation of the John experience in [the exposition on] Mark's Gospel (MG 272f. etc.). This 'most narrow of all doors', seen from within is the door of the ego zero-point, through which we see the Johannine consciousness passing through, of the zero-point where everything past is extinguished and everything future begins. This narrow door seen from without is the door of the grave, through which Lazarus, the sick man of Bethany, now goes through, led by Christ the initiator. This passage through the narrow gate, through the gate of the grave, which in the initiation drama of Mark's Gospel we found presented in the picture of the poor widow (Mark 12:41ff.) who threw her last farthing into the offering box. (That is it not necessary to give up the 'reality of the outer event', for the sake of the suggested pictorial character of this event in the drama of initiation, was already emphasized in the exposition on Mark's Gospel.)

When in this way and in this sense the dark depths of the Earth are penetrated and illumined with consciousness, when in this way as is the case in the Lazarus-events, the *depths of the grave* are enlivened with consciousness, then the experience of the grave itself already carries in itself the seed of the resurrection, citizenship of the resurrection. The sign of the earthy grave, the Saturn-Uranus sign of the Waterman, carries in itself the Mystery of the Light, which then in the following sign of the Fishes is completed. In this way we experience the end of John 11 and in John 12 the one risen from the grave in the ♓, in the same sign that later with the Resurrection of Christ is linked above all with the Resurrection morning. It is specially important, that the sign ♓ everywhere, also especially in John's Gospel, is the sign of *love that serves*, love that in a new, devoted, divine sense unites with the Earth. This will become clearer in the details of John 12.

In the constellation ♓–♍, the rhythm of the Lazarus-events in John's Gospel meets that of the Lazarus-events of the consciousness of the one becoming John in Mark's Gospel, who likewise in Mark 14 leads to the constellation (♍–♓) (MG 282ff.). We observe how the one rhythm relates to the other. In Mark's Gospel we experience, as it were, the heavenly side of the event in the bright, upper signs, which point to the experiences of the Johannine consciousness; in John's Gospel in the grave of Bethany the earthly side of the event, the Lazarus-event in the lower dark zodiac signs lying opposite, which are the same as those of the Mystery of Golgotha.

Christ's Deed

With this agreement of the rhythmical sign of the Lazarus-Mystery with the Mystery of Golgotha, not only does Lazarus-John in his initiation in anticipation participate in the whole Mystery of Golgotha as such and in himself. That experience sets him in the position to bring to completion what he soon lives through 'under the cross'. But a still deeper aspect first results when we look at the whole subject not only as an experience of Lazarus and a suffering of Lazarus, but look upon it *as a Deed of Christ.* Then the close relationship of the Lazarus-event to the Mystery of Golgotha becomes fully clear.

From the exposition on Mark's Gospel, we recall (MG 191ff.) how the death of Christ, his dying into and offering Himself into the Earth not first on Golgotha, but as it already begins in the *Transfiguration*, already there reaches a certain climax. Also the rhythmical signs of the event of the Transfiguration (♐ ♑ ♒ ♓) clearly speak of this connection with the event of death on Golgotha. The meaning of this event of death, which remains obscure with the others, is taken into the consciousness of John. From here the *Mystery of Golgotha* will also become understandable that Christ is shown to us already as One struggling in full agony (MG 291ff.).

But the event of raising Lazarus, so rich in Mysteries, takes place *after* the Transfiguration. And this deed Christ fulfilled as one already dying, dying by sacrificing Himself into the Earth. Basically it is not at all that the Mystery of Golgotha follows the Mystery of Bethany only 'on foot', but the Mystery of Bethany actually stands in space and time and spiritually even already completely within the Mystery of Golgotha. And precisely this—revealed through the zodiac sign—this connection with the event of the death of Christ gives the deepest solutions to the riddles and Mysteries of the event that took place in and around the grave at Bethany. In what follows we seek to present these things more clearly.

From such people who not only keep to the purely external wording of the gospel but also to the communications of the spiritual researcher, one can frequently hear how the Lazarus-secrets of John 11 are taken not at all as the actual experience of death, when they say, it was indeed 'only' an initiation. Such remarks and views, which have nothing to do with what Rudolf Steiner himself wanted to tell us, are very far removed from an actual understanding of the 'communications of the spiritual researcher'. At the root lie certain misunderstandings concerning the essence of initiation in general, as well as the special events told in John 11 (especially 11:14).

Firstly, it is a mistake to assume that initiation-events of the pre-Christian times must have been something simply harmless—in the case of Lazarus, and here Steiner has expressly indicated, Christ Jesus Himself did use certain forms of the pre-Christian Mysteries. Much rather in Ancient Egypt it was already quite normal that the initiation-procedure led to a tragic ending, that the candidate for initiation succumbed to the dangers of initiation. Apart from other 'dangers of initiation', that already in the 'preparation' could result in the death of the pupil of initiation, the process of withdrawing the etheric body in order to produce the sleep of death, the death-paralysis in the candidate—that condition in which the higher spiritual experiences were to be impressed into the released or loosened ether-body—was extremely critical and dangerous, leading to a situation really hard by the borders of death (one cannot say 'on the edge of the grave', for the grave was already present in its full reality in this process). And the danger—about which Steiner has indicated—during the course of the development of mankind, of the ether-body pressing into the human physical body, became ever greater towards the time of the Mystery of Golgotha. The human physical body became increasingly hardened and materialized; the strength to withstand the dangers of such a process became ever less. All the other members of the group of Twelve whom Christ originally intended (probably all of them except one) to lead to initiation, none would have had the power. For all of them the process of Lazarus was the sure and final end. What earlier was called the disciples' 'failure in initiation' really had this serious physical other side—this failure always lay in the death-sign of ♏, in which for Lazarus lay the beginning of his initiation-experiences.

Only a physical body worked through, purified and fired-through to a completely different degree by the 'I' is able to undergo the Christ-initiation, ultimately still depending on the old procedures of the Lazarus-initiation. And we appreciate, too, how critical the case of the one disciple was, who went through those procedures finally to became the disciple of Christ. We take everything right into the physical as seriously as possible, when we hear of the critical dangers and attacks he still had to overcome in his initiation (MG 218ff.). We have an inkling with what devotion and at the same time terrible care Christ Jesus concerned Himself with the becoming of the one, on whose initiation, after the failure of the others, lay the redemption and the future of the whole development of mankind and the Earth. We can understand ever more deeply and better the *Mystery of Gethsemane*. There the one, with such self-sacrificing care from Christ led to initiation by Christ, returned to Christ for the sake of humanity the service which he had attained (MG 299f.).

But perhaps we do not yet sense to what degree of devoted, directed self-sacrificial effort proceeds from Christ into the 'raising of Lazarus'. We recall the stage once again how already in the *Transfiguration on the Mount* Christ was one dying, dying into the Earth, self-sacrificing into the Earth. With this dying into ever higher degrees, until we see Christ in Gethsemane as One struggling already in full agony,

Who alone placing all His strength on dying into the earthly body, He Himself could no longer hold out in the physical body till the hour of Golgotha.

The 'awaking' or 'raising of Lazarus' falls into the middle of this dying process of Christ Himself. Yet we already sense more clearly that it was more than just a temporal connection. A spiritual, indeed a spatial connection also governs here, right into earthly substance. And we dare to express it: *precisely through this dying, this dying in sacrificing Himself into the Earth, Christ* alongside what this dying otherwise effected for all the others *also made possible the raising of Lazarus*. Only by shining His love with the rays of the Sun, dying into the Earth, illuminating from within the dark earthly material—and the human body, before whose Mystery we are standing, is a integral part of the 'Earth'—only through this did Christ draw out the life of resurrection from the grave of the Earth, in which Lazarus lay encapsulated in the sleep of death. And no other hierophant than Christ Jesus would have been able to awaken in this case the dead man closed off in the slumber of the grave.

Beyond such often easily expressed opinions—despite John 11:4—that with Lazarus it was no death at all, it would have been indeed 'only an initiation', we have now become somewhat more reflective. To decide the question whether really and without question it was a 'physical [brain] death' or only one on the most extreme borders of death, to the point of coming hard by real death, a death-catalepsy,[90] we do not regard as valid.

It is certain that the one *unique* event in the whole history of the Earth and mankind is narrated here in John 11. This event is likewise as unique as the earthly change of Christ Himself. *Never before and never after in this unique manner is an earthly-physical human body snatched from the grave of the Earth and the forces of decay, from which, already in the grip, it was ripped away.* Furthermore, not any hierophant or other of any pre-Christian or Christian Mystery-centre would have been in the position to perform such a deed of initiation. The hierophant could only be the One in which the Godhead Itself has taken on a body.

The Forces of Decay

The actual Lazarus-Mystery of John 11 seems to us to contain this *entrance of the forces of decay*. Precisely in this point the gospel speaks characteristically so mysteriously (John 11:39). In the most mysterious manner of all there lies over John 11 (already encountered in John 9, with the Healing of the Blind Man) that *Mystery of decay*, for which in recent literature—in the earlier alchemical literature it was already well-known—especially the Russian writer Dostoyevsky was on the track. Compare what is contained in the chapter on the 'Marriage in Cana'. In this area in particular the Mystery of Death meets that of the new birth (*materia prima* and *materia ultima* of the alchemists).

Purely theoretically it would again be possible to say, John 11:39 would not at all be speaking of an objective fact, but only a subjective opinion Martha had erroneously formed, and now uses as an objection or just as the reason to hinder opening the grave, to heave away the stone. But only too clearly we feel that the matter in the gospel is not meant like this. Far rather the smell of decay was so present, indeed had become so strong, that it also penetrated through the closed grave. John's Gospel means nothing other than that the forces of decay that really had taken hold of the physical body of Lazarus, were wrested away through Christ Jesus, through the *word* of Christ Jesus (11:43). Here again we recall what Rudolf Steiner relates in his first lecture-course on John's Gospel on the 'breathing the air of death' as the initiation-process in connection with the Mystery of the Healing of the Blind Man. What was said earlier, that between John 9 on the Healing of the Blind Man and that of the Raising of Lazarus (John 11), an intimate connection governs, becoming ever clearer, indicating the Johannine Mystery. This inner connection even a certain relying on the external wording becomes understandable, especially when, similar to John 9:3 on the blindness of the one born blind, also to 11:4 where Christ speaks of the chronic illness of Lazarus, it is to reveal the divine: 'that the Son of God [*the divine experienced in the 'I'*] is thereby revealed' (δοξασθῇ translators misunderstand: '*geehrt werde/ verherrlicht werde/ verherrlicht wird*' [Luther, Zwingli rev. (Zürcher Bibel)]—equivalent to 'might be glorified' [KJV/AV]; 'may be glorified' [RSV/NIV]).

From 'I' to 'I'

After all that has been discussed in the exposition, we can say this revelation of the divine 'I' expressed in the 'raising of Lazarus', the seventh and last of the 'seven signs' of Christ in John's Gospel, also the highest degree of all revelation manifesting the 'magic of the "I"', embraces the divine love in the 'I' (cf. Part One, Chapter 6). Out of all the foregoing, we know that this 'magic in the "I"' cannot work only from outside.

Such a one-sided manifestation from outside contradicts the divine nature of the 'I'. It would annul the essence of the 'I' itself. *Only from 'I' to 'I' can that activity sustain itself which comes about standing before Christ.* Why was this revelation of the divine love, this love revealed only with Lazarus-John, why was it not possible with the other disciples? The answer already lies in what was spoken directly before. Of the details, the following has still to be said.

The whole riddle, the whole Mystery of the raising of Lazarus is already found basically expressed by the disciples in the verses at the beginning of the chapter (John 11:3 and 5), 'whom the Lord loved', v. 3: 'he whom you love is ill', v. 5: 'Now Jesus loved Martha and her sister and Lazarus.' The Mystery frequently encountered in the exposition, how in the soul-being, in the whole love of both sisters of Lazarus, Mary and Martha, an inner Mystery of John's being is revealed, appearing here especially in the light of day. This love we initially encounter in Luke 7 with the yet nameless 'sinner' and 'adulteress', who anoints with costly ointment the feet of Christ Jesus, watering them with her tears and drying them with the hair of her head. Later (John 12, Mark 14) a similar event takes place directly before the Mystery of Golgotha. Here the woman is no longer the 'sinner'; she acts like a priestess, performing a sacramental deed on Christ before the great event of death. Here she is no longer the 'nameless' one; here—emphatically only in John' gospel—she carries the name Mary (Mary Magdalene). Between both events there lies in John's Gospel that significant episode of Chapter 8, where Christ raises the 'adulteress'—condemned by 'the Jews'—to herself and to the light of a higher virginity (see Section II, 'The Crisis').

As mentioned earlier, we neither need to identify this woman with Mary Magdalene, nor want to identify her like this at all. Yet we can find in the whole event a *picture* for that which had once taken place in the soul of Mary Magdalene as an inner transformation. In this transformation she received—in a higher sense—the 'nameless' name Mary. Here—this is deeply expressed in the significant pictures of John 8—her debt is wiped out of the 'Book of Destiny', so that her *Eternal Name*, her *name as Mary* can shine again in the other book, in the 'Book of Life'. Earlier we sought to understand this inner change. In this *becoming Mary* of the sister-soul at the same time a picture can be found for the *becoming John* of the *nameless disciple*, whom we experience in John 11 as the *invalid, Lazarus*. For precisely through his whole Mystery-past, the one bound with Cain's curse on mankind

(MG 273ff.) is here released from this curse. *In the dying of Lazarus, the resurrection of John takes place.* Over the grave of Bethany, in the magic of Christ's word, Abel and Cain are reconciled (discussed and demonstrated in MG 226f.). In the exposition on Mark's Gospel (MG 120ff.) is was shown how far the awakening of Jairus' daughter (Mark 5) is part of the context, how far all three raisings from the dead in the gospels (Luke 7, Mark 5 and John 11) contain an indication of the Johannine secrets, the Mystery of John.

The Mystery of Love

In the light of all these connections, let us look back at the beginning of John 11:3 & 5. We recognize all the more how in this a *Mystery of love* is revealed. We find the deeper explanation for that which made possible for Christ Jesus the deed of awakening in Bethany. This deed of awakening was only possible out of that deep love which united the whole sphere of Christ Jesus with that of the disciple whom He loved. In that sphere of love the two sisters as the actual bearers of the soul-element were fully involved, so involved that their serving love appears as the outer reflection of everything the disciple brought to his Lord and Master. Not for nothing does the beginning of John 11:2 suggests one of the sisters once anointed the Lord and had dried His feet with her hair. It appears more correct to relate this to Luke 7 as anticipating John 12, yet both point in the same direction—a Mystery lies in it, as precisely this burgeoning love rising out of the depths of mankind's Fall (cf. also John 8), of Cain's curse on mankind. It can become that completed, unconditional offering of the self that like a sacred chalice was able to receive into itself the *awakening love* of Christ. In this self-revealing love, also in and on the sister-souls, the Johannine 'I' could open itself to the Christ-'I', the awakening love of Christ.

Only where this 'I', full of opened-up love governs the 'I', can the love of Christ be revealed as an *awakening love* raying in and illuminating the depths of the grave. Here we look deeply into the Mystery of John 11 that is hidden in the words, 'I am the resurrection and the life', that is, in the 'I', revealed in the divine magic of the 'I', is revealed the love that overcomes death, life-awakening love: the 'I' itself bearing the power in itself out of the perishing decay building up the imperishable, non-decaying resurrection body.

In this sense Martha, who still expects help for her brother from some sort of external interception of divine power (11:34), is pointed by Christ towards the full power of the 'I': 'I am [the 'I' is] the resurrection and the life. Who believes in me [his/her 'I' devoted to the 'I'], s/he will live, even though s/he dies. And as a living person who trusts the 'I' [her/his heart's security resting in the 'I'] s/he will overcome death, and participate in the life of the future times.'

What in this deep, devoted love passes between the disciple and the Master from 'I' to 'I', what was revealed outwardly with the whole attitude of Mary Magdalene, this is what enabled Christ Jesus to perform the deed of the awakening of Bethany. As One dying into the Earth, sacrificing Himself by dying into the Earth, He was able to perform the deed of awakening. Similar to how already with the Healing of the Blind Man penetrating the dark material of Earth with the essence of cosmic light (John 9:6), He penetrates the earthy grave with the rays of His divine love as with the *tincture of light.* The already commencing light-processes of decay were penetrated by the divine rays of love of the cosmic life in the 'I' of Christ. By sacrificing His own bodily sheaths in death into this earthly grave, Christ Himself was able to tear away the sheaths of His friend from the earthly grave and its forces of decay. He Himself, the dying Christ, reveals the Mystery of love overcoming death, awakening life, the highest magic of the 'I'. *The raising of Lazarus is wrested from the death of Christ.* This is what the heavenly script, the language of the zodiac proclaims, when in it the heavenly sign standing over the Lazarus-events of John 11 agree with those of the event of Golgotha.

***

Thus, there also stands the Mystery of love over the grave of Bethany, over the raising of Lazarus. But this love out of which Christ speaks, 'The good shepherd lays down his life for the sheep' (John 10:11) and 'Greater love has no man than this, that a man lay down his life for his friends' (John 15:13), did He not mean *all* His disciples, all people and beings in general? Did He not speak the second of the quoted sayings to the *whole* group of disciples, adding immediately, 'You are my friends....'? These Farewell Discourses of Christ no doubt contain—as the later observations will show more clearly—in the 'Chapters on the Disciples' (Chapters 13–17) the most illuminating of all revelations of a divine love sacrificing itself; no doubt there speaks a strong human love out of the sadness of the disciples, out of the enthusiastic devotion, and the glowing confession of Peter. But alongside all this love and devotion stands the tragic turning away in Gethsemane, the betrayal of Judas, Peter's denial and the flight of the disciples.

With the weakness of the human condition of living in the body this love of the disciples was all-too-human; it was not yet strong enough to offer the human vessel to the divine love. Whether it blossomed already out of the depths of Cain, the Fall of humanity—this love, to which John 11:2 contains an indication, was still another; it contains in itself a Mystery of the chalice in which also the Mystery of the raising of Lazarus is contained. One has only half-understood the love and Christ's sacrifice of love if one does not see how this love, if it is to effect the highest in the human being, wants to be laid hold of *out of the inner depths of the 'I' and in the freedom of the 'I'*; like everything which in the highest sense of the word is the activity of Christ, it has to be wrested in human consciousness in the 'I'. This was the deeper reason, the cause, why the love of Christ, as much as He had it for everyone, could only be an *awakening love*, a love bursting the fetters of the grave, a love overcoming death directly. The *love awakening life, awakening consciousness* is revealed in the raising of Lazarus.

Thomas

Yet in this direction, John 11 contains alongside the actual Johannine secret, a significant Mystery. Probably no other disciple of Christ could meet Him in consciousness, as Lazarus could, able to have directly received the love of Christ as an *awakening love*. Apart from Lazarus no one had the strength to live dying into the grave, in a loving dying to experience the awakening love of Christ Himself, to walk through the gate of the grave in the hands of the highest Leader of souls. But while the others lacked the inner strength, the strength of consciousness, of the 'I', yet the *longing* lived in one of them, and this was *Thomas*: 'Let us go that we may die with him' (11:16). The strength to participate directly he did not yet possess, *yet he lived with it in his longing*. For this reason, Thomas is the first who after the Resurrection of Christ comes to a kind of initiation-experience. Of them all, he sensed the most deeply the Mystery of the 'disciple whom the Lord loved'. He is the one who, with the strongest forces of longing rising up towards this love that governs between Christ and the 'disciple He loved', takes this love into his inner part, the one who participated the most deeply in the whole Mystery of death and the re-awakening concerning the grave of Bethany. In his longing lives the initiation which was not yet directly attainable for him.

There exists in human life a laming longing that we learn increasingly to overcome, if the strength of Christ becomes stronger in one's soul. But there exists another longing, awoken and inspired by Christ Himself, allowing our wings to grow towards everything that encompasses the highest aims of human becoming. This longing carries in itself the strength to become the greatest love. Such a longing is received by the *Holy Spirit*. As John was the *disciple of love*, Thomas in this sense was the *disciple of longing*. We should not only see him as the 'doubter' but as the *disciple of the great longing*. We may recognize how especially for our time there lies in this *longing of Thomas* the strength to mature towards the Johannine age of love, as an age of mankind's future in which death in its form today has been overcome.

***

The forces of Transfiguration conveyed to the being of the disciples out of the dying of Christ, John's Gospel calls the forces of the *Holy Spirit*. This becomes especially clear in two places, John 7:39 and John 12:16. Through this the meaning becomes clear of the Transfiguration-process itself (Mark 9), which at the same time was a process of dying, a beginning of dying. Likewise the shining revelation of love in Christ's Farewell Discourses, the disciples' experience of the Risen One and the Pentecost-event itself. Only through the dying of Christ were these revelations of the Holy Spirit possible. And already in that wonderful tenderness and inwardness of the language, the first beginnings we already noticed in John 10, there lives this complete *revelation of the Holy Spirit* flowing out of the dying of Christ. There we also find (11:12, 15, 17 & 18) the many indications of the dying of Christ.

Moreover, this tenderness and inwardness of the language in John 11 we find particularly moving already before the meeting with the two sisters in the conversation of Christ with the disciples, especially [John 11:11], 'Our friend Lazarus has fallen asleep, but I go to awake him out of sleep' (ταῦτα εἶπεν, καὶ μετὰ τοῦτο λέγει αὐτοῖς· Λάζαρος ὁ φίλος ἡμῶν κεκοίμηται, ἀλλὰ πορεύομαι ἵνα ἐξυπνίσω αὐτόν). Out of the dying of Christ, out of that which is now increasingly revealed as the *Holy Spirit* in the dying of Christ, we see this tenderness blossoming.

The whole language of John 11 thus speaks how Christ, in performing the raising of Lazarus was already dying, how in His own dying lay the force of that awakening. With the shining forces of His own passing, Christ penetrated the darkness of the Earth, in itself dying. The bodily sheath of Lazarus was, as it were, the first piece of Earth which was penetrated by the enlivening, shining forces of Christ. And the Deed of Golgotha only continues that begun over the grave of Bethany, in the Deed of Bethany.

We saw the Deed of Bethany was already a dying of Christ into everything earthly and earthly-human, showing itself especially in the manner He participated in the mourning of human beings, and how He overcame this mourning.[91] Moreover, *Christ's weeping* over the events of Bethany (11:35) belongs to the Mysteries of John 11. 'How can Christ, the Living One, Christ the Vanquisher of death, weep over death?' one would like to ask here. Did He not know that He would wrest the disciple whom He loved from the chains of death; did He not Himself speak about it (11:4), that the illness would not be unto death, but to 'reveal the Son', the divine in the 'I'? Why then this weeping over death—if it really was a physical death that had here taken place?

But here Christ was not weeping over death, but how human beings experience death. Dying into the darkness of the Earth and the darkness of humanity, Christ learnt, *God learnt, He who descended out of the realm of life*, where death was not known, *now for the first time knows what death means for human beings*. He experiences now the whole hopeless mourning, how it is bound up with death as the essence of human nature, with the passing of a loved one. *This human experience, too, Christ now takes on Himself, as He sacrifices Himself into the earthly-human situation*. He experiences death in the heart of human beings, who are left standing so helpless and hopeless before the Mystery of death. And so deeply was He united with everything human that to Him, too, this mourning for the dead that lives in human beings overcame Him completely spontaneously.

Here, we can be struck most deeply, wonderfully, when further in the gospel account, the *motif of the stone* appears. It has to be rolled away from the grave; it raises difficulties and considerations (11:39), until finally the mighty word of Christ allows the stone to be heaved away. The *motif of the stone*, which we met so significantly in John 8—also Mark 16:3 is to be recalled—appears here again before the soul, again with the clear feeling how the outer stone is a picture for the stone lying on the human heart. But the strength of Christ, the light of Christ, the word of Christ takes the stone from human hearts—'the grave of the soul opens', as the Easter Epistle of The Act of Consecration of Man [the Eucharist of The Christian Community] declares. In the words of Christ, Who calls with a mighty voice to the one who has died (11:43), love lives that overcomes death, bursts the chains of the grave. *In this life-awakening love, the highest magic of the 'I' is revealed.*

And Christ performs the Deed of Bethany out of the complete power and fullness of the cosmic-'I' in the cosmic light, in which the twelve sacred heavenly powers are active. Out of this heavenly rhythm, and not out of some kind of earthy measuring of time, we would describe the indication to the 'twelve hours of the day' in 11:9. Every Deed that He performed, every step that He took—Rudolf Steiner points significantly in his little book *The Spiritual Guidance of Man and of Mankind* [GA 15, Lecture 3, 8 June 1911]—Christ accomplishes under the influence of the whole cosmos, the involvement of all the cosmic forces, received from all twelve sacred, heavenly powers. And the star-Mystery of the twelve sacred heavenly powers becomes in the Deed of Bethany the Mystery of the Earth.

***

During the time that Jesus of Nazareth pursued His ministry and journeys as Jesus Christ in Palestine in the last three years of His life—from the age of thirty to thirty-three—the entire cosmic Christ-being continued to work in Him. In other words, Christ always stood under the influence of the entire cosmos; He did not take a single step without cosmic forces working in Him. The events of these three years in Jesus' life were a continuous realization of His horoscope, for in every moment during those years there occurred what usually happens only at birth.

Während Jesus von Nazareth als Christus Jesus in den letzten drei Jahren seines Lebens vom dreißigsten bis zum dreiunddreißigsten Jahre in Palästina auf der Erde wandelte, wirkte fortwährend die ganze kosmische Christus-Wesenheit in ihn herein. Immer stand der Christus unter dem Einfluss des ganzen Kosmos, er machte keinen Schritt, ohne dass die kosmischen Kräfte in ihn hereinwirkten. Was hier bei dem Jesus von Nazareth sich abspielte, war ein fortwährendes Verwirklichen des Horoskopes; denn in jedem Moment geschah das, was sonst nur bei der Geburt des Menschen geschieht.

(Rudolf Steiner. Lecture 8 June 1911. GA 15.)

3.
He who was raised. Mary Magdalene (John 12)

Although it corresponds to the facts and is a true key to the riddles and Mysteries of the gospels that in the sickness and dying of Lazarus, the becoming of John, the resurrection and initiation of the disciple of Christ takes place, a doubt could still be raised. The question could be asked, why in John 12:1-9, 10, the already raised (awakened) one is still called Lazarus. Indeed, in this chapter Lazarus is mentioned, later on (John 13:23, 19:26, 20:2, 21:20) 'the disciple whom Jesus loved'. In John 11:3 & 5 this is also said of Lazarus. The riddle is actually already resolved in the addition (unjustly suppressed in some editions of the text) in 12:1: 'Then Jesus six days before the passover came to Bethany, where Lazarus was which *had been dead* [ο τεθνηκως, Stephanus New Testament 1550], whom he raised from the dead' (KJV/AV). Also with the raising in John 11:44 it is clearly and significantly said: 'And *he that was dead* [ὁ τεθνηκὼς] came forth, bound hand and foot with graveclothes, and his face was bound about with a napkin' (KJV/AV). *The picture of the one risen from the grave, who had just climbed out of the grave*—this the language of the gospel wants to tell us in all clarity—*is completely that of the dead man, of the invalid, of Lazarus.*

The whole atmosphere of the grave surrounds Lazarus. Initially he stands before us as a living corpse. Mysteriously, in his whole appearance the essentially living encounters the Mystery of the corpse. Something Saturnine, deathlike, is still clinging to the newly arising Sun-filled life. As well as in the rhythmic sign of the raising of Lazarus, the Jupiter-Sun signs ♐ and ♓ the Saturn-signs ♑ and ♒ encounter each other. In certain artistic presentations—e.g. in the drawing by Thylmann[92]—this corpse-like element of the newly risen one is clearly expressed. Moreover, after the awakening, he still carries for a certain time this atmosphere on his person; he appears, spiritually seen, still as wound in grave-cloths, his face covered with a napkin (as already expressed in MG 276f., cf. also the following, MG 277f. There it is pointed out how especially the riddle of the disciple who no longer recognizes the Temple at the beginning of Mark 13 finds a deep and meaningful explanation in the connections with that fact)—consequently also in John 12 Lazarus is still mentioned. Only gradually does this deathlike picture retreat. This (spiritual) view of the one still bound in the grave-cloths is always linked for us with the picture of the blooming life, of the non-withering beauty rising out of the depths of the grave, of the 'disciple whom the Lord loved', the 'disciple who does not die' (John 21:23).

Out of the *tincture of light*, out of the *forces of the seed* of the light which in the rays of Christ's love sink down, sacrificing themselves into the darkness of the Earth—this sacrifice, this dying into the Earth began in the Transfiguration, continued in the Mystery of Bethany, and was completed in the Mystery of Golgotha—this new non-withering life came into bloom. Christ Himself pointed in John 12 towards the Mysteries governing the processes—not only in the Mystery of Golgotha but also in Bethany—with the words (12:24): 'Truly, truly [Amen, amen] I say to you [the 'I' says to you] unless a seed [a grain of wheat] falls into the Earth and dies, it remains alone; but if it dies, it bears much fruit.' And like a serious admonition, the word of Christ is spoken of the departure of the light that now sacrifices itself into the earthly darkness (12:35, 36):

> The light is with you for a little longer. Walk while you have the light, lest the darkness overtake you; he who walks in the darkness does not know where he goes. While you have the light, take the light into your 'I' [usually translated 'believe in the light'], that you may become sons of light.

The Transfiguration process in John 12:38ff. is not identical with what is told in Mark 9, but it is a symptom of the cosmic light which dies ever more into the Earth, sacrificing itself into the Earth. The sign of the cosmic light, which is connected with the earthly element that descends inclining into the Earth, is in the gospels always the ♄. Consequently, this sign of the ♄ stands over the Transfiguration episode of John 12, as well as over the Transfiguration of Mark 9. (Notice especially the relationship of John 12:28 to Mark 9:7.) It also stands over the raising of Lazarus, as well as over the Resurrection of Christ Himself—as of a new, higher level of His connection with the Earth.

Karl Thylmann, 'Lazarus' (woodcut 17 cm x 12 cm) 1915.

As with Christ Himself—one thinks especially of the 'Washing of the Feet' standing in the ♓ in John 13—so with the newly risen disciple of Christ in the sign of the Fishes the serving love there is also revealed, in which he from now on takes an active part in the earthly Deed of Christ, and helps to accomplish the Mystery of Golgotha (MG 289ff.). All this is also expressed in that now—always reflecting the events in the consciousness of the disciple of Christ—the sister-soul, as Mary Magdalene, participates in this serving love. She, freed from the curse of Cain on mankind, performs a deed of love. The one-time 'sinner' (Luke 7:37ff.) now like a priestess performs a sacramental Deed, an introduction of the Mystery of Golgotha itself on Christ (John 12:3). The whole priestly element is expressed in the consciousness of John, its whole relationship to the effect of the Mystery of Golgotha is now newly created through the initiation. Likewise, in the conversation of the other disciples—only Judas is mentioned in John's Gospel—the fact is expressed that they failed in the initiation.

Thus, as John 12 allows us to glimpse the disciple of Christ raised out of the grave, at the same time we glimpse the sister-soul Mary Magdalene, linked with the Fishes, to the sign of resurrection and serving love, at the same time the sign of the Virgin. And we recall how we always recognized the constellation ♓–♍ (or ♍–♓) as the *constellation of the Last Supper*. Also in the beginning of John 12 (v. 2) an 'evening meal' is mentioned; resulting out of the event of Bethany an esoteric evening meal is celebrated there.

The outer withdrawal of Christ from the people corresponds to the 'dying into the Earth'. His outer seclusion is intensified through the news spreading of the Deed of Bethany (John 11:47f., 54ff.). Two Greeks, who want to speak with Him, can consequently not achieve their aim (John 12:20ff.). We see Christ Jesus here speaking differently from the dying Buddha, who still directly before his passing into *nirvāṇa* grants a final conference at the request of a new disciple, who had already been dismissed by one of Buddha's own disciples (cf. the author's *Hingang des Vollendeten*, 119f.). In the 'Mystery of the Earth', which with Christ plays a quite different role than with Buddha, we find the explanation of this difference. The aspect of the zodiac may be mentioned. This 'farewell to the outer world' is characteristic of the sign ♍ (cf. Rudolf Steiner, *Man in the Light of Philosophy, Theosophy and Occultism*. Christiania, 2-12 June 1912. GA 137). Of all signs the Virgin is the sign of the Mysteries of the Earth (cf. John 12:24) that in the gospel is always significantly united with the Mystery of the Last Supper (♍–♓).

Details on the question of John 12:12-16 (the Entry into Jerusalem) have already been discussed in the exposition on Mark's Gospel (MG 250ff.). Here, too, the aspect governing the whole chapter of the 'farewell to the outer world' (♍) is important for judging the situation (in the context of John 11:54ff.). One will be able at least to take what was said there as a hypothesis.

***

Into the governing events of the Light sinking down and self-sacrifice into the Darkness in John 12, into its Last-Supper experiences of transfigured dying immediately before the Mystery of Golgotha, there occurs a last *division of spirits*, a last *crisis*, a last 'judgment' (as it is usually translated) or 'verdict'. In no other passage in John's Gospel is this 'crisis' as a 'division of the spirits' so expressively told as 12:31: 'Now is the judgment of the world; now the prince of this world is cast out.'

He who was raised. Mary Magdalene 277

As was observed earlier, to all the other parts of John's Gospel the Lazarus Chapters (11 & 12) are inwardly related. Initially, we relate them in the first place to the first five 'Mystery-Chapters' as the fulfilment of the Mysteries in the Christian Mystery. But then also to the five ensuing Chapters [13–17], the 'Chapters on the Disciples', to which they relate as an 'affair of the group of disciples' (in the eminent sense). And Chapters 11 & 12 are inwardly strongly related to the two chapters on the Passion (18 & 19), expressed in the shared zodiac signs discussed here in detail. Naturally, the Lazarus Chapters also stand close to the 'Chapters on the Resurrection' (20 & 21), (cf. the great 'I'-motif of John 11: 'I am the resurrection and the life'). Finally also the end of John 12 shows (12:31 & 37ff.) they relate to the five 'Chapters of Crisis' (6–10).

After the language in what has preceded being already filled with tender inwardness, we now perceive it intensifies in the Farewell Discourses about to follow. In the shining revelation of the Light of Christ, we hear once more the whole seriousness of the 'words of judgment', as we know them out of the earlier passage, 12:48: 'He who rejects me and does not receive my sayings has a judge; the word that I have spoken will be his judge on the last day.'

***

The Raising of Lazarus, c. 1000 – c. 1130 with Head of Christ (detail). Chichester Cathedral, UK (photo: Nicholas Servian FIIP).

IV.
The Last Supper and Leave-taking from the Disciples
(John 13–16)

The Last-Supper constellation ♓–♍ already reached in John 12 also remains openly visible standing over the ensuing 'Chapters on the Disciples' (13–16) containing the Farewell Discourses. At the beginning of John 12 stands the scene of the evening meal in Bethany in the house of Mary Magdalene. The sign ♓ allows us initially to behold the re-awoken Lazarus, and the sign ♍ to behold Mary Magdalene. Over the following 'Chapters on the Disciples' stands the great Last-Supper of Christ itself. The whole section (Chapters 13–16, or 17) takes place against the background of the great Last Supper that before His passing Christ celebrated with His disciples. The details of this Last Supper in John's Gospel are told differently from the other gospels (Matt. 26, Mark 14 and Luke 22), yet this Last-Supper background of John 13–16 is already clearly expressed at the beginning of John 13:2-4; it is most clearly apparent in the connection between the two passages John 13:23 & 25 and 21:20.

With the cosmic rhythm, the question could only be whether the Virgin should appear as the primarily emphasized Last-Supper sign (that is, ♍–♓ instead of ♓–♏), as over the Last-Supper beginning of Mark 14 the sign ♍ was taken as primary (MG 282). In the different presentation of John's Gospel the sign ♓ appears as primary, ♍ as secondary. Firstly, because, as already expressed, the Last Supper as such (♍) in John's Gospel, unlike Mark's Gospel, does not stand in the foreground but only in the background. And then, because the scene of the Washing of the Feet at the beginning of that chapter (John 13:1-20) with the most positive clarity points towards the sign of the Fishes as the one which in the first instance is emphasized (the 'Fishes' appear on the human body as the feet, MG 32). And finally, because in the rhythm of John's Gospel, the light upper signs (to which ♍ belongs) step back altogether, and the lower, dark signs (♏ ♐ ♑ ♒ ♓), the ones of the Johannine initiation, altogether stand in the foreground with the primary emphasis. Only over the entrance of John 1 we found, as a 'Prologue', the bright signs of ♉ and ♈, and ♎ standing over John 6–10 already shows the transition from the bright to the dark, and moreover possesses there an emphasis coming from ♏. So it appears right to take on a constellation standing over John 13–16 in the form ♓– ♍.

The *great awakening Deed of Bethany* guaranteeing the human future *after the Mystery of Golgotha*, also creates the provision for all the later earthly work of the other disciples of Christ. After the tremendous event, Christ then turns with His complete love, with a self-sacrificial love unique in the whole history of mankind, to those who *initially were not able to follow Him* (John 13: 33 & 36). The other disciples, who initially failed in the initiation, were initially unable to achieve the level of consciousness achieved by the one, the great disciple of Christ, Lazarus-John. The love of Christ could be revealed on the one, whom He led living through the depths of the grave of Bethany, as the *awakening love*, as the power awakening immediate life and consciousness. On the other hand, it is shown as the love *carrying and protecting* the others who were too weak to follow Christ so far. Through Christ's love they are *preserved* through the great crisis, through the great *darkness of consciousness*, which now breaks over them and comes in Gethsemane to such a shocking consequence. They are carried right through to the Resurrection and the great *awakening of consciousness* in the festival of Pentecost and are hence protected for their great future earthly tasks, which they as yet would not have been able to fulfil. Christ clearly sees beforehand this tragic consequence of Gethsemane, the flight of the disciples, the denial of Peter, and He speaks about it most expressively in the Farewell Discourses (John 13:38, 16:32). To Peter He says that he will deny Him, Christ; to the disciples He says they will all leave Him. No weakness and darkness in the heart of the disciples remains hidden to Christ. All the tragedy of what was coming He clearly sees in advance and bears it all in His consciousness. The end of the Farewell Discourses (John 16:32) contains the clearest indication about all this. It is the frequently cited passage, where the σκορπισθῆτε of the Greek text (from *skorpizein* 'scatter', 'bring into isolation'), already in the sounds of the word, clearly points to the power of death in the Scorpion, working in the darkness region of the disciples' consciousness. All the more brightly appears the great revelation of humanity of *carrying and protecting love*—of the love that protects

His own, bearing the weaknesses of His own—of Christ offering Himself for His own. Yet before the Sacrifice for the whole of mankind stands the sacrifice for the disciple called to convey sacrifice further into humanity.

Towards this carrying, protecting love of Christ, the one disciple whose destiny forms the mysterious background of both previous chapters (John 11 & 12) takes an active part—or one rather gradually increasing towards the active part. Already the beginning scene of John 12 (cf. on this Section III, Chapter 3 of the present work) seems to us to point to this active role and task of the disciple of Christ (cf. also MG 282ff.). It is also expressed in the picture of this one disciple resting 'close to the breast of Jesus' during the Last Supper. This picture reveals him as the only one fully to experience communion with Jesus. Later in the Acts of the Apostles, indeed already in the Resurrection (John 20) and even earlier in the experiences of Golgotha (cf. John 18:15 & 16), the strength streaming from the role of the one, of the disciple John (as we would like to name him) is already prepared in the great communion of Christ's Last Supper.

Notwithstanding these connections with both previous chapters—which we take besides as containing the fulfilment of the Christian Mystery of initiation, the 'Mystery-Chapters'—a completely new section of John's Gospel begins with Chapter 13. In so far as the destiny and the task of the disciple, of the entire group of disciples, now stands completely in the middle point, we take these four chapters—in a certain sense John 17 joins as the fifth—in the actual sense of the words as the *Chapters on the Disciples*. In the exposition of Mark's Gospel, from the beginning we could lay hold of the point of view of the initiation of the disciples and their destiny. Not so specifically does the destiny of the disciples stand in the centre for John's Gospel, which in the first instance is the *gospel of Christ*. Far rather with John's Gospel it appears that the disciple-motif, which in Mark's Gospel is poured out like a substance over the whole work, in John's Gospel finds its stamp in a separately reserved section (Chapters 13–16), that forms, as it were, the concentrated content of these chapters. What the dramatic destinies of the disciples means not only for them, but what they signify for Christ comes above all to the fore.

With this, it is not said that in John's Gospel, too, the disciples' motif of destiny does not sound already earlier in individual passages. Already John 1 points in all clarity to this destiny of the disciples, to the fact of the group of disciples in the making; in John 2:11 & 17 and

The Last Supper and Leave-taking from the Disciples   281

in the Jordan episode of John 3:22 they are mentioned; in John 4:27-38 in the episode with the Samaritan woman at the well certain difficulties in understanding appear. Then in John 6:16-21 we found in the 'Storm on the Lake' already a picture is indicated of the beginning of the crisis of the disciples, and at the end of the chapter John 6:60ff. this appears in all clarity. This conclusion of John 6 touches closely on events in John 8:27-33 (see MG 187ff.). The more the others retreat as the result of their crisis, the more we see the Mystery of the one who becomes the bearer of the Christ-initiation appear in the foreground. We see the Mystery already before the Lazarus-Chapter, initially shimmering initially quietly and as if from afar through separate places in the gospel narrative.

In John 8 (Christ and the Adulteress), in John 9 (Healing of the Blind Man), in John 10 (announcement of the Johannine path of initiation) certain connections are revealed pointing to the Mystery of John. How this Mystery governs the two Lazarus-Chapters was discussed in detail. Therewith this theme is concluded, and like Christ Himself, John's Gospel turns from Chapter 13 onwards full of love towards the other disciples. The most advanced disciple, who in John's Gospel steps back completely in the deepest self-abnegation regarding his name and in his person, turns now with all the greater selfless love to the destiny of the other [Peter]. He is called to help carry the destiny of the one who once saw as his future task to ray out his own helpful strength.

In the shining revelation of love of the Chapters on the Disciples and the Farewell Chapters, John 13–16, that power and spirituality that we have to see flowing directly from the dying of Christ—which by this time indeed in a certain sense has already begun—that power which in the gospel itself (John 7:39, 12:16, 20:22) is described as that of the *Holy Spirit*, the same power that later in the Pentecost event (Acts 2) comes to the climax of its revelation. In the whole shining, loving mood that is already revealed in the *language* of John 13–16, and which in John 17 reaches its height revealed as this *power of the Holy Spirit* proceeding from the dying Christ, this is already felt here. In another more intimate sense—this, of course, is the case for the whole of John's Gospel, for all the gospels generally—the Farewell Discourses with the crowning 'Great Intercession' of John 17 are an immediate inspiration and revelation of the *Holy Spirit*. As a substance this 'Holy Spirit' shines and flows in these Farewell Discourses, in the whole revelation of Christ's love that they contain. In this revelation of love the whole language of John's Gospel gains a luminous power that can be felt as something unique in all the literature of humanity. In John 17, in the Great Intercession, the 'High-priestly Prayer', this shining power of the language also reaches its climax.

***

With the 'Washing of the Feet' at the beginning of John 13 the actual *esoteric part* of John's Gospel begins. A completely direct experience of death, an experience of Christ with death and of marital union with the depths of the Earth is poured over this whole chapter and the one following. The increasing tenderness and inwardness of the language, noticeable from John 10 onwards, reaches the characterized illuminating power.

The situation of these chapters, above all the thirteenth, is exactly that which Leonardo da Vinci has portrayed in his earthly deteriorating, spiritually imperishable, tremendous picture of the Last Supper. Rudolf Steiner once remarked (*Inner Realities of Evolution*. Lecture, Berlin, 7 Nov. 1911. GA 132) that an inhabitant of another planet, for example, someone from Mars who knew nothing of earthly conditions, if suddenly presented on the Earth with this picture would be able to experience the meaning of the whole Earth-evolution. In a moment carried by destiny, the great Turning Point of Time, all the Mysteries of the past and the future, how the far past works over into the farthest human future, all this, Steiner says, could be experienced in this picture. In the Last-Supper event (♓–♍) sacrificing divine love is revealed in the becoming of the Earth and of humanity.[93]

In the middle point of the whole drama of the scene of the Last Supper stands the critical moment when Christ dips the morsel into the dish and gives it to the betrayer (John 13:26). In his lecture, Steiner helps us to recognize how the Mystery of the 'origin of evil' here finds its expression: the whole manner by which, in cosmic beginnings, the good willed by the advanced divine powers themselves calls up the adversary. This resistance—revealing the nature of 'evil'—is taken up by divine love into its aims, by its divine foresight that wants to lead the creature to freedom, and out of freedom, to love. In this whole dramatic event of the Last Supper, the manner in which Christ took the dark deed of the betrayer on to Himself, into His own divine consciousness, we divine as belonging to the most difficult things. He has to will this dark deed itself, because without it the great Mystery for the advance of the Earth and mankind could not be brought to effect.

Only John's Gospel allows us to divine what the deed of Judas meant for Christ Himself. This finds its most moving expression in the Great Intercession or the 'High-Priestly Prayer' (John 17:12). What for the other disciples is but the transition through a difficult crisis, for Judas calls into question the destruction of the whole Incarnation (John 17:12), and only a consideration of the context of repeated earthly lives would here open the possibility of a solution to the tragedy, an atoning view.

We have but half understood the chapters with the disciples, the 'Farewell Discourses of Jesus' (John 13–16), if we only recognize the shining strength and revelation of love in the language, failing to see at the same time how these chapters are full of dramatic events and dramatic tension. Here Christ takes into His consciousness not only the betrayal of Judas, Peter's denial (John 13:38) and the flight of the disciples from Gethsemane (John 16:32), but also the weaknesses of each individual disciple—as this develops in specific individual cases in this section of the gospel. First the one, then the other disciple turns to Christ with his objections, his difficulties in understanding. Whoever here only regrets the apparent interruptions to the shining revelation of love in the flow of Christ's words, does not see how to Christ it depends precisely on releasing all the hidden, underground difficulties of the disciples and somewhat to correct and adjust their consciousness. The 'Farewell Discourses of Jesus' are not merely 'addresses' but *deeds*, full of the magic of Christ.

***

The sign of the Fishes standing so clearly and spiritually, reveals itself in its highest cosmic meaning over the scene of the Washing of the Feet at the beginning of John 13, as indeed over this whole section of the gospel. As the sign of the Divine inclining so deeply to the Earth, as the *sign of serving*, of the self-sacrificing *love* this is nowhere so revealed as in this Washing of the Feet of the disciples performed by Christ. We find the most poetic expression for all this in Christian Morgenstern [1871-1914], not only in his well-known poem, '*Die Fußwaschung*' ['The Washing of the Feet'] (which, with reference to what Rudolf Steiner gave in his lecture-cycle *The Gospel of St John*, illuminates more the cosmic-symbolical side of the Washing of the Feet), but especially in the last verse of the poem '*Faß es, was sich dir enthüllt*' ['Take in what is disclosed for you'] (in *Wir fanden eine Pfad* [1914]—'We found a path'):

Faßt ein Herz des Opfers Größe?	[Can the heart grasp the immensity of the sacrifice?
Mißt ein Geist dies Opfer ganz?—	Can the mind measure this sacrifice's extent?—
Wie ein Gott des Himmels Glanz	How a God exchanged the firmament's splendour
Tauscht um Menschennot und—blöße!	For human need and human nakedness!]

In these words the most inward spirituality, the divine meaning and gospel meaning of the sign of the Fishes is most succinctly expressed.

Everything narrated in John's Gospel from the Washing of the Feet in John 13 onwards, alongside the direct historical significance, also has an *esoteric meaning*—of course, in the last resort the whole of John's Gospel, too, in so far as it is taken as meditation content is of comprehensive, transcendent importance. In Christian esotericism of earlier times the Washing of the Feet was always taken as the picture of a specific experience on the path of Christian initiation—on the path of initiation there follows the Flagellation, Crowning with Thorns, Bearing the Cross, Crucifixion, Deposition, and Resurrection. As the human being treads the Earth with his feet, in the 'Washing of the Feet' he takes on the earthly element and the sacrifice of himself to the Earth quite directly into his deeds of will, just as Christ places quite directly for His spiritual followers as a decisive example what He did in the Washing of the Disciples' Feet (John 13:14 b& 15). *The Mystery of the Earth of the Washing of the Feet in the sign of the Fishes is at the same time the Mystery of the Christian initiation of the will.* For this reason the Fishes appear full of significance also over that 'Feeding of the Five Thousand', as an indication of the Christian initiation of the will in humanity's future.

If we look from the aspect of the cosmic zodiac to the planets, we find the revelation of Jupiter of the sign of the Fishes—the spiritual [memory] of the 'Ancient Sun', the primordial Sun-existence, in Christ sacrificing Himself to the Earth. Then, in the Fishes, in the sense of earlier tradition and star-wisdom, alongside the dominating position of Jupiter (pointing to the spiritual Sovereignty of Christ) a special 'elevation'—that is, a position of influence, not of domination—of Venus. Heavenly love, *Venus Urania*, rules in the

Scales, in the sign of the I-AM of Christ. Here, in the Fishes, Venus is revealed especially as *serving love*, as the deep self-declination of the Divine to the Earth.

***

The first words of John 13 point to the innermost being of the *carrying and preserving love* of Christ, Who 'having loved his own who were in the world, he loved them to the end'. Unlike human love that can so easily repeatedly become weak or wear out, experience or cause disappointments, this love of Christ really lasts to the end, εἰς τέλος, till the 'consecrated fulfilment', as that word is used in the language of the Mysteries. Those who themselves in their love do become repeatedly weak and falter, are not able to remain constant to the divine experience to the end, until the consecrated fulfilment, Christ carries through their weakness of consciousness, their sleep, darkness and crisis of consciousness right through until the great reunion. Alongside all the sorrow, uneasiness, and feeling of death, this mood and hope of reunion decisively penetrates (John 6:22) the Farewell Chapters of John's Gospel. A mastery in the whole presentation of John's Gospel is revealed precisely in how it unites and strongly emphasizes with this whole tenderness and inwardness, this whole bright revelation of the love of Christ yet at the same time the critical seriousness of the Last-Supper experience. That the disciples initially could simply not bear this abundance of divine love, that they, as it were, fall to pieces at the communion of this love in the Last Supper—this motif too sounds repeatedly with emphasis throughout.

One of the most disturbing passages is the one where to the warning words 'where I am going you cannot come', He adds 'as I said to the Jews'. He has to remind His own of this terrible saying, uttered in the dispute with the Jews, when the 'crisis' reached its height (John 8:21), 'I go away, and you will seek me and die in your sin: *where I am going, you cannot come*'. Only through His sacrificial death, through the whole magic and self-sacrifice already present in the 'Farewell Discourses', can He effect a different, more hopeful solution to the crisis for the disciples. In a significant manner, He shows those not able fully to open up to the divine love a way how they can now completely out of the human element from one to another develop this love, are able to ascend towards this divine love (John 13:34, 'A new commandment I give to you, that you love one another; even as I have loved you, that you also love one another'). The love that governs between those who are united or want to unite with Christ, is the touchstone for how far the growth of the divine in the heart is developed.

The disciples 'I'-extinguishing crisis of consciousness is revealed most shockingly at that dramatic climax. As Christ dips the morsel into the bowl, they look towards him 'who lay close to the breast of Jesus'. In them all lived the anxious question, which in John 13:22 is only gently suggested but in Matthew (26:22) and Mark (14:19) is expressed in the words, 'Lord, is it I?' (whereby the Greek μήτι ἐγώ εἰμι appears in Matthew as the direct negative of ἐγώ εἰμι, 'I am'). Between 'I am' and 'I am not' stands here the anxious question, 'am I (—or am I perhaps not)?' And right into the external scene, painted pictorially with effective drama, the words (appearing with the exit of Judas) 'and it was night', the darkness of consciousness. At the same time, the episode helps us to recognize the fully vital description of the outer event, frequently so characteristic for John's Gospel (John 13:28 & 29), right into the most tangible details.

Peter's crisis is linked here to that of Judas. After the temperamental and fiery beginning with its excess of warmth and burning devotion (John 13:6ff.), the indication of Christ extinguishes this fire. The ensuing night of consciousness (John 13:39) is deeply disturbing. The indication of the crisis of Judas produced a rigid benumbing in the heart of the disciples; the indication of Peter's crisis resolves the alarm spoken of at the beginning of John 14. And so in a series all sorts of individual crises and difficulties in consciousness are revealed in each disciple. For the many characteristics left in the dark in the gospels, the individual disciples supply a valuable contribution in John 13 to 16.

Thus first we see (John 15:4) how *Thomas* cannot himself find the way that he had seen his friend following, the 'disciple, whom the Lord loved', the way to which the whole longing of his heart was pulling (John 11:6). This is the *way of the 'I'* (John 10:9), that is the truth and the life (John 14:6), the way that begins as a path of knowledge and ends as the path of life. He cannot yet see it with his spiritual eyes. The doubt in his understanding that still clouds his spiritual vision is then healed through the Risen One (John 20:27 & 28).

The difficulties of Philip are revealed as similar. These originate from a sphere of early clairvoyance—linked with the 'land east of the Jordan'. He would always behold the *Father* in the supersensory sphere, and cannot recognize the spiritual-physical standing in reality before him (John 14:8 & 9). And the 'other Judas' (John 14:22) who cannot conceive why Christ can only reveal Himself to him who offers the vessel of love, who is able to open himself in full devoted love to the divine.

Everything spoken in these 'Farewell Discourses' of Christ concerning His *passing to the Father* remains the darkest thing for the disciples. In his communications on John's Gospel, Rudolf Steiner expressed the great insight how Christ speaks here of the Mystery of death, from the *Mystery of the Father* hidden behind the Mystery of death. Here he presents death as the 'ever-living Father', the 'seed of life', Who has to enliven the earthly [world], in order that it does not fall out of life, in order that it can be taken up again into life. The true figure of death—Rudolf Steiner tells us—Christ places before humanity. What to the human being is veiled as death He unveils as the reality of the ever-living Father.

> Only in this way could the divine Father-Spirit save the memory of the divine origin, that He imparts the *kindness of death* to everything that is striving in the material [world].

In the Mystery of the Father, Christ unveils the true name of death. Here at the same time, as the initiation story of Mark's Gospel shows, lies the decisive point with all the instruction to the disciples, with all the initiation of the disciples. They are to grasp the Mystery of death, of the death of Christ, of the Mystery of Golgotha—and here is shown precisely their understanding is always weak, as insufficient (Mark 8:32; MG 179ff., 189ff., 198ff.). Only one, as we saw, was able to grasp the meaning of death, overshadowed by the power of Elijah-John in the 'Transfiguration of Christ on the Mount', to become the apprehender of the Mystery of Golgotha (MG 197f.). The one [Peter] who abode with Him on the Mount, also a beholder of the Transfiguration, blinded by the Sun-splendour of Christ, still cannot grasp the great Mystery (Mark 9:5). Even the revelation of the Mystery of death so overwhelmingly demonstrated by Christ the disciples do not comprehend.

All this we see working into the Farewell-Discourse Chapters of John's Gospel. The disciples probably divine that Christ with the *passing to the Father* is speaking of His standing directly before His progress to death, but only as a vague pressure. All this lay as the dread of death on their hearts; they are not yet able to grasp the hidden Mystery of life hidden in death. John 16:5: 'But now I am going to him who sent me; yet none of you asks me, Where are you going? But because I have said these things to you, sorrow has filled your hearts.'

Yet above all the disciples' anxieties, difficulties of understanding, shine the great, comforting sayings of Christ of the *way* and of the *vine* of the 'I', 'I am the way, and the truth, and the life' (John 14:6): the 'I' is the way, on which the knowledge becomes again life. And 'I am the true vine' (John 15:1), ἐγώ εἰμι ἡ ἄμπελος ἡ ἀληθινή: the vine of the 'I' is that which *cannot be wiped out (aletheia), the power anchored in the eternal, of the never running dry, of the never extinguishable consciousness.* (In the words *aletheia, alethinos* of the Greek text, as we showed earlier, lies this meaning.) The inner Mystery of the 'I' is thereby expressed.

And Christ leads ever nearer in the last hour with His own towards the great *Mystery of the cosmic Father.* He shows the disciples how the Christ-strength of the 'I' has to be strengthened that it may now unite with the Mystery of the Father-death sunk to and living in the earthly depths (John 14:12, 14:28), and how as a consequence of His going to the Father, His marriage with the depths of death of the Earth out of the spheres of cosmic light flows the revelation of the *Holy Spirit*, how the spirit as comforter and advocate can come to them (John 16:7). Not as something simply resting in itself, but as the great *cosmic dynamic* there shines in this section the *Mystery of the Holy Trinity*—Christ in the 'I' between Father and Spirit. It is the *Holy Spirit, Who brings the world to awareness* (ἐλέγξει 16:8, from ἐλέγχειν *elenchein*, which Luther translates as *'strafen'* ['punish'] and KJV/AV as 'reprove', RSV & NIV 'reprove', 'convict'.) With this it is important to consider that the original and meaning of all 'punishment' alone justifiable before the spiritual world is a 'bringing-to-awareness', or consciousness. In this bringing-to-consciousness all crises, all 'verdicts' are concluded. For, thus Christ wants to say to His own, full consciousness wants to awaken in you. But now you are in a sleep of consciousness, 'I have yet many things to say to you, but you cannot bear them now' (John 16:12).

Such a 'bringing-to-awareness', restoring of consciousness, is fully a part of the 'Last-Supper events'. Between the Last-Supper narration of the three other gospels and the Last-Supper Chapters (13–16) of John's Gospel there exists a precise higher synopsis and synthesis. The former tell more the outer proceedings of the Last Supper. John's Gospel tells the inner processes, the inner side of the event. This is also the meaning, when the Last-Supper constellation (♓–♍) of the cosmic rhythm is recognized over the Farewell Chapters of John's Gospel.

The Last Supper and Leave-taking from the Disciples 289

This whole Last-Supper celebration of Christ with His own is the time of cosmic farewell of world-historical unique seriousness and greatness. Christ has to leave behind apparently alone in the earthly world those united to Him in love, whom He has drawn from the enclosing sleep of consciousness, and whom He still needs to use for His earthly work. He will lead them through all the night of consciousness, yet He knows over all the heart-breaking anxiety of the great farewell there shines the joy and the conviction of the eternal reunion, 'So you have sorrow now, but I will see you again, and your hearts will rejoice, and no one will take your joy from you' (John 16:22).

We experience with Buddha's passing *only* seriousness and the sadness in the great farewell (see the author's *Hingang des Vollendeten*. Stuttgart 1925. 126). In John's Gospel there stands over all the seriousness of the farewell the *reunion in the Resurrection*. This inwardly links these Farewell Chapters (John 13–16, and 17) with the two Resurrection Chapters (20 & 21), which likewise are 'Chapters on the Disciples' forming a septenary (cf. Part One, Chapters 4 & 6).

In this light of the Resurrection and of the eternal reunion, the Farewell Discourses of Christ over the *Star-Mysteries of the world of the Father* (John 14:2, and Part One, Chapter 7), all the Mysteries of the *Eternal Name* and the supplication in the Eternal Name, the *eternal supplication in the 'I'* (John 14:13ff., 15:7, 16:23ff., also Mark 11:23ff. and MG 269f.), are allowed to shine for us. On the *innermost full power of the 'I'*, on the inner omnipotence and magic in the 'I', which, however, can be exercised in full harmony with the cosmic harmony of the Eternal Name, with His last words He recalls something still preserved for them in the lap of the future, which He can still prepare for them, Christ for His own. Thus, He leads them finally to a *divining insight of the Mystery of the Father* (John 16:29-31), which as a fact rightly existing before the spiritual world is then included by Christ in the *Great Intercession*, the 'High-Priestly Prayer' (John 17:8). With the power of this prayer, He will carry them now through their crisis, vouching for them, for their whole being and work in the future.

V. THE GREAT INTERCESSION
(John 17)

In the Great Intercession or the 'High-Priestly Prayer'—as not without reason Christ's prayer to the Father-God, the great dialogue of the Son with the Father in John 17, has always been called—Christ's Farewell Discourses of the Chapters on the Disciples in John's Gospel finds its crowning conclusion. The 'esoteric section' of the gospel arrives here at its actual climax, from which streams of light and warmth are seen to flow towards all regions of the world, all time and space. With the great motif of the *'"I" that has overcome the world'*, we saw the Farewell Discourses end (John 16:33). In John 17 we see—or we hear, for increasingly John's Gospel becomes for us something of symphonic, cosmic music, something to be perceived with the inner ear—how this tremendous 'I' of Christ, which has overcome the world, intercedes this prayer for those remaining in the world. These are His own united with Him in love, and all human beings who find and can find their way to Him, the way to the 'I' in the love opening to the divine 'I' (John 17:20).

What Christ still entrusts to the disciples as a final sublime testament, what He could still say of the Mystery of the *power of prayer*, of *prayer's power of authority in the 'I'* (John 16:23ff.), this He confirms and fulfils now Himself in world-historic, unique greatness. Shining over this *tremendous prayer of intercession*, all the *Mysteries of the Eternal Name* focus on this world-event of all future worlds, through which as in no other section of John's Gospel we feel we are directly raised and transported as into cosmic heights. The *growing power of light in Christ's words* that we already could experience in what preceded it, has here raised itself to a truly *cosmic starlight* that flows over all the words of Christ. Cosmic profundities of the stars and cosmic Mysteries of the stars shine and sound, into which only the initiate, the disciple of Christ who has gone through the Johannine Initiation is able to see and hear. *Revelation of the Holy Spirit* as it flows out of the sacrificial death of Christ here reaches the climax of its shining power. It is as though, before uniting Himself with the dark depths of the Earth in the Mystery of Golgotha, all the *Star-Mysteries of the cosmic heights* shine in the words of the Great Intercession of Christ.

Thus we feel, looking at the cosmic rhythm of the heavenly zodiac over this Chapter 17 of John's Gospel, that spiritual being, herself the one who governs the cosmic Mysteries of the stars, the great cosmic provisions for the way, is the spiritual being of the great cosmic intercession, the *heavenly Virgin*. She, as the bearer and giver of the cosmic bread of the stars (MG 133ff.), together with the Fishes forms *the Last-Supper constellation*. We beheld this Last-Supper constellation already over the previous chapters of the great Farewell (John 13–16) which, together with the Great Intercession (John 17) present the pentad, the five Chapters on the Disciples. We experience here the Fishes especially strongly as the sign of Christ's inclining to the Earth, of [His] serving love. This, before the final union, or marriage, of Christ with the depths of death of the Earth is followed in the 'High-Priestly Prayer' by the great elevation to the cosmic, starry heights. All this here is *fullness of cosmic light*. We will most appropriately characterize the uniqueness of this John 17 that stands out in blinding light above all other sections of John's Gospel, by feeling how of the two signs of the Last-Supper constellation the one dark one, the sign ♓ steps back, and alone the starry light of the heavenly Virgin, the spiritual being of cosmic intercession shines over this chapter of the *Great Intercession*. It appears inwardly meaningful when, contrary to the dominance of the lower darker zodiac signs in all the other chapters of John's Gospel, this most light-filled of all the chapters is felt as only ruled from one of the upper, bright heavenly signs.

***

The meaning of this 'cosmic intercession' can only be rightly understood when it is seen how here Christ wants to lead His own through consciousness to freedom, to the free laying hold of the divine. In this *joy* (χαρὰν), which Christ wills to be fulfilled in His own (John 17:13, cf. 16:24), in this *joy in the 'I'* there lies at the same time, if we rightly take the nuance of the Greek, the *freedom*, the feeling of free space. Also through the intercession of Christ people do not receive something in their sleep, but the strength is radiated to them which leads them towards awakening out of their spirit-sleep, so that in the inner freedom of their awake consciousness they can lay hold of the 'I' that is offered to them if they want to lay hold of it. That the path to freedom and to life opening up to His own, which is meant by Christ through the power of the intercession, is a path leading through knowledge, speaks clearly in the saying of the intercession (John 17:3), 'And this is eternal life [the 'future cycles of time'], that they know Thee [Father] as the latent Divinity in the Unity of the Universe of the never-extinguishable consciousness, and the [out of thy star-radiance] commissioned, healing [Saviour] Jesus as the Christ.' Thus Christ's Great Intercession is a *prayer in the 'I', from the 'I' and to the 'I'*.

If in meditative devotion we have followed the whole exposition up to here, we can feel how much the *Great Intercession* is the esoteric centre, the *heart* of the whole Gospel according to John. Something releasing and freeing is imparted from here to our heart, taking away an oppressive weight that previously can creep upon us, especially with the inner devotion towards the content of the gospel meant here. For something oppressive would lie in it, if with all devotion to John's Gospel we have to say to ourselves: Well, something indeed great and tremendous, something unique, pointing to the human future, is in this Christ-message from the 'I' that intensifies and is transfigured from chapter to chapter of this gospel to ever higher revelation. It is:

- a new wine of life (John 2);
- a new health (John 3);
- a stream of living water (John 4 & 7) will flow from this 'I';
- a new birth will take place out of it (John 3);
- forces of the starry bread of life it would give out of it (John 6);
- it wants to raise us to a new virginity, to inner freedom (John 8);
- it wants to open a new beholding to us (John 9);
- the way of life and of the future of mankind shines in the 'I' (John 10);
- it is strong enough to burst the gates of the grave itself (John 11);
- the resurrection and the life is enclosed in it (John 12);
- it is even the power of the never extinguished consciousness, rooted in eternity (John 15).

Great and tremendous, profound and truthful is the power of the 'I'. Yet precisely through John's Gospel, we now have to experience how people are still unable to comprehend this 'I', because they have estranged themselves from the divine prototype. They hate the 'I'; they raise stones against Him; the divine tidings from the 'I' only stir up chaotic division, wild conflict in the heart; we see how, dividing and judging, they conjure up the crisis, as it works on them. Finally, we perceive how even the disciples of the Lord are not able to comprehend this divine message of the 'I' in their ultimate depths; they are not able to offer the human earthy vessel to the divine 'I'. They cannot find the 'path of life', except for the one disciple. He is led by Christ Himself, under unspeakable difficulties, passing through the gate of the grave itself; pressing on he finally does find it.

From these tidings, from this 'I' itself, which indeed even today still lies in the far future, how with all the weaknesses and shortcomings in our being, how can we but feel ourselves repulsed by something in all eternity hopelessly unreachable? Does not this whole great message of John's Gospel ultimately but bring one's own powerlessness all the more strongly to consciousness?

Nevertheless, in such thoughts there would live only the whisperings of the adversary, that would make us forget that this 'I' in John's Gospel bringing us tidings and revelation is at the same time *love*; it knows it is inwardly united with everything that lives and suffers. The *full power of the 'I'*, consequently, carries the *power of the Great Intercession* in itself. The *power of love* ultimately is that:

- which allows the wine of life to flow to human beings,
- which opens the eyes of the Man Born Blind,
- which raises to light the one fallen through error in love,
- which ultimately overcomes the forces of decay themselves and bursts the portals of the grave.

To this *full power and authority in the 'I'* there also belongs the *love in the 'I'* that takes on all the necessities of the other, all the weaknesses and denials of the other into its innermost being, all the innermost petition. Finally, it can speak of itself, 'Greater love has no man than this, that a man lay down his life for his friends' (John 15:13). Here it is the love that for the sake of human weakness cannot yet be *awakening love* (as between Christ and Lazarus), yet reveals itself as the *carrying and protecting love* (as between Christ and the disciples). This love, that ultimately never divides or excludes but always only unites, leads aloft to the divine heights of human nature and on these heights can work to unite everything. Not that we directly gain the link to the divine 'I', *but that we can find in it the Great Intercession of Christ*, and through the power of this intercession the connection to the divine 'I' itself. *This is the sublime meaning of John's Gospel.*

And this intercession of Christ had the strongest of all, the world-historic, unique power and authority, because in death itself, in going through the depths of death of the Earth, this intercession vanquishes the power and authority of death. That One married to death, speaking the sublime words of John 17, gives to the words of this prayer their power and authority, that out of the dying and self-sacrifice of Christ, the revelation of the Holy Spirit flows, gives the words the fullness of light from brilliant cosmic, starry light. The words of the One dying for His own, Christ sacrificing Himself, uniting Himself in marriage to the Earth's depths of death carry a cosmic seed, a cosmic power of a seed and a power of the Sun. Moreover, in this *Mystery of the seed* and the depths of the Earth (cf. John 12:24, here too in the sign of ♍) a Mystery of the heavenly Virgin is enclosed.

Not for nothing did Christ so speak to the disciples of the *power of prayer*, the *prayer of the 'I'*, that it makes clear to them how this omnipotence in the 'I', this power and authority of prayer yet can only be practised when and as far as the 'I' is united in love with the divine and consequently also with everything that lives. And so He says, 'If you abide in me' (cf. also Mark 11:25, MG 269f.). Of this stellar love, this love revealing itself in the starry harmony of the universe, this love allows Christ to go into death for His own. The power of the intercession victorious through death gives John 17 the world-historical precedent.

From this *Great Intercession* of Christ proceeds the force that becomes helping forces in our life and work wherever people are entrusted to our care. The 'new commandment to love one another' points in this direction, which Christ gives to His own, 'that you love one another; even as I have loved you'. The rays of cosmic love from the intercession of Christ penetrate everything; they can brighten and warm the lowliness of daily life and all human work and all work for humanity. This can be a reason why John the initiate, the inspirer of John's Gospel, was also allowed to hear this most intimate, this most esoteric of all cosmic revelations and revelations of Christ that flowed to him. This completely sublime *dialogue between the Son and the cosmic Father*, the highest and most intimate of all revelations that were given him that he may listen, this most star-illuminated of all spiritual revelations was nevertheless entrusted to him for those around him and those who are to come.

Moreover, those who have died, united to us in love, and precisely those who after divesting earthly connections have passed over into the stellar contexts to prepare the connections for a new earthly life, to spin the webs of a new earthly dress, can in the meditative devotion from us receive from us cosmic rays of love of the 'High-Priestly Prayer'.[94] This can become provisions for the way (♍), which the connections between us and them link increasingly firmly and inwardly. Within this inner connection of the forces of the intercession of Christ coming to life in the stellar harmony, or music, we weave and work with them on the *'star-dress of love'* of which we know, that it is the *'I'*, in the language of fairytales that is expressed as the *star-Mystery of the 'I'* (Part One, Chapter 5). Here our feelings, awakening and coming to life with Christ's intercession flow together with them as expressed by Christian Morgenstern humanly so beautifully and simply in the poem *'Leis auf zarten Füßen naht es'* in *Wir fanden einen Pfad*.

Die in Liebe dir verbunden,	[Those united in love to you,
werden immer um dich bleiben,	will always remain around you,
werden klein und grosse Runden	will describe small and large circuits
treugesellt mit dir beschreiben.	faithfully joining with you.
Und sie werden an dir bauen,	And they will build in you,
unverwandt, wie du an ihnen,—	unceasing, as you in them—
Und, erwacht zu Einem Schauen,	and, awakened to One beholding,
Werdet ihr wetteifernd dienen!	they all will contend to serve!]

Also this bearing and protecting love building on and leading up to the other, belongs to the *full authority of the 'I'*, to the magic of the *'I'*. *Only in this love receiving the other in our own inner being is the 'I' fulfilled:* 'Father, I desire that they also, whom thou hast given me, may be with me where I am, to behold my glory which thou hast given me in thy love for me before the foundation of the world.'

***

The actual star-Mystery of John 17 is presented in Part One, Chapter 7, 'The Star-Mystery of the Eternal Name'. All the cosmic star-Mysteries of John 17 shine before us once more in the cosmic light. Then the most precipitous transition of John's Gospel to John 18 takes place. Here we see in Christ's great progress to death, the Star-Mystery completely passes over into the *Mystery of the Earth*, into that Mystery of the Earth which is found softly sounding in John 8 & 9, until in John 11 it could be placed into the greatness of that Mystery. Here John 17 came to us as a final rising light of the stars, as if suggesting a farewell to the Mysteries of the stars, and the transition to what follows like that black, F-minor passage in Beethoven's *Ninth Symphony*, when the starry shimmer in the dark earthy depths goes out, when the stars, as it were, themselves sink into the Earth, and a darker, blacker veil, the veil of Golgotha, expands over the whole spiritual fields of vision. Also in this encounter of Star-Mystery and Earth-Mystery from starry heights to earthly depths is revealed the Mystery of that sign, which at the same time is the sign of the elemental level of the Earth and the highest stellar life-ether, the Earth-sign and life-ether sign of the Christ Son-cross, which is also the sign of the *heavenly Virgin* shining over the great cosmic prayer of Christ.

VI. Suffering and Dying
(John 18 & 19)

1. The Mystery of the Earth (♍)

The 'Great Intercession' of Christ (John 17) lies completely in the light raying from the *Mystery of Golgotha*. This prayer—spoken in the spirit—of the Son to the Father, receives its whole strength, its whole magic, in that it is spoken from the spiritual place where 'words are deeds', that it is spoken by the God, Who, incorporated in the earthly physical body, is about to sacrifice innocent Body and Blood for guilty mankind. He had already begun to die into the Earth and mankind, when we intimately understand what plays into the events of the 'raising of Lazarus', in the 'Washing of the Feet', in the Last Supper and in the Farewell to the disciples. Unlike a merely natural event, this Mystery manifested by God works in the consciousness of humanity in order to achieve its full effect. For this reason there is the whole self-sacrificial effort of Christ to awaken the consciousness of the one disciple initiated by Christ that he recognize directly and actively participate in the great Mystery. For this reason, too, the great sacrificial love of Christ that He in farewell to the disciples turns to those who now are asleep in consciousness, in order to lead them to their later awakening and to their earthly tasks. The spiritual efforts of Christ for the sake of the disciples concludes in the magical deed of the Great Intercession.

A connection is thereby shown to both Passion Chapters (18 & 19), to the previous 'Chapters on the Disciples' (13–17) and to the two

Lazarus-Chapters (11 & 12). The ending of John 11 (v. 47ff.) helps us clearly to see how the impression of the deed performed by Christ becomes the earthly-human reason for His earthly death, in which the Jewish fear of the Romans played a role. The Jews, fearing the destiny of their Temple, saw in the handing over of Christ Jesus the only possible way out (MG 246f.). The High Priests, after the great deed of Bethany, want to prepare for Christ Jesus that destiny that in pre-Christian times always followed the betrayal of the Mysteries.

The end of John 11 indicates the earthly-human causes of the Mystery of Golgotha; John 12 indicates its divine origin and its divine meaning. Consequently, the indication to the Mystery of the seed dying into the Earth (John 12:24) and at the end of the chapter (John 12:37-50), the reference to the crisis of humanity, in which lies hidden the actual divine necessity of the Mystery of Golgotha, the deeper spiritual ground for the earthly dying of Christ. Certainly, there previously lit up—we recall the Cleansing of the Temple (John 2:17ff.)—the connection of the whole happenings of the gospel with the event of Golgotha. But the section John 6–10 contains the actual and direct indication to this: *In the great crisis of the 'I' in humanity lies the direct spiritual reason for the divine necessity of the Mystery of Golgotha.* Divine love could not allow the crisis conjured up to lead to the destruction of humanity, could not allow humanity to succumb in this crisis. In the darkness that is not able to comprehend the light, Christ sacrifices the divine substance of light, the seed of light, the *tincture of light*, sacrificing Himself in order to lead the Earth and humanity again to the light.

Thus a direct connection governs between both Passion-Chapters (18 & 19) and the Chapters of Crisis (6–10), to which the end of John 12 once more points. The intention of the Jews to stone Him (8:59, 10:31) carries in itself in a seed-form the whole cross of Golgotha. As the five chapters of the crisis (6–10) with a pair make seven, so do the five with the two Golgotha-Chapters make seven chapters, in an eminent sense *Chapters on Humanity*. The whole destiny of humanity is contained in them. *As in no other moment of world-history, the destiny of humanity is decided on Golgotha.*

From *star-heights* and *star-Mysteries* we began our observations of John's Gospel and were led increasingly into *earthly depths* and *earthly Mysteries*. This transition from Star-Mysteries to Earth-Mysteries can be felt as a great leading motif in John's Gospel. In star-heights lies only the one side of the World-Mystery, in earthly depths the other. After the shining once more of all the stars and star-Mysteries of the

Eternal Name in John 17, John 18 leads into the dark depths of the Earth and of humanity. We experience the Mystery of Christ uniting in marriage to the Earth in the Mystery of Golgotha.

**

Here, too, we cannot move on in our observations without considering the person whose act of knowledge it was, through which alone we have the possibility to speak on the *Mystery of Golgotha* as an *earthly event*, of Christ's earthy deed and deed for humanity, and that person is Rudolf Steiner. For this expression 'earthly event' itself we are indebted to him. What was said earlier with the Healing of the Blind Man, and with the story of Lazarus has here to be repeated: without the key offered by Rudolf Steiner we could never have gained such insights into the Mystery of Golgotha, into the Mysteries that it contains of the Earth—without the key, such a work as this could never have been written.

But one should remember those for whom such talk of the 'Mystery of Golgotha' still makes problems, who cannot harmonize this with their principles of knowledge. They would be prepared to admit Christ Jesus as a wise teacher, a loving teacher of humanity, perhaps indeed as the 'God-man' even prepared to take compassion on His destiny. But they do not want to understand how far the Christ-Event means something for the Earth. When they read, moreover, in Rudolf Steiner (*The Gospel According to St John*. Cassel, 6 July 1909. GA 112) how through the drops of blood flowing from the wounds of the Crucified the Earth takes into itself new shining forces, how if a being with clairvoyant forces from a distant planet could have been able to look at the Earth, they would first have seen how the aura of the Earth had become increasingly darkened during the pre-Christian age. Now with the event of Golgotha it has been lit up in new colours. The Earth was penetrated with an astral light that little by little will become an etheric one and then a physical one. The first beginning of the Earth becoming a Sun was given at that time when the blood flowed out of the wounds of the Redeemer on Golgotha—then it will at first appear to them [those who have problems reading about this] that their earthly thinking has to break down at the extent of such a cosmic vision [cf. the author's study *The* Parsifal *Christ-Experience in Wagner's Music Drama*. Anastasi 2015. 46].

To understand such 'communications of the spiritual researcher', we may recall what has been said in the astronomical introduction to this book about the possibility of thinking to reach towards a different image of the concept of 'matter' than is usual for people. This is of a spiritual concept of matter, towards which also all natural-scientific explanations, hypotheses and theories lead and increasingly urge. Already this natural-scientific picture of 'matter' increasingly dissolves into a system of forces, behind which people already today begin to divine the fact of 'consciousness' as an actual reality. We gain the correct view of matter and spirit when we behold the reality in the light of the spiritual [viewpoint], of consciousness, and behold in 'matter' the 'shadow of light'. If spirit did not stand behind *all* matter then the origin of consciousness out of mere matter would be the Mystery pure and simple, the Riddle of all riddles, which with all worldviews would remain standing as an insoluble remainder (the famous '*Ignorabimus*', 'we shall never know', of Dubois-Reymond).

The way leading to the spiritual concept of matter always meant here is given in the *whole of anthroposophy*, for which a special research such as the present attempt can never be a replacement. However, the reader who has followed in meditative devotion the observations to this point will also be able to find in John's Gospel itself the path towards a spiritual picture of the earthly sphere and consequently towards an understanding of the Deed of Golgotha as an Earth-Mystery, of a spiritual event that laid hold of the Earth itself and transformed it.

Before our natural-scientific, materialistic age today, there was an age that was closer to the spiritual comprehension of the *Mystery of the Earth* as meant here. From early Manichaeism onwards until the alchemy of the medieval Middle-Age Rosicrucians we find Imaginations of light and darkness regarded and taught as the two primordial principles: in Christ the *seed of light* had been sacrificed into the darkness. Here the alchemical concept of *tincture* frequently appears; the Christian thoughts of Jakob Boehme, too, played a significant role. It is a remarkable fact that with this presentiment or recognition of the Mystery of the Earth (in the alchemical sense) there also always goes, hand in hand, a significant deepened understanding of the Bible, something reaching far beyond accepted theology. It is amazing to what spiritual heights an understanding of the Bible has developed in some of these writings deriving from this spiritual direction of the Middle Ages, lasting right into the eighteenth century.[95]

The creation story of Genesis—which appears to the smart materialists of today so easily as mere 'children's fairytales'—the story of Noah and other passages of the Old Testament suddenly reveal their whole profundity, the whole richness of their cosmogonic Mystery. The 'Song of Solomon' contains behind its apparent eroticism a completely different meaning resting on the profundities of the Mystery of the Earth. And the methods especially searching for these occult, alchemical Mysteries, throws light right into the New Testament, right into the depths of John's Gospel. The writer, or inspirer of this gospel himself in the writings and spiritual striving of that time [beginning of the modern age] was celebrated as 'John the alchemist'.

Several matters resulting from our observation over the connection of the Johannine Initiation with the 'alchemical' meaning of the sign of the Crab (MG 241f., 262f., 280f.) appear again before the soul. We recognize how very much the Mystery of metamorphosis and transfiguration of the earthly through the spiritual lies in the meaning of all Johannine perception. The 'alchemical motif' of transforming the Earth, of *transubstantiation*, belongs absolutely to the Johannine motifs. Only an approach from such an observation divining something of the 'chymical', of the earthly secret of the Mystery of Golgotha, would again unlock the full depths of John's Gospel. Today this still lies in the future.

Yet already today we can recognize how this 'chymical' motif of the earthly secret penetrates John's Gospel from the beginning, from the 'change of water into wine' at the Wedding in Cana, to the wound in the side of the Crucified from which flows *blood and water* (John 19:34). In the story of John 8—Christ, who writes the obligation of the adulteress in the Earth—we found the earthly Mystery significantly inserted. Even more in John 9, in the story of the Healing of the Blind Man, where the spiritual rays of the light of Christ communicate to the earthly substance the forces of light which open his eyes. To a still higher degree these spiritual rays of Christ's light and love are manifest in the raising of Lazarus; they penetrate the depths of the grave itself in order there to conquer the forces of decay. In the physical vessel of Lazarus penetrated by the rays of Christ's love this 'transformation of the Earth' first begins. From Golgotha onwards, it takes hold of ever-greater earthly contexts.

From the 'raising of Lazarus' to the earthly Deed of Christ on Golgotha is but one step. Lazarus was not able to awaken him*self*. Without the help, without the words of love of Christ the Initiator, he would have succumbed conclusively to the earthly forces of death and decay. At Golgotha the power of Christ worked directly as the power of His own Self. In the earthly sheath of Jesus of Nazareth fully penetrated by the power of Christ, united in marriage to the earthly depths, here the divine archetypal Light carries the *light in the 'I'* Itself, carries in Itself the force to call up the dying Earth-existence to new life. Here all the *magic of the 'I'* is concluded in the Resurrection of Christ. In this, His magic overcoming death, that 'I', which the people living at that time could not bear, awakening division in their souls, is revealed as the *primary source of divine love.*

On Golgotha is accomplished the division of spirits, the *crisis*. For this reason, both Passion-Chapters belong inwardly with those of the crisis (John 6–10). The most direct indication is contained in John 12:31 (RSV): 'Now is the judgment of this world [νῦν κρίσις ἐστὶν τοῦ κόσμου τούτου]; now shall the ruler of this world be cast out.' In the Kassel lecture-course, Rudolf Steiner points out (*The Gospel of St John*. Kassel, 24 June–7 July 1909. GA 112) in the last lectures, how what is narrated of the death on Golgotha has to be directly thought in connection with the transfiguration process. The final influence—at work in all humanity and human corporeality—of the luciferic-ahrimanic beings is expelled. The body of Christ no longer contained anything of what the human being pledges to the death-forces of the adversary and to which he is indebted. Christ's death consequently was completely without debt and was representative. *The divine 'I' (Christ) Itself between on the one side Lucifer and on the other Ahriman—here the tremendous crisis, the division of spirits, takes place.*

With the section on the crisis (John 6–10), there may already have appeared expressively before the soul that special image by Rudolf Steiner intended for the building in Dornach, the first Goetheanum. This is the *artistic image [the wooden statue] of the Representative of Humanity between the two adversaries* as the spiritual image, as the Imagination of mankind. In the gospel, the dramatic climax of this crisis comes where, before the stoning by the Jews, Christ apostrophizes the adversary of mankind himself (John 8:44, 'your father the devil ...'). We may behold this [artistic] Imagination of mankind ultimately in the deeply moving, tremendous language of world-history as the earthly scene, as the earthly-historical event in the crucifixion group of Golgotha, *in the scene of Christ Jesus crucified between the two malefactors* (John 19:18).

Of these two malefactors Luke's Gospel (Luke 23:39-43) clearly shows how they are essentially different. The one reflects the luciferic nature, the other bears in himself that of the ahrimanic nature. On the hill of Golgotha the Mystery of the Earth and of mankind was revealed. Here was decided and accomplished that human Deed which was present before us in the earlier 'Chapters on Humanity' (John 6–10) as the great problem. The decisive and judging picture of John 8 has its counterpart and supplement in the picture of deepest love and deepest suffering, in the picture, in the middle between the two malefactors, of Christ Jesus.

2.
Gethsemane
(John 18)

The cosmic rhythm with the 'Great Intercession' (John 17) has led us to the 'Virgin' and her stellar revelation that now becomes earthly revelation, carrying in itself the Mystery of the Earth in the Passion of Christ, in the *Mystery of Golgotha*. This cosmic rhythm now proceeds downwards via the Scales towards the dark signs of the zodiac. In the narration of John's Gospel it is characteristic how before the beginning of the actual events of suffering the *I-AM* of Christ is revealed in full divine majesty in the *Scales*. This sign still clearly stands over the entrance of John 18. Once more the Scales holds the middle between the light-filled heights of the Great Intercession (♍) still echoing on, and the darkness of humanity that now approaches Christ (♏). The struggle for the world and the victory for the world by Christ in Gethsemane, also accomplished in the sign of the Scales (MG 291), already lies behind us; this victory is not explicitly narrated by John—the intimate supplement to John's Gospel, as often, is Luke's Gospel, 22:38ff. (MG 298). But the mood of the great victory, that which spiritually is expressed in the sign of the Scales, continues to work at the beginning of John 18. In John's narration much more than in the narration of the other gospels, Christ's I-AM comes to the fore (♎). We think of the moment when the word 'I–AM' (v. 5) sounds from the mouth of Christ—thus sounds Christ's answer to those seeking Him, asking for 'Jesus of Nazareth' ('I am he'—literal translation of the Greek ἐγώ εἰμι)—the persecutors led by Judas fall to the ground as if unconscious. With lamps and torches, with all the dimness of earthly lights, these people seek Christ, the Light of the World, in whom their true, forgotten 'I' stands before them. They are not able to bear the gaze or hear this voice of this 'I' (cf. John 8:38, 43).

Once more there is revealed in this process of Gethsemane the shocking picture of the crisis of mankind. In the constellation shared in common (♎ between ♍ and ♏) the connection is revealed between John 18 and the Chapters of Crisis (6–10). A most tremendous revelation of mankind is placed before us at the beginning of John 18. In the striving and searching of humanity all the gloom and disturbance, all the darkening flowing from the adversary into all areas of life and knowledge, can be viewed and understood in the light of the tremendous Imagination of humanity at the beginning of John 18.

To this revelation of the I-AM of Christ in the most disturbing of all antitheses there stands in John 18 the darkening of the 'I' and the extinguishing of the 'I', as revealed in Judas, Peter and Pilate, the *I-am-not* (οὐκ εἰμί) that comes to the light of day especially in Peter's denial. As the I-AM of Christ stands in the sign of the Scales, the darkening of the I, this 'I-am-not' stands in the dark sign of ♏. The daemonic power of Mars governing this sign (Part One, Chapter 3) is revealed in the misuse of the sword by Peter, as in all the forces of Imperial Rome in the Mystery of Golgotha. The world-historical tragedy of Pilate, like the crisis of Judas and Peter, has already been discussed in the exposition of Mark's Gospel (MG 303ff., 321ff.). The motif οὐκ εἰμί ('I am not') with Peter's denial found only in John's Gospel as the 'I'-gospel, and the closely related gospel of Luke, most clearly expresses the extinguishing of consciousness (♏). And with Pilate there lies the same thing in his question, 'What is truth?' (John 18:38), when we recall how 'truth' (ἀληθείᾳ, *aletheia*) in John's Gospel that is anchored in the eternal, in the I-AM of Christ (♎), is the never extinguishable consciousness. Facing the revelation of the 'I' of Christ, all of Pilate's Mystery-wisdom, all his initiation-knowledge, breaks down.

Among the motifs of John 18 is that of the *unnamed youth* (John 18:15), behind whom we always sense the disciple of Christ (♍). Already here he would like to stand helpfully beside Peter who is moving towards his most difficult crisis, just as he accompanied him to the grave on the morning of the Resurrection. And we experience—or believe we may take an indication from John's Gospel (18:15)—that he belonged to an esoteric group, to which the Jewish High Priest himself belonged (cf. John 11:51), and to which it appears that Joseph of Arimathea and Nicodemus also belonged.

3.
Ecce homo
(John 19:1-15)

The consciousness-extinguishing power of death of the Scorpion, announced already in the betrayal by Judas, in Peter's denial and in the question of Pilate, comes to its most shocking revelation of humanity in the *cry of the Jews to crucify*, already suggested at the end of John 18. In John 19, seeing Christ Jesus scourged, crowned with thorns, in the purple mantle presented by Pilate before the Jews, the motif reaches its climax. In the *Ecce-homo* scene of John 19 (19:5 Ἰδοὺ ὁ ἄνθρωπος, 'Behold the man!') the crisis of humanity in John 6 to 10 is completed, increasing to its dramatic climax in the stoning by the Jews. In the stoning by the Jews, as we saw, lie the motifs of John 19; ultimately they contain the Crucifixion itself.

The main complaint of the Jews against Christ Jesus is that 'he made himself the Son of God' (John 19:7). Because, as in John 10, Christ speaks by the divinity of the Son, of the *divinity in His own innermost 'I'*, the second stoning of the Jews is immediately provoked. This indication of the divine Mystery releases fear and fright in human souls that are caught in the power of the adversary. This beholding of the divine in the 'I' is that which the human soul darkened by the power of the adversary (♏) can least easily bear.

Beholding the deeply moving scene of the *Ecce homo* and the calls of the Jews to crucify, we take some sentences from Steiner's lecture-cycles, initially the one on Mark's Gospel (10th lecture, Basel, 24 Sept. 1912. GA 139):

> There, before all humanity, stood ... the human being in the form originally given to him by divine-spiritual powers. There He stood, but ennobled and spiritualized by Christ's three-year sojourn within the body of Jesus of Nazareth... Here the human being stood at the moment when the Mystery of Golgotha was being accomplished, in the image of His fellowmen. Before such a man His fellowmen should have stood and

worshipped, saying, 'Here am I in my true nature, here is my highest ideal. Here am I, in the form to which I can attain only through my most ardent striving, a striving that can come only from the depths of my soul. Here I stand before that in myself which is alone worthy of reverence and worship, the divine in me!' ... mankind ought to have possessed that self-knowledge. But what did this mankind do? It spat upon the Son of man, it scourged Him, and led Him forth to the place of execution. That was the dramatic turning point ... what was described as actually happening, instead of recognizing himself, man is described as having crushed himself under foot, as having killed himself because he did not recognize himself. Yet only through this lesson, this cosmic lesson can he receive the impulse gradually to attain for himself his true being within the wider perspective of Earth-evolution!

This one statement by Steiner is closely related to another in the first lecture of the cycle *Christ and the Human Soul* (Norrköping, 12 July 1914. GA 155):

Let us assume that in Christ Jesus we have before our spiritual eyes that which must appear to humanity as the most important fact in the whole universe. And then let us set in contrast to this feeling the outcry, the fury, of the enraged multitudes in Jerusalem at the time of the condemnation before the crucifixion. Let us observe that the High Court of Jerusalem held it above all things necessary to question Christ Jesus as to His relationship with the divine, as to whether He claimed to be the Son of God. And let us bear in mind that the High Court held such a claim to be the greatest blasphemy that Christ Jesus could have uttered. An historical scene is there before us—a scene in which the people cry out and clamour for the death of Christ Jesus. And now let us try to picture to ourselves what this shouting and rage signified historically. Let us ask: What ought these people to have recognized in Christ Jesus? They ought to have recognized that Being Who gives meaning and significance to life on Earth. They ought to have recognized that Being Who had to accomplish the Deed without which earthly humanity cannot find the way back to the divine. They ought to have understood that humanity has no significance apart from this Being. People would have to strike out from the evolution of the Earth the word 'human being' if they wished to strike out the Christ-Event.

Now let it come home to us that this multitude condemned and were enraged against the Being Who actually makes man upon the Earth human; Who is destined to give to the Earth its goal and purpose ... We are told nothing less than that humanity had reached a point where it had lost itself, where it had condemned That which gives purpose and significance to the Earth-evolution. And out of the cries of the enraged multitude could be heard ... 'We do not wish to be human beings; rather do we wish to cast away from us that which gives us any further meaning as human beings.'

Here, characterized by Steiner with such expressive words, the disturbing power revealed in the call to crucify that darkens and extinguishes human consciousness for the human being and his knowledge of the human being, is none other that what we here always call from the cosmic point of view the death-power of the Scorpion. Death in the heart of man is here in the sign of the Scorpion revealed in a disturbing manner.

***

Christ's saying about the divinity of the Son, the divinity in the 'I', that this divinity to the estranged Jews can only appear as a shocking outrage, a terrible blasphemy, awakens deadly terror in the heart of Pilate filled with Mystery-premonitions and Mystery-notions. With him it touches a point where partial Mystery-knowledge is mixed with vague superstition. John 19:8: 'When Pilate heard these words, he was the more afraid.' He is dimly aware that everything in these unique legal [!] proceedings, the event of humanity taking place in Jerusalem, lies in a sphere of highest initiation-Mysteries and Mysteries of mankind—superseding all the initiation-knowledge of the time. And it seems like a conscious playing with the secrets of initiation, the way he leads out Christ Jesus, scourged, crowned with thorns, in a purple mantle, how he utters the *Ecce homo* over Him—this saying points to Mysteries of mankind overreaching his own knowledge. He presents Him before the Jews as their king—as 'king' in the sense of the Mysteries (MG 328).

Far above what notions of these things were present in Pilate's consciousness, we have to thank Rudolf Steiner, who in his book *Christianity as Mystical Fact* [GA 8] first expressed the insight that quite objective facts of initiation Mysteries were presented on the plan of world-history, in all their details, in the events of the Mystery of Golgotha. What hitherto took place half-real, symbolically in the secrecy of the initiation temple was played as the 'open secret' on Golgotha before the eyes of mankind.

Apart from everything that is or counts as historical, the whole event of Golgotha is a picture of that spiritual event which in every drama of human consciousness, which here we always call the 'Christian initiation', i.e. as the initiation leading to full consciousness of the soul, is everywhere objectively present. As an inner event it unites with the experiences of this Christian initiation. In this sense the *Scourging, Crowning with Thorns* and *Crucifixion*—the previous *Washing of the Feet* forms a first stage of the spiritual path of becoming meant here—apart from what they signify as historical events in the purely earthly, physical world, are certain 'etheric experiences' of the Christian path of initiation. With its Mysteries, the five dark signs of the zodiac always link in a special way. These 'etheric experiences' can be intensified as far as receiving the stigmata, as far as becoming outwardly visible stigmata in individual, historically attested occurrences, even in modern times. Not, however, in such cases that can partly be traced back to inheritance and abnormal physical-etheric constitutions. The true nature of Christian initiation corresponds to a focussing in the fully conscious situation, from the 'I' right into physical manifestation.

In earlier times, in what is called 'early Christian initiation', such experiences were only possible when the one seeking initiation had to abstain for a long period from any contact with outer life. He had to live inwardly into the gospel scene in a condition of complete outer and inner solitude. The nature of the path of initiation corresponding to the level of consciousness of humanity today, of the 'consciousness soul', of the most difficult but also the most effective of all paths of initiation, consists precisely *in standing fully in the whole life of humanity* and find there the experiences referred to here. The 'Washing of the Feet' is not yet realized when through meditation of the gospel scene the etheric feeling of the water is awakened flowing around the feet, but where the effect being released through the forces of will strongly connect with the earthly situation in 'serving love' (♓). The 'Scourging', too, not already when scourging blows are experienced in the imagination, actually not yet when the experience of 'the blows of destiny' remains a purely individual one, but only when the feeling is raised from the individually human into the feeling for humanity. That means where everything human is so strongly experienced at first hand and sympathized that in the suffering of humanity the suffering of Christ is really experienced. The feeling is present for that which causes the divine to suffer with what people do, when the mere human feeling and suffering become a sympathizing of the *divine suffering towards mankind*, when the stage is achieved called in Wagner's *Parsifal 'durch Mitleid wissend'*, 'learning through compassion'.

The *Washing of the Feet* relates to the Mystery of the divine *will*;
the *Scourging* relates to that of the divine *feeling*,
the *Crowning with Thorns* relates to that of the divine *thinking*.

Only when in the 'I' it is experienced how everything in human thinking that is fixed in the earthly-material realm, how all intellectual cleverness and 'scientific character' in the lofty 'world of truthfulness' concerning space, time and matter is felt as terrible pain and inhuman mockery, how before the spiritual world all earthly-human thinking and imagining in oneself, all human imagining to an excessive degree is fundamentally wrong and askew, how to the Beings of the spiritual world, how to Christ Himself our materialistic thinking today causes boundless pain, only then is an inkling apparent what the 'Crowing with Thorns' signifies in the spiritually real sense.

That person will stand closest to such an experience of 'Crowning with Thorns' who does not arrogantly look down on normal thinking and the normal 'scientific character' as something he fancies he has overcome, but who knows how to use correctly and surely these forms of thinking and imagining in the sphere of practical everyday life, for which they are allotted and for which they are to a certain degree necessary. Such people remain thereby aware of the painful division between the world of the senses that gives birth to the mechanical thinking and the spiritual life in the world of truthfulness. They can contain a feeling how all human wisdom is [as Paul says] 'foolishness before God'. When they can feel all this so strongly that they can feel the pains in their own body as if the sharp thorns of the crown of thorns were pushed into their own head, then—whether the outer stigmata appears with them or not—they have attained the level of the Crowning with Thorns.

4.
Golgotha
John (19:16ff.)

The Washing of the Feet, the Scourging and Crowning of Thorns are immediately related to the will, the feelings and thinking. *Bearing the Cross* and the *Crucifixion* relate to the 'I'; they reveal directly how the divine-spiritual 'I' is placed in earthly-human corporeality. What is present as spiritual Imagination in ancient mythology—think of the *Edda* where Odin hangs on the World-Tree, and in Platonic knowledge [*Timaeus*] of the World-Soul crucified for love of the world—becomes on Golgotha an earthly-physical event, an event that in the higher sense is at the same time a 'spiritual picture'. The Crucifixion is a spiritual picture for the relationship of the 'I' to earthly-physical corporeality; bearing the cross is such for the whole course of earthly life, when seen and experienced from the spiritual side. What is particularly evident with certain experiences, what becomes a special revelation, for example, during long and difficult illness, appears true for the *whole course of life*.

However, this conscious experience of bearing the cross and of crucifixion in the 'I' also leads to the experience of descent from the cross and resurrection. The one experience carries the other with it. In all experiences of the pain of initiation there takes place in reality a loosening and dissolving of the etheric life from the bonds to the physical. With the stations on the path of initiation, Buddhist spiritual schooling already speaks of 'degrees of loosening'.

***

In the events of the Scourging, Crowning with Thorns, and the *Ecce homo*, in the spiritual background there appears the darkening of humanity of the Scorpion. From bearing the cross onwards, the *Archer* is revealed in the actual events of the Crucifixion and of the cross. At the place (John 19:17) where it says 'and he went out, bearing his own cross', we locate as the transition from the Scorpion to the sign of death of the Archer. Moreover, in that the event leads from the Archer to the Goat and the Waterman (to which the 'entombment' is allocated), there also appears in the cosmic rhythm of the gospel, where the sign:

♐ belongs to the cross of the Son of the etheric,
♑ to the cross of the physical, or of the Father,
♒ to the 'cross of the Spirit'—
the *three crosses on Golgotha* (further details, MG Appendix 1, 343–63).

The planetary aspects are revealed, as:

♏ the daemonic side of Mars,
in ♐ Jupiter (in its relationship to 'Ancient Sun'),
in ♑ Saturn,
in ♒ Saturn-Uranus.

In the etheric sign of ♐ the Mystery of the new source of life, the new etheric life-stream is revealed on the cross of Golgotha. In the [poetic work] 'Twelve Moods', Rudolf Steiner gave words for ♃ in ♐ [fifth line], '*Im Sterben erreift das Weltenwalten*', 'In dying, there ripens prevailing of worlds'. The hour of death on Golgotha becomes the hour of birth of a new world. That is the life-and-death revelation in the Archer. Novalis expresses this in his *Hymns to the Night*: 'His sacred mouth emptied the dark cup of unspeakable wrongs. In horrible anguish the birth of the new world drew near.' Also what follows is still a revelation of the Archer:

> Hard he wrestled with the terrors of old Death; heavy lay the weight of the old world upon him. Yet once more he looked kindly at his mother; then came the releasing hand of the Love eternal, and he fell asleep.

Thus there also lies in this Mystery the 'birth hour of a new world' in the heavenly sign of the Archer the 'Mystery of the Mother' (John 19:25-27), in which at the same time the Mystery of the one becoming John, the becoming of the 'disciple of love' takes place. This was discussed earlier in the exposition of Mark's Gospel (MG 331f.).

In the *union of the disciple of Christ with the Mother under the cross*, which is the heavenly counter-picture of all earthly unions of love, the *magic of the 'I'* is completed, in which the whole possibility of the becoming of the new world lies hidden. On the cross of Golgotha the last and highest of all 'I'-Mysteries of John's Gospel is completed. The 'Mystery of the Mother' already indicated in the 'Marriage of Cana' is here completely revealed.

And within the 'Mystery of the Mother' a 'Mystery of the Sister' lies secretly included. John's Gospel lets us see 'the Mother-sister', the 'other Mary', who stands with her under the cross, as in Mary Magdalene the sister of the Disciple of Love himself (in the characters of his Mystery Dramas, Rudolf Steiner has expressed this 'Mystery of both Marys'). A Mystery of highest love is concluded in beholding the sister-soul. What this 'sister-soul' signifies in the becoming of the Disciple of Love has often been mentioned here, and in the story of the 'Resurrection' it will become more clearly revealed what it means that the sister, Mary Magdalene, stands with the Disciple of Love under the cross. If we can behold in the presentation in Mark's Gospel this 'becoming of the Disciple of Love', then we see here in the presentation of John's Gospel as the ending of Christ's earthly work itself, the magic of Christ on the Earth. The *Mystery of Love* itself is concluded at the cross of Golgotha in that which happens through Christ between the Mother and the Disciple of Love, and what the sister-soul—both sister-souls—directly experience as they look on and receive into the depths of the heart. And in what happens there lies the overcoming of the Fall of mankind. In the Fall of mankind lies the origin of the old world; in the overcoming of this Fall of man lies the seed of a new world.

The Mystery of the word from the cross 'I thirst' (John 19:28) also belongs to the heavenly revelation of the 'Archer', discussed earlier in the chapter on the 'Samaritan woman at the well' (John 4). It is very significant that the heavenly sign of the Archer, or the constellation ♐–♓, stands over the whole Mystery-encounter of Christ with the Samaritan woman at the well. We recall how it has to do with this Mystery-encounter in John 4, with the *Mystery of the old and the new source of life* (cf. John 4:13, 14). Similarly, we experience now at the cross of Golgotha in the heavenly sign of the Archer the source of the new spring of life out of the zero-point, in which the old disappears. And as in John 4 Christ, although He knows He is the bringer of the new Water of Life, asks the Samaritan woman for a drink out of the exhausted source (John 4:7). By sitting, thirsty in the hot midday sun, we hear Him on the cross spiritually calling out the word of thirsting to the world. *In Him, in Whom in Himself the fulfilment of all longing, the stilling of every thirst is completed, He takes on Himself all the longing of mankind, the thirsting of a whole world ...*

It is also significant that to the constellation ♐–♓ lying over the encounter with the Samaritan woman at the well and over the cross on Golgotha, is linked the Mystery of the 'sixth hour' (the midday hour) (cf. John 4:6, Mark 15:33, John 19:14). In the Mystery-encounter with the Samaritan woman at the well (John 4), decadent remnants and late echoes are apparent of the Mysteries of Isis and Osiris, shone over with memories of Zarathustra. In the *Mystery of the union of the Disciple with the Mother and Sister* that takes place under the cross of Golgotha in the sign of the new source of life (♐), one can also find the conclusion of the Mystery of Isis and Osiris. In Christ there ends at the cross (i.e. in the 'I') the early Egyptian Mystery, in which Isis appears as mother, spouse and sister of Osiris (MG 261ff.). And the significance of ♃ in ♐ is revealed in a new Christian Mystery-meaning. The Isis-Mystery of the early Mysteries becomes under the cross of Golgotha the *Mystery of Mary*, the *Mystery of both Marys*.

The life-and-death revelation of the Archer can also be Imaginatively seen on the cross of Golgotha, which is placed before us as a picture of newly germinating, sprouting life on the Tree of Death. The *Tree of Knowledge* in Paradise, through the Fall of man becomes the Tree of Death; the dry, sterile wood of the cross takes into itself again the forces of the *Tree of Life*. From the earlier account, we know how the *picture of the Tree of Life and of the Tree of Knowledge* expresses the polarity of the *higher and lower kinds of ether*, of the *Eternal Feminine and the Eternal Masculine*, for those forces which were united with mankind in Paradise, were then pulled apart through the Fall of mankind (cf. Genesis 1:27). From this aspect the *union of the disciple with the mother under the cross* is revealed in a new, higher light.

***

With the word from the cross hinting at the conclusion of the cosmic Deed of consecration, 'It is finished' (τετέλεσται, John 19:30), one can imagine the transition from the Archer to the Goat. The Goat 'sign of a turning point' becomes here the sign of the Turning Point of the World (MG 344f.). The mood of this dark sign of Saturn finds its best expression in the words of Novalis (*Hymns to the Night*), 'Only for a few days a deep veil hung over the roaring sea, over the quaking land'. Mark's Gospel speaks of the *darkness at the cross* as lasting three hours (Mark 15:33). John's Gospel does not mention the darkness at all; all this lies between the lines. The entry and the mood of the heavenly sign of the Goat with the narration of Golgotha is actually hardly to be found in the express words, but—if we may also use here the analogy that offers itself of the

Johannine style with a symphonic musical style—far more in the *feelings*, comparable to a musical pause or fermata lying between the lines.

The sign of the Archer lying in the etheric cross of the Son speaks of a revelation of the etheric stream of life. The Saturn-sign of the Goat lying in the cross of the Father—in which lies the Christmas event of the birth of Jesus—points wholly to the Mystery of birth and of physical existence, which is now on the point of becoming a *new Earth*. The veil of the *Mystery of the Earth* lies over the whole event in the heavenly sign of the Goat. This Mystery of the Earth is expressed in particular in the narration of the *piercing of the spear* (John 19:34), of the wound in the side, out of which flowed *blood and water*. Taken purely physiologically, this initially appears as nothing special. And historically seen, it could initially be taken only as a confirmation of the arrival of death. Many expositors take 19:35 in particular as directed to those who for whatever reason are inclined to doubt the ensuing death on the cross of Jesus of Nazareth.

That this explanation clinging completely to externals does not meet the Johannine meaning and the spiritual backgrounds of this passage of the gospel becomes most clear from the first letter of John, where we read (I John 5:5-8):

> Who is it that overcomes the world but he who believes that Jesus is the Son of God? This is he who came by water and blood, Jesus Christ, not with the water only but with the water and the blood. And the Spirit is the witness, because the Spirit [the living breath, *pneuma*] is the truth [*aletheia*, the light of the never-extinguished consciousness]. There are three witnesses, the Spirit, the water, and the blood; and these three are one.

It is as though a Mystery of four elements—water, fire, air and light-filled earth (resurrection-earth, changed earth)—shimmers through here, a Mystery of metamorphosed Earth that met us already with the Marriage in Cana. There the Mystery of the *water and wine* immediately recalls the revealed Mystery in the narration of the piercing of the spear, revealing the Mystery of the *water and blood*.

The streaming blood from the wound in the side of the Crucified carries in itself the *tincture of light*, which like a star-seed is planted into the darkness of the Earth. Between the *change of water into wine* at the Marriage in Cana and the *Mystery of the water and blood* with the wound in the side of the Crucified lies the *chymical Mystery* of John's Gospel. The manner of expression of John 19:35 causes us to feel that here a Mystery is indicated, not contained directly in the words, but lying between the lines. And this Mystery is a Mystery of the Earth, a Mystery of the light-filled Earth of resurrection, the virginal *prima materia* of Christ's Blood streaming from the wounds of the Crucified.

In the *Parzival* of Wolfram von Eschenbach (Book 9) it is said how through the deed of Cain, through the blood of the first fratricide, the Earth lost its virginity, its 'maidenhood'. What was lost is regained through Golgotha; there a beginning of regaining the virginal state took place. Wagner expresses the same thing in his musical language in the *Karfreitagszauber* [the 'Good Friday music' of his *Parsifal* Act 3].

The saga lets the spear of the Roman legionary that pierced the side of the Crucified become the Sacred Spear of the Grail. And in Wagner's *Parsifal* we find this Spear of the 'spear-thrust' of Golgotha as the *Christ-symbol of the 'I'*. This has a deep meaning, because in everything that takes place at the cross, the Mystery of the 'I' is fulfilled. In the stream of blood and water of the spear-thrust everything finds its expression that takes place between the 'I' of Christ and the physical plane of the Earth, of Mysteries of metamorphosis (transubstantiation) of the Earth and of higher alchemy taking place at the cross of Golgotha. What takes place here is also called the *Mystery of the Holy Grail*. In the blood of Christ streaming from the wound in His side caused by the spear-thrust, the *Mystery of the Holy Grail* is revealed, with which the saga then closely connects with Joseph of Arimathea, also named in John's Gospel (John 19:38).

With the wound in the side of the spear-thrust the *number five* (the pentagram—the five-pointed star ☆ is also a symbol of the 'etheric body') *of the five 'sacred wounds'* is concluded. In Lecture 7 of his lecture-cycle on Mark's Gospel, Rudolf Steiner shows how this 'number five of the sacred wounds' contains a revelation of the 'I'. A human body, as it has become today—Steiner claims—would have to fall to pieces under the force of this 'I', if this 'I' in its whole unbroken divine fullness could again enter this body. (For this reason also the indication of the destruction of the temple of the body at the miracle of transformation at the Marriage of Cana, standing inwardly in connection with the events at the cross, John 2:19-21.) The vulnerability of a Siegfried, an Oedipus, an Achilles, indicates the strong counter-effect of the higher 'I' on the earthly corporeality. If the unbroken 'I' could completely enter into a human body, and if clairvoyant vision could see this process, then—according to Steiner—on such a body not only *one*, but *five wounds* would be seen, with the five wounds of Christ on the cross (the four marks of the nails and the spear-wound). And here what is initially meant as an *experience in the etheric* is revealed on the cross of Golgotha in the physical world. Through the Christian path of initiation what is revealed in the physical world can become again an etheric experience. In the whole rhythmic construction of John's Gospel there is shown at the same time the methodical sequence of stages of this Christian path of initiation.

***

The whole context of the Mystery of the spear-wound with that of the miracle of transformation in Cana standing in the constellation ♒–♌ helps one to feel at this place in the gospel narrative the proximity of the sign ♒ (as, on the other hand, the motif of the 'source of life springing from the cross' points towards the Archer). With the *entombment* (John 19:38-42) we enter completely into the sign of the Waterman, which in the gospel [see MG] everywhere is the sign of the entombment. From the dark Saturn-sign and Earth-sign of the Goat, we move into the other Saturn-sign, brighter and less earth-heavy, the sign of the Waterman, shone over by *Uranus* with starry light. This sign of the Waterman belongs to the cross of the Holy Spirit and of the astral level (in the 'Holy Spirit' is revealed the transformation and transfiguration of the astral realm). In earlier astrology it was called the 'fixed' (tamas) cross [The term is from Vedic astrology, referring to the qualities of 'fixture' or 'earth'—*Ed.*]. Over this sign, in which we have to think this whole gospel-passage, there lies *the tranquillity of the spirit* (John 19:38ff., in a certain way already 31ff.), over the whole *Mystery of the Entombment* itself.

If we experienced in what preceded, in the dark Saturn-sign ♑ the deepest earthly darkness, there lies over the Uranus-sign ♒ something like starlight and stellar brightness. In the dark depths of Earth in the Saturn-sign ♑) all the starlight and stellar brightness was absorbed—a moment in Bruckner's 9th Symphony, first movement, expressing this Mystery was already mentioned in the earlier exposition—now everything can be felt in the Uranus-sign ♒: deeply connected with the Mystery of the starry heavens, as if out of the depths of the grave of the Earth, out of the depths of the bedrock—think of the D-minor of Bruckner's 9th Symphony (see Fig. IV)—lit up with starry brilliance and glittering, as if the Earth now itself would be preparing, initially only visible to the spiritual eye, to shine again as a star.

Already the Blood flowing from the wound in the side of the Crucified, from all of Christ's wounds, reveals this shining and glittering starlight to spiritual vision [see the author's study *The Parsifal Christ-Experience in Wagner's Music-Drama*, Anastasi 2014. 42f.]. Cosmic starry powers unite themselves in the flowing Blood with the darkness of the Earth, working in the darkened substance of the Earth as the *tincture of the light*, the revelation of highest *alchemy of the Earth*. Already with the whole episode of the spear-thrust, the shining of Uranus—which is always a supersensory shining—mixes with the dull darkness of Saturn. And the episode of the entombment is completely shone over by this light of Uranus, this starry glittering. We feel here all the Mysteries, which between the depths of the grave and the bedrock of the Earth and the upper world of the stars, to which Uranus is the mediator, truly the *tranquil stars* are governing. We recall the saying of Novalis:

> I know not whether anyone ever truly understood the rocks and stones, but such a one certainly must have been a sublime being [Novalis. *The Novices of Sais*. 2. Nature]

and the serious word of Goethe in his Freemason-poem 'Symbolum':

> *Stille ruhn oben die Sterne*   [The stars on high are silent still;
> *Und unten die Gräber*   Silent the graves, nor make reply.]

In these words is gently indicated, and as if from afar, how in the Saturn-Uranus sign of ♒ Mysteries of the Deposition with Star-Mysteries flow together.

Thus, in the narration of Golgotha, the rhythm of John's Gospel has led us from the revelation of the etheric stream of life in the Jupiter-sign of the Archer into the depths and darkness of the Earth in the Saturn-sign of the Goat, from there to the star-revelation of the grave in the Saturn-Uranus sign of the Waterman. Thereby, too, *the three crosses of Golgotha in their spiritual significance*:

- the *Christ-cross of the Son* (♐),
- the *Earth-cross of the Father* (♑), and
- the *cross of the Holy Spirit* (♒)

are impressively presented before us.

In a profound *Star-Mystery* of the Earth, the Johannine narration of Golgotha sounds out in the episode of the Deposition (John 19:38-42). Joseph of Arimathea and Nicodemus, the esoteric pupils of Christ, take part in this Mystery in conscious collaboration (John 19:38 & 39). In these depths in Mysteries of the Earth-alchemy emerging in this passage, the *Mystery of the Resurrection* is directly prepared. To this the final chapter of this work is dedicated.

VII. Resurrection
(John 20 and 21)

The tender, gentle experience of the resurrection morning at the beginning of John 20 has a counter-picture in a spirit of recent times. Moved most deeply in his whole being by the Johannine spirit, the poet *Novalis* relived this experience of resurrection, which like a breath of the resurrection and of the meeting with the Risen One spreads over his life and his poetic creations.

We know how his heart was connected with the young girl Sophie v. Kühn who was still but a child. After hardly half-a-year acquaintance the death of this child, who was just on the threshold of womanhood, suddenly ripped him out of all dreams of earthly happiness. We take some passages from Novalis' letters, which give eloquent witness to the impression of the event on the young poet's soul:

> Since 19th March the girl on whom my whole soul hung, since 19th March my Sophie is dead. It would not be easy to find somebody else who went to meet the future more joyfully. She was the soul of my life. There is nobody easy to find with a more desolate outlook before him. My wishes and needs were, like hers, so limited—and even these limitations destiny found too big, and exiled me and her into the space occupied by a grave. She surrounds me continuously—everything that I do, I do in her name. She was the beginning and will be the end of my life. Her sufferings are wounds to me, which will only be healed by the balsamic air of a better world. It is an inexpressible feeling to have known an angel like her, a beloved like her in such terrible battles.

To Schlegel he writes how clear it has become to him:

> what a heavenly coincidence her death had been—a key to everything ... My love has become a flame which by degrees consumes everything earthly.

To Caroline Just (five days after Sophie's death):

> Her suffering I will never ever overcome. The martyrdom of this heavenly soul remains a crown of thorns for the rest of my days. If my woe became a soft flame that would consume me, so that a soft breath of air would transform me into a heap of ash, should Sophie not support this wish?

Already before Sophie's death he writes in premonition in a letter: 'The ashes of the earthly roses is the motherland of the heavenly ones.' This recalls a deeply meaningful saying in the *Fragments*: 'All ash is pollen; the [flower] chalice is heaven' (Novalis, *Sämtliche Werke*. ed. Kamnitzer, Bd. 1, pp. 266, 271, 269, 253; Bd. III (Fragmente) Nr. 3—p. 49 = p. 27 of the separate volume of fragments.).

Out of these impressions from his life, out of this whole world of his inner life Novalis fashioned as a short fragment the second part ('The Fulfilment') of his novel *Heinrich von Ofterdingen.* Here too a deep inspiring young love, through the death of the loved one, is suddenly ripped apart.

Slowly there loosens the mood of painful mourning from the lonely wanderer in the mountains. A gentle longing arises in its place. Then he perceives in the spirit out of the tree a voice that like the Mother of Jesus speaking to him of her Child, Who has overcome death, and the Pilgrim recognizes the voice of the once beloved … A ray of light proceeding out of the tree changes the experience increasingly to a vision, a beholding, amongst surging figures he recognizes the beloved, who waves to him with a friendly smile … The vision disappears, but the Pilgrim now feels free from the fearful pressure from the pains of loneliness, the pain of loss, of the inner emptiness.

> Voice and language renewed their life within him, all things seemed more known and prophetic than before, so that death appeared to him a high revelation of life, and he viewed his own fleeting existence with child-like and serene emotion. The future and the past had met within him, and formed an eternal union. He stood far from the present, and the world was now for the first time dear to him, when he had lost it and was there only as a stranger in it, who would yet wander but a while through its diversified and spacious halls.

When he then sings to the lute of the meaning of the sacred mother-love, he is not aware at first how a young girl standing upon the rock, kindly greets him like an old acquaintance, and invites him to her mother's house. Stepping under a tree, and looking up with an indescribable smile, she shakes many roses from her apron upon the grass. On the way to the mother's house the following dialogue arises between them.

> 'Who has told thee about me?' asked the pilgrim.
> 'Our mother.'
> 'Who is thy mother?'
> 'The Mother of God.'
> 'How long hast thou been here?'
> 'Since I came from the tomb.'
> 'Hast thou already been dead?'
> 'How could I else be living?'
> ...
> 'Wouldst thou like to remain with me?'
> 'Indeed I love thee.'
> 'How long hast thou known me?'
> 'O! from olden times; my former mother, too, told me about thee.'
> 'Hast thou yet a mother?'
> 'Yes; but really the same.'
> 'What is her name?'
> 'Mary.'
> ...
> 'Whither are we going?'
> 'Ever homewards.'

From this resurrection-dialogue of heavenly reunion, unique in world literature, fine and hidden threads link to John 20, to the meeting of Mary Magdalene with the Risen One, 'early, while it was still dark' (20:1), breathed over with such etheric tenderness. That short dialogue of joyful reunion and loving recognition, where in the short exchange of both exclamations, 'Mary', 'Rabboni'—she answers the Risen One *calling with her name*, 'my Master!'—a world of most inexpressible feelings and experiences is condensed.[96] Is it not, as though the spirit of the Risen One Himself enlivens both dialogues?

Full of expression are the words 'early, while it was still dark'. The night of the grave still appears to lie over everything, combining with the mood of the resurrection-morning. The words remind us to think of Mary living through the night of the grave. The world of day-consciousness was extinguished for her standing with those under the cross (John 19:25). Through deepest love (John 11:2) and deepest suffering which she in consciousness had gone through, she had followed the Beloved into the night of the grave and of death. Like Lazarus, awakened out of the slumber of the grave, she, the sister, had experienced the 'way right through the narrow gate'. In this she experienced something like an 'Initiation'. She experienced the night of the grave and of death differently from someone still caught in the sleep of mankind. In the realm that sleepers otherwise unconsciously enter every night in sleep, here she enters with a slowly brightening consciousness. When the consciousness of the day—in which those were caught who still dream in the sleep of humanity—was extinguished for her, a higher consciousness was slowly awoken in her. That which is not yet perceptible to the dull senses of those still caught in the sleep of mankind slowly became perceptible to her.

In the lecture-cycle *The Effect of Occult Development on the Self and the Sheaths of Man* (The Hague. Lecture 6. 25 March 1913. GA 145), Rudolf Steiner shows how leaving the physical, spatial world in deep sleep, we enter the etheric world. Today we are mostly completely unconscious in deep sleep. Seen Imaginatively (that is, with a picture-consciousness), the world we enter is none other than that world, described in Genesis 2 out of such a picture-consciousness as the 'world of the blossoming Paradise garden'. In its plants and living beings—if we were fortunate enough in this situation 'inwardly to awaken'—we would be able to behold the construction of our own physical corporeality and its organs in the Paradisal splendour of their original primordial past. For the spiritually developed clairvoyant, Steiner gives us to understand, such a moment is really possible. The vision of inner 'waking up while asleep' is linked to this 'experience of the Paradise garden'. Those not clairvoyant, but inwardly receptive, are perhaps able to receive an impression of the 'blossoming Tree of Life' upon seeing a sleeping child.

This 'etheric world' for people today mostly passed in sleeping is also that in which Mary Magdalene, walking with the Crucified right through the night of the grave and the darkness of death, finds herself slowly awakening. The delicate breath of such an 'etheric experience' lies over the whole opening episode of John 20, 'early, while it was yet dark'. In this 'world of the blooming Paradise garden' she encounters the 'heavenly gardener'. This is the reason why, first waking slowly in consciousness, she takes the Risen One for the gardener. The experience of the etheric Paradise Garden is spread for her over the garden of the grave of Golgotha, as over everything earthly and physical. In her inner experience she is still with the Father, with Death, and slowly at first she wakes up to the consciousness of the nearness of the living Christ. Where the earthly gaze at first sees the empty grave (20:1-10), the etheric eye then sees both angelic figures (20:12), that is, the spiritual vision completely within, turning in the opposite direction to the day-consciousness—the early Indians and Jakob Boehme speak of the 'turned gaze' (20:14) of the inner eye. She sees the Risen One. And only in the spiritual perception of her own name does seeing turn into recognition.

The delicate, etheric breath lying over the whole experience is revealed especially when Mary—this is not said in so many words but it clearly lies between the lines of the gospel text—full of the joy of reunion and loving devotion, out of the whole love that united her to the Master, with arms open for the Risen One, however, hears from Him the words, 'Do not hold me, for I have not yet ascended to the Father …' The whole narrated experience here at the beginning of John 20 has this over-delicate quality about it, which also intellectually cannot at all be touched. In reality what appears here indeed is more than something merely etheric. Here a delicate, initially still super-sensory physical shoot is revealing itself, which as the 'heavenly seed', as *the tincture of the light* in the earthly dying of Christ has planted itself into the earthly darkness. It is the first virginal seed of the 'new Earth', as it appears in the super-sensory realm but more than the merely etheric resurrection-figure.[97] Yet all this is bound with the etheric, still as breathed over by the etheric; at first everything is as in a threshold area between the etheric and the super-sensory physical. Only through the more confined contact with the forces of the Father, as took place in the event of the 'Ascension', does the seed grow on the physical plane.

With all this we touch again on what, at the beginning and the end of the chapters on Golgotha (Section VI), has been termed the '*Mystery of the Earth*'. And this spiritual Mystery of the *virginal Earth*, the *light-filled Earth*, the *Resurrection-Earth*, the *prima materia* of the great processes of metamorphosis of the Earth, is revealed in the earthly sign ♍ (the Virgin) that at the same time is a sign of the life-etheric. It is the 'grain of wheat' mentioned in John 12:24, that has to fall into the Earth and die in order to produce much fruit. There, too, as we see, the heavenly sign of the Virgin standing over this chapter points to the Mystery of this 'grain of wheat'. There, too, we stand, as here in the chapter on the Resurrection, in the constellation ♓– ♍. There, too, is revealed, as here in the sign ♍ Mary Magdalene, the one become maidenly again, the sister-soul of the 'disciple of love'. Through the 'cosmic rhythm', as through nothing else, the inner connections of the gospel become revealed.

Thus, gradually the constellation of the Resurrection Chapters (John 20 & 21), initially John 20, in its whole contexts becomes more deeply understandable. Already when we take the 'early, while it was still dark' (20:1), at first merely as chronology, the sign ♓ is revealed, the sign of the 'hour before sunrise' (MG 27). And this sign ♓ is an expression that in the resurrection of the 'I' of Christ, which already descended into the Baptism in the Jordan, now unites with the Earth on a new level of becoming. Like the ♍, the ♓ is an etheric sign, expressing the whole breath lying over these Resurrection-Chapters. And what is linked to the sign ♍, not only indicates Mary Magdalene meeting us as the first at the grave, as the first to experience the Risen One, but through Mary Magdalene it also indicates the virginal Mystery of the Resurrection-Earth, the light-filled Earth (♍ is an Earth-sign, as also a sign of light and a sign of seeing), the virginal *prima materia* of the tremendous process of transforming the Earth. This is for the first time revealed here; in the 'New Jerusalem' of the Apocalypse it is fulfilled.[98]

The Apocalypse speaks of the 'great supper of God', of the 'marriage supper of the Lamb' (19:9, 21:2 & 10, 22:17), and we also recall how we always met the constellation standing over the Resurrection Chapters ♓–♍ (or ♍–♓) as the 'Last-Supper constellation'. It is the same constellation that also rules over the Mystery of the grain of wheat in the Parable of the Sower (Mark 4) and the Feeding [of the Five Thousand].

Finally, we found the constellation ♓ as that of the 'Chapters on the Disciples' (John 13–16); it previously governed the events of the Jordan in John 1 and 2. Here, too, connections hold sway. For, as said earlier (Part One, Chapters 4 & 6), the Resurrection Chapters are once again Chapters on the Disciples. The narration of the first calling of the disciples contained in the Jordan Chapters is in a certain sense, though not exclusively, such a Chapter on the Disciples. Even John 12 is related in various ways to the events with the disciples, and it places us before the raised Lazarus, as John 20 and 21 does before the resurrected Christ. There, as here (John 20), Mary Magdalene plays a decisive role.

***

The fact that both Resurrection-Chapters of John's Gospel are again 'Chapters on the Disciples' gives us an important key to understand them. Along with the Risen One Himself, not even does John stand in the actual focus of these chapters, but the group of disciples as such. Christ's *carrying and protecting love*, as it is so radiantly revealed in the Farewell Chapters and finally in the 'Great Intercession', carries the disciples through their crisis, right through their sleep of consciousness. It creates the possibility that those who, in their earthly life, are not able to maintain their connection with Christ, the Initiator (Mark 4:50, John 16:32), are able to find Him again as the *Risen One* in another sphere of existence, *so that to the great heart-breaking farewell, the reunion can follow.* In the sorrow of parting itself lies the strength of reunion. The great *motif of reunion* links John 20 & 21 with the Farewell Chapters 13–16. Thereby also John 20 & 21, 'Chapters on the Disciples', through which the pentad of the earlier 'Chapters on the Disciples' (John 13–17) are made up to a septenary. It is just as significant, as revelatory, that out of the rhythm of the whole the constellation arising in this, as in those chapters, is the same (♓–♍).

The full awakening of the disciples out of the sleep of consciousness brings first that Pentecost-experience narrated at the beginning of the Acts of the Apostles. Like an indication of this event, a deep spiritual experience of communion[99] of the disciples with Christ can be felt in connection with the words 'The peace be with you' (John 20: 19 & 21), receiving the breath of the *Holy Spirit* (20:22). Already in an earlier passage of John's Gospel (7:39, cf. 12:16) this Being of the *Holy Spirit* was indicated, revealed *through the Death and the Transfiguration of Christ*, appearing only after the Death and through the Death. Over the whole Resurrection Chapters of John's Gospel there lies the *revelation of the Holy Spirit*.

***

The character of these chapters on the disciples becomes apparent also in the leading role Simon Peter (outwardly) plays in the group of disciples, at the beginning of the resurrection events (John 20:2ff.). As later in the Acts of the Apostles, we see already here the 'disciple whom the Lord loved' standing at Peter's side helping and inspiring him. Already in the story of the Passion he took on this task, as it appears, precisely through the Initiation he went through (John 19:15ff.), without at the time being able to protect Peter from his deep fall.

Why was it actually not this disciple—so perhaps we will ask here—who in his vision of the 'New Jerusalem' becomes the deepest proclaimer of all the Resurrection-Mysteries? Why was it not 'the disciple whom the Lord loved' who, as the Christ-Initiate stood under the cross; why was it not he who first beheld the Risen One?

But like this, the question is not rightly posed. We have to remember just here what role the sister-soul, Mary Magdalene, always plays in all this, what proceeded with the 'disciple of love'. Regardless of her physical presence, her experience appears—as we saw at several places (MG 284f.)—always to reflect in the soul what the disciple of Christ experiences in the spirit. Seen like this, her vision then appears in John 20, too, as a reflection of everything that the disciple of Christ experiences from his sleep of the grave in Bethany onwards, until the place where he with both Marys and the Mother stands under the cross. We know how he already was close to physical death, already touching the sphere of decay. Still like a corpse, as wrapped in gravecloths, he appears to spiritual vision some time later as precisely the one risen from the grave. In the Initiation-story of Mark's Gospel (MG 330ff.), it was shown in a significant moment (Mark 13:1), how before the spiritual eye of the one who outwardly is still not fully given back to the world of day-consciousness, in the dawning distance already the *shining temple of the New Jerusalem*, the resurrection-Earth of the future begins to shine forth. He consequently no longer recognizes the old temple of stone and bronze that was so deeply connected to his earthly destiny, the temple which he frequently passed by with the Lord, and he asks Christ Jesus about it. We saw how deepest Mystery-contexts begin to shine in this passage of the gospel. He sees all this as in the dawning distance. *'Noch blendet ihn der neue Tag'*, 'Him dazzled by new shining day' [Goethe. *Faust* II, 12093, towards the very end]. He who is still as if blinded by the light of the new world that first surrounds him, the world of day-consciousness, is no longer able to receive, to perceive this, *'wahrzunehmen'* [literally, 'to take true']. Thus we see him, too, sleeping in Gethsemane (MG 299), even if just here we can recognize how his sleep, the sleep of an initiate, is of another kind, spiritually more alive than that of the other disciples.

As he completely lives through and suffers the experience under the cross, he was more than ever dead to normal earthly consciousness. He had witnessed there the world-historical, unique event, the ultimate that could be experienced and suffered in the whole process of the becoming of the Earth and the development of humanity, all that could be experienced and suffered *in this way* only *once*. He was there, from the earthly aspect, himself as at the end; in his outer experience he would not have been much different from the other disciples (still in the sleep of consciousness), indeed, outwardly seen, he who in reality had suffered twice through the night of the grave (the second time spiritually) might have appeared still more dead than the others.

What with the others came from their failure to experience; with him came from an over-abundance of experience. *His* experience of resurrection in its full, true greatness still lies in the future, in a still far future. What he experienced in the slumber of the grave of Bethany and on Golgotha, still needed basically a full, long earthly life—for he is indeed still a young man in years—in order to mature to that which he then only later, towards the end of his life, experienced on Patmos. This appeared in the 'Apocalypse' as a testament written for posterity. Only in the 'Apocalypse of John' do we find the actual tremendous experience of resurrection of the disciple of Christ, only there is it fully described. In what he describes there as the majesty of the *Son of man*, of Christ resurrected from death *in the midst of the seven golden candlesticks* (Apoc. 1:9-20), in this *experience of the living Christ*—which here is a fully spiritual, not only an etheric experience—lies, as it were, that side of consciousness of his resurrection-experience. In the light-filled 'new Earth' of the 'heavenly Jerusalem', which is revealed to him at the end of the Apocalypse, in the 'Last Supper of the Lamb and the Bride' lies the earthly side, the alchemical, the 'Mystery of the *Chymical Wedding*', the *earthly Mystery of the Resurrection*.

The two sides of the resurrection-experience appear like the male and female [principles]: the 'transformed Earth', the virginal light-filled Earth of the *New Jerusalem* is the Bride, the 'I' resurrected from death, Christ, is the Bridegroom. What only in a distant future of the Earth will be revealed in full light, rests today like a seed in the being of the Earth and in man's being. This seed, by becoming increasingly consciously received by the human soul, allows the Earth itself to mature its transfiguration and metamorphosis, its resurrection in future times. To behold all this as something already of the present, was and is what John could experience of the resurrection at the end of his earthly life.

It is not as if John had himself experienced nothing of the resurrection-event of Golgotha. But, as already mentioned, precisely the experience of Mary Magdalene at the beginning of John 20 appears at the same time to reflect that which was prepared in the disciple of Christ as a resurrection-experience on the higher 'I'-stage. The 'I'-experiences of the disciple are reflected etherically in the receptive sister-soul. And the etheric nature of these experiences which, as a gentle breath lies over the whole chapter, is, as it were, a picture for his own experience. For the disciple of Christ everything is initially like a seed, everything initially is only like a gentle presentiment of the future. The earthly eye of this disciple sees, as does that of Peter, initially only into the empty grave. What the masculine soul, the conscious soul cannot as yet grasp, is there initially in the feelings, the feminine soul.

It is deeply grounded in the Mysteries of Christianity, that initially the feminine, the sister-soul, experiences the Risen One. Thus through everything that at the beginning of John 20 is narrated about Mary Magdalene, at the same time tenderly points to the experience of John himself. Even in the way Mary Magdalene, obeying a direction of the Risen One to tell the group of disciples of the things He said to her (John 20:18), there lies a reflection of John's role as helper with regard to the other disciples.[100]

Thomas

The interest turns from Peter and John especially to that disciple who was not present at what is narrated in John 10:19-23, a premonition of Pentecost. This disciple, who although during the earthly life of Christ Jesus could not find initiation, yet in his *longing* was the most strongly connected with that which Christ did accomplish with the 'disciple whom the Lord loved' (John 11:16). John is the *disciple of the great love* (which is always reflected in Mary Magdalene); *Thomas* is *the disciple of the great longing*. And such a longing out of spiritual depths, not flowing out of earthly desire, carries in itself forces to realize and draw towards what in the present could not yet become reality. There exists in life a longing that alienates the human soul from Christ as the fountain-head, but also such a longing which does bring us close to this fountain-head. In this sense Thomas is the 'doubter', yet at the same time the 'disciple of the great longing'. He is the original for our present age attuned to the doubt of the understanding, so attuned that precisely the most advanced soul has initially to go through this intellectual doubt.

The Mercury-sign of the Twins, aligned to Thomas, the 'Twin' (John 11:16) (MG 338), is on the one side really a sign of intellectual doubt, on the other hand a sign of the highest Initiation (John 4, with the chapter 'The Samaritan woman at the well' (and MG 86ff., 178ff. On both sides of Hermes-Mercury see the chapter on the planets, Part One, Chapter 4 above). The story of the Resurrection in John's Gospel

(John 20:24-29) shows how Thomas, through the strength of longing present in himself, finds the way from the more lowly, cosmic revelation of his own being to the higher revelation. *After the earthly death of Christ Jesus, Thomas is the first disciple*, who, similar to the 'disciple of love' before him, *finds the way to Initiation*. The concern here is an *initiation-process of the most tremendous kind*, in no way a mere embarrassment of the 'doubter'—although the one fact does not exclude the other. Even an embarrassment stirred-up in the soul's depths can become a 'way to Initiation'. The concern here, though, is the spiritual experience narrated in John's Gospel.

Moreover, the words (John 20:29), 'Heavenly blessed [μακάριοι] are those who have not seen yet inwardly become aware'—who before they behold, have already inwardly perceived (Luther & KJV/AV): 'Blessed are they who have not seen and yet have believed', do not need at all to be taken as a value judgment—although initially it suggests this. It can mean that there are people whose inner hearing is still given as a blessed inheritance, whereas the actual advanced souls are those who initially have to struggle through intellectual doubt, but then from the 'I' penetrate through to beholding, from beholding they pass towards inner hearing, to Inspiration, to an opening of the forces of the heart. Precisely in our age this way can be seen as the advanced, contemporary path. We can feel such an age as the 'age of Thomas', preceding the actual Johannine Age lying in the future, perhaps a still far future.

Thomas' experience of Resurrection and Initiation, even though still in the etheric region, is still a degree more conscious and thereby at the same time closer to the earthly-physical than that of Mary Magdalene. The touch, still forbidden to Mary Magdalene, is precisely offered to Thomas (John 20:27). Something inconceivably great, unique in world-history, is suggested in the progress of this narration. [To use anthroposophical terminology,] we advance, as it were, from the 'sentient soul' to the 'mind-soul', in order in the later Johannine-apocalyptic Resurrection-experience to attain the level of the 'spiritual-soul'. Everything in the Resurrection-experiences narrated in the final chapters of the gospel are but preparation, lying in a sphere that is not yet that of full spiritual awakening. Even with Thomas we have to imagine that his initially still half-dreamt 'initiation' becomes fully conscious only with the experience of Pentecost, that is, only then does it become fully real.

The Paradisal Garden, the Stream & the Holy City

In several respects Thomas' experience relates to that of Mary Magdalene. Mary experiences the *Paradise Garden*; Thomas experiences [the invitation] to place his hands into the marks of the nails of the Crucified-and-Risen One (John 20:27), into the greatest etheric stream and stream of life in the world, that springs afresh on Golgotha, the new *river of Paradise* (Gen. 2:10 also MG 339f. and chap. 1, 5 above).[101] In his initiation Thomas directly experiences the essential substance of Christ's saying (John 7:38), 'He who receives me into himself, as the scripture has said, out of his heart shall flow rivers of living water'. This etheric stream of life changes all the dead thinking of intellectual doubt into *living thinking*.

- The resurrection-experience of Mary Magdalene lies in the sphere of the feelings;
- The resurrection-experience of Thomas lies in the sphere of thinking.
- The Johannine experience of resurrection lying in the future carries in itself the decisive inspiration of the will.

The resurrection-experiences of Mary and of Thomas reveals the picture of the *garden* and of the *stream*—of the stream which springing in the free mountain heights then flows down to the lowlands of humanity. We find only in the Apocalypse—the fulfilled resurrection-experience of John—the picture of the *city*, the Holy City of the 'New Jerusalem', which contains the Mystery of the new, metamorphosed Earth, the light-filled Earth, of the 'white stone' (or 'stone of the wise'; Rev. 2:17). All development of humanity in consciousness and of the 'I', moving on from natural existence to existence in the city, all city-culture, is connected precisely with the development of the 'I', or ego. So, too, the path of Initiation of the awakened 'consciousness-soul'[102] leads from the *Paradise of primordial beginnings* to the *Holy city of the future*.

The Resurrection is only fulfilled in this *Holy City*, which is built no longer out of dead earthly material but out of the world of the 'upper light', out of the forces of the advanced un-decaying substance, the virginal, super-sensory light-filled Earth, the 'transformed Earth'. Only here is the 'I' advanced to its whole full power of authority in the earthly-physical realm, to build the Earth afresh out of the forces of un-decaying substance; only here is the 'I'-experience of resurrection united to the events of the [planet] Earth. As an invisible, hidden becoming within the 'dying Earth-existence' [as the Creed of The

Christian Community expresses the fact] all this is already present today. The awakened 'I' feels and lays hold of its potential strength, coming to fulfilment in the future. This becoming takes its beginning in that which, invisible to the earthly, physical eye, has been raised out of the grave of Golgotha.

Fishing, Feeding and the Future

As in the dawning distance, like a Fata Morgana, or superior mirage, all these pictures of the future lie over the final Chapter 21 of John's Gospel. With the fishing catch at the beginning, the Feeding and Lord's-Supper experience at the end, once more we are placed in all clarity into the Last-Supper Constellation ♓–♍ standing over the whole Resurrection Chapters. With the 'great Feeding' of John 6 the 'bread' as the etheric element was primarily emphasized. With this exceptional resurrection-encounter in the final chapter of John, as a vision of a most distant future, the *Fishes* stand in the foreground as the symbol of the becoming *ego-strength*, of the future 'super-sensory members' of humanity (John 21:11). The number given there points to Mysteries of the Johannine Initiation and the standard measurement of far-reaching, future 'cycles of time'.[103]

Here, too, the zodiac sign of the Fishes corresponds to the fact that the whole experience takes place between night and morning, comparable to dreaming and beholding that we experience before waking up (MG 27, top). With the earlier experience the disciples initially encountered difficulties in recognizing Christ (Mark 6:49), and they also do here (John 21:4). In both accounts the shore is a picture of the solid land of day-awake consciousness, in which recognition gradually occurs. The 'disciple whom the Lord loved' is the first to recognize the Risen One. Here, too, he precedes the other, Peter, to whom is lent spiritual help. The whole event lies far removed from normal daytime experience.

One notices everywhere how the experiences the disciples went through with Christ Jesus come to light now in a completely different level of consciousness, pointing to the distant future—as in this 'breakfast' [v. 12] which the disciples share with the Risen One there lives again the earlier Feeding (Mark 6, John 6), in the fishing catch itself there lives again the earlier fishing catch and call of Simon-Peter (Luke 5:1-11), and in the triple question of Christ to Peter (John 21:15ff.) lives again 'Peter's denial'. In particular, there lies an exact inner connection, researchable for a spiritual psychoanalysis (also the question John 13:23-25 has its counter-picture in John 21:20-22).

Especially the final episode (John 21:15ff.) expressively shows—as does the whole content of both Resurrection Chapters—how a sleep of consciousness, a constraint of silence on the consciousness of the disciples, in this case of Peter, slowly begins to loosen. When he spoke the 'I am not' (οὐκ εἰμί) in his denial (John 18:17 & 25) his consciousness was deeply darkened by the adversary, as if extinguished. He does not perceive with these words the spiritual gaze of Christ directed to him; the event remains for him completely unconscious, or in the deepest sub-consciousness.[104] Yet nevertheless the presented objective experience creates in the soul a counter-picture, which now in the sphere of consciousness of the Resurrection, as it were, finds the substance in order to be re-enlivened and revealed. This is perhaps the reason why the evangelist narrates with such detail the whole story of the denial of Peter, to whom he would rather show kindly consideration and keep silent (John 18:15-27). For the concern here is not with some subsidiary episode, but with a part of the tragedy of mankind with difficult consequences of comprehensive, world-historic significance. This says a lot for the genuineness—contested by some—of John 21, which exists at least in the spiritual sense.

Thus Christ's triple question, 'Simon, son of John, do you love me?', reflects Peter's triple denial 'I am not'. The whole of John 21 is a chapter of reflection; it unrolls for us occurrences of reflection. Deepest Mysteries of the most distant future of humanity are reflected in it, appearing like a Fata Morgana on the horizon of the future. Like an anxious question of destiny and question of the future, finally there arises the riddle of the two disciples, whom from the narration of the Resurrection onwards we have seen increasingly joining together in outer manifestation. The one is the spiritual helper of the other, who appears in the first instance called to work outwardly as the 'rock' of the Church in the making.

- This disciple always appears somehow linked with the Mystery of fish and catches of fish—as the picture for the human task of the visible Church—think also of Peter's 'fisherman's ring'.[105]
- The other disciple is the one who has found the *way of life*, overcome the sting of death (MG 123, 209ff., 229f.)—the 'disciple who was not to die' (John 21:23), that is, for whom earthly death no longer has significance, because he lives and works constantly in Christ's earthly

sphere, 'remains' (μένει 21:22 & 23, whereby we recall how this word always points towards the Mystery of the connection to Christ and connection to the 'I'). This disciple, who awoke in himself the Virgin (♍), is inwardly united with the Mystery of the virginal Earth, the Resurrection-Earth, the metamorphosis of the Earth and future of the Earth.

Thus there still appears at the end of John 21 the constellation (♓–♍) actually opposite both disciples as the mysterious antithesis (if with ♓ we think not so much on the immediate meaning of this sign for Christ, but in a certain way on its meaning here revealing Peter).

With the one disciple we see the Mystery of the temporally-conditioned, earthly visible Church in its most earthly mighty manifestations. With the other, we see the 'disciple of love' (John 21:30) and Inspirer of John's Gospel (John 21:24) united to the Mystery of the super-temporal, the 'invisible Church', the eternal 'I'-future of humanity.

Und schwer und ferne	In vain we ask, with yearning fond,
Hängt eine Hülle,	The form of that which lies beyond:
Mit Ehrfurcht, stille	Interrogate them, as we will,
Ruhn oben die Sterne	The stars on high are silent still;
Und unten die Gräber.	Silent the graves, nor make reply
	The dearest lips therein that lie.

(a verse from the poem 'Symbolum' by Goethe, tr. Arthur John Lockhart)

[*Prose tr.*: And heavy and far hangs a sheath, with awe, silent the stars rest above and down below the graves.]

What to the One just risen from the grave, from the one dazzled by the rays of the new light, standing before the spiritual eye like a dawning distant future (MG 315f.), that which like a distant Fata Morgana forming the dawning future-background and future-prospect of John 21, is the light-transfigured Mystery of the *New Jerusalem*. Then there appears in clear outlines the great vision, which as the *Apocalypse of John* is like a final and cherished testament to posterity, to the spirit whom we thank for the inspiration of John's Gospel. In this *tremendous vision of the New Jerusalem*, in the becoming of the resurrection-Earth, the *Last-Supper event* of humankind is fulfilled (♓–♍), which is also indicated by John as shining over both Resurrection-Chapters. Only there, in the *Supper of the Lamb and the Bride*, in the great *Chymical Wedding*, in this final and highest content of Johannine vision, is the Johannine revelation of the 'I' fulfilled, is the future of the consciousness of mankind in the *Apocalypse in the 'I'* fulfilled.

The Figures of the Zodiac

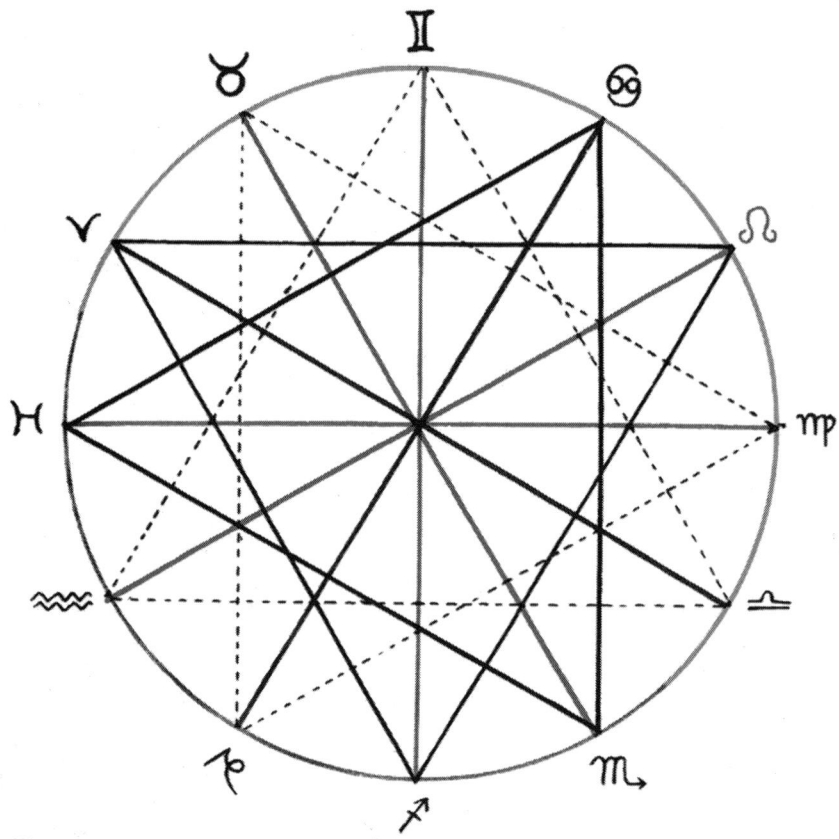

FIGURE I *is already given in the book* Mark's Gospel, the Cosmic Rhythm. *The three crosses in the zodiac (MG 401ff.) are shown through the different colours: the physical cross ('Cross of the Father') in blue, the ether-cross ('Christ-Cross of the Son') in green, and the astral cross ('Cross of the Spirit') in red. The 'triangle of the four evangelists' (MG 356ff.) are emphasized in this figure through stronger and weaker lines (John and Mark), and through stronger and weaker dotted lines (Luke and Matthew).*

The Figures of the Zodiac 335

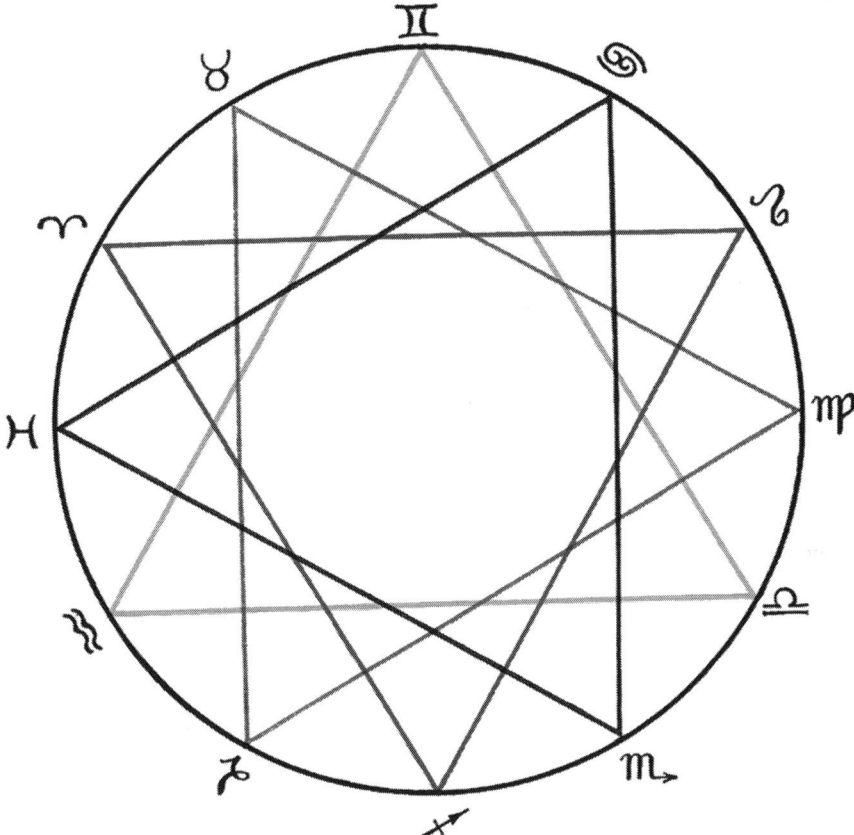

FIGURE II *is taken from the book by Dr Günther Wachsmuth,* The Etheric Formative Forces in the Cosmos, Earth and Man, *Bk 2, p. 15. The position of the axes is reversed (with Wachsmuth ♈ ♎ is the traverse axis, ♋ ♑ the longitudinal axis) for a certain point of view, initially only decisive for the Christ-cross (traverse axis ♓ ♍, longitudinal axis ♊ ♐) to allow it to appear as the 'cross of the middle'. For the position of the axes as chosen by Wachsmuth the Johannine triangle (sound-ether, blue) the apex would stand with the point above, which is likewise significant.*

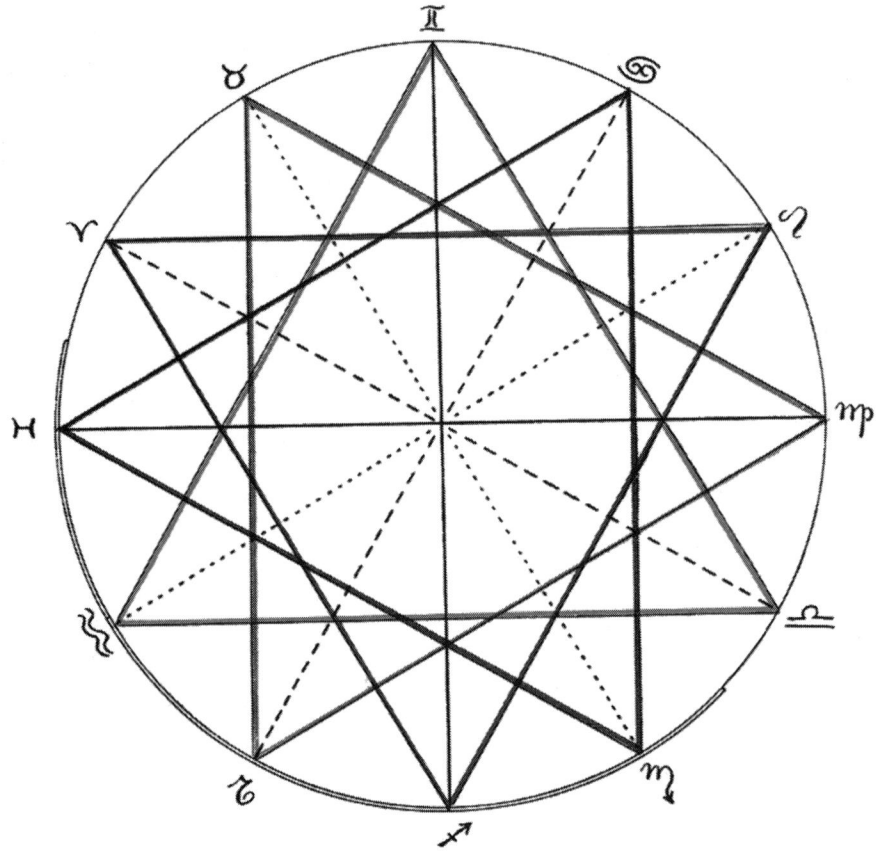

FIGURE III is to be thought as the summary of the first two figures.

The Figures of the Zodiac 337

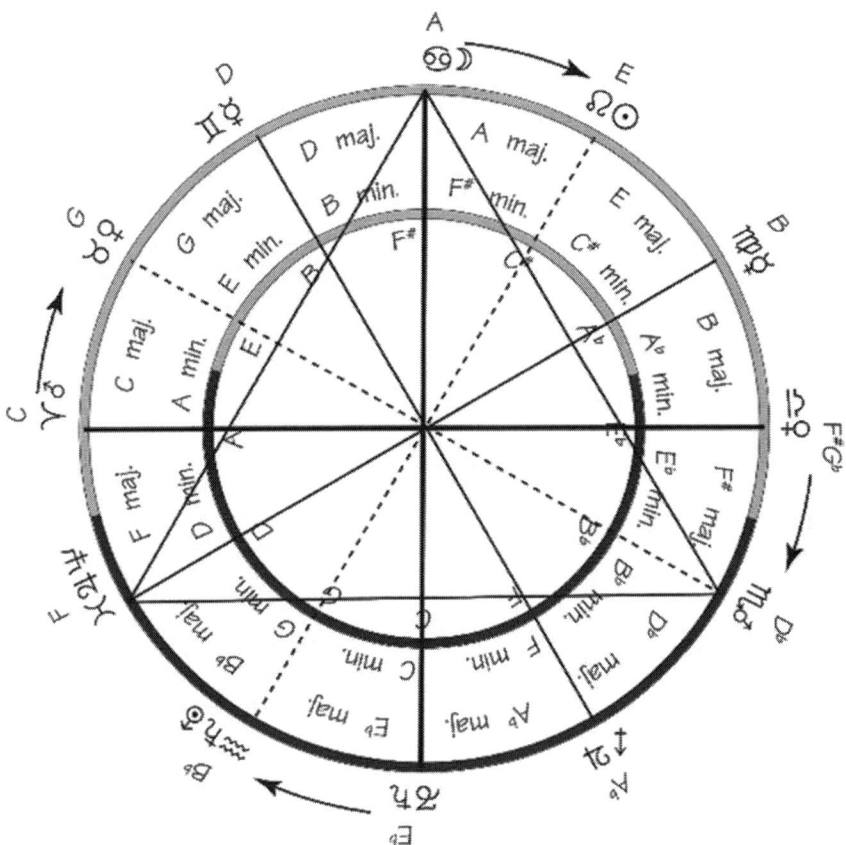

FIGURE IV (the tone-zodiac) appears in the author's publications on the musical keys [The Essence of Tonality *and* The Language of Tonality. *Anastasi; TL forthcoming*]. *It serves to show musical and tonal phenomena, as they correspond to the character of John's Gospel, mentioned at various places in the book (e.g. pp. 10, 49, 77, 101, 121f., 127f., 258f., 290, 314, etc.).*

APPENDICES

Rhythmical Events in the Gospel

Hermann Beckh

(*Die Christengemeinschaft*, 6. Jg. Nr. 11. Feb. 1930. 334-38)

The old Indian word *ṛta* (pronounced 'rita'), for which, amongst other translations 'law, order, use, sacred cosmic order, truth', we find especially a threefold meaning: firstly, the course of the year, regulated according to the stars that move on the eternal ordering on their pre-ordained paths, and finally of religious ritual of sacrifice in harmony with the annual events of the permanent order of the stars in their courses.

Recalling the Latin *ritus*, this Indian word *ṛta* comes from a root from which also the Greek word *rhythmós* derives. According to its innermost meaning, it means a *rhythmical event*, expressing the thought that the eternal divine being, where it reveals itself in earthly time, is expressed in *rhythmical events*. Not only the events of the year like the stars in their courses, but also the sacred order of the cultic rites of sacrifice are based on such a rhythm, *ṛta*, and everything rhythmical appears as a revelation of a higher lawfulness. The inner being of everything cultic is here stated; the inner nerve of the cultic events is shown. And what concerns the early Indian ritual of sacrifice is shown to be true in this sense also for the Christian rite. The sacrifice of the Mass of the Catholic Church and the Act of Consecration of Man of The Christian Community are based again on the course of the stars, constructed on the rhythm of the stars measured on the rhythmical events of the course of the year.

In pre-Christian Mysteries, too, in the Eleusian, likewise the Adonis and Attis Mysteries, this regard for the rhythmical events in the course of the year plays a significant role—the eternal change and rotation of growing and withering, ripening and fruiting, becoming and passing away, death and resurrection. What is meant, however, is initially always but a natural event reflected in the human soul, a revelation of the course of nature falling to the human soul. The significantly new, innovative and unique thing about the Christian event lies in the fact that what in blossoming and decaying and in the fresh growth of the plant-world is merely a revelation of nature. What—in the Mysteries of Eleusis—the soul could dimly divine as the secret of its destiny, becoming manifest throughout long periods of human history, was placed on the plane of earthly history as an *historical event* in the death and Resurrection of Christ. Thereby, the secret is gently indicated why in the Christian ritual, the Mass of the Catholic Church as in The Act of Consecration of Man in The Christian Community, initially the concern is not to celebrate some mere natural event, a mere revelation of nature. An historical fact, the sacrifice of Christ Jesus for humanity, is celebrated. Nevertheless, in this sacrificial celebration that appears woven so significantly with the rhythmic events of the course of the year, the externals also of this Christian ritual always change, fashioned according to the different times of the year.

The Gospels

At the same time, a new and remarkable light falls on the Christian gospel, especially on the Gospel according to Mark. In this narration of the Christian gospel of the earthly life and earthly death, of the death and Resurrection of Christ Jesus, regardless of the historical character of the narrated events, nevertheless it can be understood why a rhythmical element can be found that recalls the rhythmical events in the course of the year, on the eternally regular change of blossoming and withering, growth and ripening, becoming and decaying, sleeping and waking, summer and winter, day and night. All these are meanings also contained in the Indian word *ṛta*. In the book, *Mark's Gospel: The Cosmic Rhythm*, the attempt was made to point to the connection of the gospel narration with the rhythmic events of the year. Thereby the following came into consideration.

In the early Mysteries, in which the soul was led through specific experiences, initially revealed out of natural events, the concern was for a specific inner path of becoming, a specific path of stages of spiritual development that was always called *Initiation*. The human soul was brought into a certain rhythmic accord and harmony with higher Mysteries of nature and Mysteries of existence. In this connection, what was experienced in the early Mysteries and was protected as a deep, inviolable secret—to betray this was punishable with death— also this *initiation-event* was placed on the plane of world-history in the suffering, death and Resurrection of Christ Jesus. But it was done so that what was experienced in the earlier Mysteries as a divining parable was now published abroad. What in pre-Christian times was long before divined and prophesied stood there in the Mystery of Golgotha as the fulfilment of all the Mysteries.

That is why the entire appearance of Christ Jesus, especially in the 'raising of Lazarus', to the Jewish Pharisees and High-Priests appeared as a betrayal of the Mysteries, worthy of death. This placing of the Mysteries openly on the plane of world-history in the Mystery of Golgotha did not mean that everyone had to experience the Mystery. Much rather, as Novalis [Sophie, in *Heinrich von Ofterdingen*] expresses it: 'the great secret is revealed to all, and remains forever unfathomable. Out of pain is the new world born, and the ashes are dissolved into tears for a draught of eternal life.' Only *one disciple stood under the cross* (John 1:25), after the others in Gethsemane had abandoned their Master in a confusion of consciousness, that is, only one consciously participated in the great Mystery. In this experience, as the gospel indicates, the 'Mother' and Mary Magdalene take a certain part. For actual humanity it remained, and to a considerable extent still remains, a Mystery. This fact sufficiently shows what significance the Initiation of the one disciple—fulfilled under the cross—has for the future of humanity, as the secret of the new, the Christian initiation presented in the disciple John. The initiation of the earlier pre-Christian Mysteries is discharged at the cross on Golgotha—which, again, stands in mysterious connection with the Mystery-events of Bethany, the 'raising of Lazarus'—through the new Christian-Johannine Initiation.

Understanding what was said of the historical revelation of Christ connected to the revelation of nature in the early Mysteries, illuminates without more ado all the variety of pre-Christian, yet also the Christian initiation-events. These initially must have to do with how an understanding and living with the Mystery of Golgotha is connected with the revelation of nature, with the rhythmical events of nature. No initiation exists that does not concern the soul brought into accord and harmony with this eternal rhythm of blossoming and withering, growth and ripening, becoming and decaying, birth and death. And for all recent training of the soul, such a significant book for all 'modern initiation' as *Knowledge of the Higher Worlds: How is it Attained?*, Rudolf Steiner points to the importance of this beholding of the eternal facts of blossoming and decaying, becoming and dying away for the development of higher organs of perception of the soul.

The narrations of the life of Christ in the gospels are something other than only external, historical reports. That they otherwise have the character of 'initiation writings' is emphasized by Rudolf Steiner. In the future this will become increasingly known and understood.

One can certainly read such a document as Mark's Gospel, simply interested in what is told of the deeds and experiences of Christ Jesus and the group of disciples. But one can also read the account as a very significant portrayal of the Christian-Johannine path of initiation, of the initiation of the disciples. One can especially recognize the experiences of John leading to his initiation by Christ. This point of view nobody can forcefully open up; it cannot be proved in the normal sense through some kind of 'convincing' arguments—for it concerns precisely those areas that leave the soul free, not to be compelled. It can only be said that, for those who have opened themselves to this point of view, Mark's Gospel becomes something more important than it was before. In John's Gospel one can find the way to Christ; in Mark's Gospel such a person can find the way to John in a completely special sense. And it will dawn on him when precisely in Mark's Gospel this rhythm, essential for all initiation, becomes more obvious in a completely special way, so obvious that also someone so completely distant from representatives of all mysticism, all occultism, and all anthroposophy as [historian and philosopher] Arthur Drews [1865-1935] became aware of the fact of this rhythm.

Such persons—especially Arthur Drews in a here and there genial, though often plainly in a fantastically strange manner—however, introduce into the fact of this 'cosmic rhythm' that cannot be denied, all kinds of possible 'astral mythology' and astronomical connections. The fact of this rhythm becomes at first only mutilated and obliterated. What for itself is to be taken seriously is changed into a mystical frivolity, which Drews, who consequently also denies the historical reality, naturally does not personally advocate but merely finds an interesting superstition. Thereby the many accounts by Drews and others have failed to lead readers, introduced to such great cosmic views, to approach the significant and honourable Christian gospel with its wonderful and sublime questions of the gospel-rhythm. In many respects they have rather deterred people.

The Cosmic Rhythm

For comprehending the governing rhythm of Mark's Gospel, what has to be seen is that the stars in the abstract are not at all necessary. This rhythm can be understood purely from observing the events of the year. The events of Mark's Gospel—all one, whether we take the events of Christ of the three years (which as such in Mark's

Gospel are not at all obvious), or whether we take the Johannine Initiation-event that inwardly follows the events of the three years—lie basically in the same sphere in which we stand in experiencing the year and, what is especially important, likewise in experiencing the Christian Eucharist, The Act of Consecration of Man. For this reason the objection is invalid, for example, that for those initially searching only for the Christian experience in the Eucharist, taking the cosmic view of the gospel should be something completely distant and 'far-fetched'.

Precisely being present at the Eucharist creates favourable circumstances to experience the rhythmical element. A premature introduction of extensive astronomical aspects in a justified and understandable manner can appear detrimental here. The eternal rhythm of blooming and withering, becoming and decaying, governs by death and resurrection in the course of the year, in the Eucharist, as it does in the Christ-events and the process of initiation in the gospel. This rhythm can be recognized as something for itself, as understandable and illuminating on its own terms. We notice at the corresponding place of the rhythm—this concerns the threefold return of the same section or 'sign' [over the three years]—a similar or meaningfully-related event always returns. For example, the voyage on the Lake of Galilee and the Storm on the Lake is found always at a quite specific place, clearly given through the gospel-rhythm. At a specific point the descent always follows the ascent and the new ascent follows the descent (the details have to be viewed out of the whole presentation). Thus, without all the 'astral mythology', the 'cosmic rhythm' meant here can become clear on its own terms, and from all that has been said we can well understand precisely in the gospel what such a rhythm signifies.

But when 'the signs of the zodiac' are discussed, won't there be an incessant reference to the stars? Here too it is not as many people imagine. Recall much rather what was given at the beginning—the three meanings of the word *ṛta* . To the revelation in the events of the year specific movements of the stars proceed in parallel, specific events in the starry heavens, in the Sun, Moon and stars. The word *ṛta* (rhythm) also relates to this eternal ordering of the course of the stars. What since olden times have these movements of the stars in connection with the events of the year—as with the events of the day—always been for humanity? Initially simply the great *cosmic clock* given simply through the nature of the thing, according to which ultimately all our earthly clocks join and are attuned. If one wanted to establish in the heavens the section of the Sun's heavenly arc corresponding to the annual events, one looks up to the starry heavens. The 'zodiac pictures' came about, whose unity of twelve once again is connected with the course of the Moon, with the unity of the twelve months. (The question whether and how far an earlier consciousness of humanity really experienced the starry heavens in pictures can for the moment rest on one side.)

Sign and Constellation

This aspect of the *cosmic clock* is not the last but the first, initially more important point, for considering the whole question. During the time when Christ walked the Earth, one looked up to the starry heavens, and found how the Sun:

- with the spring equinox entered the constellation of the Ram,
- in the summer solstice into the constellation of the Crab,
- in the autumn equinox into the constellation of the Scales, and
- in the winter solstice into the Goat.

This connection no longer exists like this today because of the retrograde motion of the spring equinox. Orientating to the [actual] starry heavens:

- the spring equinox today lies in the Fishes,
- the summer solstice in the Twins,
- the autumn equinox in the Virgin, and
- the winter solstice in the Archer.

Yet we stand from the point of view of the course of the year even today in the Crab, when the Sun in the summer solstice goes backwards again, commencing its 'crab's walk', when the increasing shortening of the day ensues. Even today, seen from the Earth, in the Scales, when in the autumn day and night are provisionally equal in duration, we 'enter into the Scales'. In astronomy, by dividing the whole heavenly arc into twelve equal sections, one is actually calculating with these sections as 'signs' and differentiating them from the constellations. The sign, even when it retains its name from the constellation (which it no longer indicates today) in the abstract, nevertheless regarded purely from the earthly side, is a specific section of the rhythm of the year having nothing directly to do with the fixed stars.

And so we can understand the rhythms of Mark's Gospel without concerning ourselves with the stars, simply out of these 'signs', these rhythmic sections of the course of the year. Only the fact exists that, precisely in the age of Christ's earthly life, sign and constellation coincided, that is, the place of the rhythmic 'sign' was really decided by the constellation by which it carries the name. This agreement was at its most complete in the hour of the Mystery of Golgotha. For this reason it can appear meaningful to point—as happens in the book on Mark's Gospel—from the sign to the constellation, to the actual heavenly picture. For in the time of Christ's earthly life this heavenly picture, like a great 'cosmic script' stood there for the earthly event. Later the relationship was displaced and in the future will be displaced ever further. This should here initially be stated as a purely astronomical fact, about whose spiritual background much can be said, much conjectured. Yet this would have to form the subject of a further special article. In such an article one can pursue the question of sign and constellation further, and some other star-Mysteries and questions.

The Indian Yoga Mystery and the Awakening Deed of Bethany

Hermann Beckh

(from *Die Christengemeinschaft*, 8. Jg. 8, November 1931. 225-32)

With the Indians, certain sacred texts, the *Upanishads*, form the mystical, esoteric supplement and completion of the *Vedas*, the basic Indian bible. Upanishad (stress on the third syllable), literally means, 'sitting down near'. A teaching is meant that the pupil receives personally from the spiritual teacher in intimate, or esoteric, conversation. We know how the philosopher Schopenhauer loved the Upanishads, which he knew in a Latin translation. He said about them, 'They will be the comfort of my life and the comfort of my death', and he placed them during the night beside his bed.

One Upanishad text of wonderful significance is the Kathaka Upanishad (with Kathaka, stress on the first syllable) in a way that still today touches people. It declares the great, riddling questions of death and immortality connected to all human existence. It shows us today not only how the early Indians thought about these issues, but beyond this allows us to discover a significant connection between the Indian Mystery and the Christian Mystery. In what follows, this connection will be explored, and then the general question of how the riddle of death and immortality in the Upanishads is answered out of the Indians spirit.

*

The Raising of Lazarus and Yoga[106]

The centre piece of John's Gospel, in the chapter on Lazarus (John 11:25), Christ Jesus utters the saying allowing the decisive solution of all human questions on immortality, the fulfilment of all human hopes of immortality; it allows to shine before us in the 'I': 'I AM [the 'I' is] the resurrection and the life.' Christ's saying is linked to Christ's Deed, giving to His words their true power, which only gives the saying its true power—the awakening of the 'invalid' of Bethany, of Lazarus, out of the three-and-a-half-days slumber in the grave (John 11:39).

Rudolf Steiner gave a key to understand this mysterious, and for the consciousness of today possibly scandalous process, by stating in his book *Christianity as Mystical Fact* [GA 8] and in his lecture-courses on John's Gospel [GA 103 and 112] that it concerns here an initiation process, about the founding of the new Christian, Johannine Initiation. But in the way Christ carried out this Initiation process on Lazarus links to an earlier form of initiation, to the Indian Yoga-initiation. For the latter, it would have been characteristic that the candidate for initiation was immersed into a three-and-a-half-day sleep of death by his teacher, by the initiator. The higher members of the human being, which already in sleep are loosened but in death are completely separated from the physical bodily sheaths, would have expanded far. They would have received in this condition the immediate impressions of the spiritual world. After re-awakening they would have been imprinted into the physical sheath. The re-awakened one would then arise out of the slumber of the grave as a knower in a higher sense, an 'initiate'.

If we follow this explanation given by the spiritual researcher, we will see in it a significant bridge between the Indian Mystery and the Christian Mystery. Light is shed over a certain mysterious section repeatedly met in the documents on Indian Yoga and other mystical writings. All sorts of schooling methods in meditation, breathing exercises and other exercises are described in such texts, often interesting and explicit, but only up to a certain point. Then, we are made aware, would come the most important part that cannot be publically transmitted but only personally communicated from the teacher to the pupil. Such a kind of secrecy and way of holding back knowledge might have been justified with an earlier level of pre-Christian Mysteries.

Today, we feel repulsed and possibly insulted in our human dignity. This feeling is fully justified in the Christian age of the consciousness-soul, [a technical term for] the soul fully developed in the consciousness of the 'I', or ego. Everything that appears in the direction of mystical secrecy has to awaken mistrust in the soul carrying the contemporary level of consciousness. This soul, on the other hand, will trust the Christ-Event as that Event through which what was veiled earlier in the Mysteries is now placed on the plane of world-history. Through the Mystery of Golgotha, Rudolf Steiner says in the book *Christianity as Mystical Fact*, the earlier Mysteries have been revealed. (Here we can also think of Novalis' words [Sophie in *Heinrich von Ofterdingen*]: 'The great secret is revealed to all, and remains forever unfathomable.' [The quote continues: 'Out of pain is the new world born, and the ashes are dissolved into tears for a draught of eternal life.']

Does this becoming-revealed also apply to the Indian Yoga-Mystery in question? Indeed, and the Lazarus Chapter, John 11, indicates how and where it becomes revealed, if we attempt to use the key given by Rudolf Steiner. For that which was not communicated publically, that which could only be personally experienced from the teacher, could never have formed the content of a communication clothed in abstract words. It had to do here with nothing other than the experiences out of the spiritual world, brought about for the candidate by the teacher through the means of this three-day slumber in the grave, or sleep of death. The etheric organization of the early Indian matured to become receptive in a special manner for such a procedure, difficult to understand today. During the descent of humanity, this receptivity, this strength of the inner organization, increasingly disappeared.

Today, such a procedure for the Westerner would bring certain death. Only from Indians, from fakirs and yogis who through their own will were able to control their heartbeat, are able to go through a process of being buried alive. Scientifically credible examples exist. Such a case is that of the hatha yogi and fakir Sadhu Haridas [who in 1837 survived a forty-day internment].[107] These are decadent remnants of what was fully alive and extant in the early Indian primordial past. Such deeds, however, are not the concern with what Christ Jesus achieved with Lazarus.

A special power of the etheric organization was at work as with the early Indians—and in the few credible cases with Indians of today. In the Deed of Christ at Bethany the Christ-'I' was revealed. With His rays of love, His power of love in the 'I', Christ, dying by sacrificing Himself into the Earth, penetrated the bodily sheaths of Lazarus, locked into the slumber of the grave in Bethany. This dying of Christ begins in the Mystery of Bethany, indeed it had already begun with the Transfiguration (further details, as well as the whole context of the raising of Lazarus, is contained in the author's book on *John's Gospel*, 319-358, also on *Mark's Gospel*, 189ff., 209ff., 241ff.). No other disciple than the one of whom it is said that Jesus 'loved him' and who himself was able to open completely to this divine Love, could receive the Love of Christ as an awakening Love.

Today, we see here a unique event of world-history that could only be carried out by Christ. Subsequently, it no longer played a role as a form of the new, Christian initiation. Outwardly seen, however, an agreement, emphasized by Rudolf Steiner, exists between this raising of Lazarus and the early-Indian Yoga-initiation. We then understand several seemingly insignificant things that Indian Mystery-texts tell of the communication between teacher and pupil. The pupil comes to the spiritual teacher and initially learns nothing in words about the world-secret. He has first to perform only humble duties. The decisive thing is not the visible and audible, but what takes place invisibly and inaudibly between teacher and pupil, how the pupil is received by the spiritual sphere of the teacher. The divine initially speaks silently before it can be revealed in words. And through the whole personal communication, such a riddle to us today,[108] between teacher and pupil, this receptivity is achieved in the pupil. This enables him to penetrate through the three-and-a-half-day sleep of death and to experience the secret never to be conveyed in words.

Thus the Lazarus Chapter of John's Gospel in a certain way does contain the revelation of the decisive Yoga-secret always suppressed in the Indian documents. And we recognize, or experience, how the fulfilment of the Indian Yoga-Mystery is to be found not in today's decadent Indian practice but in Christianity.

*

So far, we have followed the communications of the spiritual researcher and have tried to apply a key given for the Lazarus Chapter on John's Gospel for the Yoga-Mystery. An objection should not be ignored, which an Indologist of today will raise, by a scholar who researches Indology only out of the documents that have come down to us. He would say: If that process of a three-and-a-half-day sleep of death reminding us of the Lazarus-event in John's Gospel is of such importance for the Indian Yoga-Mysteries, how does it come about that the Indian Yoga-documents do not communicate such a process to us anywhere? And it is true we do not find anything explicitly about this in the usual Yoga texts. That the often recurring, mysterious passage, 'now would come the most important thing, but this could only be experienced personally from the spiritual teacher', relates to those events, today appearing so dark—this will never be accepted and admitted by such an Indologist.

And yet there exists an Indian text—and here we arrive at the decisive point—where the secret of the three-and-a-half-day sleep of death, or slumber of the grave, is touched on. Of course, not mentioned in such a way that the scholar could be convinced, who stays completely with the externals of the words and of the document. But yet in such a way that the one who seeks to penetrate into esoteric deepening into the secret of the text can form an enlightened connection. The text meant here is the Kathaka Upanishad, mentioned at the beginning. It tells of the Brahman youth, who descends into the realm of death. After remaining there for three days and three nights, he receives from the god of Death the teaching concerning the Yoga-Mysteries. He then returns as a knower, an initiate, into the world of the living. Especially when we place in this brevity the essential motif of the Upanishad, we will understand what is essential here and will be surprised to meet the viewpoint, mentioned by Rudolf Steiner as decisive, with all clarity also in the Indian context.

For what else stands here before us than the great motif going through all pre-Christian and Christian Mysteries and their initiations, that the first step of each true initiation is the 'approach to the portal of death', that only from death can the highest secrets be found. And that in the actual essence of initiation something is experienced in life which otherwise is experienced in going through the portal of death. It is here also significant that the name of the Indian god of Death, Yama, at the same time means the first level of the Yoga schooling, a level of self-discipline and moral purification. The name of the Brahman youth, too, calls up Mystery connections in us. He is called Nachiketa, meaning literally 'the one who does not think intellectually'; he also reminds us of the 'pure fool' of the Grail legend 'Parsifal'. (This interpretation is given by Wagner, whereas the form of the name Parzival, Percival, is another one, but which especially relates to the penetrating through the experience of death.)

The most significant thing for the Christian, the Lazarus connection, however, remains with the Upanishad the three-and-a-half-day sojourn of this youth in the dwelling of the god of Death. He then leaves as a knower, one who knows the highest Mysteries (Yoga). And the motif of the three-and-a-half-days agrees exactly, for then in the Upanishad after the course of the three days and three nights, that is on the fourth day, the teaching through the god of Death follows. Whoever at this point wants to understand, will understand. And only for those who want to understand are the Mystery documents of all peoples written, the Indian not least. Their style is such that for those who think and search the literary side, the depths and richness of the content remains closed.

In what follows, we give indications on as much content of the Kathaka-Upanishad that can illuminate the treatment of the riddle of immortality in early India.

*

An early Brahman brings the *'Allhabeopfer'*,[109] full of the power of religious belief. The early Indian recognized and measured the reality of the religious experience, of the 'belief' in the ability and willingness to sacrifice that arose out of himself. The Upanishad pictorially describes how the sacrificial cows are being driven away—cows for the early Vedic Indian mean the most important of his earthly possessions, his 'capital'. Moreover, the religious interest gathers around the cow, as the Rigveda shows, in which the Indian reveres the sacred forces of the Earth—*one* word (*go*) still signifies Earth and cow. But the son of the Brahman, that youth, who, as we heard, carried the name of the 'pure fool', looks thoughtfully at the passing cows; these grass-eating, milk-giving animals seem a somewhat weak gift. To him a sacrifice seems to be incomplete to which the most precious thing is missing. And the most precious possession for the Indian Brahman was his own son. So the youth asks his father, 'Little father, to whom do you give me?' The father is angry, because the son has criticized his sacrifice, 'I give you to Death'.

And already we see the Brahman youth below in the dwelling of the god of Death. The Indian storytelling style habitually passes over the details and connections, leaving it to the listener's imagination. Essential to the Indian story here is only this, that for the Indian youth, the 'pure fool', the path to Death was nothing fearful; he only makes general observations on his way, such as, that already many have gone before him, and many will come after him, and that human beings are like the fruits of the field, they ripen and are cut down. And then how the seed starts another cycle. We believe we hear through this Indian text many things reminding us of Homer and the Greek Demeter-Mysteries of Eleusis. The thought of reincarnation also appears to come to light in it. But for the pre-Christian Indian it is characteristic that this thought does not contain anything comforting to him and it is no solution to the riddle of immortality.

The Indian of primordial times, still dreaming in the primordial consciousness did not know the fear of death because he did not experience it as we do today. Even the earthly connections to which he felt his bodily sheaths contained were for him still something spiritual. This, of course, changed in later times, but the literary documents—

this is characteristic for Indian culture—still in a certain way contain the mood of primordial times. Only in the Assyrian-Babylonian epoch—one thinks of the Gilgamesh epic—do we find the dread of death, prior to the sinking into the earthly element.

Thus the Brahman youth of the Kathaka Upanishad with a peaceful heart enters the dwelling of the god of Death. He has no fear of death, but the god of Death has more fear of him, when after three days—before the youth arrived he was away on a journey—he enters his dwelling again and hears now that the Brahman has dwelt there without being hosted and without the customary honours of a visitor. (At this place, in the ninth verse, the motif so important for us of the three days and three nights is mentioned in the account.) In order to understand all this and especially to understand the strange fear of the god of Death before the Brahman, who himself does not fear Death—one has to know what the Brahman meant for the Indian consciousness of culture, as the bearer of the sacred priest-forces, the divine power of the word and of prayer, of those forces which the Indian called Brahma, and revered as the Divine in the universe. Reverence for the spiritual life was as great in those days as it is small today; one feared this power which was also able—for example, the story of Elijah in the Old Testament—to appear as a dangerous destructive-bringing fire. Consequently, the god of Death demands water be brought for the feet of the Brahman, in order to quench the fire of the Brahmans. In order to make good his unintentional shortcomings, he also offers to grant the Brahman three wishes.

As a first wish, the youth asks to make peace with his father. As a second wish, a mystic heavenly fire (developed through a certain meditation or ritual) which grants bliss in the heavenly world. Both wishes are immediately fulfilled by the god of Death. What is meant by the second wish is only understood rightly if we know how the Indian person looks at the condition in the heavenly world—in the theosophical literature today called Devachan [in anthroposophy, simply 'the spiritual world'—*Tr.*]—as something that only passes as temporary, not the ultimate thing for which to strive. The mere 'continuation of life after death', the Indian certainly knows as a fact, but he does not find it worth striving for in the higher sense, although it is a blessed continuation. Each reincarnation, after all, appears to the pre-Christian Indian as painful. For him, to cut off a return into a suffering earthly existence is the highest goal of longing.

But then there arises the big question, what actually will become of the human being with this great passing over? The answer to this great riddling question is what the Brahman youth asks as his third wish from the god of Death. The question is placed in such a way that is appears to us almost modern—and this is something unusual in the style of this Indian text—whereby, of course, we take into account that the words which we simply relate to the normal riddle of death, are for the Indian person perhaps only related after many rebirths, though perhaps also related to the 'great passing' that can already be experienced here, called by Buddha the *parinirvāṇa*. The youth's question is: 'Concerning the doubt, when a human being has passed away—the one says that he is [exists], others say that he is not—this I would like to know, taught by you, [O Death]. This is my third wish.'

The way the question is expressed seems to us very modern, even if the meaning we connect with it is different from that of the Indian. Increasingly clearly we recognize that what the Indian longed for was not at all immortality in the usual sense, but eternity, the deathless life (Buddha, too, used this word) beyond space and time. Was this deathless life of eternity perhaps after all only the great Nothing? This question is what the Brahman youth here with concern lays before Death himself.

And here we see Death, who fulfils the first two wishes easily and point-blank, immediately becomes unsure, seeking to wriggle his way out, in order to avoid the answer. Even the gods, he says, would have doubted, and the matter is not easy to discern. 'Choose another wish, don't press me further, let me off this wish.' But the youth remains adamant, even though the god of Death offers him all kinds of earthly allurements, riches in land, beautiful women, all kinds of earthly possessions and earthly delights, long life and many children. 'Every new morning takes the fire of life and the light of life away' (this thought already occupied the early Vedic Indian very much), 'and also a fully lived life is yet only a short thing, yours, O Death, are carriages, dances and songs. Not through riches is the human being satisfied; how can we desire riches, if we look you in the eye [O Death]?' And the youth persists in his request: 'The pure one chooses the wish, and none other, that penetrates into the secrets.'

*

So far, Chapter One. Following this Chapter Two begins with the great teaching of the god of Death about the secrets of Yoga, stretching over four further chapters. Not their details, however rich and remarkable, are of significance. But what is important is the viewpoint that the question concerning immortality in the highest sense is more than a mere temporary continuation in heavenly bliss, which finds its end in a new earthly life is not answered in an abstract, theoretical way, but the calling up of the active soul-forces, which through heroic adjustment—this concerns the genuine Yoga—battles for immortality as meant here, eternity.

Immediately at the beginning of the teaching, the god of Death brings a picture that reminds us of the Greek legend of Heracles, of the story of Heracles at the dividing of the ways, where the two women approach him. The one offers him sensual pleasures, the other the higher life. The seeker of the path is placed before these decisions, between what is the favourable and what is the better one. Says Death to the Brahman. 'But you, youth, have decided for the better one, for true redemption.' And when he speaks of what the pupils can only personally experience from the teacher, this sentence, after all that we now know about it, especially in this Upanishad with this teaching communicated by Death himself, has a quite special justification, a special meaning, hardly imagined by the Indologist of today. 'Without a teacher,' says the god of Death, 'here indeed there is no entrance; but you have found the entrance with the right teacher [with me, Death].'

In rich pictures of the primordial cosmic wisdom the teachings of the god of Death pass before him. Some things remind us of Greek, some of Egyptian Mystery wisdom. In Chapter 4, Aditi (immortality) is mentioned, the divine Mother and goddess of the mystical primordial consciousness, from the primordial Motherhood of the world, which connects with the cosmic breath. The Egyptians, too, know Aditi as a name of Isis (a connection of Indian and Egyptian culture that is hardly recognized in research). This leads ever deeper into the secrets of Yoga, where also the 'Tree of Life', as we call it, the 'sacred fig-tree whose roots are in heaven and whose branches touch the Earth', as it appeared to the Indian, plays a role, until at the end the god of Death expressively calls his proclamation *Yoga*.

This is the word for the Indian central Indian Mystery that touches the Mystery of Lazarus in John's Gospel, the path of knowledge and meditative endeavour (this last word is the literal translation of the Indian *Yoga*). Yoga means active endeavour, *practice* (in contrast to all mere theory), whereby we have to think that for the Indian the path of spiritual endeavour (concentration) is the practice of all practice.

*

With this our observations reach again the starting point. With it, the essential thing is not the Indian concept of immortality, going into mysticism and losing itself with its negative evaluation of repeated earthly lives, overcome in Christianity. Rather the important thing is that connection which inwardly unites the Mystery motif of three-and-a-half-days in the grave (or the dwelling of Death) as it meaningfully echoes in that Indian Upanishad with the Mystery of Bethany as it stands before us in John 11.

The Heavenly Jerusalem

> Beckh agreed to write an article on the *'heavenly Jerusalem'*. To our surprise, his contribution took the form of poem. Beckh's enthusiasm had broken the simple, elementary track; he could not make his contribution other than in an artistically lilting, poetic form. And with this unfortunately little-known poem, he shows his homeland is the spiritual world of Novalis.
>
> (Rudolf Frieling, 1937).

This poetic offering of Hermann Beckh's surprised his six colleagues who collaborated for the little volume on the Apocalypse, *Gegenwartsrätsel in Offenbarungslicht* ('Present-day riddles in the light of revelation'), Stuttgart 1925. 105-121. Based on passages from the vision of John on Patmos we know as the Apocalypse (Book of Revelation) concluding the New Testament, Beckh's poetic lines may possibly owe something to passages from Victor Hugo's (1802-85) gigantic dream-vision *La Légende des Siècles* (1859-83) ('The legend of the ages', also translated as, 'The legend of the centuries'). Beckh himself acknowledges the holistic visions and thoughts of the spiritual-scientific fragments of Novalis (the early German Romantic poet and philosopher, 1772-1801). Partly bursting the constraints of neat prose, Beckh, following the lead of this poetic soul with whom he felt at home, conveys in iambic metre an elemental vision of some essentials on the human struggle in the light of progressive Christianity.

For the task of writing on the concluding vision of the Bible—the picture of the fulfilment of the Earth—the writer no doubt felt he had to risk everything for this ultimate theme by attempting a poetic mode. Like a sketch-book, a workshop, or an 'improvisation', in facing pictures from the Apocalypse existential demands will inevitably use whatever lends itself as relevant to the high spiritual theme—Beckh's own love of the mountains, traditional pictures, fairytales, Christian liturgy, Wagner's 'Parsifal' and the Grail story, alchemical and spiritual-scientific insights—above all following Novalis, poet and miner, as pathfinder to express the unity of star and stone, of man and the world, the self and its Creator.

A spiritual experience as a five-year-old in the mountains convincing him of human pre-existence was decisive for Beckh's life, and it was later recreated at specific turning points. Something of the incredible pain of compassion for his fellow human beings he experienced is also reflected in this poetic offering (see Beckh's autobiographical memoirs in the biography by Gundhild Kačer-Bock, *Hermann Beckh: Life and Work*, TL 2021, 46).

This rendering in English making no poetic claims, nevertheless hopes to remain faithful to the author's intentions—(A.S., 2014, rev. 2020).

The New Jerusalem
Hermann Beckh

A clear winter's day enticed me
into the solitude of the high mountains. Today the mountains are
not only the great grave, a heap of rubble
of the Earth, of the lonely dying one
that longs to disappear again into world dust.
They are a mirror today of the eternal Light,
which shone in the primordial beginning, of the virginal
crystal formative forces that are revealed in rock crystals
and in the tender miraculous starry snowflakes
of pure cosmic light.
Today everything earthly is covered
with a radiant dress of heavenly light,
from myriads of snow-crystals
a shining countenance of the Sun
glitters towards me reflecting the heavens,
in that which, falling out of the heights of heaven,
has then become the tender earthly covering.

Only out there, where on the far horizon
the widths of the flatland grow broad before the eye
and where in the nebulous grey fog
the towns of the people begin to disappear, heavy darkness weighs,
dark stripes of blue-black billowing fog.
Is it the pressure
of daemonic shadows on human souls?
Does there not shine
to them also the brightness of eternal Light?
Does it not penetrate to their dark sheaths?
'The cosmic Light shone into the darkness'—

thus it is written—'and the darknesses
comprehended it not'. But up here,
here in the freedom of the mountains,
in the pure light, the clear cosmic-'I' shines pure;
there speaks in the profound blue ether of the sky
out of the widths of the world the sublime primordial Mystery
of the Darkness, which yet did comprehend the Light.
And from the foothills of the Alps, which the winter
has bequeathed the the bright, radiant dress,
where the spring flowers already prophesying
blossom at the edge of the snow, now in mid-winter,
the gaze is lifted towards those scented distances,
and yet in the clear light of the winter's day
the snowy mountains as if within reach,
that glisten there in eternal white.
As if condensed out of the clouds,
like a revelation of super-sensory beings,
like the shining Temple of the distant Grail,
ether-light stands thus before the astonished gaze,
like the mysterious town of Arkturs,
the town of the ice-flowers and crystal-plants
beheld by the fairytale eye of Novalis.
And in the soul's divining dawning
there the picture of the Holy City condenses,
which with golden walls transparent like crystal
with gates pearl-like for the spirit-eye
of the seer on the holy island of the sea
showed itself in the loneliness of his soul,
and which in the coloured light of the gemstones
reveal twelvefold sublime cosmic-forces of stones
and cosmic-forces of stars:

'And behold! He led me in the spirit
on to a high and sublime mountain
and showed me the Holy City Jerusalem,
descending from the world above
of pure heavenly light and radiating
in the splendour of revelation of the divine world.
And I, John, saw the Holy City
like a virgin who, in a white dress
adorned like a bride, prepares herself for the wedding.'
A festive moment of existence, well do I feel it,

is the one which conjures this shining picture of revelation
for me before the eye of my soul,
the moment when the veils,
which otherwise cover up the spiritual before the sensory gaze,
seem to lift lightly, only a little,
and where the 'I' comes to itself again
'weaving in widths of space and depths of time':
where the 'I' is again connected to the cosmic light,
and in this cosmic light with everything which otherwise
radiates to it in the mirror of the outer world,
where it begins to divine again:
the force which there weaving in the ether-light
of the snow-crystals enchants constellations of stars,
and which out of this in the soft spume of the flakes
condenses winter's white earthly cover,
the force, which in being
has been hardened, fashions the mountain crystal,
which in the heavy stone the counter-pole of weight:
wants to reveal light, this force
am I – – – I am this too,
who, to this world, which today in the light of the heights
radiates towards me, has given death—
to the world which as the valley of the shadow of death
appeared often to me, is at other times
as a great grave of dust and rubble – – –
the rocky grave where the exalted-power of Moses
was laid to sleep by the Father-God,
afterwards, on the holy mountain height once more,
for the last time in his life there shone for him
the eternal Light of the divine I AM,
after he had heard once more in the Light
the eternal primordial Word, which once revealed itself
to him tremendously by speaking:
'I am I, Who was and is and will be.'

The power of the gods which once created the universe
and entered into the human 'I', it has
separated this human 'I' from the universe.
Thereby this universe has died,
has become a grave for what lives.
In one lightning flash of sudden understanding

the obscure words of Novalis light up:
'Whether perhaps Nature have been turned
to stone by the gaze of God?—
or for sheer terror at the advent of man? ....'

For the power of the gods creates in the primordial beginning
the human divine 'I' in the Spirit-light;
through the power of the Earth the earthly 'I' grew in him
and only in the becoming of this earthly 'I'
the power in earthly matter became dead stone.
The human 'I' which created this death
also possesses the power to transform it,
since Christ has connected Himself with the Earth.
Only in Him do I find my true 'I',
that is raised above all powerlessness,
into which the sickness of sin has banished it.
And as awakening to myself in musing,
I recognize in the resting thought:
Yea! Also in yourself, in the depth of your soul,
there slumbers the germinating-power of the eternal 'I',
which like a grain of corn has been sown
into everything that dies in earthly being.
Christ has planted it there. Also in you
it rests buried, also in you it awaits
the resurrection. Only if you too
burst in yourself the dark husk of the grave,
you can become a co-creator in creations of soul
working at Earth's transformation,
at its resurrection, which the Earth then
experiences in a new and transfigured being,
when what of the old Earth is dying
will one day have fallen into dust and ashes,
so that the living, the new Earth
can spring forth out of that which as ash
of the living is dispersed in the universe.
And again I hear a profound saying of Novalis
within my soul, when he speaks of the One,
'Who out of love moves for us
gave Himself completely for us, and into the Earth,
laid Himself as a Foundation-Stone of a divine City.'
In the secret, which in this word
He speaks to us, a veil is lifted

off the secret which John beheld,
where from the high mountain he saw
(which spirit-led he had climbed in spirit)
the divine Holy City, Jerusalem,
in its bridal, virginal adornment.

There, that city of our human present-day,
the large city that on the far horizon
in the dusty haze hides from the eye,
the city which once delighted the heart of the child,
when I, a stranger, entered it for the first time
in early youth, which still today
awakens in the heart joyful memories,
she too is built up out of what has died,
out of dead earth's rigid, stony matter,
and what moves in it carries the seed of death.
One day the following word will become truth for it too:
'Woe! she is fallen, the great city!'
Into the earthly grave there returns what arose from it.
Yet that holy city of the future of the Earth,
which John's seer-eyes behold,
did not arise out of the dark earthly ground,
she is not from below; she is from above,
from the realm of the incorruptible, of the ether-light.
As in the snow-crystal ether-spume
a bright cosmic starry life
is condensed to a tender veil of earthly matter,
as all earthly matter has this starry life
as its being's true origin,
thus in that bright city the life
but returns to its starry origin,
no longer polluted by decay
held in enchantment here below.

The human 'I' which created the enchantment
in stone and plant as in its own being,
alone has the power to free the fetters
when, having gone through the cleansing of many lives
and trials of suffering,
it re-unites with the star-borne 'I'
which descended to earth in Christ.
From starry ether-light earthly matter

will then be lit through again.
And this earthly material flooded by heavenly light
will become the new Earth, germinating,
which will know only development, growth and unfolding,
but no longer any decay.
It is the Earth, which the one consecrated by God,
illuminated by Christ's light, was allowed to behold
in the pure revelation of cosmic light,
about which he spoke the transfigured words:
'And I beheld a New Heaven
and a New Earth: for the first Heaven
(which as the upper world of the radiating light
separated itself from the weaving of earthly matter
in the primordial beginning of creation) has passed away,
with it the Earth, as it was before,
and also the sea—no more to be seen.'
Then the voice from the throne becomes true:
'Now the dwelling of God is with men,
and He, the Holy One, will live with them.
They will be His faithful people,
and as their divine "I" He will live with them.
Death will be overcome, and every tear
God Himself will wipe from their eyes.'
'Behold I make all things new'—in these words
is enclosed the secret of *transformation*:
already when on Golgotha Christ
burst victoriously the dark covering of the grave,
when His corpse dissolved and disappeared,
and when in light-transfigured corporeality
the disciples then beheld the Risen One,
then the transformation of the Earth had begun
which shall continue into future cycles of time.
Since then the Holy City is unfolding,
although still hidden to earthly senses,
but the deeper sensing of the heart beholds
it everywhere already in the present
where human beings in shared faithful work
build a place for spiritual life,
and where the purest sacrificial forces of the heart
unite with the sense for noble form.
Everything outer may appear as dead,
may even be fallen and rotten,

yet there rises still visible to the finer senses,
out of what is dying, in a tender outline
the bright beautiful picture of the becoming.
Like everything dead we humans carry
in ourselves as the decay of spirit,
spreading its stench everywhere,
yet even penetrates everything that in ourselves
our 'I' has shone through, and life's creative breath
has enlivened, into everything earthly.
And nothing of all this that in this way
the human being has wrestled from his own being,
remains lost for the Earth's future.
With what he thinks in the spirit, feels in the heart,
what in deeds he reveals through his will,
what in doing he embodies into matter,
what his whole being expresses,
he carries the new earthly seed in himself.
And though in these earthly days he still
feels distant from such soul-creating,
in soul-*depths* it has already begun.
In the heart the Foundation Stone has been laid
upon which one day the city shall be founded,
which shines in uncorrupted nature,
a shining Temple of divine, eternal being.
Within, as a living pillar there lives
the human being who overcame the past,
and who received the name 'I' from God
(around which the eternal name Eve
is wound as a Mystery of the virgin bride).
And it is only the nightmare of decay
(the Sphinx which plunged into the abyss)
which today still hides this from the senses.

And like awakening from a dream of the future
my eye turns towards the horizon,
to that sombre blue layer of fog,
which distantly covers the widths of the flatland
like that dismal and dark realms of shadows,
of the Fates in Novalis' fairytale world,
who forever spin further the old [patterns]
and towards that which stirs eternally youthful,
sets itself childlike creatively into existence

they contemplate ruin—in vain—in poisonous hate.
In the fog I behold the mark of decay,
as it weighs Sphinx-like on the earthly souls.
From the beings who dwell down there
it hides the world of light in the heights,
destiny full of grace has given me
to look from this mountain today.

Well do I feel: before the foggy, Sphinx-like
dark, daemonic pressure in human souls
is not expelled by the clear light of the 'I'
as long as decay reigns Medusa-like
in soul-darkness and soul-dullness,
in drives and passions,
as long as it is not overcome there,
until then the 'I' cannot be master
in its outer husks,
until then earthly matter remains enchanted,
and in the soul there only remains the light-filled divining
of the distant divine city.
Change has to begin within
before it can be revealed
full of light
one day in outer earthly being.
There where the fog weighs down in the depths,
down there you too have to continue dwelling
working among your human brothers
until all the nightmare darkness is overcome,
and only the memory of what you have beheld here,
what was experienced in the pure light of the heights,
you take with you as a comfort into those depths.

While thus lost in thought,
see there, all at once,
the fog of memories' weaving pictures is grasped
before my soul lives another picture
(this too I experience wandering in the mountains)—
there the fog does not remain in the blue of the widths,
darkening it penetrated into the mountains,
breathlessly thrust by the wild wind's bride,
who whips them into shreds.
The foggy shreds' chaotic, fantastic forms,

they became daemonic forms
and before the inner gaze of the soul
there appeared the wild chase of the Apocalyptic riders
with pale reddish sulphuric armour,
with horses whose heads, lion-like,
blow sulphurous billows out of their nostrils
and whose tails are made of snake-heads
have power over mankind.
Ghostlike everything lives in them
that resists the higher 'I',
that holds the soul in the fog of greed.
They are the powers that rule in the fog,
dealing their imprint onto human souls
robbing them of the view of heavenly light,
and give them over to death's power of decay.
And in the soul itself there reigns decay.
Here first it must be overcome,
erroneous drives have to be transformed,
which have estranged themselves from starry life
where lies their beings' purest source.
Only then can starry life shine again
in the rigid stone which today still surrounds the grave
in which the human 'I' is bound.
Only then the earthly body is also able
to tear itself away from the power of decay,
the Earth itself can unite with Heaven
(as it separated from heaven once
in the primordial beginnings of creation …).

The purifying transformation
which in purity of thought, light-filled, works
draws the human soul from the powers of decay
with its counter-picture
working in the earthly realm of matter
works against rot and decay,
in the *salt*, condensing out of solution,
builds forms that meaningfully, sublime,
in earthly being can reveal to the spiritual gaze
the secrets of the spatial world
where the crystal-form becomes the temple-form,
the cube as long as wide, as long as high.
Carrying the eternal measure of spatial forming

as formative force within itself, the human 'I',
which overcame the fog of decay
(still it hangs on the coarser sheaths,
which then the soul discards, as
the 'forecourt, given to the heathens').
And this measure the human being also carries
into the city where no temple shines
for then the divine Light shining in him,
is the temple itself because then everything
has become a single temple and all life
has become a sacred temple service.

From these future pictures I am led away
by memory to a past year,
where I found myself in a fairytale world
of wonderful snow and ice-crystals.
But unlike the outer world today—
which shone in fresh green of May,
and burst with the spring's flowery adorning.
But only within the world was of snow and ice.
And in this world of snow and ice-crystals
a familiar fairytale picture was created for me, [Snow-white]
the picture of a child which as white as snow
as red as blood, as black as ebony wood,
on a high mountain in a crystal coffin
lay in a sleep of death,
wept over by friendly animals showing pity,
owl and raven, nocturnal birds,
fluttered around; the dove of light hovered above;
the child, who suffering, lovingly, sacrificed itself
to the darkness, which spinning the threads of envy
planned evil to it, but only sleep of death
could bring, that could not cloud
its pure being with the poison of selfishness.
Thus in death it appeared sleeping—
the radiant colour of life,
life's blossoming colour remains,
the fresh red of its cheeks, because the decay
could not reach its bright being.
There it lay in its coffin of crystal,
until it woke at the green bush
(it was a sprouting sapling of the miraculous tree

the Tree of Life growing in Paradise).
The young sovereign power of the cosmic 'I'
could waken it there to full life
making *Snow-White* Queen of the World
kissed awake by the cosmic starry love.

The profound secret of the *Holy Grail*
I recognize in the simple fairytale scene:
the sufferings of Christ and the Resurrection
of the flesh which is the coffin of the Spirit.
That which on Earth resists decay,
the pure strength of the stone which in the crystal
is revealed as power of cosmic light,
becomes the coffin of the body of the pure child
that overcame the sickness of decay,
which became healthy again as a starry being
where the stone's crystal purity lives,
its weight overcome.
This substance of life that has become a crystal coffin
penetrated by ether-light
that is removed from the power of decay
is the *Holy Grail*.
In the crystalline becoming of the etheric,
there time, which serves decay,
becomes again space. This is the secret of the Grail.
Time which in the world of decay
is the destroyer of being for man:
For he who experiences will-less becoming and dying away,
it is controlled by the awakening 'I',
which takes up becoming and dying into the will
which then experience eternity in both.
And through eternity transformed
time becomes space. That etheric being,
which only experiences itself in the becoming of time,
(in the same way as the plant yearns to reveal its etheric being
in the germinating, growing, flowering, bearing fruit
as a being of time),
it then becomes penetrated by the essence of space,
which in a crystalline, spatial form is imprinted.
In this transformation works the power of the Grail.

The same elevated secret of starry light
that is sealed in the realm of stones,
is beheld by the seer in the most sublime picture:
in the soul's separateness, the Leader showed him
on holy Patmos, in the picture of the Holy City Jerusalem,
which to him had descended out of cosmic light,
appearing in revelatory splendour,
like a bride adorned for her wedding.
Where time becomes space, where ether-beings
mysteriously wed to the earthly world,
and where in the light of the spirit this is beheld,
transfigured earthly-heavenly being appears
in the full circle of twelvefold ether-colours,
(so too the mere ether time-being
speaks in the sevenfold bow of colour).
'Is there anyone who already understood the secret
of the stones and the stars,' so speaks Novalis,
'I cannot say I know, but certainly
it must have been a sublime being.'
To the one who spoke this and he who has given to us
the Revelation, this secret was known.
The 'I', which has become the lord in the forces of space,
can in the body, the un-decaying one,
then unfold a twelvefold starry life,
which in the gemstones' twelvefold coloured light
is revealed reflected twelvefold on earth.
This twelvefold stellar life which in stones
is reflected twelvefold the seer saw
in the bright ground of that divine city,
and that twelvefold exalted cosmic power,
which out of the twelve starry signs radiates to us,
there builds up the human body,
which is un-decaying, undying like a gemstone,
which again is a temple divine.
Once, in distant pre-earthly Paradise,
there the human body was etheric-divine,
the green garden still in the land of Eden,
also the Ark, which life-saving,
swam then on the wild waves of the Deluge.
In the temple then it found its exalted symbol,
which Solomon created through Hiram's art.

In Jesus it became the pure human Body,
which in the bright divine City of Earth's future
is transformed again into the cosmic Temple
and out of the pure being of the crystals,
in which weave the cosmic forces of the Twelvehood,
there sprouts a new, bright Tree of Life,
which unites ether-force of time with the force of space,
that brings healing to all human beings
through the healing balsamic force of its leaves.
It is watered by the eternal stream of life,
the sacred fourfold stream of Paradise,
that is sealed in the world cross,
the source which quickens all those who thirst
at the Supper of the Lamb and the Bride
(which is the living New Earth).
In its blossoming and fruit-bearing
the same starry Twelve is revealed.
It gives its fruit each month.
The order of space is imprinted into the course of time,
when space and time are transformed through eternity.

I had lost myself in distant contemplation.
The Sun of this short winter day sinks,
and cold darkness descends on the mountain.
The world of the light of the heights has disappeared,
sunk down is the splendour of its revelation.
The world again is a wide grave.
Yet in the heights the stars still quietly shine;
the brightest is the Star of Christmas.
And what was beheld in the light of the height
continues to live as warmth thankfully in the heart,
as comfort in life and hope for the future.
And even if my path still leads over graves,
and I have still to carry death,
yet there shines on the path from cosmic distances
the holy solemn light of the silent stars.

Karl Thylmann, 'Snow-White' (woodcut 30 x 32 cm) 1914.

John and the Word

Hermann Beckh

(from *Die Christengemeinschaft*, 08. 5. Jhg. 1928. 101-05)

The biblical Pentecost-experience with its speaking of tongues (Acts 2) is not the climax of the Christian experience of the Word. We can deeply feel the cosmic Mystery—called in certain traditions, right into Freemasonry, the 'lost Word'—by entering into the biblical creation story, the story of the Fall, and of the building of the Tower of Babel with the confusion of languages (Gen. 1–2). This word, lost through the Fall of humanity, the creative Word of the Sun—this means the cosmic Word carrying in itself the enlivening Sun-forces. Where actually was it to be found, when in Christ in the 're-enlivening of the dying earth-existence' [the Creed] took place? With which name did the re-finding of the lost Word of the Sun attach itself? This re-enlivening of the creative Word of the Sun already seen as a vision in the early Teutonic mythology connected to the name Vida, the re-newer, is connected in the Christian tradition with the name John, Johannes, [Heb.] Ioannes. In the magnificent I-O-A, I-A-O of the name Ioannes (John), in the bright [German] vowel I (*'ee'*), in the sounding wonder of A (*'ah'*), and in the embracing O (*'oh'*) there lies directly expressed, for a eurythmical feeling for the sounds, the secret of this word and of the cosmic Sun-rhythm pulsing in it.

A direction of a theological research far removed from all spiritual research, already discovered in Mark's Gospel the cosmic rhythm resting on the annual course of the Sun through the twelve signs of the zodiac. Another approach built more on a spiritual basis finds the fact of the existence of this rhythm in Mark's Gospel fully confirmed, even if it basically cannot follow the details of the still materialistic 'astral mythological-theological' observations [of Arthur Drews and other writers] on the gospel. In the narration of Mark's Gospel it can indeed be shown how the triple course of the Christ-Sun through the twelve, sacred heavenly signs is expressed. In this at the same time we can feel how this triple course is inwardly connected with the I-A-O of the name Ioannes. These are also secrets of the Johannine Initiation presented in the narration of Christ's life in Mark's Gospel. In all twelve signs, meaningful secrets of this Initiation occur in the recurring of the same sign; the same point is reached again yet lifted on to a higher level. What at first was, as it were, seen in the light, in the picture and image (I–'*ee*'); on the second, higher level like an inner hearing (A–'*ah*'); until on the third, highest level, brought down right into the depths of corporeality, is experienced and embraced in its inner being (O–'*oh*').

This article cannot aim to show and prove all this in detail. This is reserved for the author's book *Mark's Gospel: The Cosmic Rhythm*. There the reader will find the detailed exposition to what can only be indicated here.

In anthroposophy the technical terms Imagination, Inspiration and Intuition are coined for the three stages of consciousness that are also revealed in the vowels of John's name: IOANNES. Through the three levels of Imagination, Inspiration and Intuition passing through all twelve, sacred heavenly signs, John penetrates the secret of the great cosmic Sun-rhythm, I-A-O. Through this he becomes Ioannes (for John in a higher sense is not a personal name, but a grade of initiation), a re-discoverer and re-enlivener of the lost Creator-Word of the Sun. With closer inspection, it can be shown particularly in the 'sign of the word', in the zodiac sign of the Bull—relating in the human organism to the larynx, the forces of speech—how the important events relating of the initiation of John take place. John 10 is full of the Mysteries of the re-enlivening word.

Facing the Bull on the circle of the twelve zodiac signs lies the sign of the Scorpion, which through the Fall of man has become the sign of death. In the course of the year in the Northern Hemisphere, when natural life, as it were, receives the sting of death in November, the Sun stands in this sign. The forces of generation, the human sexual forces, stand under this sign. In conventional physiology it is known how these forces stand inwardly connected to the forces of speech [breaking of boys' voices, etc.]. Originally, according to an ancient spiritual tradition, in this region lives the Mystery of the solar life, felt in the picture of the Sun-eagle (in early ecclesiastical images, John was portrayed amongst the evangelists as the Eagle).

Through the Fall of man, the origin of this Sun-life was struck by the adversary. Life is killed; the Eagle has become the Scorpion, carrying the sting of death, the poison sting of sin. The essence of the Christian, Johannine Initiation consists in overcoming this sting of death; the Scorpion is transformed again into the Sun-Eagle. If we follow the narration of the gospels in their depths, we see that John alone achieved this. The other disciples initially still succumb to the powers of death. In Judas' betrayal, in Peter's denial and in the flight of the disciples in Gethsemane (Mark 14:50), this finds its most devastating expression.

In these events there comes to completion that which with a careful observation can be followed throughout the gospel as a 'crisis of the disciples'. And it can be shown—shown in detail in the exposition on Mark's Gospel—how this crisis always appears at a decisive point, when in the rhythm of the gospel narration, the death-sign of the Scorpion is once again reached.

Only John within the narrated events of the gospel becomes in this sign the one who overcomes. He reconnects with the original, virginal forces of human nature. The two usual signs of Scorpion and the Virgin show this relationship; they are actually the same sign, only that the characteristic arrow or sting for the Scorpion is missing with the Virgin. The original, virginal forces are already shown on the first stage of the great Sun-rhythm in Mark 5, where in v. 41 at the raising of Jairus' daughter, the words are spoken: 'Maiden, I say unto you, arise.' Thereby we feel this 'raising of Jairus' daughter' is not only an outer event but at the same time it belongs to the process of John's Initiation.

Old legends tell how the deep impression of the raising of the youth of Nain, experienced by him who later became the disciple 'whom the Lord loved', had the effect that he falls into silence, into a kind of sickness, which then leads to the chronic illness that precedes Christ's raising of Lazarus [= 'one who is sick'], as the disciple is called in John 11. Rudolf Steiner has shown how all this points towards the secrets of John's Initiation. Out of an experience of deepest silence, out of a silence that resulted from a strong experience that changes the soul, we see arising the rebirth of the creative Sun-word in John.

Facing him stands the other disciple, Peter, chosen by Christ as the 'rock of the Church'. Peter is connected with the ancient forces of the word. These were alive in humanity's primordial past, but not yet ego-carrying. These ancient forces of the word live in Peter as something he should grow beyond, in order in freedom to find the true power of Christ, the creative Sun-word. Yet it is always shown how he cannot separate himself from them. As the one who speaks prematurely, Peter stands opposite the one who is silent for so long. He blurts out the great secret of Christ's being, but he speaks too soon (Mark 8). After Peter's shining confession of Christ at Caesarea Philippi, there immediately follows the darkening of Peter's consciousness that shows his incomprehension of the sacrificial death on Golgotha. It causes Christ to say to Peter, 'Get behind me, Satan.'

This section of Mark's Gospel (Mark 8, at the end) stands in the death-sign of Scorpio always standing over the crisis of the disciples, as is shown by observing the rhythm of the whole. At the 'Transfiguration on the Mount' as well, Peter still does not grasp the meaning of the sacrificial death that already begins there. He wants to remain on the heights and to 'build tabernacles', or huts, there; we can feel how John, the silent one, increasingly penetrates silently into the meaning of the sacrificial death during the Transfiguration overshadowed by the power of Elijah. John is the only disciple to stand under the cross on Golgotha. So we see—at this place in Mark's Gospel we are to pay attention—how, soon after the Transfiguration, he relinquishes his silent stance and becomes the spokesman (Mark 9:38). From now on he, as it were, takes hold of the word. It is not without deep significance that, as the rhythm of the gospel shows, this section has to be thought in the sign of the Bull, the forces of the word.

And John, the re-awakened one, becomes one who re-awakens the lost creative Word that the other disciples during the time of the earthly ministry of Christ Jesus, bound by the forces of death, are not able to find. In the story of Peter, the denial following Gethsemane, which sounds like a negation of the Christ I-AM, 'I- am-not' is the climax of this darkening of consciousness. The mysterious story of the sword, with which Peter in Gethsemane cuts off the ear of a servant of the High-Priest—if we follow the interpretation of Emil Bock in his *Studies in the Gospels*—has something to do with the misuse of old forces of the word. Right into the Acts of the Apostles, that is, right into later times of the infant Church, these things with Peter can be followed up. These forces play into the whole manner in which, in the Church founded on Peter's rock, in the Petrine Christianity right up to the present, a use of words can still be found that is not quite free from past forces of consciousness of humanity [e.g. at the time of writing the Mass was still celebrated in Latin—*Tr.*].

The Johannine 'I-am' faces the 'I-am-not' of Peter. Because John out of the I-AM of Christ was able to overcome the death-forces and regain the lost Sun-Creator-Word, is the reason why the Prologue of his gospel makes such a primordial tremendous impression on us. Seen purely intellectually, one could perhaps find in the gnostic and Alexandrine writers similar words on the cosmic logos, but with John we receive the clear impression how with rich, inner authority he writes these words opening his gospel. He writes with an authority he alone possesses, because he alone was the one who overcame the forces of death. He alone has truly re-found the Lost Word, uniting with it with the depths of his being. The re-found creative Sun-Word itself, we feel, speaks through the mouth of John in the first sentence, as in all the following sentences, of John's Gospel. And in John's Gospel it is shown how the human being can find again the heights of the Lost Word in Christ: 'I AM the Way, the Truth and the Life.' How the human being of today and of the future can find this way forms the content of John's Gospel; how John himself found it forms the content of Mark's Gospel.

***

The other disciples failed because they were still in the crisis that finds its climax in Gethsemane. They could not initially find the path that leads towards re-finding the Sun-Word. Yet this does not mean that they are excluded for good from their Christ-task and task of humanity. The 'Farewell Discourses' and 'High-Priestly Prayer', which are narrated in John's Gospel in particular, show even in the crisis with what love Christ guards the consciousness of the disciples, seeking to keep them and lead them towards their future task. Not in order to rise above them did John go ahead in his initiation, but in order later to be able to help them, the weaker ones, with stronger forces.

Rudolf Steiner has pointed towards the deep sleep of consciousness, which sunk ever more strongly on to the disciples, the deepest moment taking place in Gethsemane. Peter's denial, besides Judas' betrayal, is the most shocking expression of this sleep of consciousness. Even though they experience at Easter the Resurrection of the Risen One, the sleep of consciousness still lies over the disciples. And we understand the meaning of the biblical Pentecost-event correctly when we recognize here the sleep first disappears from the consciousness of the disciples, through the power of the Risen One with which the helpful forces of John are united. Like scales this sleep suddenly falls from the eyes of the disciples.

Out of a depth of suffering, which initially supersedes their grasp—only John was strong enough to stand under the cross—the whole miracle of cosmic Love that was at work on Golgotha was revealed to them. Again, it is as though they are overcome as by a storm-wind by that which is revealed to them here. Forces of the cosmic Word overcome the consciousness of the disciples and the others in their circle. This is expressed in the whole appearance of 'speaking in tongues', so strangely described in the Acts of the Apostles. In these events the disciples in a certain way find the Word lost since ancient times. In the story of the Tower of Babel and the confusion of language, in tremendous pictures the Bible points towards the way it became lost. Unlike John, however, they do not find it in the full freedom and calmness of the 'I'. Something still of the old, past forces of consciousness of humanity is revealed in it. In the essay, 'India and Pentecost',[110] this thought is further developed with regard to India.

Rudolf Steiner's Last Address

Dornach, Michaelmas Eve, 28 Sept. 1924 [GA 238]
Translated by George Adams

My dear friends,
   It has not been possible for me to speak to you on the last two days. But today—the day when the Michael mood of dedication must pour its light into all our hearts, I did not want to let pass without speaking to you at least a few words. That I am able to do so is due entirely to the loving and devoted care of our friend Dr Ita Wegman. And so I hope that I will still be able to say today what I desire particularly to say to you on the occasion of this festival.
   In recent months we have frequently spoken, my dear friends, of the in-streaming of the Michael-Power into the spiritual events of man's life on earth. And it will be one of the more beautiful results that can follow from our anthroposophical understanding of times and seasons, if we are really able to add to the other festivals of the year a rightly ordered Michael Festival. That however will only be possible when the might and power of the Michael-Thoughts, of which today men have no more than a dim feeling, have taken hold in a number of human souls who will then be able to create the right human starting-point for such a festival.
   What we can do at present is to awaken, in this Michael-time, the Michael-mood in our souls by giving ourselves up to thoughts that will prepare the way for a future Michael Festival. And such thoughts are especially stirred to activity within us when we turn our gaze upon all that we have seen taking place—partly on Earth, partly in super-sensible worlds—through long periods of time, in preparation for all that can now be accomplished for human evolution in the course of this present century by souls who in full sincerity feel themselves drawn to the Michael-Stream.
   That you yourselves, my dear friends, in so far as you truly and honestly incline to the Anthroposophical Movement, belong to these souls—this I have endeavoured to make clear to you in the lectures of the last weeks and especially also in the lectures where I spoke to you directly of the *karma* of the Anthroposophical Society. We can however carry these considerations a little further, and that is what I want to do today.

Let us now bring before our souls beings who are intimately connected, and will always be intimately connected, with the Michael-Stream, in the sense in which we have described it here. Let us direct our gaze to beings who in at least two successive incarnations made a powerful impression on great numbers of their fellow-men, beings who, however, only show themselves in their true unity when we recognize them as successive incarnations of one and the same being.

When we look back into olden times, we see rise up before us within the traditions of Judaism the prophetic figure of Elijah. We know what significance the prophet Elijah had for the people of the Old Testament, and therewith for all mankind; we know how he set before them the goal and destiny of their existence. And we have shown how in the course of time the being who was present in Elijah appeared again at the very most important moment of human evolution, appeared again so that Christ Jesus Himself could give him the Initiation he was to receive for the evolution of mankind. For the being of Elijah appeared again in Lazarus-John—who are in truth one and the same figure, as you will have understood from my book *Christianity as Mystical Fact*.

And further we saw that this being appears once more in that world-painter who let his artistic power unfold in marvellous depths of tenderness, as it moved hovering over the Mystery of Golgotha. And we saw how the deeply Christian impulse that lives in Raphael, as it were impelling into colour and form the very nature and being of Christianity itself—we saw how this impulse rose again in the poet Novalis. In the poet Novalis stands revealed in wondrously beautiful words what Raphael had placed before mankind in colours and forms of rarest loveliness. We see, thus following one another in time, beings who are brought together into a unity when incarnation is understood.

We know—for I have often spoken with you of these things—how, when man has gone through the gate of death, he enters the world of the stars. What we are accustomed to call 'stars' in the external, physical sense are no more than the outer sign and symbol of spiritual worlds which look down upon us and take their share and part in all the deeds of the evolution of mankind.

We know that man passes through the Moon-sphere and through the spheres of Mercury and Venus, through the spheres of the Sun and of Mars, and of Jupiter and Saturn. And we know that when, together with the beings of these spheres and together too with other human souls who have also departed from the life on Earth, he has elaborated his *karma*, he then turns back again to earthly existence.

Bearing this in mind, let us look for a moment at Raphael and see how he passes through the gate of death, and how he enters the realm of the starry worlds, the realm of spiritual evolution, taking with him the power of his art, which already on earth shone with the bright light of the stars. We behold, my dear friends, how Raphael enters the Moon-sphere, and we see how he comes into association here with the Spirits who live in the Moon-sphere and who are the spiritual Individualities of the great original Leaders of mankind, with whose wisdom Raphael, as Elijah, had been deeply inspired. He meets these Moon-Beings, and he meets too all the souls with whom he has lived in earlier stages of Earth-evolution. We see how he unites himself spiritually with the spiritual origin of the Earth, with that World of Being which first made it possible for man to be, and for the Earthly to be impregnated with the Divine. We behold Raphael, as it were, completely 'at home', united with those with whom he had most loved to be in the Elijah-existence, inasmuch as it was they who at the beginning of Earth-existence set the goal for the life on this Earth.

Then we behold him wander through the Mercury-sphere where, in association with the great Cosmic Healers, he transforms for his spirituality the power that had been his to create what is so infinitely whole and healthy in colour and line. All that he has painted, whether on canvas or as a fresco on the wall, for the help and comfort as well as for the unending inspiration of such as can understand—all his work that was so radiant with light, showed itself now to him in the great cosmic connection in which it is able to stand when it passes through the Beings of the Mercury-sphere.

And thus was he, who on Earth had unfolded so great a love for art, whose soul had been aflame with love for colour and for line, transplanted now into the sphere of Venus, which in turn lovingly bore him across to the Sun, to that Sun-existence which lived in all his incarnations so far as they are yet known to us. For it was from the Sun that he, as the prophet Elijah, brought to mankind through the medium of his own people the truths that belong to the goals of existence.

We see how in the Sun-sphere he is able to live through over again in a deep and intimate sense—in another way now than when he was on Earth as a companion of Christ Jesus—he is able to live over again what he underwent when, through the Initiation of Christ Jesus, he, Lazarus, became John.

And all that he has painted in shining light for the followers of Christ Jesus—he now beholds all this pour its rays into the cosmic transformation of the human heart.

And we see further how what he thus had at the foundation of his life penetrates, wisdom-filled, the sphere of Jupiter. In this sphere he is able in wisdom to enter into a relation of understanding with such spirits as Goethe—the spirit, that is, that afterwards became Goethe—as well as also with spirits who had gone astray on other paths, but who nevertheless led over World-Being and World-Thought into the realm of the magical. The foundation is laid for his magic idealism in the experience he had of the evolution of the later Éliphas Lévi. And we behold too how he partakes in all that was living there in Swedenborg.

And now I must draw your attention to something in the life of Raphael that is of very great significance. A personality who was most deeply devoted to Raphael—Hermann Grimm—set to work four times to write a life of Raphael. His *Life of Michaelangelo* he brought to a beautiful completeness, but he never succeeded in drawing any picture of Raphael's earthly life that gave him satisfaction. In his own view all he wrote was unfinished and incomplete. The first book he undertook was intended to be a biography. What is it? Nothing but a reproduction of old anecdotes told by Vasari! No biography of Raphael at all, but something altogether different—a description of what Raphael became on Earth after his death, in the respect and recognition of his fellow-men. Hermann Grimm relates what people have thought of Raphael—what the Italians, the French, the Germans have thought of Raphael in the course of history through the centuries. What he gives us is a biography of the Raphael-Thought as it has lived here on Earth since his death. He finds the way to tell what remains of Raphael in the hearts and minds of men, what lives of him still in their reverence and understanding. But he does not find the possibility to give a picture of the earthly life of Raphael.

After Hermann Grimm has made the attempt four times over, he says: all that one can really do for Raphael as a personality is to write of how one picture passes over into the next, as though it had been painted by a super-sensible being who had simply not touched the Earth at all with his earthly life. The pictures are there, but one can look right away from Raphael who painted the pictures and reproduce the sequence of what is expressed in their inner content. And so, shortly before his death, Hermann Grimm began to speak once again about Raphael; yet once more he made the attempt to put pen to paper and write about him. This time, however, he spoke only of his pictures and not about the earthly personality of Raphael at all.

The truth is, my dear friends, this earthly personality of Raphael was completely yielded up and was only present through what Lazarus-John gave to this soul to be poured out into colour and line for all mankind. Such was the life of this being. And it was so, that this Raphael life could only be, as it were, absolved in another life of thirty years—in Novalis. And so we see Raphael die young, Novalis die young—one being, who came forth from Elijah-John, appearing before mankind in two different forms, preparing through art and through poetry the true Michael-mood of soul, sent down by the Michael-Stream as messenger to men on Earth.

And now we behold the wonderful artistic power of Raphael come to life again in Novalis in poetry that stirs and enraptures the hearts of men. All that through Raphael was given to human eyes to see—of this could human hearts drink deep, when it came again in Novalis. When we consider the life of Novalis, what an echo we find there of the Raphael life for which Hermann Grimm had so fine an understanding! His beloved dies in her youth. He is himself still young. What is he going to do with his life now that she has died? He tells us himself. He says that his life on Earth will be henceforth to 'die after her', to follow her on the way of death. He wants to pass over already now into the super-sensible, to lead again the Raphael-life, not touching the Earth, but living out in poetry his magic idealism. He would fain not let himself be touched by Earth-life.

When we read the *Fragments* of Novalis, and give ourselves up to the life that flows so abundantly in them, we can discover the secret of the deep impression they make on us. Whatever we have before us in immediate sense-reality, whatever the eye can see and recognize as beautiful—all this, through the magic idealism that lives in the soul of Novalis, appears in his poetry with a well-nigh heavenly splendour. The meanest and simplest material thing—with the magic idealism of his poetry he can make it live again in all its spiritual light and glory.

And so we see in Novalis a radiant and splendid forerunner of that Michael-Stream which is now to lead you all, my dear friends, while you live; and then, after you have gone through the gate of death, you will find in the spiritual super-sensible worlds all those others—among them also the being of whom I have been speaking to you today—all those with whom you are to prepare the work that shall be accomplished at the end of the century, and that shall lead mankind past the great crisis in which it is involved.

This work is: to let the Michael-Power and the Michael-Will penetrate the whole of life. The Michael-Power and the Michael-Will are none other than the Christ-Will and the Christ-Power, going before in order to implant in the right way into the Earth the Power of the Christ. If this Michael-Power is able verily to overcome all that is of the daemon and the dragon—and you will know what that is —if you all, who have in this way received in the light of the Michael-Thought, have indeed received it with true and faithful heart and with tender love, and will endeavour to go forward from the Michael-Mood of this year, until not only is the Michael-Thought revealed in your soul, but you are able also to make the Michael-Thought live in your deeds in all its strength and all its power—if this is so, then will you be true servants of the Michael-Thought, worthy helpers of what has now to enter Earth-evolution through anthroposophy, and take its place there in the meaning of Michael.

If, in the near future, in four times twelve human beings, the Michael-Thought becomes fully alive—four times twelve human beings, that is, who are recognized not by themselves but by the Leadership of the Goetheanum in Dornach—if in four times twelve such human beings, leaders arise having the mood of soul that belongs to the Michael Festival, then we can look up to the light that through the Michael-Stream and the Michael-Activity will be shed abroad in the future among mankind.

Because this is so, my dear friends, I have made the effort today to rise up and speak to you, if only in these few short words. My strength is not sufficient for more today. May the words so speak to your soul that you receive the Michael-Thought in the sense of what a faithful follower of Michael may feel when, clothed in the light-rays of the Sun, Michael appears and points us to that which must now take place. For it must even be so that this Michael-garment, this garment of Light, shall become the Words of the Worlds, which can transform the Logos of the Worlds into the Logos of Mankind. Therefore let my words to you today be these:

> Springing from Powers of the Sun,
> Radiant Spirit-powers, blessing all Worlds!
> For Michael's garment of rays
> Ye are predestined by Thought Divine.

He, the Christ-messenger, revealeth in you—
Bearing mankind aloft—the sacred Will of Worlds.
Ye, the radiant Beings of Aether-Worlds,
Bear the Christ-Word to Man.

Thus shall the Heralds of Christ appear
To the thirstily waiting souls,
To whom your Word of Light shines forth
In cosmic age of Spirit-man.

Ye, the disciples of Spirit-Knowledge,
Take Michael's Wisdom beckoning,
Take the Word of Love of the Will of Worlds
Into your soul's aspiring, actively!

*

Hermann Beckh himself humbly and briefly acknowledges the experience of the 'Last Address' by Rudolf Steiner inspired his exposition of Mark's Gospel, and again in the Foreword to the present study on John's Gospel. 'Without the inner work on what was then received, the whole present work would not have been possible' (*Mark's Gospel: The Cosmic Rhythm*, TL 2021 48). The spiritual research came to fruition in the writing of that book, when the *occasion* was offered by the appearance of the 'astral mythology' of Arthur Drews and others.

The 25-year-old Ralph Kux, the first male eurythmist, recollects:

> This last address was like a tremendous ritual. It was also received as such by the listeners. As Rudolf Steiner entered the hall and as he left after he had spoken the tremendous words of the Michael verse, everyone present in deeply stirred concentration rose to their feet, something that did not usually happen. He looked very pale and we had the impression that he summoned his last strength in order to be able to manage this. He spoke unusually fast and urgently.

(Ralph Kux, Willi Kux. *Erinnerungen an Rudolf Steiner*. Ralph Kux. *Eurythmie und Musik* [in one volume]. Stuttgart: Melinger Verlag. 1976. 24. Eng. tr. in MS. A.S.)

Beckh's biographer writes:

> The year 1924 brought an abundance of lectures and courses by Rudolf Steiner up to then unequalled. His activities intensified to a hitherto

undreamt extent. The climax took place in September, in which Steiner frequently gave five lectures daily: for the craftsmen working on the Goetheanum, for the actors, the priests, the priests with the doctors, and for the members [of the Anthroposophical Society]—that is, for all those present in Dornach. After the end of the course given on the Apocalypse of John, the last lecture of which took place on 22 September, the priests had to return to their communities. By this time Hermann Beckh also belonged to those few of the group of priests who were able to remain a few days longer in Dornach. Rudolf von Koschützki and Gottfried Husemann were also in this fortunate position. They heard the last *karma*-lecture [in GA 238] on 23 September. On the following day, Rudolf Steiner spoke in the morning to the workers. The lecture announced for the evening for the members had to be cancelled, something that had never happened during all those long years. People were shocked and full of concern. Rudolf von Koschützki describes how, with Hermann Beckh, he was on his way to the lecture:

> It was already dark and was raining. A car came towards us down the hill. The driver stopped and said, 'The lecture is cancelled; Dr Steiner is taken ill'. Professor Beckh then stepped closer to learn more. When the car moved on, Beckh was very concerned and said, 'Now it starts with him just as with Buddha'. The latter's organism apparently refused to take any further earthly nourishment. Nobody could recall a single announced lecture by Steiner ever having to be cancelled. But he wanted to speak to his friends one more time. We waited from day to day till for his recovery sufficient to hold the lecture. As he ascended the speakers' desk we saw he looked terribly wretched and struggled for breath. Then he became increasingly animated, until after twenty minutes he stopped and left the room [Rudolf von Koschützki. *Fahrt ins Erdenland*. 1952. 332].

The people present were deeply moved. At first absolute silence ruled; the people did not dare to move. 'Then Professor Beckh got up with the words, "*Das war erschütternd!*—That was most astonishing!" More or less silent, we left the room.' So it was reported by someone who was present (Chlothilde Votteler. 'Letzte Ansprache Rudolf Steiners' in *Mitteilungen aus der anthroposophischen Arbeit in Deutschland*. 1978. 258).

That was the farewell. After this day, Michaelmas Eve 1924, Rudolf Steiner spoke no longer to the Members [of the Anthroposophical Society, though he continued to write, for example the *Anthroposophical Leading Thoughts* for the weekly newspaper *Das Goetheanum*]. He could no longer leave his sickbed and died 30 March 1925. Those who had experienced this farewell have kept the memory their whole life long, feeling it an inner duty through it to have felt more strongly and closely united with Rudolf Steiner and his task for humanity.

In this 'Last Address' that remains a fragment, Rudolf Steiner spoke again of Elijah and his mission as a forerunner of Christ, as already in that first lecture that Hermann Beckh heard thirteen years previously, on 14 December 1913 in Berlin. For him a circle closed on this Michaelmas Eve 1914.

[Gundhild Kačer-Bock. *Hermann Beckh: Life and Work*. TL 2021, 98f.]

Perhaps Dr Rudolf Steiner was even speaking in particular to Professor Dr Hermann Beckh?—A. S.

Book Reviews

Book Reviews of Mark's Gospel: The Cosmic Rhythm *by Prof. Dr Hermann Beckh*

'This work of the well-known many-sided scholar and expert of Oriental languages, music, theology and law, introduces something totally new and unique in the realm of biblical research. In a thoroughly spiritual as well as deeply founded and artistic manner, Prof. Beckh unfolds the cosmic and mystical connections between the event in Mark's Gospel and the starry pictures of the zodiac. Moreover, he notes how they mirror in the human organism and the 12 musical keys. In a special illumination stimulated by Rudolf Steiner's lectures on Mark's Gospel, the writer follows the pictures of the gospel. Like a fascinating journey through many levels, the heights and depths of Christian initiation appear before the reader's eye. This gospel may have already inspired abundant research and exposition, but it is mostly taken as a simple and devotional chapter. For the layman as well as the theologian, this work by Prof. Beckh will be a source of spiritual joy and elevation. The book's dignified and tasteful format contributes. A further work on similar lines on John's Gospel is in preparation.'
Bremer Nachrichten, May 1929.

'... these "influences of the stellar facts and solar-rhythms in the gospel narratives" are based—according to the "anthroposophical spiritual manner of contemplation"—on Christ, a heavenly being, uniting with the earthly vessel of Jesus of Nazareth; the spiritual Sun-being united with the Earth! Prof. Dr Hermann Beckh pursues this thesis throughout his abundantly rich and beautifully presented book, producing a continuous exposition of the gospel. With great acuteness all these mysterious connections are uncovered with the zodiac.'
Neue Zürcher Zeitung, April 1929.

'The Orientalist and Buddha-researcher Prof. Beckh has put into this book an abundance of new and novel thoughts. Earlier Drews, Stucken, Erbt and others spoke of connections between the gospel narratives and the events in the starry sky; not one of them however had found the key recognizing that the gospels as books of Christian initiation. Written from higher levels of consciousness, they allow the so-called contradictions to disappear. Beckh shows us the cosmic Christ in the earthly life. Rudolf Steiner first recognized in full clarity and taught this reflection of heavenly events. It can be deeply moving how far Beckh's manner of contemplation opens the door to the secrets of the gospel, to what depths we can accompany the path of initiation of the disciples. Such a commentary as this on a gospel has hitherto not been written. Whoever impartially occupies himself enough with it, is offered the possibility of a religious deepening opening up unimagined worlds.'

Hamburg Fremdenblatt, December 1929.

'… brilliantly accomplished, we find here the fruit and penetrating power of the anthroposophical method of observation in a book of life of humanity. Only through this method can we recognize Judas, Peter and Pilate in their human limitations as tragic personalities, as Hermann Beckh is able to do. Having read the book, you await with intense interest the appearance of the sequel on John's Gospel …'

Anthroposophie, January 1929.

Beckh's most recent publication deserves special attention for several reasons. He attempts in his own way to show in detail the influence of the stars in the details of Mark's Gospel. In the figure of Christ Jesus they are revealed in every moment from the baptism in the Jordan to the Mystery of Golgotha. Beckh follows a path indicated by Rudolf Steiner in his book, *The Spiritual Guidance of Man* (GA 15). The special interest of the present book is to observe how the anthroposophical way of spiritual-scientific knowledge inspired a personality such as Beckh's to these anthroposophical and astrosophical studies. They initially don't appear to be his professional task in the strict sense of the word. And yet if, with understanding, you inwardly follow with sympathy Beckh's development, from his professorial seat in Indology to this book, you can see the logical line of destiny allowing him in this life, especially tangibly to experience the cosmic-earthly stream of development from ancient India up to the present.

In this book—which will be followed with a sequel on John's Gospel—Beckh summarizes all his knowledge and insights in order with them to illuminate the cosmic-starry revelations brought through Christ. He accomplishes this right into the style, not only researching scientifically, but experiencing with a religious and artistic sensibility.

In the midpoint of the exposition stands the Apostles' drama of Christian initiation, the greatest drama of world-history. With strong, holy seriousness Beckh has worked out how Christ with and in the souls of the disciples struggles for the balance between cosmos and earth, between God and man, spirit-world and sensory world. With great love he immerses himself into Christ's work of initiating the souls of the twelve Apostles. With this seriousness and with this love, Beckh dares to approach the Mystery surrounding the two great figures, John the Baptist and John the Evangelist and Apocalyptist. To a high degree Beckh has enriched the thoughts of each true pupil of Dr Steiner's anthroposophy, concerning in intimate consecrated hours with this great triad—John the Baptist, Christ, and John, the disciple whom the Lord loved—in order to experience these thoughts in the centre of their concern as a seed of a new cosmic rhythm of the Christened Earth.

Mark's Gospel is written in the sign of the Lion. It is the sign in which the great cosmic Christ-Sun reigns. In the human organism it is revealed essentially at work in the heart-forces. Both Johns are impulsed by the virtue of courage, where they are pure, by the courage of 'great love'. Beckh rightly calls John the 'Disciple of Love', for his 'I' in the truest sense of the word is a child of Christ's love, engendered and brought to birth in the act of initiation, in 'the awakening of Lazarus'.

Something of this courage of the sign of the Lion flows through Beckh's thoughts which he follows right into the details of the apostolic, Christian movements from the individual disciples to the present day. Much becomes clear as though present, experienced by each individual human soul in their way, as the *'drama of Christianity'*, as far as the quarrels of the confessions and the sects. This is shown as especially significant with the spiritual impulses of Judas and Peter. The betrayal by Judas and the threefold denial by Peter are part of the whole 'flight before the cross' by the whole group of disciples. They consequently cannot experience the Mystery of Golgotha with full consciousness. Only John is able to do so, out of the strength of the love of Christ. Thus Beckh finally leads the reader with John, the disciple and Apostle of Love, before the three crosses on Golgotha.

This book, however, is not intended only as a religious and artistic treatment, but at the same time a special reminder to self-knowledge. This reminder is not expressly made, but certainly emerges as the inner result of such thoughts as Beckh expresses, climaxing in the question of readers to themselves: 'Am I able with John to stand before the three crosses on Golgotha?'

Dr Bruno Krüger in *Das Goetheanum*, 9. Jahrgang, Nr. 3. 19 January 1930. 22f.

Book Review of John's Gospel: The Cosmic Rhythm, Stars and Stones by Prof. Dr Hermann Beckh

Hardly two years after the appearance of the book on *Mark's Gospel: The Cosmic Rhythm*, there appears as a kind of sequel, though also understandable on its own—once again a significant book. After that first beginning, to present and appreciate Mark's Gospel with its narration of Christ's mission pre-eminently in the light of the cosmic rhythm, one can meet the announced appearance of the sequel of such a manner of exposition with a certain expectancy. How will Prof. Dr Beckh be able to achieve this task in relation to the 'I'-Mystery of Christ? With this new title he succeeds surprisingly in making a significant advance in the soul-aspect of the stellar-earthly influence and its characterizing the 'I'-activity in the human being and the world.

The first thing to be emphasized is the beautiful perfecting of the style, which corresponds to the manner of exposition in rhythmic repetition, and at the same time reveals with constant inner development the path of initiation of John's Gospel in its mutual significance for the human being and the world. Although he deals with the most difficult regions of knowledge, Beckh knows how to unlock these in a manner that with a really serious study and familiarity can be available to *everyone*. The abundance of material, which Beckh offers us, is kept together through the great inner thread; the whole thing harmonizes to a tremendous composition. The attentive reader is called to co-operate with the account that is able to transmit to him at the present time the urgently necessary deeper understanding of the gospels.

In a pleasant contrast to many astrological utterances, Prof. Dr Beckh avoids outer sensationalism in order to evoke something popular; he also avoids one-sided and specialist technical terms. The whole work is traversed and glows through with an elevated enthusiasm for the sublime, world-encompassing mission of Christ in the cosmos, in the stream of time, in the world of the stars and in the earthly world. With the anthroposophical manner of knowledge gained from

Dr Steiner, the work is presented as a completely free, autonomous and self-creative achievement. As such it is a beautiful testament to the creative strengths of the human individuality through the awakening force of anthroposophy, without which this work would not have been presented to human beings to attain self-knowledge.

Out of the rich abundance of the content the great rhythm of initiation may be taken as especially important, which coming out of the pre-Christian ages of the Earth, is crystallized in John the Baptist. From him it is led through the Jordan-Baptism to the initiation of Lazarus-John, which was the first Christian initiation. The motif of the 'Johannine triangle' in the stellar realm of Fishes, Crab and Scorpion, shone over by Uranus, sounds like a basic chord through everything. And what sounds into earthly manifestation, through the great discord of the crisis of humanity through the 'Scorpion', is harmonically resolved through the initiation of John to the 'Eagle'. To recognize, to experience this as the greatest of all transubstantiations, all metamorphoses, becomes the leading-thought of the whole book. The expositions relating to this, already contributing many valuable things in the 'cosmic rhythm of Mark's Gospel', are deepened through John's Gospel. Something of the Johannine Eagle's vision and eagle's flight of thought striving for the light pulses through the author's bold flight of thoughts, directed towards and working aloft to the cosmic-'I', in which he seeks with great love to place himself into the soul of John.

In the beautiful chapter on 'giving the name', Beckh has valuable things to say on the great rhythm of breathing, the starry constellation and the earthly zodiac, constellation and zodiac signs, on human destiny and the Christ-'I' in mutual interpenetration. 'Everything that concerns the "I" as the human member that is for the future and which only exists today in seed-form, belongs to a higher world than the earthly zodiac and the planetary connections of destiny, pointing us to the real worlds of the stars' (p. 121).

The various etymological word-studies of the author with a comparison of the relationships of the languages contribute to a further enlivening of the whole and lead in the same way to yet other paths to understand the 'cosmic word'. Expositions like those on 'body' as Sun-dress, 'life' as Moon-dress, on 'light' as Star-dress, and 'love' as Cosmic-'I' (Cosmic Word) in connection with the changes of the incarnation of the Earth illuminate the tremendous Primordial Word in the beginning of John's Gospel, concerning the metamorphosing creative power of the Cosmic Word, that with eagle's pinions circles the universe.

With his manner of exposition, Beckh deeply illumines the connections of the Mystery of Golgotha with the Ancient Egyptian, Persian and Indian Mysteries of the past, and with the 'I'-Mystery of the future. It is very interesting to follow the development of the author of his studies in language out of the soul of the ancient epochs of the peoples to the stellar script of the cosmos. The intimate connection of both languages—the language of the divine stellar script and the human stellar language of words—as it is also shown in Wolfram's *Parzifal*, becomes especially clear through Beckh's explanations.

Right into the tangible details he points with this stellar script and the cosmic language of Christ to the possibility of cosmic-earthly prophecy, as lies before us in the Apocalypse of John in grandiose pictures, signs and symbols.

The nature of the three crosses, the physical (of the Father), the etheric (of the Son), the astral (of the Holy Spirit) in their relationships and influence for the will, the feelings and the thinking of the human soul, as well as their metamorphosis through the reception of Christ become clear in many mutual constellations of the stellar clock in the cosmos. The 'Word in the primordial beginning' in the sign of the Bull and the Ram, the 'Jordan Baptism' in the sign of the Fishes, the 'Marriage in Cana' in the sign of the Waterman, the 'Conversation by night with Nicodemus' in the sign of the Goat, the 'Samaritan woman at the well' and the 'Healing of the Centurion's son' in the sign of the Archer, that of the 'invalid in Bethesda' in the sign of the Scorpion, and so on, then the great crisis of humanity, 'and the darkness comprehended it not', in the further events in the signs of the oscillating Scales, between the Virgin and the Scorpion seeking the balance; furthermore, the raising of Lazarus-John and the great Mystery of the cross with the Resurrection of Christ Himself become for us in reading the cosmic starry clock revealed as *the* rhythm, in which the inner human being walks initially unconsciously. While awake during the day, in the rhythm of clock-time we experience its everyday destiny.

Thus, the cosmic extent becomes humanly accessible. We experience the core of the Mystery-drama of all time, how through all the pictures and events right through John's Gospel the seed is laid and nurtured, in order in the human 'I' to un-bind the will to join Christ and therewith again to go to the Father: 'I go to the Father'; 'No one comes to the Father, but through me' (through the 'I') …

The book is raised to the highest seriousness in the presentation of the crisis of humanity in the sign of the Scorpion, which *alone* John overcomes; it is changed to the sign of the Eagle. For this reason the Eagle is also the occult sign of John's Gospel. This crisis, before which humanity stands anew today, becomes at the same time the 'verdict' for human beings, whether they want to entrust themselves to the adversary of the depths or the divine in the heights. At the division of the ways Christ stands as the 'love in the primordial beginning'. Therewith, Christ becomes the 'Lord of destiny'. Cf. John 3:19: 'This is the separation and the decision: Light has come into the world, but men loved darkness more than the light, because their deeds weighed on their destiny.' Beckh impressively works out the motif of 'changing destiny' through Jesus Christ in the scene with the woman taken in adultery, as the motif of the *Richtens*, judging out of the 'I', in the sense of *Aufrichten*, getting up, straightening up.

We receive strong stimuli out of the cosmic-earthly stellar constellation with the initiation of Lazarus-John which, in itself and in its relationship to the Mystery of Golgotha forms the actual culmination of John's Gospel, as the one-off, unique example of initiation of *those* human beings who decide out of free-will of love of the I-AM to become 'imitators of Christ'.

For a time there came through Frau Dr Steiner's worthy decision to publish Dr Steiner's lecture-cycle on John's Gospel in book form, somewhat earlier the Apocalypse of John in duplicated form. Whoever seriously works through this with the seriousness with which Beckh studied them and inwardly re-experienced them, will through both of Beckh's works with quite special deepening of the soul gain much that will contribute a deeper understanding of the lecture-cycles of Dr Steiner.

Dr Bruno Krüger, in *Das Goetheanum*, 9. Jahrgang. Nr. 42. October 19, 1930. 333f.

Bibliography

HERMANN BECKH, Orientalist, university lecturer, co-founder of The Christian Community, independent scholar

* 04-05-1875 D-Nuremberg
† 01-03-1937 D-Stuttgart

Tr. from the German, A. S. 2014
(http://biographien.kulturimpuls.org/detail.php?&id=48)

HERMANN BECKH, as a cultural researcher, exponent and lecturer, belongs to the exceptional figures of the Anthroposophical Movement before World War II.

He was the son of Eugen Beckh, co-owner of a factory for metal thread; his mother Marie, née Seiler [outlived her son]. His sister was twelve years his junior, to whom he was closely connected—she died already in 1929. Beckh grew up in a prosperous, sheltered situation. He was a highly gifted yet sensitive child, who possessed a fine ability to differentiate colours, musical sounds and moods of nature. At five years old in the mountains, which he greatly loved all his life, he experienced a body-free condition that convinced him that human beings live through a pre-natal existence in the super-sensory world.

At school it was apparent that he possessed an exceptional memory. The teaching methods put him off all subjects so that he could not decide on a profession. Nevertheless, a brilliant *Abitur* [school finals] earned him a scholarship to the Maximilianeum in Munich, where in particular the future members of the Civil Service studied. His original plan was to study national economics, because he hoped in this subject to be able to work for the social development of humanity. Through his fellow students he was increasingly stimulated to study law—he became by chance a judge, without a real decision to enter this profession, as he himself said. He ended his studies with his prize-winning work on *Die Beweislast nach dem Bürgerlichen Gesetzbuch* ['The onus of proof according to the code of civil law'], but practising as a judge he soon saw that it was impossible for him to be a judge all his life, when he actually wanted to help human needs. So at that moment when he stood directly before a position in the Civil Service, he broke from this professional path and began again from scratch. He began to study Indian and Tibetan philology, was promoted to Berlin in 1907 with his work on Kalidasa's 'Meghadūta' ('The Cloud Messenger'). With his inaugural dissertation a year later, a further work on this text, he became one of the few specialists in the Tibetan language to teach at the University of Berlin and worked on the manuscripts in the *Königlichen Bibliothek* (Royal Library).

In 14 December 1911 Beckh heard for the first time a public lecture by Rudolf Steiner (on the prophet Elijah; in GA 61. 194-220). From then on he concerned himself intensively with Rudolf Steiner's basic books. After a personal conversation with him, he became a member at Christmas 1912 of the Anthroposophical Society. A few weeks after Rudolf Steiner admitted him to the Esoteric School. During the course of 1913 he experienced a decisive climax in Steiner's career. In February the first Annual General Meeting of the newly-founded Anthroposophical Society, in August the Munich Summer Conference with Rudolf Steiner's Third and Fourth Mystery Dramas, the very first public eurythmy performance, Rudolf Steiner's lecture as well as the Christmas the lecture-cycle in Leipzig on *Christ and the Spiritual World* (GA 149), through which he received important impulses for the development of a renewed study of the stars. Despite the War, at Easter 1915 he could spend some days in Dornach and perceived the progress of the building of the Goetheanum.

In 1916 Beckh was called up for War-service. Shortly before the two small volumes of *Buddha und seine Lehre* in the Göschen series were published—the climax and in a certain sense also the end of his academic activities. Firstly, he was sent to the Balkans, after which he was called to the *Institut für Seeverkehr und Weltwirtschaft* [Institute for Shipping and World Economics] in Kiel, where he had to evaluate the economic articles in the Scandinavian newspapers. For this he had to learn the Scandinavian languages, so that he had now mastered English, French, Italian, and the Scandinavian languages, along with Greek, Latin, Hebrew, Egyptian, Syriac, Sanskrit, Tibetan and Old Persian (the language of the *Avesta*). His War-service responsibilities—from August 1918 in the Berlin Foreign Service—lasted into the post-War period.

Alongside this he began again to lecture in the University of Berlin, but he saw that his professional future no longer lay in this realm, so he searched for an opportunity to work for the future of human development. He gave up his teaching post for Tibetan philology and went on leave from the University. When an extension of his leave was denied, and instead of becoming a Professor without a Chair, in November 1921 he wrote to have his name withdrawn from the list of private tutors. This was the end of his academic career.

Already in 1920 Beckh offered himself as an anthroposophical lecturer. He gave lectures on linguistics at the Anthroposophical Conference of 1921 and in March 1922 at the Berlin Conference, where he led the day on [*Sprachwissenschaft*] philology under the theme 'From dead philology to living philology'.

However, the question of a satisfying life's task still remained open. When Beckh then learned of the preparations for the founding of the Movement for Religious Renewal, he decided there and then to join the founding group. Here the possibility was opened through the words and language of a renewed rite to find a completely new access to the word and to the sounds of speech. And he recognized that something of a future Christianity was wanting to come into being, was what he desired and intuited since as a 16-year-old he had attended a performance of Wagner's *Parsifal* in Bayreuth. Thus he was one of the oldest of the 48 personalities who in September 1922 with Rudolf Steiner's help called The Christian Community into life.

Still during the same year, Beckh moved to the newly built Urachhaus in Stuttgart. In the group of colleagues he took up a special position from the beginning. Unlike the others, he was not a priest serving a congregation, but could engage his strengths in free activity as a tutor in the Seminary, as lecturer, researcher and writer and still celebrate the sacraments at various locations. This freedom to study enabled him also to attend lectures at the Goetheanum in Dornach, to contribute in cultural contexts such as the Schopenhauer Society and the Astrology Association, for he was concerned to represent the aspects won out of anthroposophy wherever people wanted to hear them.

The themes on which Beckh lectured ranged widely. Initially, proceeding from his academic work, there were considerations on language and presentations of Eastern traditional wisdom. Soon he began to concern himself with questions of music, particularly the music of Wagner and the essence of tonality, and its connection with the forces of the stars, making his realm of study these stellar forces in the sense of a renewing of early Egyptian wisdom in astronomy and astrology. He sought to discover the cosmic lawfulness of the zodiacal influences in their various effects and reflection in all areas, in the ancient languages and their sounds, in music and the colourful circle of musical keys, in the Mystery wisdom of earlier epochs of human history, in the gospels and in human destiny. Thus his life's work did finally reveal a uniform thread.

Beckh was not a bookworm, but a human being with an impulsive temperament and a heart capable of enthusiasm. The little chores of daily life often presented obstacles, but his being and striving was always directed to the highest; thither he aimed to steer the thoughts of his listeners. With Rudolf Steiner and the Goetheanum he felt deeply connected. Experiencing the Christmas Conference 1923 in Dornach of the General Anthroposophical Society, and his presence at Rudolf Steiner's 'Last Address' to the members on 28 September 1924 (in GA 238), he felt as the climax of his life.

After he died on 1 March 1937, after a difficult period of suffering (cancer of the kidneys), Friedrich Rittelmeyer said of him, 'A singularly unique scholar, a rare wrestler for the spirit, an enthusiastic spirit-prophet has completed his rich life and has inscribed his name forever into the moving history of our time'.

Gundhild Kačer-Bock (1924-2008),
Beckh's biographer

The Works of Prof. Dr Hermann Beckh

'An abundance of books came into existence whose significance perhaps will only be properly appreciated in the future.'

Lic. Emil Bock,
'Hermann Beckh' in *Zeitgenossen Weggenossen Wegbereiter*,
Stuttgart: Urachhaus 1959. P. 132.

*

Die Beweislast nach dem Bürgerlichen Gesetzbuch
'The burden of proof according to the Code of Civil Law'
Prize essay, awarded distinction from the Law Faculty the University of Munich.
München und Berlin 1899. Download: http://dlib-pr.mpier.mpg.de/m/kleioc/0010/exec/books/%22103926%22/

Ein Beitrag zur Textkritik an Kālidāsas Meghadūta
'A contribution for the text criticism of Kālidāsa's Meghadūta'
Doctorate dissertation approved by the Department of Philosophy of the University of Berlin 1907.

Die tibetische Übersetzung von Kālidāsas Meghadūta
'The Tibetan translation of Kālidāsa's Meghadūta'
Edited and with a German translation, Berlin 1907/2011.

Beiträge zur tibetischen Grammatik, Lexikogaphie, Stilistik und Metrik
Habilitationsschrift. Berlin 1908.
'Contributions to Tibetan grammar, lexicography, style and prosody'
Inaugural dissertation.

Udānavarga
A collection of Buddhist sayings in the Tibetan language
Berlin 1911 (also reprinted by Walter de Gruyter, 2013).

Verzeichnis der tibetischen Handschriften
'Catalogue of Tibetan MSS in the Royal Library in Berlin' (Vol. 24 of the

Manuscript Catalogue)
First division: Kanjur (Bhak-Khgur)
Berlin 1914/2011/14.

Buddha und seine Lehre
Vol. 1: *Das Leben*. Vol. 2: *Die Lehre*.
Sammlung Göschen. Berlin & Leipzig 1916. Third edition 1928.
Later one-volume editions, Stuttgart: Urachhaus 1958/98/2012. Tr. into Dutch and Japanese.
Eng. tr. *Buddha's Life and Teaching*, TL 2019.

'Rudolf Steiner und das Morgenland'
in *Vom Lebenswerk Rudolf Steiners*
Ed. Friedrich Rittelmeyer, München: Chr. Kaiser 1921
Reprint by HP, Univ. of Michigan (www.lib.umich.edu) (download: www.archive.org).
Eng. tr. 'Rudolf Steiner and the East' in *Hermann Beckh and the Spirit-Word*, Anastasi 2015. 33-65; also in *The Source of Speech*, 16-71.

Der physische und der geistige Ursprung der Sprache
'The physical and the spiritual origin of language'. Stuttgart 1921.
'*Es werde Licht!*'
'Let there be light!'
The primordial biblical words of creation and the primordial significance of the sounds in the light of spiritual science. Stuttgart 1921.
Etymologie und Lautbedeutung
'Etymology and the significance of speech-sounds in the light of spiritual science'
Stuttgart 1922/2013.

All three essays on language (above) reprinted in
Neue Wege zur Ursprache, Stuttgart 1954
Eng. tr. *The Source of Speech*, with all relevant essays and articles. TL 2019.

Anthroposophie und Universitätswissenschaft
'Anthroposophy and University Knowledge'
Breslau 1922. Eng. tr. in *Hermann Beckh and the Spirit-Word*, Anastasi 2015. 71-101; also in *The Source of Speech*. TL 2019, 181-207.

Vom geistigen Wesen der Tonarten
The Essence of Tonality: An Attempt to view musical Problems in the Light of Spiritual Science. With diagrams. Breslau 1922. Third edition 1932. Eng. tr. Anastasi 2008.

Der Ursprung im Lichte. Bilder der Genesis
'Our Origin in the Light: Pictures from Genesis'. Stuttgart 1924. Eng. tr. 'Genesis' with 'Zarathustra', in *From the Mysteries*. TL 2020.

Von Buddha zu Christus
From Buddha to Christ
Stuttgart 1925 (tr. in Norwegian, Oslo 1926); Eng. tr. of short digest Floris Books 1978. New Eng. tr. of full text, with additions, TL 2019.

Das neue Jerusalem
'The New Jerusalem'
A poetic work, in the collaborative work *Gegenwartsrätsel im Offenbarungslicht* ('Riddles of the present in the light of revelation'), Stuttgart 1925. Eng. tr. incl. in *John's Gospel: The Cosmic Rhythm—Stars and Stones*. TL 2021. 358-72; also in *Alchymy*. 100-13.

Der Hingang des Vollendeten
'The Passing of the Accomplished One and his Nirvāṇa (Mahāparinibbāna sutta of the Pali canon)'.
Translated and with an Introduction. Stuttgart 1925/60.
Eng. tr. 'Buddha's Passing', TL forthcoming.

Zarathustra
Stuttgart 1927
Eng. tr. in *From the Mysteries* with 'Genesis', TL, 2020.

Aus der Welt der Mysterien
From the Mysteries
Seven articles (reprinted). Basel 1927. Eng. tr. as triple book with 'Genesis' and 'Zarathustra', TL 2020.

Der kosmische Rhythmus im Markus-Evangelium
Mark's Gospel: The Cosmic Rhythm
Basel 1928/60/97. Eng. tr. Anastasi 2015. Rev. ed. TL 2021.

Der kosmische Rhythmus, das Sternengeheimnis und Erdengeheimnis im Johannes-Evangelium
John's Gospel: The Cosmic Rhythm—Stars and Stones
Basel 1930. Eng. tr. Anastasi 2015; expanded and corrected ed. TL 2021.

Das Christus-Erlebnis in Dramatisch-Musikalischen von Richard Wagners 'Parsifal'
The Parsifal=Christ=Experience in Wagner's Music Drama
Stuttgart 1930. Eng. tr. with 'Richard Wagner and Christianity' (1933) and essays by Emil Bock (1928) and Rudolf Frieling (1956), Anastasi 2015; TL forthcoming.

Vom Geheimnis der Stoffeswelt (Alchymie)
Alchymy: The Mystery of the Material World
Basel 1931/37/42/2007/13. Eng. tr. with appendices, TL 2019.

Der Hymnus an die Erde
'The Hymn to the Earth': From the Old Indian Atharvaveda: A memorial to the oldest poem and to the early Aryans. Stuttgart 1934/60. Eng. tr. TL, forthcoming.

Psalm 23 aus der Heiligen Schrift
Psalm 23: Newly translated from the original text and set to music, op. 7. Stuttgart 1935.

Die Rosen von Damaskus
'The Roses of Damascus'. 'Thibaut von Champagne'. The ballad by Conrad Ferdinand Meyer. For solo high voice with piano accompaniment set to music, op. 8. Stuttgart 1937.

Die Sprache der Tonart
The Language of Tonality in the Music from Bach to Bruckner with special reference to Wagner's Music Dramas
Stuttgart 1937/87/99. Eng. tr. Anastasi 2015. TL forthcoming.

Richard Wagner und das Christentum
'Richard Wagner and Christianity'
Stuttgart 1933. Eng. tr. incl. in *The Parsifal=Christ=Experience in Wagner's Music Drama*. Anastasi 2015.

Indische Weisheit und Christentum
'Indian Wisdom and Christianity'
Articles: 10 reprinted and 9 from the literary estate
Stuttgart 1938. Eng. tr. in *Collected Articles*, TL forthcoming (2022).

The Mystery of Musical Creativity: The Human Being and Music
A recently discovered history of music in Ms (1936):
Five chapters pub. in three articles in *Der Europäer,* Basel
09.2005/09.2006/02.2007-08.
http://www.perseus.ch/archive/category/europaer/europaer-archiv
Full restored text translated into English, TL 2019.

The Language of the Stars: Zodiac and Planets in Relation to the Human Being with a chapter on the Anthroposophical Soul-Calendar (1911-12) (1930-33) by Prof. Dr Hermann Beckh and *The Cosmic Rhythm in the Creed: for readers of Beckh's books* (1930-31) by Dr Rudolf Frieling, with an Introduction and Reviews by Rudolf Frieling and others, translated from the German by Maren & Alan Stott, edited by Neil Franklin, Temple Lodge Publishing 2020.

Collected Articles of Rev. Prof. Hermann Beckh (1922-1937). Over 70 items translated into English, ed. Neil Franklin, TL forthcoming (2022).

Three further publications:

(1) *Hermann Beckh: Leben und Werk*
Hermann Beckh: Life and Work
by Gundhild Kačer-Bock (d. 2008)
Stuttgart 1997. Eng. tr. Anastasi 2016. TL 2021.

(2) *Hermann Beckh and the Spirit-Word:*
Orientalist, Christian Priest and Independent Scholar
Anastasi 2015. Contents includes:
    Alan Stott, 'Hermann Beckh and the Twenty-First Century'
    H. B., 'Rudolf Steiner and the East'
    H. B., 'Anthroposophy and University Knowledge'
    H. B., 'Meeting Rudolf Steiner'
    Numerous appreciations by Beckh's colleagues and his biographer; introducing the 'Collected Works of Prof. Hermann Beckh'.

(3) *Festschrift in Honour of Hermann Beckh*
Published on the centenary of *Buddha und seine Lehre* and the publication of the English translation *Buddha's Life and Teaching* also the first publication of Beckh's *The Mystery of Human Creativity: The Human Being and Music* and the English translation of Gundhild Kačer-Bock's biography *Hermann Beckh: Life and Work*.
Contents includes:
    Prof. Hermann Beckh: 'Steiner und Buddha' (1931; previously unpublished)
    Prof. Hermann Beckh: 'Buddhism and its Significance for Humanity' (1928)
    Prof. Hermann Beckh, 'The Little Squirrel, the Moonlight Princess and the Little Rose', illustrated by Tatjana Schellhase
    'Prof. Hermann Beckh' by Johannes Lenz (Berlin)
    Manfred Krüger (Nuremberg): 'Daniel Simeon and Asita the Sage'
    Oliver Heinl: 'Prof. Dr Hermann Beckh—Pioneer linguistic work in the light of Christ'
    Susana Ulrich-Alvarez Ulloa (Öschelbronn): 'The Search for the Lost Word'
    Katrin Binder (Nottingham): 'Buddha's Life and Work one hundred years on'
    Alan Stott (Stourbridge): 'Hermann Beckh: Musician' (a lecture, Dornach, April 2016)
    Rosemaria Bock (Stuttgart): 'Recollections' (with photos)
    Gundhild Kačer-Bock (1924-2008) Memories & Appreciations.

'Beckh Rarities', containing 'The Essence of Tonality', 'The Parsifal =Christ=Experience in Wagner's Music Drama', 'Buddha's Passing' and 'The Hymn to the Earth' (planned for 2022)

Note: Useful sources for texts by Beckh:
www.rudolf-steiner-bibliothek.de/
bibliothek@goetheanum.ch/
archiv@christengemeinschaft.org/

Endnotes

1. H.B. 'Rudolf Steiner in der Geschichte des lebendigen Wortes.' *Die Christengemeinschaft*, May 1925. 44-9. Eng. tr. in *Collected Articles of Rev. Prof. Hermann Beckh*, TL forthcoming (2022); also in *Hermann Beckh & the Spirit-Word*, Anastasi 2015, 21-32.
2. Gundhild Kačer-Bock, *Hermann Beckh: Life and Work*, TL 2021, 179.
3. Michael Ward, *Planet Narnia*, OUP, Oxford 2008, 30.
4. Michael Ward, op. cit., 43. The popular version, Michael Ward: *The Narnia Code*, Paternoster 2010; also a DVD, same title, 2011. Concerning the space trilogy, see Sanford Schwartz, *C.S. Lewis on the final Frontier: Science and the Supernatural in the Space Trilogy*, OUP, Oxford 2009.
5. Neil Franklin, Boehme and Blake scholar, traces Beckh's development in 'Farther Up! Hermann Beckh: Passing through four levels of consciousness, 1916-1931' in *The Language of the Stars*, TL 2020, 503-20.
6. Presented in H. Beckh, *Buddha's Life and Teachings*, Temple Lodge, 2019.
7. Issues raised by musicians are discussed in the Introduction to *The Language of Tonality*. Anastasi 2015, TL forthcoming.
8. H.B. letter of 26 Jan. 1936, in G. Kačer-Bock, op. cit. 266.
9. Norman Nicholson. *Collected Poems*. London: Faber & Faber. 1994. 68.
10. From now on, MG stands here for *Mark's Gospel: The Cosmic Rhythm*, Temple Lodge (TL) 2021; MG is followed by the page number. On what is meant here by 'rhythm', cf. the author's 'Rhythmisches Geschehen im Evangelium' in the monthly journal *Die Christengemeinschaft* VI. II. Feb. 1930. 334-38. Eng. tr. in MG, Appendix II, also pp. 341-47 above.
11. Cf. H. Beckh, *The Essence of Tonality* [Anastasi 2008] and *The Language of Tonality* [Anastasi: 2015. Both TL, forthcoming].
12. A unique and illuminating way to overcome the materialistic thinking in the realm of astronomy from the purely mathematical aspect is shown in the valuable and interesting book by Dr Wilhelm Kaiser, *Die geometrischen Vorstellungen in der Astronomie*, 2 vols, with supplements (Basel: Rudolf Geering Verlag 1928), especially for those who, in this overcoming of a certain materialistic manner of thought do not remain with things beyond the Earth but are able to draw consequences also for the Earth. The danger is avoided of placing a starry cosmos volatized to abstraction facing a material (in the normal sense) Earth, left as it was. For such readers, the Earth and cosmos become again essentially spiritual, in a spiritually accurate meaning also justified by anthroposophy, enabling the Earth again to become a 'star amongst stars'. (In this meaning, Walter Johannes Stein, in his Introduction to *The Ninth Century and the Holy Grail*. London: Temple Lodge 1991.)

13 As in all astronomical science and all astrological practice based on experience, on a very decisive occasion, significant for humanity—namely the laying of the Foundation Stone of the first Goetheanum on 20 September 1913—the founder of the Anthroposophical Movement noting that 'Mercury stands as the Evening Star in the Scales', takes into account the *sign* and not the constellation. Mercury, that is, the astronomical Mercury, during the course of the day, entered the sign of the Scales, and stood at the stellar midday 0° 9' Scales, that is, as regards constellations, in the constellation of the Virgin. On the other hand, the 'occult Mercury', that is, the astronomical Venus—the meaning of these expressions will be explained later—stood in the sign of the Lion 22° 35'; that is, if you take into account the reality and at the same time the great expanse of the constellation of the Lion, the 'occult Mercury' also stood in this constellation.

14 The astrological direction of research resting on Indian Theosophy names the 'three crosses' in the zodiac with expressions of Indian Sankhya-philosophy: the Rajs Cross (pron. 'Radshas'), the Sattva Cross, and the Tamas Cross. The Christian expressions used here as in MG do not contradict the spirit of Indian primordial wisdom as shown in the fact that the Indians themselves connect the trinity of 'Gunas' Rajas, Sattva, and Tamas with their divine trinity Brahma, Vishnu, Shiva, corresponding to the Christian Trinity of *Father, Son* and *Spirit*. [See Beckh, 'Indology and Spiritual Science' in *The Source of Speech*, TL 2019.]

15 Meanwhile, as we went to press, a wandering star still farther than Neptune has been discovered by an American astronomer, and has been named 'Pluto' [May 1930]. The—here and there doubted—existence of this far distant outer planet appears to be confirmed. It would show that the total number assumed in the present work of 'middle' or 'central' planets between the narrow planetary world and the actual 'world of the stars' is still larger. Astrologers have been long concerned with this new discovery, and even expect one or two more.

16 Today this is no Utopian, or 'fantastic' astrological, alchemical assumption. The research of Frau Kolisko (Stuttgart) has shown that what has long been known as an old, spiritual view, is becoming increasingly placed on an empirical basis.

17 To avoid a possible confusion, *uranós* is of course meant. In *The Language of the Stars*, TL 2020, p. 241, the Professor uses the picture of a train, which we might say comes from a station down the line, whereas beyond that fact it hales from the original station of the entire journey—*Tr. note.*

18 Expressed poetically by George MacDonald: 'Out of the everywhere into the here'—*Tr.* Prof. Beckh writes: This initially simple fact, verified by experience, of the birth-horoscope also shows how, like a heavenly script, the outer planets relate to the spiritual activity of the stars. Also for the

time being, all the spiritual imaginations on the 'spirit in the stars' and the cosmic origin of the human being, which are hidden—with sufficient devotion to the facts that can be gleaned, observable purely empirically, of the relationship between the firmament at birth and the destiny of birth (karmic gifts, potentials)—can bring strongly felt convictions, even deeply disturbing things. Indeed many people today, simply only with an 'empirical attitude' resting on natural-scientific thinking, approach the subject in question. Where astrology is pursued in such an as yet inadequate spirit it should here in no way enter as part of the discussion.

19   For the astronomical contemplation we are concerned here with the relationship of the Sun's middle-point to the course of the Earth in the periphery; for the spiritual contemplation with the relationship of the Earth middle-point to the periphery given by the apparent course of the Sun.

20   This concept underlies, for example, the fiction of the well-known writer C.S. Lewis. See endnote 3—*Tr.*

21   Cf. Albert Steffen, *Legensgeschichte eines jungen Menschen*, Dornach and Stuttgart 1928, p. 126, below:
> The heart of Christ beats for everyone. What an astonishing thought, that once a human being has lived who carried the pulse-beat of mankind through death! This rhythm is immortal; it lives for evermore on the Earth. Human beings cannot stand still until they recognize Him and make Him their own. They sense that something in them in confirmation is saying: Do not rest until you are in the middle-point of mankind, that is, *where the Earth is [a] Sun, in the heart.* Nowhere besides. Only here is freedom and love, One for All. *Seek Christ here ...*

On this, see R. Steiner, *Occult Physiology*, lecture-course Prague 20-28 March 1911. GA 128.

22   Some people, not without reason as it appears, relate the Uranus-activity to the triangle Waterman–Twins–Scales, and the Neptune-activity to the triangle Fishes–Crab–Scorpion. (Cf. to these 'trigons', or triangles, in the zodiac the figures at the end and MG Appendix 356ff.) The former triangle is also that of the element of air, the latter as that of the element of water. From the viewpoint of the various kinds of ether (MG 356f., 360) the Uranus-trigon would align to the light-ether, the Neptune trigon to the sound-ether, which in many respects agrees with the spiritual nature of both planets. The triangle of the sound-ether—as already touched on in MG, and here presented in more detail—is the *Johannine triangle*.

23   This 'Uranus viewpoint' coming to the fore very strongly in John's Gospel, uniting with the 'spiritual essence of the Sun' and the origin of Christ out of the spiritual sphere of the Sun primarily emphasized in anthroposophy, we take from the last lecture of Rudolf Steiner's lecture-course *Life between Death and Rebirth* (Berlin, 5 Nov. 1912 – 1 April 1913 [GA 141]). In Lecture 2

(20 Nov. 1912) the discussion is how the impulse bound with Christ and the Mystery of Golgotha initially descends from the spiritual nature of the Sun to the Earth, yet is deeply grounded in the universe. It belongs in the spirit to even more profound regions than that of the seven planetary spheres. These planetary spheres point to the context of the 'Ancient Moon' (that is, the most recent of the earlier incarnations of planet Earth). The Christ-impulse points to contexts of the 'Ancient Sun', that is, a much earlier situation in the primordial past.

24 The harmonic aspects (trigon, or triangle, sextile, etc.) of a spiritual science of the stars is based on the equilateral *triangle*; the disharmony (opposition, quadrature, etc.) is based on the *cross*. All fulfilment of the creative element rests on the cross and triangle within the circle.

25 Many things in this direction, expecially concerning Venus, are contained in *Nine Lectures on Bees* by Rudolf Steiner to the workmen at the Goetheanum (GA 351, 9 lectures, 1923).

26 See the author's two articles in *Gäa Sophia*, Vol. III, Völkerkunde, Dornach 1929. 183-212 Eng. tr. in *Collected Articles*, TL forthcoming (2022).

27 The double nature of the Moon touched on here also has a purely astronomical aspect. *One* side of the Moon essentially always faces the Earth, the other side always faces the cosmos, the starry realms. Here the Moon *mirrors the universe*, as on the other side it *mirrors the Earth*. The spiritual side of this astronomical fact Rudolf Steiner discusses in the lecture, Dornach 27 July 1923 [GA 228. Eng. tr. in *The Golden Blade,* London: RSP 1988. 43-9; online www.rsarchive.org]. The earthly-hardening tendency of the Moon's being is the antithesis of the other tendency, revealing a cosmic mirroring of primordial wisdom.

28 Friedrich Creuzer, *Symbolik und Mythologie der alten Volker*, Vol. 2, p. 111f., in the chapter on 'Hermes'. (Ref. details obscure; Beckh possibly used a later edition than the first, available on the internet—*Tr. note.*)

29 The concluding bracket sign, missing in the text, is supplied here as a suggestion—*Tr.*

30 For the early Egyptians the star Spica ('the sheaf') was in the constellation of the Virgin, as similarly the fixed star Sirius and the planet Venus, is an Isis-star, a revelation of Isis. This relationship of the star Spica in the Virgin to Isis-Venus is today especially visible, since, as a result of the precession of the equinox, the Venus-sign—the Scales—lies in the constellation of the Virgin (the star Spica in the Virgin stands today 22° Scales; this is a way of expression that one has to get used to, if the important difference between sign and constellation is to be clearly conceived [tropical and sidereal zodiacs]).

31 See Günter Wachsmuth, *Etheric Formative Forces In Cosmos, Earth & Man* (1932). Sacred Science Institute 2006 (deluxe hardbound ed.); Borderland Sciences Research (simplified facsimile edition). Download from

<www.scribd.com>. Wachsmuth significantly differentiates within the light-ether the *cold light* that connects with the higher life-element (life-ether and sound-ether), and the 'warmth-light' aligned to the lower element of warmth-ether. Cf. the author's *From the Mysteries*. TL 2020, 71, 133f.

32 Of great interest for all the questions touched on here is Friedrich Christoph Oetinger, *Das Geheimnis von dem Salz*, München: Pfüger-Verlag 1924; Nabu Press 2014. [Oetinger (1702-82), Lutheran pastor and follower of pietism, wrote over 100 works covering almost all branches of science, frequently under his pseudonym 'Elias Artista Hermetica', that influenced poets and his contemporaries.]

33 Cf. 'The name Eve' in *From the Mysteries*, TL 2020, 176-84. In this form of the name, the secret of the Egyptian Isis-Mysteries, whose initiate was Moses, has gone over into the Hebrew culture. The name Eva ('Eve before the Fall of man') is also an expression of the above-mentioned 'virginal secrets of the Earth', the *prima materia* of the alchemists.

34 This is not to be understood as if the lower ether would only be for the man, the higher ether alone for the woman—although echoes of this are to be found physiologically—but through the Fall man *and* woman are pulled down into the sphere of the lower ethers. The higher ether is the 'lost Tree of Life'. Through Christ both man and woman can find once again *each in themselves* union with the etheric stream, the Tree of Life.

35 The full text, German and English, of 'The Twelve Moods' is included in Rudolf Steiner, *Eurythmy: Its Birth and Development* (GA 277a). Rudolf Steiner Press 2019. 73-5.

36 Cf., for example; John 3:19 NIV, 'This is the *verdict*: Light has come into the world...'; αὕτη δέ ἐστιν ἡ κρίσις ὅτι τὸ φῶς ἐλήλυθεν εἰς τὸν κόσμον ...
John 9:39: Εἰς κρίμα ἐγὼ εἰς τὸν κόσμον τοῦτον ἦλθον,
AV/KJV: For *judgment* I am come into this world.
John 5:22.: οὐδὲ γὰρ ὁ πατὴρ κρίνει οὐδένα, ἀλλὰ τὴν κρίσιν πᾶσαν δέδωκεν τῷ υἱῷ ...; NIV 5:22. Moreover, the Father *judges* no one, but has entrusted all *judgment* to the Son, ...

37 On the connection of each supersensory human member with the stages of cosmic development—'Ancient Saturn', 'Ancient Sun' and 'Ancient Moon', in the cosmological sense of *Esoteric/ Occult Science*—compare MG 84. The 'Moon-dress' of the fairytale, the astral body, is also allocated in this sense to the stage of evolution termed 'Ancient Moon', the 'Sun-dress' to the 'Sun' and the stage of '[Ancient] Sun-evolution'.

38 Much recent astrology names these three crosses in the zodiac with Indian expressions, taken from Sankhya-philosophy, as the *tamas, sattva* and *rajas* crosses. The Christian expressions used here correspond to the Indian, in so far as the Indians themselves connect *rajas* (spoken 'rad-schas') with Brahma, *sattva* with Vishnu, *tamas* with Shiva, whereby the

trinity Brahma, Vishnu, Shiva appears as the Indian parallel to the Christian Holy Trinity.

39 Luther translates 'that his works would not be *punished (gestrafet)*', the meaning of the word ἐλέγχειν in the N.T. Greek is 'convict, bring to consciousness' [in Classical Greek, 'to bring to shame']. Luther's translation is no longer understood today but means the same.

40 One thinks of an ammonite or similar fossil, of the visible connection of the fossilized impression to the positive fossil. Similarly, normal consciousness holds the impression of spirit-reality in the sensory sphere for the reality itself.

41 Cf. also Exodus 32:31-33 (in the 'story of the golden calf'): So Moses returned to the Lord and said, 'Alas, this people have sinned a great sin; they have made for themselves gods of gold. But now, if thou wilt forgive their sin— and if not, blot me, I pray thee, out of thy book which thou hast written.' But the Lord said to Moses, 'Whoever has sinned against me, him will I blot out of my book.' Compare, too, Psalm 69:28: 'Let them be blotted out of the book of the living; let them not be enrolled among the righteous.' The 'book of the living', like that in which the 'Eternal Name' is written, is not only an apocalyptic or New-Testament motif, but a universal-biblical motif.

42 Out of John's Gospel itself one can list the places for the 'incorrect belief', the incorrect, or lesser effect of the Name: John 1:50, 2:11, 2:23f., 3:2f., 4:48, 6:30, 7:3-5, 11:47f., 12:17-19; for the 'correct' belief, correct submission and security of heart proceeding from the 'I' to 'I': John 1:12, 4:42, 10:4, 10:16, 14:12, 16:31, 17:8, 20:29, 20:31.

43 Many interesting things can be found, even if written in a completely materialistic spirit, in the great works of J.G. Frazer, *The Golden Bough: a Study in Magic and Religion*, London 1911. Similarly, Edward B. Tylor, *Primitive Culture*, London 1903.

44 Not for nothing, in the *Fragments*, Novalis indicates that here two problems are present on quite different levels. He speaks of *two forms* of etymology: 'Etymology is of different sorts: genetic [and] pragmatic.' Cf. on all this, the author's publication 'Etymology and the Meaning of Speech-Sounds in the Light of Spiritual Science' in *The Source of Speech*. TL 2019, 112-33.

45 Christoph Rau's unjustly neglected, concise work on the composition of the Fourth Gospel studies the rhythms of certain words, *Struktur und Rhythmus im Johannes-Evangelium*, Stuttgart 1972, Eng. tr. in MS. Later, Rau offers an explanation of the miraculous draught of fishes drawn uniquely from the text itself: the gematria of *logos* (62) *phos* (63) and *agape* (28) = 153 fishes. Chr. Rau, *Die Vier um den Einen*, Bochum 2008, Eng. tr. 'The Four around the One', SteinerBooks forthcoming—*Tr*.

46 Compare the *m* in the German word *stumm*, Latin *mutus*, Indian *muaunam*, 'to keep silent', *muni* the silent one, the holy one. Connected to this is the

m in words for 'death, dying': Indian *mr* (mar), Latin *mori, mors*, Hebrew *mavet* [NB the best OT dictionary gives *mavut*, which is more similar to the Egyptian given here—*Ed.*], Ancient Egyptian *mwt* (*maut*).

47 See the author's 'Genesis' in *From the Mysteries*, TL 2020.

48 For this reason, the *m* appears in many languages in words that describe something female, especially the words for *mother* (already Ancient Egyptian *mut*, Lat. *mater*, Gk. μήτηρ *meter*). This touches with the *m* words about water (Heb. *ma'i* water, *yam* sea, Lat. *mare*), if we think of the 'waters of birth' and the 'primordial water of the etheric' as the 'female-maternal world'. The *m*, too, of what is moon-like shows in many languages the inner relationship to the water-element on the one side, and to the feminine on the other side. In the name *Maria*, Mary (Heb. *Miryam*)—we recall *'stella maris'*—this connection comes to the fore. See further, the author's 'Etymology and Meaning of Speech-Sounds in the Light of Spiritual Science', in *The Source of Speech*. Temple Lodge 2019. 112-33.)

49 In the author's essay 'The physical and the Spiritual Origin of Speech', in *The Source of Speech*, TL 2019. 134-53, with the world *'Mensch'*, man, the different viewpoints with words of the same meaning in various languages are pointed out. Words deriving from the root *man*, 'thinking', of the Germanic and Indian languages point towards the spiritual element in the human being. The Greek word points more towards the soul-element of the human being turning upwards towards the spiritual, whereas the Latin and the Hebrew words (*homo, adam*) initially emphasize the connection with the Earth.

50 This is the meaning of Beckh's text, *vom unrichtigen Alleinsein*. The Mystery-aspect of this saying is not discussed—*Tr. note*.

51 Cf. An outstanding exposition on the twelve groups of 'Truly, truly' sayings in John's Gospel based on lectures delivered in 1879: Andrew Jukes, *The New Man and the Eternal Life: Notes on the reiterated Amens of the Son of God* (London: Longmans Green 1881/ Kessinger Publishing 2009/ General Books 2012/ Nabu Press 2014, etc., also downloadable from <www.archive.org>). Jukes concludes by relating the series to the traditional threefold mystical path (grouped as 4+4+4 sayings); the unity of twelve may also be fruitfully related to the annual zodiac rhythm, independent of the great rhythm Beckh discovered in John's Gospel—*Tr*.

52 Cf. 'Amen' is one of God's names: *El-Amen*—'God [whose name is] Truth' (Is. 65:16)—*Tr*.

53 Rudolf Steiner once spoke of how specific beings in the cosmos, out of cosmic intelligence, bring about this harmony of the self-woven *karma* with that which is present in the birth constellation. (If one is so inclined, one may think of an abstract, philosophical equivalent for such a thing in Leibnitz's 'pre-established harmony'.) Whether and when a soul can enter into

earthly life is, as it were, characterized through the moment in which the outer constellation harmonizes with the star-tapestry of self-woven destiny. Numerous riddles of earthly life and also the love between the sexes lead ultimately in this sense towards this star-Mystery.

54 In the last lecture of the cycle *Life between Death and Rebirth* (Berlin, 1 April 1913. GA 141), important for all these questions, Rudolf Steiner speaks—and already in the earlier lecture on the planets—of the regions referred to here (*Uranós* of the Greeks) as the 'region beyond the Saturn-sphere'. The passage allows us to link a Uranus-impulse of Christ with a Sun-impulse of Christ.

55 Perhaps there lies a significant and important transition to all this in the existence of Uranus and Neptune, those two planets distant from the Sun we recognized earlier as appearing to us like mediators between the world of the seven planets and the upper stars. These two planets have been objectively present although only discovered in relatively modern times. One gradually increasingly recognizes how meaningful their fine and distant rays are for all human relations and contexts. People became receptive at the beginning of a new age, when human beings, as it were, began to free themselves from the narrow confines of the planetary septenary. They began to make steps towards the higher starry world beyond Saturn. The spiritual significance of those two Sun-distant planets has been revealed and many things still remain reserved for the future of mankind.

In modern times experts in this area believed they observed how in horoscopes the 'old planets', whose influence affects human destiny, in a certain way step ever more into the background, whereas the rays of the far-distant planets, predominantly that of *Uranus* for the spiritual manifestation of the human individuality begin to be increasingly decisive. In this a transition and a symptom could be seen for how human beings are about to grow into the world of their eternal source; thither they are destined to grow.

56 This occult connection of Eagle and Scorpion—or 'Eagle and Snake'—lives in the ancient myths and Mysteries of humanity, right into the Egyptian hieroglyphic alphabet built on the 'polarity of the sounds' and Nietzsche's waking dream in *Thus spake Zarathustra*.

57 See the article 'The Sacred Primal Word of Zarathustra with excerpts from the Avesta' in the author's *From the Mysteries*, p. 130f. mentioning the Gatha verse of the Avesta regarding the discussed experience of sound.

58 Cf. words for light in different languages in the author's essay 'The Physical and the Spiritual Origin of Speech' in *The Source of Speech*, TL 2020, 134-53.

59 What is meant as 'mistranslated' does not of course relate to the expression 'the true light', which only requires further explanation, but to 'which lighteth every man that cometh into the world', as the Latin Bible translation does (which Luther uses for his translation). Luther mistranslates the

Greek ἐρχόμενον (coming) which as a nominative relating to φῶς (light) gives the far better, really the only possible, meaning: 'the light... coming into the world'.

60 The 'was' (Greek ἦν) at the beginning, speaking of the divine-eternal Being, stands here facing 'there was' (ἐγένετο), where the historical appearance of the human initiate is mentioned.

61 The emphasis here on the Baptist's part would seem to derive from Rudolf Steiner's spiritual research—*Tr.*

62 Concerning the 'Mystery of the two Jesus children', cf. Rudolf Steiner's book *The Spiritual Guidance of Man and Mankind* [GA 15], and the illuminating explanations in Emil Bock's *Studies in the Gospels*, Vol. 2, no. 23 'The Mystery of Jesus' Childhood'. Edinburgh: Floris Books 2011. [See also the first theological study: Christoph Rau, *The Two Jesus Boys*, TL 2019.]

63 *Editor's note*: In the section here devoted to the Wedding at Cana, Professor Beckh expands his observations made in *Mark's Gospel: The Cosmic Rhythm* regarding the motif of Feeding (*Speisung*) which consistently points to the Pisces-Virgo axis of the Etheric Cross. Underlying these observations is the particular indication made by Rudolf Steiner, which is clearly set out by Sergei Prokofieff in *Anthroposophy and The Philosophy of Freedom* (Verlag am Goetheanum, 2006; Eng. tr. TL, 2009.)

While the 'normal' intellectual thinking of every day is destructive of substance, the sense-free Moral Intuitions fostered in the second part of *The Philosophy of Freedom* are 'substance forming' (Prokofieff, Chapter 2). Through the Mystery of Golgotha the new formation can receive 'the forces of the Resurrection Body of Christ' (ibid.). That this was Rudolf Steiner's view in connection with *The Philosophy of Freedom* is demonstrated by Prokofieff who refers to Steiner's lecture of 5 September, 1921 (in GA 78): 'purely moral ideals [Intuitions] arise that work in a world-forming manner even down into materiality' (quoted by Prokofieff, Temple Lodge, p. 23). Prokofieff later examines, Chapter 14, the relation of the Grail tradition to this theme, while Professor Beckh has much of value to say also in his article 'The Name Isis' and his poetic work on 'The Heavenly Jerusalem'.

At first the underlying idea will appear strange to many but this need not be so once it is understood that 'substance' (*Substanz*) also refers to the Hypostasis (*Substantia*) of Christian theology. It would not scandalize Anglican, Roman Catholic or Orthodox to hear that Man requires to be enhypostasized in God through Christ, whose name is also I-AM. Rudolf Steiner has clarified the perceptions of the German Idealists J.G. Fichte, Schelling and Hegel, the destiny of the finite I-am of human thinking is within the absolute I-AM. If the Son is consubstantial with the Father, then man is called to find consubstantiality with the Son. In turn, that Christ's substance after the Resurrection was 'down into materiality' is the whole point of the story of Thomas—N.F.]

[64] Cf. on this relationship of the etheric-astral human origins to the sign and constellation of the Waterman, Rudolf Steiner's lecture-cycle, *The Spiritual Hierarchies and their Reflection in the Physical World*, Düsseldorf 1909 [GA 110], and the chapter on the primordial Word in the present book [Part Two, Chapter 1].

[65] A main source of knowledge for all these things can be found in the recent reprint of *Geheime Figuren der Rosenkreuzer aus dem 16ten und 17ten Jahrhundert* of Henricus Mathadamus Theosophus of the eighteenth century (EOD Network 2015; also Bauer Hermann Verlag 1988/92). In his lectures on Christian Rosenkreuz (Neuchâtel. 27 Sept. 1911, in GA 130), Rudolf Steiner points to their historical importance. In Goethe's *Faust* I, Easter Scene, we find the alchemical 'red lion'.

[66] In the second lecture-cycle on John's Gospel, Kassel 1909 (GA 112, Lecture 9) Rudolf Steiner describes the event, initially apparently subjectively— that the wedding guests, touched by the 'I'-impact of Christ, only drank water like wine—but then a page later adds an important motif, saying that it depended on the fact that the initially empty water-jars were filled with 'water drawn freshly from the springs of nature', water that had not yet lost the inner forces of the connections to elemental nature. With this the motif of the alchemical (*prima materia*) is gently touched, as from a distance. In the earlier lecture-cycle (Hamburg 1908, GA 103 Lect. 5) the 'transformation of water into wine' is still discussed in an objective manner.

[67] Thus, especially in the many pictures and deeply meaningful 'Parabola' in the *Geheime Figuren der Rosenkreuzer*, mentioned above (see endnote 65), which is a main document for the direction of research meant here. Especially remarkable are the quite public connections to many well-known *fairytale pictures* with this alchemical-Rosicrucian picture-world, especially 'Cinderella', 'The Chrystal Ball', 'Snow-White and Rose-Red' [see H.B. 'Snow-White' in *Collected Articles*, TL forthcoming (2022); also in *Alchymy*, TL 2019, 114-26], and 'The Seven Ravens' [in the Grimms' collection].

[68] Novalis, *Fragments*, ed. Kamnitzer. 650.

[69] Cf. Ambrosius Siebmacher, *Der Wasserstein der Weisen*, early seventeenth century, similar in time and outlook to the above-mentioned Henricus Mathadamus.

[70] Tr. Constance Garnett, slightly revised. New York: The Modern Library. Random House. 1963. 432-37; John's Gospel, RSV.

[71] Further details in both articles on Indian Yoga in *Gāa Sophia* 1929 and especially in *Österreichischen Blättern für freies Geistesleben*, June 1919, esp. pp. 12ff., 25f. [all in Eng. tr. in *Collected Articles*, TL forthcoming (2022)].

Endnotes 415

[72] Relating to this 'Book of Destiny' is the word πονηρὰ in v. 19, usually translated as 'evil', from πόνος 'load', actually 'burdened', i.e. burdened with destiny, fate. The word linked to it ἔργα 'works' = Indian *karma*.

[73] Here too we should observe how the inner connection of the two sections, or chapters, so different at first view (the Conversation with Nicodemus, and John at the Jordan), is clearly established through the constellation. In this connection the case is similar to John 2 and 4 (also in John 6–10). The meaning of the 'cosmic rhythm' for the knowledge of the inner connection of the gospel is everywhere evident here.

The connection of the [seven or eight] motifs in the various sections is to be observed for the 'symphonic style', so characteristic of John's Gospel:

- the Baptism motifs, John 3:23 & 38 ('I am not Christ') we found already in John 1,
- in John 2 the motif of the 'cleansing' (= baptism, 3:25) and the 'motif of the bridegroom' (3:29), also
- the 'motif of the measure' (3:34, cf. 2:6), and then the
- 'Uranos motif' (3:31 with v. 13) 'the one who is from the earth speaks from the earth; the one who comes from heaven (Uranos) is above all'; the motif 'the Father loves the Son' (3:35 with v. 16 'God so loved the world ...'); finally
- the 'motif of the wrath of God' (3:36), which is the counter-picture of the 'love in the "I"', the power of the 'I' to judge, to divide, which is mentioned in the conversation with Nicodemus (3:18-21)—the motif of the 'Book of Destiny', as we can also call it, standing in an inner relationship with the 'starry motif of the Book of Life' (of the 'Eternal Name' in the Book of Life, see Part One, Chapter 7).

[74] Plutarch on Isis and Osiris, Book 3, 46. (http://penelope.uchicago.edu/Thayer/E/Roman/Texts/Plutarch/Moralia/Isis_and_Osiris*/C.html):

46. The great majority and the wisest of men hold this opinion: they believe that there are two gods, rivals as it were, the one the Artificer of good and the other of evil. There are also those who call the better one a god and the other a daemon, as, for example, Zoroaster the sage, who, they record, lived five thousand years before the time of the Trojan War. He called the one Oromazes and the other Areimanius; and he further declared that among all the things perceptible to the senses, Oromazes may best be compared to light, and Areimanius, conversely, to darkness and ignorance, and midway between the two is Mithras: for this reason the Persians give to Mithras the name of 'Mediator'. Zoroaster has also taught that men should make votive offerings and thank-offerings to Oromazes, and averting and mourning offerings to

Areimanius. They pound up in a mortar a certain plant called omomi at the same time invoking Hades and Darkness; then they mix it with the blood of a wolf that has been sacrificed, and carry it out and cast it into a place where the Sun never shines.

In fact, they believe that some of the plants belong to the good god and others to the evil daemon; so also of the animals they think that dogs, fowls, and hedgehogs, for example, belong to the good god, but that water-rats belong to the evil one; therefore the man who has killed the most of these they hold to be fortunate.

(Further details on the question of Zarathustra in the author's *Zarathustra*, especially Chapter 2, 78ff. Also two articles 'The Sacred Primal Word of Zarathustra' and 'Isis—the star-wisdom of the early Egyptian Mysteries and its connection to Zarathustra' in *From the Mysteries*, Temple Lodge 2020, 127-69.)

[75] Or, where it nevertheless does appear—think of the lamenting songs in Jerusalem—clinging in a tragic manner on to the past, on to what is irretrievably lost. Longing, which in its right form negates the old Pharisaism, has invaded in a tragic, retrogressive form later spiritual Judaism all the more.

[76] Also in the ordering of Buddha's series of development and causes which presents the 'descent' of the soul in the Fall of mankind mirroring the ordering series of the zodiac, in the well-known formula of the 'twelve causes' (*nidāna*) the five or, with Buddha, 'six senses' appear at the place corresponding in the zodiac signs to the Archer. [Further details—yet without reference to the zodiac—in the author's *Buddha's Life and Teaching*, TL 2019, 29ff. See MG 263 for the zodiac reference where a parallel case is discussed. As there the fifth *aspect* (in Buddha's life) is aligned to the Archer, the same sign meets the fifth of the twelve causes, that of the 'six senses'.]

[77] Luther and others translate 4:22 in a non-understandable manner, something like [in English tr.]: 'You are not present consciously in your devotions, but we are consciously present in our devotions, so that progress lies with the representatives of the Hebrew influence.'

[78] Tr. Douglas Robertson, online: http://shirtysleeves.blogspot.com/2007/11/translation-of-die-lehrlinge-zu-sais-by.html

[79] ἀληθινός (*a-lethinos*) in Greek, also here again (cf. Part One, Chapter 6) 'what takes place in full consciousness', a verdict that takes place through itself, that the full light of consciousness is cast on that which has to be decided.

[80] Cf. on these questions the author's poetic attempt 'The New Jerusalem', original Germ. ed. incl. in *Gegenwartsrätsel im Offenbarungslicht*. Stuttgart 1925. 105, esp. 108ff. Eng. tr. pp. 358-72 above. The whole conception of the evolution of the Earth in anthroposophy, provided particularly by Rudolf Steiner in *Esoteric/Occult Science: An Outline*, Chap. 4, is the path to achieve full clarity concerning the line of thought indicated here.

81 Cf. Albert Stefen. *Lebensgeschichte eines jungen Mannes.* 12. Quoted in endnote 21 above.
82 Cf. the author's essay 'On the name Isis' in *Mark's Gospel: The Cosmic Rhythm,* Appendix 5, and *From the Mysteries,* TL 170-75. Here it is also shown how the Ancient Egyptian name 'Isis' I-S-T is contained in the words *'Kristall',* 'crystal' and *'Christus','*Christ'.
83 Since the charge is clear, Christ's entry in the dust could hardly consist of a list of personal names and statistics, even if these are necessary evidence in contemporary divorce cases on grounds of adultery. As Beckh suggests, serious readers will also consult Rudolf Steiner, GA 103, lecture, Hamburg 26 May 1908; GA 112, lecture, Kassel, 7 July 1909 where Steiner emphasizes the essential perspectives for concepts of sin, *karma,* merit, compensation, and so on. J. Duncan M. Derrett (similar to Beckh: Oriental lawyer, historian, theologian and independent scholar) brilliantly argues that Christ wrote in the dust Ex. 23:1b and Ex 23:7a. (*Law in the New Testament.* London: Darton, Longman & Todd 1970; Eugene, Oregon: Wipf & Stock 2005. 156-188.) The Law and Christ's attitude *because* they are personally grounded reach beyond names and statistics; what He wrote brought self-knowledge to all concerned—*Tr. note.*
84 Cf. scenes with Mr Raven in George MacDonald's final masterpiece, *Lilith: A Romance* (1895)—*Tr.*
85 This sentence will be challenged by those, like today's Sanskrit scholars and scholars in general, who only look on the written documents that have come down to us. An earlier age is ascribed to the Ancient Egyptian and Assyrian cultures than the Ancient Indian. Only the spiritual research of Rudolf Steiner gives us the key from the relatively recent age of the traditional Indian literature, in order to look back to a much older Indian culture. A 'primordial Indian cultural epoch' flourished in the age when at the spring equinox the Sun stood in the constellation of the Crab. Here too the cosmic aspect of the signs of the zodiac and with this the connection with the 'great cosmic year' is a revelation that sheds light.
86 An account of these Indian things, that are also connected with an exposition concerned directly with John's Gospel, can be found in two articles by the present writer in *Gäa Sophia* (Bk. III, Dornach 1929. 182ff.):
'*Der indische Yoga im Lichte der Anthroposophie, insbesondere der Lehre von den ätherischen Bildekräften',* 'Indian Yoga in the Light of Anthroposophy: especially the teaching of the etheric formative forces' and
'*Der übersinnliche Organismus im indische Yoga (Lotusblumen, Kundalini) im Lichte der Erkenntnis der ätherischen Bildekräfte',* 'The supersensory Organism in Indian Yoga (lotus blossoms, Kundalini) in the light of knowledge of the etheric formative forces'.

In a similar direction the article *'Der indische Yoga in seinem Verhältnis zum abendländischen Erkenntnisweg'*, 'Indian Yoga in its relation to the Western path of knowledge' in *Österreichischen Blättern für freies Geistesleben*, June 1929. 7ff.
The relationship of pre-Christian Buddhism to the Christian path is discussed in the writer's *From Buddha to Christ*, Chap. 4. 'The Path', 55-104 [also *'Der indische Yoga und das Aufweckhungsereignis in Bethanien'*, 'Indian Yoga and the awakening event in Bethany' and *'Der indische Yoga und Christus'*, 'Indian Yoga and Christ']. All the above in Hermann Beckh, *Collected Articles* ... TL forthcoming (2022).
For a general account of Yoga teaching see Hermann Beckh, *Buddha's Life and Teaching*, TL 2019, 129ff. and Buddhist meditation, 141ff. [For further work on Buddhism in the gospel of Luke, on Eightfold Path in the contexts of the eight Lukan mealtimes, see Chr. Rau. *Die Vier um den Einen*. Bochum: Dr. Dieter Winkler 2008. Eng. tr. *The Four around the One*, SteinerBooks forthcoming, and Chr. Rau. *Blicke in die Werkstatt der Evangelisten*. Stuttgart: Urachhaus 2013—*Tr. addition.*]

87   Cf. on all this the beginning of the author's *From Buddha to Christ*, TL 2019, and the article 'The Tree of Life' in *From the Mysteries*, TL 2020, 202-22.
88   The 'hidden door with the four-petalled lotus-flower' recalls the 'door with the four-leaved clover air-hole' in Strindberg's *The Dream Play*, 1902.
89   Cf. on the whole area touched on in this chapter, especially R. Steiner, *Knowledge of the Higher Worlds: How is it Attained?* Here how to pursue the 'way of the "I"'—also indicated in John 10—is explained in detail in a contemporary manner.
90   Catalepsy, from the Greek κατάληψις 'catch', is a nervous condition characterized by muscular rigidity and fixity of posture regardless of external stimuli, as well as decreased sensitivity to pain.
91   This mourning [John 11: 19, 21, 31, 33, 36] shows probably the most clearly of all, that all involved at the event took it as a serious, real death, that all calculated with the fatal outcome of the initiation-procedure accompanied by Christ as a solid fact, that none consoled himself by saying to himself, 'it's *merely* an initiation'.
92   Karl Thylmann, graphic artist, 1888-1916. The image in question here appears as a woodcut on paper. Thylmann was strongly influenced by anthroposophy shortly before WW1 in which he received a mortal wound—*Tr*.
93   The Professor mentions Leonardo's painting again in *The Language of the Stars*, TL 2020, yet refrains from detailed comment. Footnotes 15 & 16 of that book mention some later researchers who have attempted to relate the starry zodiac to the twelve disciples. See also Kurt von Wistinghausen, who followed up the portrayal of thirteen disciples in fine art of the Middle Ages. His original comments, e.g. on Leonardo's arrangement are suggestive, *Der Verborgene Evangelist*, Stuttgart 1983, 113f.—*Tr*.

94 A passage from a devotional exposition on John's Gospel (on John 15, 'the True Vine') echoes the conceptual context here: 'In all my striving to attain some ideal or perform some service, unless my heart and will are wholly captivated, there will be some self-assertion, and probably a great deal. That is why the consciously virtuous person is disagreeable. It is not virtue that can save the world or any one in it, but love. And love is not at our command. We cannot generate it from within ourselves. We can win it only by surrender to it' (William Temple. *Readings in John's Gospel*. Macmillan 1945. 260f. [1961. 251])—*Tr*.

95 A significant conclusion regarding the stream meant here is the recently republished *Geheime Figuren der Rosenkreuzer* of Henricus Matthadamus Theodophus (Altona 1783) [EOD Network 2015; also Bauer Hermann Verlag 1988/92].

96 This moment in the plainchant, antiphonally sung, liturgical Easter 'drama' of the Middle Ages is recognized by historians as marking the re-birth of drama in the West—*Tr*.

97 On this question Rudolf Steiner has spoken in detail in his lecture-cycle *From Jesus to Christ* (Karlsruhe, 5-14 October 1911. GA 131). The supersensory-physical 'phantom' [the traditional term] is there distinguished from the mere 'ether-body'. As the 'etheric body' relates to the plant world on the Earth, the 'supersensory physical body' (the 'phantom') relates to the 'crystalline forces of the cosmos'. The alchemical 'stone of the wise' (the 'white stone' of the Apocalypse) is the same entity.

98 See on this Resurrection Mystery also the author's poetic contribution 'Das Neue Jerusalem' in *Gegenwartsrätsel in Offenbarungslicht* ('Present-day riddles in the light of revelation') Stuttgart 1925. 105-121. Eng. tr. of Beckh's poetic work 'The New Jerusalem', see pp. 358-72 above; also in H. Beckh, *Alchymy: Mystery of the Material World*. Temple Lodge 2019, 100-13.

99 [The construction of John's Gospel relates to the four main movements of the Communion Service, the Mass, and most clearly in The Act of Consecration of Man.]
(1) The beginning of John's Gospel (the 'descent of Christ', Chapters 1–5) relates to the descent of the Word, to the *Gospel*;
(2) the 'crisis' (Chapters 6–10) relates to the *Offertory*;
(3) what follows (the raising of Lazarus and Golgotha) to the *Change* or *Metamorphosis* (Transubstantiation);
(4) the end of John's Gospel (both Resurrection-Chapters) to the *Communion*.

100 The nature and meaning of this helper-role is developed by Emil Bock in his *Studies*, No. 14, 'Peter and John'. Emil Bock, *Studies in the Gospels*, Vol. 2, Edinburgh: Floris Books 2011. 27-47.

101 On the nature of the 'four rivers of Paradise', see also the author's little book 'Genesis', in *From the Mysteries*, TL 2020, 31-33.

[102] The 'consciousness-soul' is alternatively called 'spiritual soul' by Rudolf Steiner, because in the light of self-knowledge what is spiritually, eternally real in experiencing the world first lights up; experience is interpreted, the basis upon which all further spiritual progress can develop—*Tr.*

[103] As with the earlier 'Feeding', the pentad of bread points to the lower forces of the human constitution, taken hold by the initiation of the will. They correspond to the five lower, dark zodiac signs. With the number [153 fishes] given in John 21:11, we are raised from viewing the whole in the picture of the Twelve to the comprehensive aspect of the 'great year': 5/12, reckoned with the number 365 days in the year—as our friend Rudolf Meyer first pointed out—rounded off yields the number 153. [On the geometry of this number as a 'fishing-net', see David Fideler. *Jesus Christ, Sun of God*. Wheaton Ill., Madras, London: Quest Books 1993. Another explanation of 153 is based on the text of John itself: Chr. Rau, *Die Vier um den Einen*. Bochum 2008. 122-25 (Eng. tr. forthcoming). See endnote 45 above—*Tr. addition.*]

[104] On the problems of psychological analysis governing here, see the author's *The* Parsifal-*Christ-Experience in Wagner's Music-Drama*. Anastasi 2014. 53ff.

[105] The 'fisherman's ring' or *annulus piscatoris* is the ring given to the Pope as a symbol of his service—*Ed.*

[106] It may be superfluous to point out that at the time of writing Beckh, along with other writers, treats Yoga = 'practice', as a respected teaching, which is not identical with what passes today for popular Yoga in the West—*Tr.*

[107] https://en.wikipedia.org/wiki/Sadhu_Haridas/

[108] It could be worth mentioning that since this was written educational debate and practice have changed. The pendulum may continue to oscillate and issues abound, nevertheless artistic and educational practice does emphasize rather more acutely and to ever earlier age-groups that pupils and students 'self-reflect'. Thereby rote-learning is to be superseded; impersonal information is to be used for creative ends—*Tr. note.*

[109] A sacrifice of all that one represents, prefiguring what is called today a 'living sacrifice'—*Tr.*

[110] *Die Christengemeinschaft* 5. Jg. Nr. 3. June 1928. 69-70; Eng. trans. in *Collected Articles*, TL forthcoming (2022).

A note from the publisher

For more than a quarter of a century, **Temple Lodge Publishing** has made available new thought, ideas and research in the field of spiritual science.

Anthroposophy, as founded by Rudolf Steiner (1861-1925), is commonly known today through its practical applications, principally in education (Steiner-Waldorf schools) and agriculture (biodynamic food and wine). But behind this outer activity stands the core discipline of spiritual science, which continues to be developed and updated. True science can never be static and anthroposophy is living knowledge.

Our list features some of the best contemporary spiritual-scientific work available today, as well as introductory titles. So, visit us online at **www.templelodge.com** and join our emailing list for news on new titles.

If you feel like supporting our work, you can do so by buying our books or making a direct donation (we are a non-profit/charitable organisation).

office@templelodge.com

For the finest books of Science and Spirit